LOUISE MÜHLBACH

"I AM A MAN. WHO IS MORE SO?"

Muhlbach—"Goethe and Schiller," Vol. Seventeen, p. 271

THE WORKS OF
LOUISE MÜHLBACH

IN EIGHTEEN VOLUMES

GOETHE AND SCHILLER

FRONTISPIECES IN COLOR FROM PAINTINGS BY
WALTER H. EVERETT

NEW YORK
P. F. COLLIER & SON
MCMII

CONTENTS.

BOOK I.

CHAPTER   PAGE

I. Introduction, ... , . . 1

II. The Trials of Life, ... 10

III. Henrietta von Wolzogen, ... 22

IV. Joy and Sorrow, ... 33

V. Charlotte von Kalb, ... 41

VI. The Title, ... 59

VII. Adieu to Mannheim! 68

VIII. Plans for the Future, ... 73

IX. The Last Ride, ... 85

BOOK II.

I. After the King's Death, ... 111

II. "Le Roi est Mort! Vive le Roi!" 120

III. The Favorites, ... 129

IV. The Maid of Honor, ... 138

V. Figaro, ... 143

VI. The Alliance, ... 157

VII. The Conditions, ... 173

VIII. New Love, ... 180

IX. The Decision, ... 189

X. The Invocation, ... 198

XI. The Will, ... 214

XII. Leuchsenring, ... 226

BOOK III.

CHAPTER PAGE

I. Schiller in Dresden, ... 236

II. Gilded Poverty, ... 245

III. Marie von Arnim, ... 252

IV. Souls in Purgatory, ... 268

V. Separation, ... 283

VI. The Song "To Joy," 293

VII. Together once more, ... 299

VIII. Goethe and Moritz, ... 314

IX. Leonora, ... 326

X. A Dream of Love, ... 340

XI. Adieu to Italy, ... 355

BOOK IV.

I. The Return, ... 360

II. Reconciliation, ... 377

III. Grim Death, ... 385

IV. Goethe's Return from Rome, ... 394

V. Estrangement, ... 404

VI. The Two Poets, ... 421

VII. The First Meeting, ... 431

VIII. Wilhelmine Rietz, ... 443

IX. Husband and Wife, ... 450

X. The Attack, ... 460

XI. Youth Victorious, ... 470

XII. Schiller's Marriage, ... 482

GOETHE AND SCHILLER

GOETHE AND SCHILLER.

BOOK I.

CHAPTER I.

INTRODUCTION.

THE honest and peaceful inhabitants of Mannheim, the capital of the Palatinate, had long since retired to rest; the streets were deserted, and the houses wrapped in darkness. Only high up in the little bow window of a corner house on the Palace Square still glimmered a faint light like the subdued gleam of a lamp in a sick-chamber.

But the watch, who had just proclaimed at the corner in stentorian tones the third hour of the morning, knew better; and, as he entered the square, he again looked up at the illuminated window, gravely shaking his head.

"Mr. Schiller has not yet gone to bed," said he to himself; "writing all night again, I suppose. But I will not stand it! Did I not promise Mr. Streicher that I would always look up at his window, and, whenever I found the light burning after one o'clock, protest against it? Well, then, I'll try it to-night, and keep my word, as an honest man should."

And in stentorian tones the watchman cried out, "Mr. Schiller! Halloo! Mr. Schiller!"

For a moment the window was darkened by a shadow, and then opened, and a hoarse voice demanded, "Who called? who called my name?"

"I, Mr. Schiller. I, the watchman, Fabian," roared the man in response.

"And what do you desire of me, worthy guardian of the worthy city of Mannheim?"

"I wish to beg of you, Mr. Schiller, to be so good as to put out your light and go to bed."

"What brought you to this strange and ridiculous idea?" exclaimed the voice from above, laughing loudly. "What does the light behind my windows concern you, a watchman and a guardian of the streets?"

"Really it doesn't concern me at all," cried the watchman. "I know that very well, but I have promised the music-teacher of my daughter, Mr. Streicher, to pay attention to your window, and every time I see the light burning in your room after one o'clock, to call you, and beg you in the name of your dear friend to be kind enough to put out your light and go to bed."

"A very ridiculous idea of Mr. Streicher," said the voice of the invisible poet, laughingly, "and I am only surprised that you should do his bidding, and take this task upon yourself."

"Don't be surprised, sir, for I am not doing it gratis. Mr. Streicher told me that whenever I had called you, and begged you in his name to go to bed, I should have to pay only half-price for the next piano-lesson of my daughter; and I beg you, therefore, Mr. Schiller, to be good enough to tell Mr. Streicher to-morrow that I have done his bidding. And hereafter do as you please, sleep or wake. I have done my duty. Good-night, Mr. Schiller

"Good-night!"

The poet rapidly closed the window, and drew the folds of the old threadbare coat which served him as a dressing-gown closer around his shivering form.

"The good and true Streicher," he murmured in a low voice, "is an honest soul, and means well, and does not know how he has injured me to-day! I was in the grandest flow of enthusiasm; all the discomforts and necessities of life had disappeared! I was no longer cold, there were no more tormenting creditors, no cares, and no pangs of love! I was in thy heaven, Father Zeus! And the messenger of my friend comes and calls me back to the cold, inhospitable earth. The fire of my enthusiasm is extinguished, and now I am sensible that there is no fire in the stove!"

He raised his large blue eyes, and glanced through the dimly-lighted space toward the high black stove, within the open grate of which only a few glimmering coals were visible.

"No fire," sighed Schiller, shrugging his shoulders, "and no wood to make one. Poor, feeble man! The fire of the soul does not suffice to warm thy shivering body, and the prose of life ever recalls thee from the Elysian fields of poetry. But it shall have no power over me. I will defy it! Forgive me, friend Streicher, but I cannot do your bidding! Your watchman calls to me to sleep, but Don Carlos calls to me to be wakeful! I cannot let the Spanish prince call in vain! Fortunately the coffee-pot is still standing in the stove. If it is yet warm, something can be done for the poor, shivering body."

He rapidly went across the room to the stove, knelt down before the fire-place, drew the brown coffee-pot from its bed of ashes, raised it to his lips and refreshed himself with several long draughts, after which he carefully restored the vessel to its former place.

Truly a strange sight, this long, thin figure in the gray-yellow flannel gown, a pointed nightcap on his head, stooping before the stove and occupying himself with a coffee-pot! If the admirers of the tragic poet Schiller could have seen him in this position, they would never have believed that the young man in this miserable apparel—the long, lean, angular figure, with the bony, homely face and yellow hair, loosed from the confinement of the queue, and falling in dishevelled masses over his sunken cheeks—that this man was the author of the three tragedies which for the last few years had filled all Germany with astonishment, admiration, and terror. Like the column of fire, harbinger of a new era, they towered on the grave of the old, licking the heavens with tongues of flame.

About ten years before, Goethe's "Sufferings of Young Werther" had flooded Germany with great enthusiasm. This wonderful book, half romance, half reality, had pierced the hearts of all like lightning—as if these hearts had been but tinder awaiting ignition and destruction at the touch of this eloquence, this passion of love, and revelling in destruction by such heavenly agents! In the impassioned and excited state of the public mind, Goethe's "Werner" had been received by the youth of Germany—yes, of all Europe—as a revelation of the spirit of the universe, as a proclaiming angel. On bended knees and in ecstatic devotion they listened to the heavenly voice which aroused their hearts from sleep with the holy sirocco of passion, and awakened them out of the tameness of prose to the passion and vehemence of poetry; to the blissful pain of unsatisfied longing and heaven-achieving love.

And now, when the excited minds had hardly quieted down, when the dazzled eyes had hardly become accustomed to the heavenly effulgence shed upon them by "Werther"—now, after scarcely ten years, another wonder occurred, another of the stormy, impassioned periods, of which Klinger had been the father and creator, with his soul-stirring dramas, had given birth to a new genius, and a new light was diffused over Germany.

In the year 1774 Goethe had published his romance, "Sufferings of Young Werther." Carried away with sympathy by his lofty enthusiasm, all Germany—yes, all Europe— applauded and hailed him as the wonderful poet who had embodied the sorrows and pangs which agitate the heart and soul of each individual, in a sublime symphony, in which every sigh and every thought of suffering, weeping, rejoicing, and exulting humanity, found expression. Schiller's first tragedy, "The Robbers," was produced upon the stage for the first time in 1782; and its effects and results were of the most vast and enduring character.

Goethe, with his "Werner," had imbued all hearts with enthusiasm for love and feeling; Schiller, with his "Robbers," filled all hearts with yearnings after liberty and hatred of tyranny. The personal grandeur and freedom of man were idealized in the noble robber Charles Moor, and, not only was this magnanimous robber the hero of all young girls, but the hearts of all the young men were filled with abhorrence of and contempt for the tyrants who had compelled this high-minded man to flee to the Bohemian forests and become a robber in order to escape the galling chains of subserviency to princes.

Enthusiasm for this champion of liberty, this robber, Charles Moor, at the same time imbued all with detestation of tyrants.

The lion-rampant which was to be seen on the printed copies of "The Robbers," and which bore the motto "*In Tyrannos,*" was only a representation of the German people, who, moved to the core by Schiller's tragedy, and made conscious of the worth and dignity of man, asserted itself in its majesty against tyranny.

"Had I been present at the creation of the world as God," said a German prince at that time, "and had I foreseen that 'The Robbers' would be written in this world, I would never have created it."

In a German city where "The Robbers" was produced on the stage, the performance had so powerful an effect on the minds of the youth, that twelve young men formed the plan of fleeing secretly from the houses of their parents to the Bohemian forests, in order to make up a band of robbers. All the preparations had been made, and the twelve juvenile robbers had agreed to meet on the following night at a designated place outside the city gate; when one of the young heroes, in giving his mother a last good-night kiss, could no longer restrain his tears, and in this manner led to the discovery of the great secret and the prevention of the plan by the arrest of the youthful band of aspirants.

As the German public was filled with rapture for the
suicidal love-hero Werther, it now worshipped the suicidal
robber-hero Charles Moor: while love then excited its trans-
ports, liberty and the rights of humanity were now the objects
of its enthusiasm.

And the poet Schiller added fuel to the flames of this enthusiasm. A new tragedy, the theme of which was liberty,
"Fiesco," soon followed his "Robbers;" and the sensation
which it caused was still to be surpassed by that excited
throughout all Germany by his third tragedy, "Louise Müllerin, or Intrigues and Love:" This was, at the same time,
an exaltation of noble love, and of the proud human heart,
and a condemnation and denunciation of the established
prejudices which arrogantly recognized nobility and gentle
birth as conferring prerogatives and privileges.

"The Robbers," "Fiesco," and "Louise Müllerin," these
were the flaring torches of the revolution which in Germany
was to work out its ends in the minds of men, as it had done
in a more material manner, in France, on their bodies. In
France royalty and the nobility were conducted to the guillotine, in Germany they were pilloried in public opinion by the
prince and court marshal in "Intrigues and Love."

Goethe had given the German public the ideal of love—
Schiller gave them the ideal of liberty. And the poet of
"The Robbers" was as warmly enshrined in the heart of the
German people as the poet of "Werther" had been.

But alas! the admiration and enthusiasm of the German
public shows itself in words and praises, but not in deeds in
material proofs. True, the Germans give their poets a portion of their hearts, but not a portion of their fortune.

Schiller had given the Germans his three tragedies; they
had made their triumphal march over every stage in Germany; but Schiller had nevertheless remained the poor poet,
whose only possession was the invisible laurel-wreath which
adorned his noble brow, accorded him by the German people.

His countless admirers saw him in their inspired thoughts

with his youthful head entwined with laurel, and would, no doubt, have been horrified if they could have seen him in his dressing-gown, the nightcap pulled down over the laurel, stooping in front of his iron stove and endeavoring to rekindle the coals with his breath, in order that his coffee might be warmed a little.

But it was a vain endeavor. The fire was almost out, the coals glowed but faintly, and the poet's breath was not strong enough to renew the flame.

"All in vain," sighed Schiller, replacing the coffee-pot on the ashes, with a disconsolate shrug of the shoulders; "where there is no fuel, there can be no fire."

He slowly arose from his kneeling position, and, his hands folded behind his back, walked with rapid strides to and fro in his little chamber. The dimly-burning tallow-candle which stood on the table, covered with papers and books, flared up whenever he passed, and illuminated, for the moment, the large rugged figure and the pale countenance, with the high forehead and light-blue eyes. At first this countenance wore a gloomy, troubled look. But by degrees it assumed another expression; and soon the flaring light showed in this dingy little room the features of an inspired poet, with sparkling eyes, and an exulting smile.

"Yes," he exclaimed, in a loud voice, "yes, it shall be so! I will append this scene to the third act, and it must be the loftiest and grandest of the entire tragedy. Not to Prince Carlos or to the queen shall Posa proclaim his sublime ideas of liberty and his plans for the happiness of the people. No, he shall hurl them in the face of the tyrant, of King Philip himself. With the lightning of his words he shall warm this rock of tyranny, and unseal the spring of inspiration in the breast of the man-despising, bigoted ruler, and make the waters of human love play joyfully! Oh, ye eternal gods, give me words, fire my thoughts, and give wings to my inspiration, that I may be able to give expression, in a flow of rapture and poetry, to that which now fills my whole soul!"

He rushed to his table and threw himself with such violence into his old stool that it groaned and cracked beneath him. But Schiller paid no attention to this; his whole soul was in his work, his whole heart was filled with enthusiasm and de-light. His hand flew over the paper, his smile brightened, his countenance became more radiant. At times he dictated to himself in a loud, energetic voice, the words which his flying pen conveyed to the paper, that they might henceforth to all eternity be indelibly imprinted in the hearts of his readers. But Schiller was not thinking of his readers, nor of the possible effect of his words; he thought only of his work. There was no room in his soul but for poetry, for the sublime and lofty scene which he wished to add to his tragedy. "Oh," he now exclaimed, his pen speeding like an arrow over the rustling paper, "oh, could the combined eloquence of all the thousands who are interested in this lofty hour, but trem-ble on my lips, to fan the spark which I feel into a flame! Abandon this unnatural idolatry that destroys us. Be our model of the eternal and the true, and—"

A severe and painful cough interrupted the enraptured poet; he was compelled to discontinue his recitation; the pen faltered in his quivering hand; and from the sublime realms of the ideal, bodily pain recalled the poet to reality.

He let fall the pen, the arrow which the gods had be-stowed, to enable him to divide the clouds of prejudice and throw open to enraptured humanity the heaven of poetry,— he let fall the pen, and raised his hand to his trembling, pant-ing breast.

"How it pains, how it pricks!" he groaned. "Is it not as if the tyrant Philip had thrust his dagger into the breast of poor Posa, in the anger of his offended majesty, and—"

Another attack of coughing silenced him, and resounded through the quiet solitary chamber. The sound struck upon his ear so dismally that he cast a hasty glance behind him into the gloomy space, as if looking for the ghost which had ut-tered such dreary tones.

"If this continues, I am hardly repaid for having fled from my tyrannical duke," murmured Schiller. "Truly I had better have remained and served out my poor miserable existence as regimental surgeon, than cough my life out as a German, that is, as a hungry poet."

But as he said this, his lips quivered, and self-reproach was depicted in his countenance.

"Be still," he exclaimed, "be still! Shame upon you, Schiller, for uttering such unmanly, cowardly words! You a poet, Frederick Schiller? you are not even a man! You aspire to ascend the heights of Parnassus, and sink down disheartened and discouraged when an evil annoys you on the way, and admonishes you that you are only a man, a mortal who aspires to climb to the seat of the gods. If you are a poet, Frederick Schiller, remember that the gods are watching over you, and that they will not cruelly abandon you before the goal is half achieved.

"No," he exclaimed in a loud voice, raising his head, and looking upward, "no, the gods will not abandon me! They will give me strength and health and a long life, that I may accomplish the task which my soul and mind and heart tell me is required at my hands. No, Parnassus stands before me, and I will climb it!" His beaming eye glanced upward in ecstasy and saw not the low dusty ceiling, the want and indigence by which he was surrounded. He gazed into immensity; the low ceiling opened to his view, and through it "he saw the heavens and the countenance of the blessed!"

A loud noise in the street awakened him from his trance. It was the watchman blowing his horn and calling the hour in stentorian tones.

"Four o'clock," murmured Schiller, "the night approaches its end!—and my candle also," he continued, smiling, as he looked at the brass candlestick, from the upper rim of which the softened tallow was falling in heavy drops, while the wick had sunk down into the liquid mass.

Schiller shrugged his shoulders. "It appears that I must

stop in the middle of my grand scene and go to bed. My good friend Streicher has in vain begged me to do so, through his musical messenger of love; and now a tallow-candle compels me to do so! What poor, miserable beings we men are! A trifling, inanimate, material thing has more power over us than the spirit, and while we oppose the latter we must submit to be overcome by the former! Therefore to bed, to bed! Farewell, my Posa! The poor human creature leaves you for a few hours, but the lofty human mind will soon return to you! Good-night, my Posa!"

The wick of the miserable candle flared up once more and then expired with a crackling noise in the liquid tallow. "That is as it should be," laughed Schiller; "the poet, like the mule, must be able to find his way in the dark on the verge of an abyss!"

He groped his way through the little room to his bedchamber, and undressed himself rapidly; and the loud, regular breathing soon announced that the young poet, Frederick Schiller, was wrapped in health-giving and refreshing slumber.

CHAPTER II.

THE TRIALS OF LIFE.

FREDERICK SCHILLER still slept, although the pale winter sun of December stood high in the heavens, and the streets of the little city of Mannheim had long since awakened to new life and activity. Frederick Schiller still slept, and, worn out by his long vigils, his work, and his cough, might have slept on for a long time, had he not been aroused by a loud knocking at the door, and an audible step in the adjoining room.

A young man stood on the threshold of the bedchamber and wished Schiller a hearty good-morning.

"I can account for this, Fritz," said he, raising his finger threateningly—"not into bed at night, not out of bed in the morning! Did I not send you my watchman as a love-messenger? But he has already complained to me that it was unavailing."

"Do not be angry, my Andrew," exclaimed Schiller, extending his hand to his friend with a cordial smile. "A poet must above all things wait upon the muses submissively, and may not show them the door when they pay him a visit at an unseemly hour of the night."

"Ah, the nine muses would have been satisfied if you had shown them out, and had graciously accorded them the privilege of knocking at your door again this morning! But get up, Fritz! Unfortunately, I have something of pressing and grave importance to communicate!"

With one bound Frederick Schiller was out of his bed. "Of pressing and grave importance," he repeated, dressing rapidly, "that sounds very mystical, Andrew. And now that I look at you, I find that your usually open brow is clouded. It is no misfortune that you have to announce?"

"No, Fritz, no misfortune, thank God, but a very great annoyance. Miserable, grovelling poverty once more stretches out its ravenous claws."

"What is it?" asked Schiller, breathlessly, as he drew the dressing-gown over his shoulders with trembling hands. "I am now composed and ready to hear all! Some impatient creditor who wishes to throw me into prison. Is it not so? Speak it right out, Andrew, without hesitation."

"Well, then, come with me into the other room. There you shall learn all," answered Andrew Streicher, taking his friend's hand and throwing the chamber door open, which he had closed behind him on his entrance. "Come and see!"

"Mr. Schwelm," exclaimed Schiller, as he observed on crossing the threshold a gentleman standing in a window-niche, whose countenance indicated that he was very ill at ease. "Yes, truly, this is my loved and faithful friend, Oswald Schwelm, from Stuttgart, the literary godfather of my career as a poet, and—But how mournful you look, dear

Schwelm! and not a single word of friendship for me, no greeting?"

"Ah, Schiller, these are hard times," sighed Oswald Schwelm. "Anxiety and want have driven me from Stuttgart, and I come to you as a right unwelcome guest. Only believe that I deplore it deeply myself, but I cannot help it, and it is not my fault. I would gladly sacrifice every thing for my friend Schiller, but I have nothing more; and painful necessity compels me to remind you of the old debt."

"Do not judge him harshly, Schiller," said Streicher, in a low voice. "Poor Schwelm's difficulties are of a very urgent nature. You know very well that at a time when no printer could be found to put your 'Robbers' in press, Schwelm guaranteed to the publisher in Stuttgart the expense incurred in its publication, because he was convinced, as we all were, that the 'Robbers' would make you a celebrated poet, and not only insure you a harvest of honor and renown, but also of money. Now, unfortunately, the money has not yet been harvested, and poor Oswald Schwelm has had the additional misfortune of losing his capital by the failure of the commercial house in which it was deposited. Since then the publisher has dunned him in an outrageous manner, and has even obtained a warrant for his arrest; and, in order to escape, Schwelm fled from Stuttgart and came here!"

"Forgive me, friend Schwelm," said Schiller, rushing forward and embracing the young merchant. "Ah, my dear friends, it seems that you have mistaken me and my future; it seems that the lofty plans formed in our youthful days are not to be realized."

"They have already been realized in part," said Schwelm, gently. "You are a renowned poet; all Germany admires and praises you! The 'Robbers' has been given on every stage, and—"

"And I have not even three hundred florins," interrupted Schiller, sadly, "not even a paltry three hundred florins to meet the just demands of the friend who confided in and gave his bond for me, and who must now become involved in danger and difficulty on my account."

"Then you have not succeeded in getting the money together?" said Streicher, mournfully. "I imparted to you two weeks ago the contents of the letter containing an anxious appeal for help, which Schwelm had written to me, and you promised to procure the money. Since then I disliked to speak of the matter again, because I knew you would surely leave no means untried to raise the amount."

"And I have left no means untried," exclaimed Schiller, with an angry gesture. "What can I do? No one is willing to lend or advance money on the pitiful capital of a poet's talent! The few florins which I have received for the representation of the 'Robbers' and 'Fiesco' have hardly sufficed to purchase the bare necessities of life; and when I begged the manager, Mr. von Dalberg, to advance me on 'Louisa Müllerin' at least three hundred florins, as he had determined to put it on the stage, he refused me, and I had the mortification of being turned off by this nobleman like a miserable begging writer."

"And your father," said Andrew Schwelm, timidly. "Did you not say that you would apply to your father, Major Schiller?"

"I have done so," replied Schiller, with a sigh. "I wrote urgently, representing my want and troubles, and begging him to have pity on his poor son, and to lend him a helping hand for this once. But it seems my words have not had power to touch his paternal heart, for until now I have in vain awaited a reply on every mail day. And it seems that the mail which comes from Stuttgart to-day has brought me no letter, for I believe the hour at which letters are delivered has long since passed. I must therefore patiently wait another three days for a reply, and the next mail will perhaps condemn me to another trial of patience. Oh, my friends, if you could see my heart, if you could estimate the pain this mortification causes me! For myself, I am ready to suffer want, to content myself with the bare necessities of life—yes, even to hunger and thirst, to attain the lofty ends to which I aspire.   The path of a poet has ever been a thorny one, and poverty has always been the companion of poetry.   This I am ready to bear.   I do not crave riches; and even if the tempter should approach in this trying hour and offer me a million, but with the condition that I should forswear poetry, and write nothing more for the stage, I would reject the million with contempt, and a thousand times prefer to remain a poor poet than become a rich idler.   But to see you, my friends, in trouble and suffering on my account, and powerless to relieve you, is truly bitter, and—"

"The letter-carrier," exclaimed Streicher joyfully, as, after a timid knock, the door was softly opened, and a man in the uniform of the Thurn and Taxis post-office officials entered the room.

"A letter from Ludwigsburg.   Ten kreutzers postage," said the carrier, holding out a large sealed letter.

"Ten kreutzers," murmured Schiller, as he nervously fumbled in the pockets of his dressing-gown and then in the table-drawer.

"Here are the ten kreutzers, in case you should not happen to have the small change," said Streicher, hastily, as he handed the carrier the money and received the letter.   "And here it is, friend Schiller.   Is it from your father?"

"Yes, my friends, it is from him.   And may the gods have been graciously inclined, and have opened my father's heart to his son's prayer!"

He hastily tore off the cover and threw open the large folded sheet.   "Alas, my friends," he sighed, "it is a very long letter, and that bodes no good, for he who gives says but little, but he who denies clothes his refusal in many prettily-turned phrases.   Let me read!"

A few moments of silence followed.   Schiller, seated on his chair, his arm resting on the table, was reading his father's letter, while Andrew Streicher and Oswald Schwelm were standing opposite him, in the window-niche, regarding him anxiously and inquiringly. They saw that Schiller's brow grew darker and darker; that his cheek became paler; and that the corners of his mouth quivered, as they always did when the poet's soul was moved with anger or pain.

"Read, Andrew," said Schiller, handing the letter to Andrew Streicher, after a long silence. "Read my father's letter aloud, that you may both know what I have to expect; that you may perceive that I am nothing but a poor, miserable dreamer, in whom no one believes, not even his own father, and who must be awakened from his illusions by harsh words. Andrew, read the lecture addressed by my father to his miserable son. To hear these unhappy words from your lips will serve as a penance, and may perhaps have the effect of bringing you to the conclusion that my father is right in giving me up. Read it, Streicher."

Streicher took the proffered letter and read aloud:

"'My Son!—Here I sit with his letter before me, and its perusal has provoked tears of displeasure. I have long since foreseen his present position, the foundation of which has already been laid in Stuttgart. I have faithfully warned him against it, given him the best advice, and cautioned him against expending any thing over his income, and thereby involving himself in debts, which are very readily made, but not so easily paid. I gave him an adequate outfit upon leaving the academy. To give him a start in the world, our gracious duke gave him for his services what, together with the little his parents were able to do for him from day to day, would have been an ample support for him as an unmarried man. But all these advantages, all my teachings, and all hopes of better prospects here, have been able to effect nothing. He has combated all my reasons, made light of my experience and of the experience of others, and has only listened to such counsels as would inevitably insure his destruction. God in His wisdom and goodness could choose no other way to bring him to a knowledge of himself than by sending this affliction to convince him that all our intellect and power, all reliance upon other men, and upon accidental and happy contingencies, are for the most part vain, foolish, and fallacious, and that it is He alone who helps all those who pray to Him earnestly and patiently.'"

"As if I had not done so!" interrupted Schiller. "As if I had not besought the great Ruler of the destinies of men, in deep fervor and humility of soul, to cast a ray of enlightening grace upon the head of him who had believed it to be his duty to follow the divine call of poetry, and who for its own sake had joyfully relinquished all other earthly prospects and hopes! But my fervid prayers were in vain; no ray of mercy has illumined my poor, gloomy chamber; and from God and man alike the poet receives an angry refusal, and is dismissed as a beggar!—Read on, Streicher! I will drink the cup of bitterness to the dregs; not a single drop of gall shall remain untasted. Read on, my friend!"

"But, Frederick," said Streicher, in a tender, imploring voice, "why impose upon yourself and us the penance of reading these hard words? Your father means well with you undoubtedly. He is a good and honorable man, but from his stand-point the world has a different appearance than from that of the heights of Parnassus. He estimates you by an ordinary scale, and that is not adapted to Frederick Schiller. That your father will not furnish you the required three hundred florins was evident from the commencement of the letter, and that suffices."

"No, that is not enough," exclaimed Schiller, earnestly. "You shall know what my own father thinks of me, that you may be under no more illusions concerning me, and not have to reproach me some day with having infected you with my fantasies, and held out hopes that would never be realized. I beg you, therefore, to read on. It seems as if the scorching words of paternal anger might in some degree expiate the criminality of my conduct. Read!"

"Well, Fritz, if you insist upon it, I will do so," sighed Streicher; and in a loud voice he resumed the reading: "'He has not been humbled by all the chastening administered to him since his departure, and experience only has made him wiser. That he has suffered from intermittent fever for eight entire months, does no credit to his professional studies; and in the same case he would certainly have bitterly reproached a patient for not having followed instructions in regard to diet and mode of living. Man is not always dependent upon circumstances, or he would be a mere machine. My dear son has never striven with himself, and it is highly improper and sinful to throw the responsibility of his not having done so upon his education in the academy. Many young men have grown up in this institution who demanded and received as little assistance, and they are now doing well, and are much esteemed and provided for. How does he suppose we poor parents feel when we reflect that these troubles would not have overtaken him, that we would have been spared a thousand cares on his account, and that he would certainly have achieved what he sought if he had remained here? In brief, he would have been happier, more contented, and more useful in his day and generation, if he had been satisfied to pursue a medium course in life, and had not aspired to take so high a flight. Nor is it necessary that a superior talent should be made manifest outwardly, at least not until the benefits accruing from its exercise can be shown and proven, and it can be said, "These are the fruits of diligence and intelligence." Pastor Hahn and Pastor Fulda are both great men, and are visited by all travelling scholars, and yet they look like other men. As for the three hundred florins, I must say that this demand has excited my great displeasure. I have never given him cause to think, "My father can and will rescue me when I become involved in difficulties." And he knows himself that I have three other children, none of whom are provided for, and from whom much has already been withheld on his account. On his prospects, hopes, plans, and promises, I can advance nothing, as I have already been so badly deceived. Even if it were possible to place some faith in them, I could not raise the money; for, although I am known as an honest man, my financial condition, and the amount of my salary, are also well known; and it is evident that I would not be able to pay a debt of from two to three hundred florins out of my income. I can do nothing but pray for my son! His faithful father, SCHILLER.' " *

"Can do nothing but pray and scold," exclaimed Schiller, emphatically. "There you see what an unworthy, trifling fellow I am. All the hopes which my family and friends entertained for me, yes, which I entertained for myself and my talents, are blighted, dissolved in smoke like burning straw. Nothing real is left but the burden of my debts, and my poverty. My good Oswald, you have had the weakness to believe in me, and to accept a draft on my future. To your own detriment, you must now perceive that this draft is worthless, and that my father was right in reproaching me for having had the temerity to attempt to make a German poet out of a Wurtemberg regimental surgeon."

"Do not speak so, Frederick Schiller," exclaimed Streicher, indignantly. "Your words are blasphemous; and all Germany would be angry with you if it heard them!"

"But all Germany would take good care not to pay my debts. While I, in holy and true disinterestedness, am ready to consecrate my ·whole being to the service of my country, and to devote all the powers of my mind and talents to its benefit, its instruction and entertainment, if I should demand of the German nation that it should also bring me an offering, that each individual who had read and seen my tragedies should give me a groschen, each one would deny that he had ever seen or read them, and, with a shrug of his shoulders, would turn from the beggar who had the temerity to require any thing of the public but its applause and its momentary

* "Schiller's Relations to his Parents and the Walzogen Family," pp. 62-68.

delight. My friends, I am very miserable, for you must know
that this is not the only large debt which troubles me. There
were other noble souls who had confidence in my success, and
allowed themselves to be bribed by 'The Robbers.' My noble
friend, Madame von Wolzogen, who gave the homeless one an
asylum on her estate in Bauerbach, when he had fled from
Ludwigsburg, did more than this. When, after a sojourn of
seven months in her beautiful Tusculum, I marched out into
the world again, she loaned me two hundred florins, which
I solemnly promised to return in a year. The year has expired, my noble friend depends on this sum to make a
necessary payment on a mortgage which is attached to her
estate, and I am not able to keep my word. I must expect
her to consider me a swindler who has cheated her with
empty promises!"

"No, Madame von Wolzogen will not think so, for she
knows you," exclaimed Streicher, indignantly.

"She will be as far from thinking so as I am," said Oswald
Schwelm, gently. "It is not your fault that you are in
pecuniary difficulties; the blame does not attach to you, but
to the German public, to the German nation, which allows
its poets to suffer want, even while enraptured with their
works. The German people are prodigal with laurels and
wreaths, but cannot be taught that laurels do not sustain life,
and that wreaths are of no avail to the poet if they do not
also prepare a home for him, where he can await the muses at
his ease, and rest on his laurels. Ah, Frederick Schiller,
when I see how you, one of the noblest of poets, are tormented by the want of a paltry sum of money, my eyes fill
with tears of compassion, not for you, but for the German
fatherland, which disowns its most exalted sons, while it
worships the foreigner and gives a warm reception to every
stranger charlatan who condescends to come and pocket German money for his hackneyed performances."

"No, no," said Schiller, hastily. "You must not abuse
and condemn the object of my highest and holiest love. As

a true son never reviles his mother, even when he believes that she has been unjust to him, so the true son of Germany must never scold his sublime mother, but must love her tenderly and endearingly, even if she should accord him nothing but a cradle and a grave. As we say, 'what God does is well done,' we must also say what Germania does is well done. And believe me, my friends, if I truly deserve it, and if, as you say, and I hope, I am really a poet, the German fatherland will smile upon me, and give me the bread of life for the manna of poetry. Men will not let him die of hunger to whom the gods have given the kiss of immortality."

"Amen," said Streicher, with a slight touch of derision.

"Yes, amen," repeated Schiller, smiling. "It was well, friend Oswald, that you awakened the patriot in me by your indignation in my behalf, for the patriot has helped me to overlook my little earthly necessities. My friends, be patient and indulgent with me. Better times are coming, and if I am really a poet the gods will take pity on me, and a day of recognition and renown will also come! To be sure, I have nothing to offer you at present but hope. The draft on the future is all I can give you, my good Oswald, for the money you loaned me."

"This draft is, in my eyes, the most beautiful coin," said Oswald Schwelm, heartily, "and truly it is not your fault that my hard-hearted creditor cannot take the same view of the matter, but demands payment for the publication of 'The Robbers.' Well, we will speak of it no more. Forgive me, Schiller, for having caused you disquiet by coming here. But, as I said before, I did not think of the ingratitude of the German fatherland, but only of the German poet who had given it 'The Robbers,' 'Fiesco,' and 'Louise Müllerin;' and I hoped that applause had made him rich. Give me your hand, Schiller, and let us say farewell."

"And what will you do, my poor friend?" asked Schiller, feelingly. "Will you return to Stuttgart, where the hard-hearted creditor awaits you?"

"No, no," answered Oswald, "I will not return to Stuttgart, for the warrant of arrest would hang over my head like the sword of Damocles! I will go to Carlsruhe, where I have an old uncle, and will endeavor to soften his heart. Do not trouble yourself about me, my friend; and may your cheerfulness and the creative power of the poet not for a single moment be darkened by the remembrance of me! We prosaic sons of humanity are often aided by accident, and find some little avenue of escape from the embarrassments of life, while you poets march through the grand portals into the temple of fame, where you are more exposed to the attacks of enemies. Farewell, friend Schiller, and may great Jupiter ever be with you!"

"Adieu, friend Schwelm!" said Schiller, extending his hand and gazing sadly at his kind, open countenance. "You assume to be gay, in order to hide your anxiety; but I see through the veil which friendship and the goodness of your heart have prompted you to assume, and behind it I detect a careworn, anxious look. Oh, my friends, I am a poor man, and am only worthy of commiseration; and it is all in vain that I endeavor to arm myself against a knowledge of this fact."

"No, you are a great and enviable man," exclaimed Streicher, with enthusiasm. "Of that we are all assured, and you also shall become convinced of it. You are ascending the mountain which leads to renown, and, although now enveloped in a cloud, you will at last attain the heights above, and be surrounded with a halo of sunshine and glory."

"I wish, my friend," said Schiller, pointing with a sad smile to the ashes in the stove, "I wish we had some of this sunshine now, and were not compelled to warm the room with such expensive coals. But patience, patience! You are right, Andrew, I am ascending a mountain, and am now in a cloud, and therefore it is not surprising that I feel chilly and uncomfortable. But better times are coming, and my health will improve, and this bad cough and fever will no longer re-

tard my footsteps, and I will be able to mount aloft to the
abode of the gods with more rapid strides. Farewell, my
friends! My writing-table seems to regard me with astonishment, as if asking why I have not brought it my customary
ovation."

"Let it look and inquire," said Streicher. "You must
make no reply, but must first break your fast, as any other
honest man would do. Come and breakfast with us at the
inn, Frederick. A man must eat, and, although I unfortunately have not enough money to satisfy this Cerberus of a
creditor, I have at least enough to pay for a breakfast and a
glass of wine for us three. Come, Frederick, get yourself
ready quickly, and let us tread the earth with manly footsteps,
and compel it to recognize us as its lords."

"No, you good, thoughtless man of the world," said Schiller, smiling; "no, I must remain here! I must work on at
'Don Carlos,' who gives my mind no rest by day or night, and
insists on being completed!"

"But promise me, at least, Fritz, that you will breakfast
before you go to work?"

"I promise you! Now go, Andrew, for the good Schwelm
is already holding the door open, and waiting for you."

CHAPTER III.

HENRIETTA VON WOLZOGEN.

"BREAKFAST," murmured Schiller, after his two friends
had taken leave of him. "Oh, yes, it were certainly no bad
idea to indulge in a hot cup of coffee and fresh sweet rolls.
But it costs too much, and one must be contented if one can
only have a cup of fresh water and a piece of bread."

He stood up and returned to the chamber, to complete the
toilet so hastily made before, to adjust his hair, and put on

the sober, well-worn suit which constituted alike his work-day and holiday attire.

After having finished his toilet, Schiller took the pitcher, which stood on a tin waiter by the side of a glass, and bounded gayly down the stairway into the large courtyard and to the fountain, to fill his pitcher at the mouth of the tragic mask from which a stream of water constantly gushed.

This was Schiller's first morning errand. Every morning the people in the house could see the pale, thin young man go to the fountain with his pitcher; and it amused them to watch him as he walked up and down the yard with long strides, looking heavenward, his head thrown back, and his chest expanded with the fresh morning air, which he inhaled in long draughts. Then, when he had stretched and exercised his limbs, breathed the air, and looked at the heavens, he returned to the fountain, took up his pitcher, running over with water, ran into the house, up the stairway, and re-entered his dingy little room.

But he brought the heavens and the fresh morning air with him, and his soul was gladdened and strengthened for his poetic labors.

To-day the fresh air had done him much good; and, after he had drunk his first glass of water, and eaten his bread and butter, which he took from a closet in the wall, he looked pleased and comfortable; a smile glided over his features, and his eyes brightened.

"How rich is he who has few wants," he said softly to himself, "and how freely the spirit soars when its wings are un-encumbered with the vanities of life! Come, ye Muses and Graces, keep a loving watch around my table, and guide my hand that I may write nothing that does not please you!"

He threw himself on the chair before the table, took up his pen, rapidly read what he had last written, and with a few strokes finished the last great scene of the third act of his new tragedy, "Don Carlos."

"Und jetzt verlaszt mich!" * recited Schiller, as his pen flew over the paper; and then he continued, in a changed voice: "Kann ich es mit einer erfüllten Hoffnung,—dann ist dieser Tag der schönste meines Lebens!" And then he added, in the first voice: "Er ist kein verlorener in dem meinigem!"

"Yes," exclaimed Schiller, in a loud voice, as he threw his pen aside, "and it is not a lost one in mine. At some future day I will think of this hour with joy and satisfaction—of the hour in which I wrote the closing scene of the third act of a tragedy, a dramatist's greatest and most difficult task. Oh, ye Muses and Graces, whom I invoked, were you near me, blessing my labors? I laid my human sacrifice of pain and suffering on your altar this morning, and my poor head once more received the baptism of tears. Bless me with your favor, ye Muses and Graces, and let me hope that the tears of the man were the baptism of the poet! Yes, my soul persuades me that I am a poet; and this new work will attest it before the world and mankind, and—"

A cry of surprise and dismay escaped his lips, and he stared toward the door which had just been opened, and in which a lady appeared who was completely wrapped up in furs, and whose face was entirely shaded by a hood.

"Madame von Wolzogen," he exclaimed, rising quickly. "Is it possible? Can it be you?" He rushed forward and seized her hand, and when he encountered her mournful gaze he sank on his knees and wept bitterly.

"Oh, my friend, my mother, that we should meet under such circumstances! That I should be compelled to throw myself at your feet in shame and penitence!"

"And why, Schiller?" asked Madame von Wolzogen, in her soft, kindly voice. "Why must you throw yourself at my feet, and why this penitence? Be still. Do not reply yet,

---

* Fragment of a dialogue between the King and the Marquis, last Scene, Act III., of "Don Carlos:"

"*King.* And now leave me.

"*Marquis.* If I can do so with an accomplished hope, this will be the most glorious day of my life.

"*Marquis.* It is no lost one in mine!"

my poor child. First, hear me! My only reason in coming here was to see you. It seemed impossible, unnatural, that I should pass through Mannheim without seeing my friend, my son, my Frederick Schiller! My sister, who lives in Meiningen, has suddenly fallen ill, and has called me to her bedside. Well, I am answering her call; for no one has ever appealed to Henrietta von Wolzogen in vain. I have ridden all night, and will soon resume my journey. The carriage is waiting for me at the corner. I inquired my way to Schiller's dwelling; and here I am, and I wish to know, Frederick Schiller, what this silence means, and why you have not written to me for so long a time? That I must know; and I am only here for the purpose of putting this one question: Schiller, have you forgotten your friends in Bauerbach? have you forgotten me, who was your friend and your mother?"

"No, no," he cried, rising and throwing his arms tenderly around Madame von Wolzogen's neck, and pressing her to his heart. "No, how could I forget your goodness, your generosity, and friendship? But can you not comprehend, my friend, why your arrival could have a terrible effect on me— could bring me to the verge of despair?"

"Only see how the poetic flame bursts forth when we prosaic people ask a practical question—when we have to remind poets that, unfortunately, we are not fed upon ambrosia falling from heaven! But I imagined that my wild boy would be once more tearing his own flesh, and terribly dissatisfied with his destiny. And I am here, Schiller, to tell you that you must think better of me and better of yourself, and not confound noble friendship with ignoble gold, which shrewd people call the mainspring of life, but which is, fortunately, not the mainspring of friendship, and—"

"Oh, my friend, if you knew—"

"Silence! The philippic which I had time to prepare at my leisure during my night ride, and which I am determined to inflict upon the capricious and wayward boy, if not upon the man, is not yet ended. Is it possible that your heart could be forgetful of and untrue to the past? And why? Because his poor motherly friend has written him in confidence that she would be glad if he would return at least a part of the sum of money she had loaned him. And what is his reply? Nothing, nothing at all! He throws his friend's letter into the fire, and—"

"Into the fire of his anguish, of his reproaching conscience," interrupted Schiller, passionately. "He was silent, because it wrung his heart to stand even for a moment in the category of those who had defrauded you. Oh, my dear friend, toward whom I feel drawn as a loving, obedient son, consider in your sensitive woman's heart if the thought of breaking my faith and becoming a traitor to you was not calculated to drive me to desperation! Confiding in my honesty, you loaned me a considerable sum of money, the more considerable as you were not rich, and were yourself compelled to borrow the money from a Jew. I solemnly promised to return the borrowed sum within the course of a year. The year has expired, the Jew urges payment; and now, when you gently remind me of my promise, I feel with shame and rage that I have broken my word, and acted dishonorably toward you; and, therefore—oh, out upon contemptible, cowardly human nature, which dares not look its own weakness in the face!—and therefore I was silent. How often did my heart prompt me, in my distress of mind, to fly to your friendship for relief! but the painful consciousness of my inability to comply with your request and pay my debt, held me back. My powerlessness to meet your just demand made the thought of you, which had ever been a source of joy, a positive torment. Whenever your image appeared, the picture of my misery rose up before me. I feared to write to you, because I had nothing to write but the eternal: 'Have patience with me!' " *

He laid his head on Madame von Wolzogen's lap and sobbed; but with gentle force she compelled him to rise.

---

* Schiller's own words.—See "Schiller's Relations to Parents," etc., p. 450.

"Stand up, Schiller; hold your head erect. It does not beseem you to despair and complain like other poor, suffering children of humanity. You, who are marching upward to Parnassus, should tread under foot the vermin of earthly cares."

"But this vermin does not lie at my feet, but is in my brain, and will drive me mad if this goes on! But I must tell you, you must know the truth: it is impossible for me to pay you any part of my debt. Oh, it is hard to say these words; nevertheless, I must not be ashamed, for it is destiny. One is not to be deemed culpable because one is unfortunate." *

"And one is not unhappy because one has no money," said Madame von Wolzogen, smiling. "One is only retarded and checked, like the fiery young steed, impatient to bound madly over the plain and dash up the mountain, but prevented by the tightly-drawn reins. But, my friend, this need cause you no unhappiness. With the strength of brave determination, and the energy of creative power, you will break the reins, liberate yourself, and soar aloft. Even the winged Pegasus bears restraint, and must suffer it; but the poet, who holds and guides the reins, is free—free to mount aloft on his winged steed. And as he soars higher and higher, the earth, with its want and distress, grows less and less distinct. Then look upward, friend Schiller, upward to Parnassus, where golden renown and immortality await you!"

"Words, beautiful words!" exclaimed Schiller. "Oh, there was a time when the hope of renown was a source of as intense delight to me as an article of jewelry is to a young girl. Now, I am indifferent to every thing. I am willing to serve up my laurels in the next 'boeuf à la mode,' and to resign my tragic muse to your dairy-maid, if you keep cows.† How pitiable is a poet's renown, compared with a happy life! And I am so unhappy that I would willingly exchange all my expectations

---

* Schiller's own words.—See "Relations to Parents," etc., p. 451.
† Ibid., p. 416.

of future renown for a valid check for one hundred thousand florins, and—"

"Be silent!" exclaimed Madame von Wolzogen, imperiously. "You slander yourself. Thank God, these utterances do not come from your heart, but from your lips; and that the blasphemies which anger provokes are in a language known and understood only by your fantasy, and not by your mind! I told you before, that it did not beseem you to grovel in the dust. But now I say: Down on your knees, Frederick Schiller, on your knees, and pray to your own genius for forgiveness for the words which you have just spoken."

"Forgiveness," groaned Schiller, falling on his knees. "I beg forgiveness of you, my friend, my mother. I am a criminal—am like Peter, who in the hour of trial denied his Lord and Saviour—and reviled that which is greatest and holiest on earth. Be indulgent, have patience with me! Better times will come! The foaming and fomenting juice of the grape will clear, and become the rich, fiery wine which refreshes and makes glad. No, I do not despair of my future, and you who love me shall not do so either, and—"

"We do not," said Madame von Wolzogen, smiling. "You are a wonderful man! You are like the changing skies in storm and sunshine—first threatening clouds, then celestial blue; before anger and despair, now joy and hope. And this, my dear young friend, is the best evidence that you are truly a poet; and if you had not known it already, this hour should assure you of the fact. I, however, Frederick Schiller, have never doubted either your genius or yourself; and I have come to tell you this, and dissipate the dark cloud that was forming between two friends.—No, Frederick, we will not permit the sun of our friendship to be darkened. We must be honest, true, and sincere to one another; but we must not be silent and withhold a word of sympathy whenever one of us cannot grant what the other requires. I know that you are embarrassed and in want; and notwithstanding all my friendship, I cannot aid you. You know that the Jew Israel demands the sum which I borrowed of him; and it is not in your power to return it, although it is very inconvenient for me, and very painful to you. But shall we, because we are needy, make ourselves poor also? Shall we, because we have no money, have no friendship either?"

"No, my dear, my great, my good lady," exclaimed Schiller, his countenance radiant with joy. No, we will strengthen and console ourselves with friendship, and it must compensate us for all else. Oh, how poor and needy one would be in the possession of millions, without love and friendship! I, however, am rich, for I have dear friends—"

"And have, perhaps, besides friends, the precious treasure of a sweetheart? Oh, Schiller, how very prettily you blush, and how conscious you look. In love—once more in love! But in love with whom, my poet, with one or with two? And is the dear one's name Margaret, or Charlotte, or Laura, or—"

"Enough, enough," cried Schiller, laughing, "the dear one's name is Love, and I seek her everywhere, and think I find her in every noble and beautiful female face that wears the smile of innocence and the dignity of beauty, that meets my gaze. My heart is thrown open to permit Love to enter as a victorious queen, and take possession of the throne of beauty which I have erected in its sanctuary at the side of the altar of friendship, on which you reign supreme, my dear Madame Wolzogen, my second mother! Ah, how I thank you for having come! Your loving hand has removed from my soul the load of shame and humiliation, and I once more feel light and free; and I can now speak to you about these disagreeable money matters with calmness. No, no, do not forbid me, my dear lady, but let me speak on. Listen! I have been sick throughout almost the entire past year. Gnawing disquiet and uncertainty in regard to my prospects have retarded my recovery. This alone is the reason why so many of my plans have miscarried, and I have not been able to work and earn as much as I hoped. But I have now marked out my future course after mature consideration. And, if I am not disturbed on my way, my future is secured. I am putting my affairs in order and will soon be in a condition to pay all my debts. I only require a little time, until my plans begin to work. If I am hampered now, I am hampered forever. This week I will commence editing a journal, the *Rhenish Thalia*. It will be published by subscription; and a helping hand has been extended to me from many places. The journal will be a success, and I shall derive from it a certain income which will be sufficient for my support. From the proceeds of my theatrical pieces I shall be able to pay off my debts by degrees, and above all, my debt to you, my friend. I solemnly promise to pay you the entire amount, in instalments, by the end of next year, and I will make out three drafts which shall certainly be honored when due. Do not smile incredulously, my dear lady, but depend upon my assurances. I am certain that God will give me health to attain this noble aim." *

"My friend," said Madame Wolzogen, with emotion, "may God give you health and strength, not to enable you to pay this little debt, but to enable you to pay the great debt you owe the world! For the world requires of you that you use the great capital of poetry and mind with which God has intrusted you, as the talent which shall bear interest to the joy of mankind and your own honor and renown. It is a high and difficult calling for which God has chosen you. You must march in advance of humanity as its poet and priest, proclaiming and sympathizing with its sorrows and sufferings, and awakening that enthusiasm which leads to action and promotes happiness. Ever keep your noble ends in view, my friend, and when the little cares of life annoy you, disregard them, as the lion does the insects that fly around his head, and which he could destroy with a single blow of his paw, did he deem it worth the trouble. And now that we have come to an understanding, and know what we are and intend to

* Schiller's own words.—See "Relations to Parents," etc., p. 452.

remain to each other, and as my time has expired, I must leave you, for my sister is awaiting me. Farewell, Frederick! Give me your hand once more, and now, hand in hand, let us vow true friendship, that friendship which is never dumb, but imparts to the sister soul its joys and sorrows."

"So let it be," said Schiller, earnestly. "In joy and in sorrow I will ever turn to you, my friend, and second mother; and I now beg you never to doubt me. You were, are now, and always will be, equally dear to my heart. I can never be faithless to you, although circumstances and fate might make me appear so outwardly. Never withdraw your love from me. You must and will learn to know me well, and you will then, perhaps, love me a little better. Let nothing impair a friendship so pure, sealed under the eye of God.* And be assured I will always love you with the tenderness of a son, although you would not permit me to become your son. I do not reproach you, because I knew you were right. I am at the starting-point of my career, and dare not yet stretch out my hand after the woman I love!"

Henrietta von Wolzogen laid her hand on Schiller's shoulder and looked smilingly into his large blue eyes.

"After the woman you love?" she whispered. "You, dear boy, admit that the woman you love has not yet been found, and that for the present your heart is playing blind-man's-buff with all the pretty young women? For instance, my daughter Charlotte is almost forgotten, because the beautiful Madame Vischerin has such lovely eyes and converses so agreeably. Then we have Margaret Schwan, who Schiller would now certainly love to the exclusion of all others, if, fortunately or unfortunately, Madame Charlotte von Kalb had not been sojourning in Mannheim for the last few weeks. She is certainly not exactly beautiful, but then she has such eyes; eyes that glow like a crater of passion, and her words are flaming rockets of enthusiasm. This, of course, charms

---

* Schiller's own words to Henrietta von Wolzogen.—See "Relations," etc., p. 452.

the young poet; he stands hesitating between Margaret and Charlotte; and will at last, because he does not know whether to turn to the right or to the left, walk straight on, and look farther for the lady of his love.   Farewell, Schiller, you faithful friend, you faithful lover!   Farewell!"

And waving her hand as a last adieu, Madame von Wolzogen left the room.   Schiller cast a confused and troubled look after her.

"Can she be right?" he murmured.   "Have I really a heart that only seizes upon an object to relax its hold again? Where is the solution of this enigma?   Have I ever loved, and is my heart so fickle that it can hold fast to nothing?"

He walked to and fro in his little room with great strides, his brow clouded and his eyes looking inward, endeavoring to unravel the mysteries of his heart.

"No," he said, after a pause.   "No, I am not fickle.   To her who loved me I would hold firmly in love for ever and ever.   But here is the difficulty!   I have never found a woman who could or would love me.   My heart longs for this sweet interchange of thought; and new sources of happiness and enthusiasm would be opened to me if this ardently-wished-for woman would but appear!   It seems the poor, ugly, and awkward Frederick Schiller is not worthy of such happiness, and must be contented with having had a modest view of love in the distance, like Moses of the promised land, without ever having entered its holy temple."

With a sigh, Schiller threw himself in the chair before the table and covered his quivering face with his hands.   But he soon let them fall, and shook his head with an energetic movement.

"Away with sensitiveness!" said he, almost angrily, "I must accustom myself to be happy on earth without happiness.   And if I have no sweetheart, I have friends who love me, and the friendship of a noble soul can well console me for the denied love of a perhaps fickle heart.   For he who can call but one soul on earth his friend is blessed, and sits at the round-table of the gods. My poor Posa, I will learn from you, and will infuse into you my own feelings. You had but one friend on earth, and the love you could give to no woman you bestowed upon humanity, upon your people. I also will open my heart to humanity, and one woman I will love above all others, and her name shall be Germania! I will serve her, and belong to her, and love her as long as I live. Hear my vow, ye Muses and gods! Germania is my love. I will be her poet and her servant; on bended knees I will worship her; I will raise her to the skies, and never falter in my devotion, for to her belong the holiest impulses of heart and soul alike. And now, Frederick Schiller, be resolute, be strong and joyful. You are Germania's lover and her son. Determine to do what is good and great, throughout your lifetime, to her honor and renown! Take up the pen, Frederick Schiller! The pen is the sword with which you must fight and conquer!"

He took the pen and held it aloft; his eyes sparkled with enthusiasm, and on his smiling lips a silent prayer trembled.

The deep silence was again unbroken, save by the rustling of the pen as it glided over the paper. The Muses gathered round the poet and smiled on his labors.

CHAPTER IV.

JOY AND SORROW.

How long he had sat there and written he knew not, he only knew that these had been happy moments of action and creation; that his heart had been full of bliss and his soul overflowing with enthusiasm, and that this high thought had found expression in words. He felt that, like a god, he was creating human beings who lived, moved, and suffered before him. But alas! he was doomed to descend from the serene heights of poetry to the dusty earth; the cares of life were about to recall him from the bright sphere of poetical visions

His door was violently thrown open, and Oswald Schwelm rushed in, pale and breathless.

"Help me, for God's sake, Schiller! Hide me! I have recognized him! He has just turned into this street, followed by two constables."

"Who? Of whom do you speak? Who pursues you?" exclaimed Schiller, bounding from his seat.

"The hard-hearted creditor from Stuttgart. Some one has advised him that I have come to Mannheim, and he has followed me with his warrant, determined to arrest me here. Of this I felt assured when I saw him accompanied by the two constables: but, hoping that I had not been perceived, I ran hastily to your room, and now, Schiller, I implore you to rescue me from my pursuers, from my unmerciful creditor; to preserve my freedom and protect me from arrest."

"That I will do," said Schiller, with an air of determination and defiance: and he stood erect and held up his hand as if threatening the invisible enemy. "You shall suffer no more on my account; you shall not be robbed of your freedom."

"Be still, my friend! I think I hear steps and whispering voices outside the door. Hide me! for God's sake, hide me, or—"

Too late! too late! The door is opened and the cruel creditor enters, accompanied by two constables.

Schiller uttered a cry of rage, sprang like a chafed lion at the intruder, caught hold of him, shook him, and pressed him back to the door.

"What brings you here, sir? How can you justify this intrusion? how dare you cross this threshold without my permission?"

To the stormy questions addressed to him by Schiller, with a threatening look and knitted brow, the man replied by a mute gesture toward the two constables, who, with a grave official air, were walking toward Oswald Schwelm, who had retired to the farthest corner of the room.

"Mr. Oswald Schwelm, we arrest you in the name of the

Superior Court of Mannheim, by virtue of this warrant, made out by the judicial authorities in Stuttgart; and transferred, at the request of Mr. Richard, to the jurisdiction of the authorities in Mannheim. By virtue of the laws of this city we command you to follow us without offering any resistance whatsoever."

"You have heard it, Mr. Schiller," said the printer Richard, emphatically. "I have a perfect right to enter this room to arrest my debtor."

"No, bloodsucker!" cried Schiller, stamping the floor with his foot. "No, you have not the right. You are a barbarian, for you desire to deprive a man of his liberty of whom you know that he owes you nothing!"

"He made himself responsible for the payment of a sum of three hundred florins; the sum is due, and Mr. Schwelm must either pay or go to prison."

"God help me!" cried Schiller, trembling with anger, and deathly pale with agitation. "Give me patience that I may not crush this monster in my righteous indignation. I will be calm and humble, I will beg and implore, for something high and noble is at stake, the liberty of a man! Be tranquil, friend Schwelm; this man shall not carry out his base intention, he shall not arrest you here in my room. This room is my house, my castle, and no one shall violate its sanctity. Out with you, you cruel creditor, ye minions of the law! You can stand before my door and await your prey like blood-hounds, but you shall not lay hands on this noble game until it leaves this sanctuary and crosses this threshold. Out with you, I say! If you love life, leave quickly. Do you not see that I am filled with the holy wrath of outraged humanity? Do you not feel that my hands will destroy you if you do not go, and go instantly?"

He threw up his arms, and clinched his fists; and, his eyes flaming, and his angry countenance beautiful with inward agitation, he was about to rush upon the men who had taken hold of Oswald Schwelm, and now looked on in confusion and terror. But Oswald Schwelm had, in the mean while, liberated himself from their grasp, and now seized Schiller's arm and held him back, gently entreating him to let the law take its course and leave him to his fate. He then turned to the officers and begged them to forget Mr. Schiller's offensive words, uttered in anger; he admitted that they were perfectly in the right, and he was ready to yield to stern necessity and accompany them.

As Oswald Schwelm approached the door, Schiller thrust him back, exclaiming in loud and threatening tones: "I will permit no one to pass this threshold. If you will not leave without him, you shall all remain here; and my room, the room of a German poet, shall be the prison of the noble German man, who is guilty of nothing but—"

"But not having paid the money he owes me," interposed Mr. Richard, "the money which he should have paid a year ago. Since then he has been continually putting me off with empty promises and evasions. I am tired of all this, will put up with it no longer, and am determined to resort to extreme measures. Officers of the law, do your duty, arrest this man, and pay no attention to the boastful words of Mr. Schiller. He is a poet, and poets are not so particular in their words. One must just let them talk on without heeding what they say! Forward now, forward!"

"No, no, Oswald," cried Schiller, trembling with anger. "Come to me, Oswald, hold fast to me. They shall never tear you from my side. No, never!—no, never!"

"What is going on here, who uttered that cry?" asked a loud, manly voice, and the broad, well-conditioned body of a man who was plainly dressed, and whose face wore an expression of good-nature and kindliness, appeared in the doorway.

"Herr Hölzel," exclaimed Schiller, with relief. "My landlord, God sends you to our aid!"

"What's the matter? What can I do?" asked Hölzel. "I came down from the floor above, and in passing your door I heard a noise and disturbance, and my Mr. Schiller cry out. 'Well,' thinks I, 'I must go in and see what's going on.' "

"And I will reply—I will tell you what is going on, my dear Hölzel," said Schiller, with flashing eyes. "We have here an unmerciful creditor and rude minions of the law, who dare to enter my room in pursuit of a friend who has fled to me from Stuttgart for help; to me who am the miserable cause of all his misfortunes. Good Oswald Schwelm pledged himself to make good the payment of three hundred florins to the printer who printed my first work, 'The Robbers.' At that time we anticipated brilliant success; we dreamed that 'The Robbers' was a golden seed from which a rich harvest would be gathered. We have erred, and my poor friend here is now called upon to pay for his error with his freedom."

"But he shall not," said Mr. Hölzel, with vivacity, as he laid his broad hand on Schiller's shoulder. "I will not suffer it; your good friend shall have made no miscalculations. Now, Mr. Schiller, you know very well how fond I am of 'The Robbers,' and that I see the piece whenever it is given here in Mannheim, and cry my eyes out over Iffland, when he does Charles Moor so beautifully; and I so much admire those fine fellows the robbers, and Spiegelberg, who loves his captain dearly enough to die for him a thousand times. I will show you, Schiller, that I have learned something from the noble Spiegelberg, and that the high-minded robber captain is my model. I am not rich, certainly, and cannot do as he did when his money gave out, and take it forcibly from the rich on the public highways, but I can scrape together funds enough to help a good man out of trouble, and do a service to the author of 'The Robbers!' "

"What do you say, my friend? What is it you will do?" asked Schiller, joyfully.

"With your permission, I will lend Mr. Schwelm, with whose family in Stuttgart I am well acquainted, and who, I know, will repay me, the sum of three hundred florins for two years, at the usual rate of interest—that is, if he will accept it."

"I will accept it with pleasure," said Oswald Schwelm, heartily grasping Hölzel's proffered hand. "Yes, I accept the money with joy, and I give you my word of honor that I will return it at the expiration of that time."

"I believe you," said Hölzel, cordially, "for he who promoted the publication of 'The Robbers' by giving his money for that purpose, is surely too good and too noble to defraud his fellow-man. Come down into my office with me. Business should be done in an orderly manner," said he, as he laughingly surveyed the room, in which nothing was in its proper place, but every thing thrown around in the greatest disorder. "Things are not exactly orderly here; and I don't believe there would be room enough on that table to count out the three hundred florins."

"Very true," said Schiller, smiling. "But you must also consider, Hölzel, that the table has never had occasion to prepare itself for the reception of three hundred florins."

"I, unfortunately, know very well that the managers of the theatres do not pay the poet as they should," said Hölzel, contemptuously. "They pay him but a paltry sum for his magnificent works. Tell me, Schiller, is what Mr. Schwan told me yesterday true; did the Manager von Thalberg really give you but eight louis d'ors for your tragedy, 'Fiesco?'"

"Yes, it is true, Hölzel, and I can assure you that this table, for my three tragedies, has not yet groaned under the weight of three hundred florins. And this may in some measure excuse me in your eyes for what has occurred."

"No excuse is necessary," said Hölzel, good-humoredly. "Come, gentlemen, let us go down and attend to our business. Above all things, Mr. Printer-of-the-Robbers, send your constables away. They have nothing more to do here, and only offend the eye with their presence. And now we will count out the money, and satisfy the warrant."

"And make out a note of indebtedness to you, you worthy helper in time of trouble," said Oswald Schwelm, as he followed the printer and constables out of the room.

Schiller was also about to follow, but Hölzel gently pushed him back. "It is not necessary for you to accompany us, Mr. Schiller. What has the poet to do with such matters, and why should you waste your precious time? We can attend to our money matters without you; and I am not willing that this harpy of a printer should any longer remain in your presence."

"My dear friend," exclaimed Schiller, with emotion, "what a kind, noble fellow you are, and how well it becomes you to do good and generous actions in this simple, unostentatious manner! You have freed me from a heavy burden to-day, and relieved my soul of much care; and if my next drama succeeds well, you can say to yourself that you are the cause, and that you have helped me in my work!"

"Great help, indeed," laughed the architect. "I can build a pretty good house, but of your theatrical pieces I know nothing at all; and no one would believe me if I should say I had helped Frederick Schiller in his tragedies. Nor is it necessary that they should. Only keep a kind remembrance of me in your heart, that is renown enough for me, although men should hear nothing about the poor architect, Hölzel."

"My friend," said Schiller, in an earnest, solemn voice, "if I am really a poet, and the German nation at some future day recognizes, loves, and honors me as such, you also will not be forgotten, and men will keep your name in good remembrance; for what a good man does in love and kindness to a poet, is not lost. Children and grandchildren will praise his good action, as if he had done it to themselves, and will call him the nation's benefactor, because he was the poet's benefactor. May this be your reward, my friend! I wish this for your sake and for my own. And now go, for my heart is filled with tears, and I feel them rushing to my eyes!"

Hölzel had already passed out, and gently closed the door, and did not hear these last words. No one saw Schiller's gushing tears; no one heard the sobs which escaped his breast; no one witnessed the struggle with himself, with the humiliations, sorrows, and distress of life; no ear heard him complain sadly of want and poverty, the only inheritance of the German poet!

But Frederick Schiller's soul of fire soon rose above such considerations. His glance, which had before been tearfully directed to the present, now pierced the future; and he saw on the distant heights, on the temple of renown, inscribed in golden letters, the name FREDERICK SCHILLER.

"I am a poet," he cried, exultingly, "and more 'by the grace of God' than kings or princes are. If earth belongs to them, heaven is mine. While they are regaled at golden tables, I am feasted at the table of the gods with ambrosia and nectar! What matter, if poets are beggars on earth—if they are not possessed of riches? They should not complain. Have they not the God-given capital of mind and poetry intrusted to them, that it may bear interest in their works? And, though the man must sometimes hunger, a bountiful repast awaits the poet on the heights of Olympus! With this thought I will console myself," he added, in a loud voice, "and will proclaim it to others for their consolation. I will write a poem on this subject, and its name shall be, 'The Partition of the Earth!'"

He walked to the table, and noted this title in his diary with a few hasty strokes of the pen.

He now wished to return to his tragedy. But the Muses had been driven from this consecrated ground by discordant earthly sounds, and were now not disposed to return at his bidding, and the poet's thoughts lacked buoyancy and enthusiasm.

"It is useless," exclaimed Schiller, throwing his pen aside. "The tears wrung from my heart by earthly sorrow have extinguished the heavenly fire, and all is cold within me! Where shall I find the holy, soul-kindling spark?"

"In her," responded a voice in his heart. "In Charlotte von Kalb! Yes, this fair young woman, this impassioned soul will again enliven and inspire me. She understands poetry; and all that is truly beautiful and great finds an echo in her heart. I will go to Charlotte! I will read her the first two acts of my 'Carlos,' and her delight will kindle anew the fire of enthusiasm."

He hastily rolled up his manuscript, and took down his hat. He cast no look at the dusty, dingy little mirror fastened to the window-frame. No brush touched his dishevelled hair, or removed the dust and stains from his dress. It never occurred to the poet to think of his outward appearance. What cared he for outward appearances—he who occupied himself exclusively with the mind? He rushed out of the house, and through the streets of the little city. The people he met greeted him with reverence, and stood still to look after the tall, thin figure of the poet. He neither saw nor heeded them. His eyes were upturned, and his thoughts flew on in advance of him to Charlotte—to the impassioned, enthusiastic young woman.

Does her heart forebode the poet's coming? Does the secret sympathy which links souls together, whisper: " Charlotte von Kalb, Frederick Schiller approaches?"

CHAPTER V.

CHARLOTTE VON KALB.

SHE was sitting at the window of the handsomely-furnished room which she used as a parlor. She had just completed her elegant and tasteful toilet; and when the mirror reflected the image of a young woman of twenty, with light hair, slightly powdered, a high, thoughtful forehead, and remarkably large and luminous black eyes, and the tall, graceful figure, attired in a rich and heavy woollen dress of light blue, Charlotte von Kalb turned from the beautiful vision with a sigh.

"I am well worthy of being loved, and yet no one loves me! No one! Neither the husband, forced upon me by

my family, nor my sister, who only thinks of the unhappiness
of her own married life, nor any other relative. I am alone.
The husband who should be at my side, is far away at the
court of the beautiful Queen of France. The sister lives with
her unloved husband on her estates. I am alone, entirely
alone! Ah, this solitude of the heart is cheerless, for my
heart is filled with enthusiasm, and longing for love!"

She shuddered as she uttered these words, and turned her
eyes with a startled, anxious look to the little picture which,
together with several others, hung on the window-frame.
She slowly walked forward and gazed at it long and thoughtfully. It was only a plain black silhouette of a head taken
in profile. But how expressive was this profile, how magnificent the high, thoughtful forehead, how proud the sharply-
defined nose, how eloquent the swelling lips, and how powerful the massive chin! It would have been evident to any
observer, that this picture represented the head of a man of
great intellect, although he had not seen, written underneath,
the name Frederick Schiller!

"Frederick Schiller,"—whispered Charlotte, with a sigh,
—"Frederick Schiller!"

Her lips said nothing more, but an anxious voice kept on
whispering and lamenting in her heart; and she listened to
this whispering, and gazed vacantly out into the street!

The door-bell rang and roused Charlotte von Kalb from her
dreams. Some one has entered the house! She hopes he is
not coming to see her! She does not wish to see any one, for
no one will come whom she cares to see!

Some one knocks loudly at the door; a crimson glow suf-
fuses itself over Charlotte's cheeks, for she knows this knock,
and it echoes so loudly in her heart, that she is incapable of
answering it.

The knocking is heard for the second time, and a sudden
unaccountable terror takes possession of Charlotte's heart;
she flies through the room and into her boudoir, closing the
door softly behind her. But she remains standing near it,

and hears the door open, and the footsteps of a man entering; and then she hears his voice as he calls to the servant: "Madame von Kalb is not here! Go and say that I beg to be permitted to see her."

Oh, she recognizes this voice!—the voice of Frederick Schiller; and it pierces her soul like lightning, and makes her heart quake.

It may not be! No, Charlotte; by all that is holy, it may not be! Think of your duty, do not forget it for a moment! Steel your heart, make it strong and firm! Cover your face with a mask, an impenetrable mask! No one must dream of what is going on in your breast—he least of all!

A knock is heard at the door leading to her bedchamber. It is her maid coming to announce that Mr. Schiller awaits her in the reception-room.

"Tell him to be kind enough to wait a few minutes. I will come directly."

After a few minutes had expired, Charlotte von Kalb entered the reception-room with a clear brow and smiling countenance. Schiller had advanced to meet her, and, taking the tapering little hand which she extended, he pressed it fervently to his lips.

"Charlotte, my friend, I come to you because my heart is agitated with stormy thoughts, for I know that my fair friend understands the emotions of the heart."

"Emotions of the heart, Schiller?" she asked, laughing loudly. "Have we come to that pass again? Already another passion besides the beautiful Margaret Schwan and the little Charlotte von Wolzogen?"

He looked up wonderingly, and their eyes met; Charlotte's cheeks grew paler in spite of her efforts to retain the laughing expression she had assumed.

"How strangely you speak to-day, Charlotte, and how changed your voice sounds!"

"I have taken cold, my friend," said she, with a slight shrug of her shoulders. "You know very well that I cannot stand the cold; it kills me! But it was not to hear this you came to see me?"

"No, that is very true," replied Schiller, in confusion. "I did not come for that purpose. I—why are your hands so cold, Charlotte, and why have you given me no word of welcome?"

"Because you have not yet given me an opportunity to do so," she said, smiling. "It really looks as if you had come to-day rather in your capacity of regimental surgeon, to call on a patient, than as a poet, to visit an intimate acquaintance."

"An intimate acquaintance!" exclaimed Schiller, throwing her hand ungently from him. "Charlotte, will you then be nothing more to me than an intimate acquaintance?"

"Well, then, a good friend," she said quietly. "But let us not quarrel about terms, Schiller. We very well know what we are to each other. You should at least know that my heart sympathizes with all that concerns you. And now tell me, my dear friend, what brings you here at this unusual hour? It must be something extraordinary that induces the poet Schiller to leave his study at this hour. Well, have I guessed right? Is it something extraordinary?"

"I don't know," replied Schiller, in some confusion.

"You don't know!" exclaimed Charlotte, with a peal of laughter, which seemed to grate on Schiller's ear, for he recoiled sensitively, and his brow darkened.

"I cannot account for the sudden change that has come over me," said Schiller, thoughtfully. "I came with a full, confiding heart, Charlotte, longing to see you, and now, all at once I feel that a barrier of ice has arisen around my heart; your strangely cold and indifferent manner has frozen me to the core."

"You are a child; that is to say, you are a poet. Come, my poet, let us not quarrel about words and appearance; whatever my outward manner may be, you know that I am sound and true at heart. And now I see why you came.

That roll of paper is a manuscript! Frederick Schiller has come, as he promised to do a few days ago, to read his latest poem to the admirer of his muse. You made a mystery of it, and would not even tell me whether your new work was a tragedy or a poem. And now you have come to impart this secret. Is it not so, Schiller?"

"Yes, that was my intention," he replied, sadly. "I wished to read, to a sympathizing and loved friend, the beginning of a new tragedy, but—"

"No 'but' whatever," she exclaimed, interrupting him. "Let me see the manuscript at once!" and she tripped lightly to the chair on which he had deposited his hat and the roll of paper on entering the room.

"May I open it, Schiller?"—and when he bowed assentingly, she tore off the cover with trembling hands and read, "Don Carlos, Infanta of Spain; a Tragedy."—"Oh, my dear Schiller, a new tragedy! Oh, my poet, my dear poet, what a pleasure! how delightful!"

"Oh," cried Schiller, exultingly; "this is once more the beautiful voice, once more the enthusiastic glance! Welcome, Charlotte, a thousand welcomes!"

He rushed forward, seized her hand, and pressed it to his lips. She did not look at him, but gazed fixedly at the manuscript which she still held in her hand, and repeated, in a low voice, "Don Carlos, Infanta of Spain."

"Yes, and I will now read this Infanta, that is, if you wish to hear it, Charlotte?"

"How can you ask, Schiller? Quick, seat yourself opposite me, and let us begin."

She seated herself on the little sofa, and, when Schiller turned to go after a chair, she hastily and noiselessly pressed a kiss on the manuscript, which she held in her hand.

When Schiller returned with the chair, the manuscript lay on the table, and Charlotte sat before him in perfect composure.

Schiller began to read the first act of "Don Carlos" to his "friend," in an elevated voice, with pathos and with fiery emotion, and entirely carried away by the power of his own composition!

But his friend and auditor did not seem to participate in this rapture! Her large black eyes regarded the reader intently. At first her looks expressed lively sympathy, but by degrees this expression faded away; she became restless, and at times, when Schiller declaimed in an entirely too loud and grandiloquent manner, a stealthy smile played about her lips. Schiller had finished reading, and laid his manuscript on the table; he now turned to his friend, his eyes radiant with enthusiasm. "And now, my dear, my only friend, give me your opinion, honestly and sincerely! What do you think of my work?"

"Honestly and sincerely?" she inquired, her lips twitching with the same smile.

"Yes, my friend, I beg you to do so."

"Well, then, my dear friend," she exclaimed, with a loud and continuous peal of laughter; "well, then, my dear Schiller, I must tell you, honestly and sincerely, that 'Don Carlos' is the very worst you have ever written!"

Schiller sprang up from his chair, horror depicted in his countenance. "Your sincere opinion?"

"Yes, my sincere opinion!" said Charlotte von Kalb, still laughing.

"No," cried Schiller, angrily, "this is too bad!"

Schiller seized his hat, and, without taking the slightest notice of Charlotte, left the room, slamming the door behind him.*

With great strides, he hurried through the streets, chagrin and resentment in his heart; and yet so dejected, so full of sadness, that he could have cried out with pain and anguish against himself and against the whole world.

When he saw acquaintances approaching, he turned into a side street to avoid them. He wished to see no one; he was not in a condition to speak on indifferent subjects.

* This scene is historically exact.

He reached his dwelling, passed up the stairway, and into the room, which he had left in so lofty a frame of mind, dispirited and cast down.

"It is all in vain, all in vain," he cried, dashing his hat to the floor. "The gold I believed I had found, proves to be nothing but glimmering coals that have now died out. Oh, Frederick Schiller, what is to become of you—what can you do with this unreal enthusiasm burning in your soul?"

He rushed excitedly to and fro in his little room, striking the books, which lay around on the floor in genial disorder, so violently with his foot, that they flew to the farthest corners of the chamber.

He thrust his hands wildly into his disordered hair, tearing off the ribbon which confined his queue, and struck with his clinched fist the miserable little table which he honored with the name of his writing-desk.

These paroxysms of fury, of glowing anger—eruptions of internal desolation and despair—were not of rare occurrence in the life of the poor, tormented poet.

"My father was right," he cried, in his rage. "I am an inflated fool, who over-estimates himself, and boasts of great prospects and expectations which are never to be realized! Why did I not listen to his wise counsel? why did I not remain the regimental surgeon, and crouch submissively at the feet of my tyrant? Why was I such a simpleton as to desire to do any thing better than apply plasters! I imagined myself invited to the table of the gods, whereas I am only worthy to stand as a lackey at the table of my Duke, and eat the hard crust of duty and subserviency! She laughed! Laughed at my poem! All these words, these thoughts that had blossomed up from the depths of my heart; all these forms to whom I had given spirit of my spirit, life of my life: all this had no other effect than to excite laughter—laughter over my tragedy! Oh, Charlotte, Charlotte, why have you done this?"

And he again thrust his hands violently into his hair, and sank groaning into his chair.

"I am unhappy, very unhappy! I believed I could conquer a world, and have not yet conquered a single human
heart! I hoped to acquire honor, renown, and a competency
by the creative power of my talents, and am but a poor, nameless man, tormented by creditors, by misery, and want, who
must at last admit that he placed a false estimate on his
abilities. Truly I am unhappy, very unhappy! Entirely
alone; none who loves or understands me!"

Deep sighs escaped his breast, and tears stood in the eyes
that looked up reproachfully toward heaven.

As he lowered his eyes, he looked toward the writing-
table—the writing-table at which he had spent so many hours
of the night in hard work; at which he had written, thought,
and suffered so much.

"In vain, all in vain! Nothing but illusion and dis-
appointment! If what I have written with my heart's blood
excites laughter, I am no poet, am not one of the anointed!
It were better I had copied deeds and written recipes, instead
of tragedies, for a living, and—"

He ceased speaking as he observed a letter and package,
which the carrier had brought and deposited on his table during his absence.

A simple letter would have excited no pleasure or curiosity; yes, would even have filled him with consternation, for
the letters he was in the habit of receiving only caused humiliation and pain. They were either from dunning creditors, from his angry father, or from theatre-managers, re-
jecting his "Fiesco," as useless, and not adapted to the
stage.

But beside this letter lay a package; and the letter which
Schiller now took from the table bore the postmark Leipsic.
From Leipsic! Who could write to him? who could send
him a package from that city? Who had ever sent him any
thing but rejected manuscripts and theatrical pieces?

"Ah, that was it!" He had also sent his "Fiesco" to the
director of the theatre at Leipsic, and this gentleman had

now returned it with a polite letter of refusal. Of course, it could be nothing else!

He wrathfully broke the seal, unfolded the letter, and looked first at the signature, to assure himself that he had not been deceived.

But no! This was not the name of the director in Leipsic; and what did these four signatures in different handwritings mean? There were: "C. G. Körner," and, beside it, "Minna Stock;" and under these names two others, "L. F. Huber," and "Dora Stock."

Schiller shook his head wonderingly, and began to read the letter; at first with composure, but, as he read on, became agitated, and his pale cheek colored with pleasure.

From the far-off Leipsic four impassioned beings wafted a greeting to the distant, unknown poet.

They wished to thank Frederick Schiller, they wrote, for the many delightful hours for which they were indebted to him; to thank him for the sublime poetry which had awakened the noblest feelings in their bosoms and filled their hearts with enthusiasm. They, two bridal couples, were deeply imbued with love for each other, and the high thought and feeling of Frederick Schiller's poems had excited emotions in them which tended to make them better and happier. They wrote further, that nothing was wanting to complete their happiness but the presence of the poet at the consummation of their union. Together they had read his "Robbers," his "Louise Müllerin," and his "Fiesco;" and while so engaged love had taken root in their hearts, grown and blossomed, and for all this they were indebted to Frederick Schiller. They therefore implored him to come to Leipsic on the weddingday. And then in touching, cordial words, they told him that they never spoke of him but as their dearest friend and benefactor. And further, they begged permission to send the accompanying package as a token of their gratitude in the ardent admiration which they entertained for him in common with every feeling heart and thinking head in Germany.

He laid the letter aside, and hastily opened the package, for he longed to see the persons who so ardently admired him.

And there they were, these dear persons, in beautiful miniatures, on each of which the name of the painter, Huber, was inscribed. How charming and beautiful were the two girlish faces which seemed to smile upon Schiller from the two medallions; how grave and thoughtful the head of the young man designated as Körner; how genial and bold the face of the painter Huber! But there was something else in the package besides the four portraits. There was a song neatly written on gilt-edged paper, a song from "The Robbers," and Körner's name was given as the composer. Moreover, the package contained a magnificent pocket-book, worked in gold and silk, and embroidered in pearls; in the inside he found a little note in which Dora and Minna had written that they had worked this pocket-book while their fiancés read his tragedies to them.

Schiller regarded these tokens of love and esteem with astonishment. It seemed to him that he was dreaming; that all this was an illusion, and could not be reality. How could he, who, but a few hours before had experienced such mortification and humiliation, he who had been ridiculed, scolded, and laughed at; how could he be the happy recipient of such appreciation and recognition? How was it possible that people with whom he was not even acquainted, who knew nothing of him, could send him a greeting, presents, and words of thanks? No, no, it was all a dream, an illusion! But there lay the letter, yes, there lay the eloquent witness of truth and reality! Schiller seized the letter with trembling hands, and continued reading.

"We must tell you, you great and noble poet, that we are indebted to you for the brightest and best hours of our life. What was good in us you made better, what was dark in us you made light; our inmost being has been elevated by your poems. Your sublime words are constantly on our lips when we are together. Accept our thanks, Frederick Schiller, accept the thanks of two German youths and two German maidens! Let them speak to you in the name of the German nation, in the name of the thousands of German maidens and youths who sing your songs with enthusiasm, and whose eyes fill with tears of devotion and delight when they see your tragedies!"

Tears of devotion and delight! Schiller's eyes are now filled with such tears. He sinks down upon his knees almost unconsciously, and his soul rises in inspiration to God. He raises his arms and folds his hands as if in prayer, and the tearful eye seeks and finds heaven.

"I thank Thee, God, that Thou hast blessed me with such happiness. I thank you, my absent friends, to whom my heart longs to fly. I thank you for this hour! I thank you, because it is the happiest of my life. Your loving greeting sounds on my ear like a voice in the desert, cheering and consoling. And I, who was crushed in pain and despair, once more arise in renewed hope and happiness. O God! when I think that there are, perhaps, others in this world besides you, the two happy couples who love me, who would be glad to know me; that, perhaps, in a hundred years or more, when my dust is long since scattered to the winds, people will still bless my memory, and pay it a tribute of tears and admiration when my body is slumbering in the grave; then, my beloved unknown friends, then I am proud of my mission, and am reconciled to my God and my sometimes cruel fate.*

"Now I know that I am a poet," he exclaimed, rising from his knees and walking to and fro with rapid strides. "It was not a dream, a vain illusion! I am a poet! These noble souls and loving hearts could not have been enkindled by my works if they had not been deeply imbued with the fire of poetry! I am a poet, although she laughed at and ridiculed me! She of all others; she who I thought would certainly understand me!"

Schiller opened the door to admit some one who knocked

* Schiller's own words.—See "Relations," etc., p. 448.

loudly. A liveried servant entered and handed him a little note.

These few words were written on the sheet of paper in almost illegible characters: "I conjure you to come to me, my friend! I have something of importance to communicate! Be magnanimous, and come at once! CHARLOTTE!"

She had appealed to his magnanimity at a favorable moment! She had irritated and mortified him greatly, but balm had been applied to the wound, and it no longer smarted.

"Go, Charles, and tell Madame von Kalb that I will come at once!"

Charles leaves the room, followed by Schiller, whose thoughts are not occupied with Charlotte on the way this time, but with the four friends in Leipsic, who love him and who did not laugh at his "Don Carlos." These thoughts illumine his countenance with serenity and noble self-consciousness. He carries himself more proudly and his face is brighter and clearer than ever before, for the recognition of his fellow-man has fallen upon and elevated him like the blessing of God.

He enters Charlotte's dwelling and passes through the hall to the door of her room.

Charlotte awaits him, standing at the open door, her eyes red with weeping, and yet a heavenly smile resting on her countenance. She beckons to him to enter; and when he had done so and closed the door, Charlotte falls on her knees before him; she, the beautiful, high-born lady, before the poor young poet—but yet the poet "by the grace of God."

"Oh, Schiller, dear Schiller, can you forgive me? I appeal to you, the genius, the noblest of German poets, for forgiveness!"

He stooped down to her in dismay. "For God's sake, my lady, what are you doing? How can you so debase yourself? Stand up. I conjure you, stand up!"

"Schiller, not until you have forgiven my error; not until you swear that that horrible scene no longer excites your anger!"

"I swear to you, Charlotte, that I feel no trace of displeasure. Good angels have wafted from me all irritation and anger with the breath of love. And now arise, Charlotte! Let me assist you with my hand."

She took hold of the large hand which he extended, with her two little hands, and raised herself up. "Oh, my dear Schiller, how I have suffered, and yet how much delight I have experienced since your departure! How fortunate it was that you had forgotten your manuscript in your displeasure! I read it once more, to strengthen my opinion as to its want of merit. But how completely had I been deceived, how sublime a poem is this tragedy, how melodious is the flow of words, how poetic is the heavenward flight of thought! Hail to you, my friend, hail to your future, for your latest poem, your 'Don Carlos,' is the most beautiful you have yet written!"

"Oh, Charlotte," exclaimed Schiller, joyfully, "is it true, are you in earnest? But no, only your goodness of heart prompted you to utter these words. In your generosity you wish to soothe the pain your condemnation inflicted."

"No, Schiller, I swear by all that is high and beautiful, by yourself, by your poetic genius, that your 'Don Carlos' will adorn your brow with a laurel-wreath of immortality. After the lapse of centuries this tragedy will be still praised and esteemed as a masterpiece; and the entire German nation will say with pride, 'Frederick Schiller was our own! The poems which excited enthusiasm and delight throughout all Europe were written in the German language, and Frederick Schiller was a German poet!' Oh, could my spirit wing its flight earthward to hear posterity proclaim these words, and to sing the song of rejoicing on the immortal grave of him whom my spirit recognized and revered while he still trod the earth in the flesh! Schiller, something seems to tell me that I am the Muse destined to consecrate the poet with the kiss of love and of pain. What can a woman give the man she honors above all others, and for whom she entertains the purest affection, what more noble gift can she bestow upon him than the kiss of consecration from her lips? Take it, Frederick Schiller, poet of 'Don Carlos,' take from my lips the kiss of consecration, the kiss of gratitude."

"Oh, Charlotte, my Muse, my friend, and let me say the grand, the divine word, my beloved! I thank you!"

He entwined her slender figure with his arms; pressed her to his heart, and imprinted a long and ardent kiss upon her lips, then looked at her with sparkling eyes, and, enraptured with her blushing countenance, his lips were about to seek hers for the second time.

With a quick movement, Charlotte withdrew from his embrace, and stepped back. "The sublime moment has passed," she said, with earnestness and dignity. "We again belong to the world, to reality; now, that we have done homage to the gods and muses, we must again accommodate ourselves to the rules and customs of the world."

"And why, Charlotte, why should we do so? Are not those rules changeable and fleeting? What men denounce as crimes to-day, they proclaim as heroic deeds at some other time; and what they to-day brand as vice, they will perhaps praise as virtue at some future day. Oh, Charlotte, I love you, my soul calls for you, my heart yearns for you. When I look upon you, all is feeling and blissful enjoyment! Let us unite the souls which arise above earthly feeling to divine sublimity; let us unite in the godlike love in which heart responds to heart, and soul to soul. Oh, do not look wonderingly at me with those profound and glowing eyes! Charlotte, have you not long since known and divined that I loved you, and you only?"

"Me only," she cried, sadly. "No, it is not so, not me only! It is love that you love in me, and not myself. Oh, Schiller, beware, I pray you; for your own sake, beware! Take back your avowal. I will not have heard it, it shall have died away inaudibly—have been erased from my fantasy. Take it back—but no, rather say nothing more about it. Let this moment be forgotten, as the last golden ray of the setting sun is forgotten. Let us speak to each other as we have been accustomed to do, as friends!"

"Friends!" exclaimed Schiller, angrily. "I say to you, with Aristotle: 'Oh, my friends, there are no friends!' At least what I feel for you, Charlotte, is not friendship! It is ardent, passionate love! But this you cannot comprehend. You do not know what love is; your heart is cold!"

"My heart cold?" she repeated, with sparkling eyes. "I not know what love is! And Frederick Schiller tells me this! The poet's eyes are clouded! He does not look behind the veil, which the usage of the world has thrown over my countenance. I know what love is, Frederick Schiller! But ought I, the married woman, the wife of an unloved and unloving husband, ought I to know love? Must I not wipe the tear of delight from my eye, suppress the longing cry on my lips, and erect a barrier of ice around the heart, that burns and glows with the flames which animate my whole being, giving warmth and light, like the fires in the bosom of the earth? If I were free, if the will of my relations had not forced me to the altar, where I fainted after my lips pronounced the fatal word of assent;* if I could name the man I love, I would say to him: 'Beloved, you are the life of my life, the heart of my heart, and the thought of my thought. From you I receive all being, and breathe all inspiration from your glances! Take me to yourself as the sea receives the drop of rain, absorbing it in its bosom! Let me be a part of your life! Let me feel that my own being merges its identity in yours! I have lost myself that I may find myself in you. My sun sets, to rise again with you to the serene heights of bliss, of knowledge, and of poetry. For us there is no more parting on earth or in heaven; for we are one, and by murder only can you make of this union two distinct beings capable of going in different directions. But I would not wander on, for separation from you, my beloved, with whom I had been

* See Charlotte.—"For the friends of the deceased," printed as MS., p. 86.

made one, would only be accomplished by shedding my heart's blood. But my lips would not accuse you; they would receive the kiss of death in silence! Therefore, if you do not wish to kill me, be true, as I shall be unto death.'"

"Charlotte, heavenly being," cried Schiller, gazing at her radiant countenance with astonishment and delight, "you stand before me as in a halo! you are a Titaness; you storm the ramparts of heaven!"

A smile flitted over her features, and she lowered the eyes, which had been gazing upward, again to earth, and regarded Schiller earnestly and intently. "I have told you how I would speak to the man I loved, if I dared. Duty forbids it, however, and 1 must be dumb. But I can speak to you as a friend and as a sympathizing acquaintance, and rejoice with you over your magnificent work. Seat yourself at my side, Schiller, and let us talk about your 'Don Carlos.'"

"No, Charlotte, not until you have first honestly and openly acknowledged why this sudden change took place, and how it is you are now pleased with what only excited your laughter a few hours ago?"

"Shall I tell you, honestly and openly?"

"Yes, my friend, henceforth everything must be open and honest between us!"

"Well, then, my friend, you yourself bear the blame."

"Myself? How so, Charlotte?"

"I acknowledge it out of friendship, your tragedy was spoiled in the reading. You are a poet, but not an orator. In the heat of delivery, my friend forgets that Don Carlos did not speak Suabian German, and that King Philip 'halt nit aus Stuckart ist.' * And now, that I have told you, give me your hand, Schiller, and swear that you will forget my laughter!"

"No, I will forget nothing that you say or do, Charlotte; for all that you do is good, and beautiful, and amiable! I

* A provincialism. It should be, "ist nicht aus Stuttgart," and means is not from Stuttgart.

kiss the loved hand that struck me, and would like to demand as an atonement a kiss from the cruel lips which laughed at me."

"No jesting, Schiller; let us be grave, and discuss the future of your 'Don Carlos.' Something great, something extraordinary, must be done for this great and extraordinary work! It must shoot like a blazing meteor over the earth, and engrave its name in characters of flame on huts and palaces alike. The poet who makes kings and princes speak so beautifully, must himself speak with kings and princes— must obtain a princely patron. And I have already formed a plan to effect this. Schiller, you must become acquainted with the Duke Charles August of Weimar, or rather he must become acquainted with you, and be your patron. Do you desire this?"

"And if I do," sighed Schiller, shrugging his shoulders, "he will not! He, the genial duke, who has his great and celebrated Goethe, and his Wieland, and Herder, he will not trouble himself much about the poor young Schiller. At the best, he will anathematize the author of 'The Robbers,' like all the other noblemen and rulers, and be entirely satisfied if his mad poetry is shipwrecked on the rock of public indifference."

"You do the noble Duke Charles and yourself wrong," cried Charlotte, with vivacity. "Charles August of Weimar is no ordinary prince, and you are no ordinary poet. You should know each other, because you are both extraordinary men. May I make you acquainted with each other? The Duke Charles August is coming to Darmstadt to visit his relations. Are you willing to go there and be introduced to him?"

"Yes, I will gladly do so," exclaimed Schiller, with eagerness. "The poet needs a princely protector! Who knows whether Tasso would ever have written his 'Jerusalem Delivered,' if the Duke of Este had not been his friend—if he had not found an asylum at the court of this prince? If you can, Charlotte, and if you consider me worthy of the honor

procure me this introduction, and the patronage of the Duke
Charles August. May he, who lets the sun of his friendship
shine upon Goethe, send down one little ray of his grace to
warm my cold and solitary chamber! I will crave but little,
if the Duke would only interest himself in the interdicted
'Robbers.' This alone would be of great service to me."

"He will, I hope, do more for you, Schiller. I know the
Duke, and also the Landgravine of Hesse! I will give you
letters to both of them, and Mr. von Dalberg, toward whom
the Duke is graciously inclined, will also do so. Oh, it will
succeed, it must succeed! We will draw you forcibly out of
the shade and into the light! Not only the German people,
but also the German princes, shall love and honor the poet
Frederick Schiller; and my hand shall lead him to the throne
of a prince."

"And let me kiss this fair hand," said Schiller, passionately. "Believe me, Charlotte, all your words have fallen like
stars into my heart, and illumined it with celestial splendor!"

"May these stars never grow pale!" sighed Charlotte.
"May we never be encompassed with the dark night! But
now, my friend, go!"

"You send me away, Charlotte?"

"Yes, I send you away, Schiller. We must deal econom-
ically with the beautiful moments of life. Now go!"

On the evening of this day of so many varied emotions,
Schiller wrote letters, in which he warmly thanked his unknown friends in Leipsic. In writing, he opened his heart
in an unreserved history of his life—so poor in joys, and so
rich in deprivations and disappointed hopes. He imparted
to them all that he had achieved; all his intentions and desires. He told them of his poverty and want; for false shame
was foreign to Schiller's nature. In his eyes the want of
money was not a want of honor and dignity. He acknowledged every thing to the distant, unknown friends—his homeless feeling, and his longing to be in some other sphere, with
other men who might perhaps love and understand him.

As he wrote this he hesitated, and it seemed to him that he could see the sorrowful, reproachful look of Charlotte's large, glowing eyes; and it seemed to him that she whispered, "Is this your love, Schiller? You wish to leave me, and yet you know that you will be my murderer if you go!"

He shuddered, and laid aside his pen, and arose and walked with rapid strides up and down his room. The glowing words which Charlotte had spoken to him that morning again resounded in his ear, but now, in the stillness of the night, they were no longer the same heavenly music.

"I believe it is dangerous to love her," he murmured. "She claims my whole heart, and would tyrannize over me with her passion. But I must be free, for he only who is free can conquer the world and achieve honor; and the love which refreshes my heart must never aspire to become my tyrant!"

He returned to his writing-table and finished the letter which he had commenced to Körner. He wrote: "I would that a happy destiny led me away from here, for I feel that my stay in this place should come to an end. I wish I could visit you in Leipsic, to thank you for the hour of delight for which I am indebted to you! Aristotle was wrong when he said: 'Oh, my friends, there are no friends!' I think of you and yours; I think of you four, and cry joyously: 'There are friends, nevertheless! Blessed is he to whom it is vouch-safed by the gods to find friends without having sought them!' "

CHAPTER VI.

THE TITLE.

CHARLOTTE VON KALB had kept her word. She had equipped Schiller with letters of introduction to the Duke Charles August and members of his family; she had also induced Mr. von Dalberg to furnish him with letters to influ-

ential friends at the court of Darmstadt. Provided with
these recommendations, and in his modesty and humility at-
taching greater importance to them than to his own reputa-
tion and dignity, Schiller journeyed to Darmstadt, in the
beginning of the year 1785, for the purpose of endeavoring to
obtain a friend and protector in the Duke Charles August of
Weimar.

Dalberg's and Charlotte's letters accomplished more than
Schiller's name and worth could possibly have done. The
author of "The Robbers" and "Fiesco," poems which lauded
freedom and popular government, and of "Louise Müllerin,"
which branded aristocracy as opposed to the rights of the
human heart; a poet who had dared to defy a prince and a
ruler could not have entered the golden gates of a princely
palace without the golden key of Dalberg's and Charlotte's
letters.

Frederick Schiller was received at the court of the landgrave in Darmstadt. The young and joyous Duke Charles
August of Weimar welcomed the poet cordially, and, prompted
by the enthusiastic praises of Madame von Kalb, requested
Schiller to read him a portion of the new tragedy.

Schiller offered to read the first act of "Don Carlos," and
his offer was graciously accepted. The reading took place on
the afternoon of the same day. A brilliant array of noblemen in embroidered court dress, and adorned with decorations, and of magnificently attired ladies, sparkling with
jewels, had assembled in the reception-room of the landgravine. She, the lover of art, the intellectual Landgravine
of Hesse, had seated herself at the side of the Duke Charles
August on the sofa in the middle of the saloon, behind which
the ladies and gentlemen of the court were standing in groups.
Not far off, and completely isolated, stood a plain cane-
bottomed chair, and a little round table, on which a glass of
water had been placed. This was the poet's throne, and this
was the nectar he was to drink at the table of the gods.

He felt embarrassed and almost awe-stricken as he entered

the brilliant court circle in his homely garb; he felt the blood first rush to his cheeks and then back to his heart again, leaving his countenance deathly pale.

"Rouse yourself, Schiller, and be a man! Shame upon you for being blinded by the trumpery and outward glitter of nobility and princely rank!" He said this to himself as he walked to the place set apart for him, feeling that the eyes of all rested on him with a cold, examining glance.

"What do I care for this pack of courtiers, this court-marshal Von Kalb and his associates?" said he to himself, defiantly. "It was not on their account I came here, and what they may think of me is a matter of complete indifference. I aspire only to the good opinion of the duke, of the friend of the great Goethe."

He looked over toward the sofa, and his glance encountered the eyes of the young duke, whose countenance was turned to him with a smile and an expression of good-natured sympathy. Schiller felt encouraged, and a smile flitted over his features.

He opened his manuscript and began to read the first act of "Don Carlos" in a clear and loud voice. His voice was full and sonorous, and his delivery, thanks to Charlotte's admonitions, was purer and more moderate; and, as he read on, his embarrassment disappeared, and the clouds lifted from his high brow.

The courtiers, who had first regarded the young poet contemptuously, now began to show some sympathy; the head, covered with light-yellow locks, with its sharply-chiselled features and large Roman nose, was, now that it was illumined with earnest thought, no longer so homely and uninteresting.

The countenance of the landgravine was expressive of the closest attention, and the reading of "Don Carlos" affected her so profoundly, that she had recourse to her handkerchief to wipe the tears of emotion from her eyes.

At times Charles August could not repress an exclamation of delight, a loud bravo; and when Schiller arose from his seat, after finishing the first act, Charles August walked for-

ward to thank the poet with a warm pressure of the hand,
and to conduct him to the landgravine, that she might also
express her thanks and sympathy.

The duke then took the poet's arm, and walked with him
through the saloon, to the disgust of the courtiers, who, notwithstanding their devotion, found it somewhat strange that
the duke could so demean himself as to walk arm-in-arm with
a man without birth or name.

But of course this was a natural consequence of the mania
after geniuses which reigned in Weimar; such abnormities
should no longer excite surprise.   Was there not at the court
in Weimar so variegated an admixture of well-born and ill-
born, that one ran the risk of encountering at any moment a
person who was not entitled to be there?   Had not the duke
carried his disregard of etiquette so far, that he had made
Wolfgang Goethe, the son of a citizen of Frankfort, his privy-
councillor, and an intimate associate?   And was it not well
known that his mother, the Duchess Amelia, as well as himself, never made a journey without picking up some genius
on the road for their establishment at Weimar?

This time Frederick Schiller was the genius whom the
duke desired to recruit.   That was quite evident, for the duke
had been standing with the poet for more than a quarter of
an hour in a window-niche, and they were conversing with
vivacity.   It was offensive and annoying to see this Mr.
Schiller standing before the duke, with a proud bearing and
perfect composure; and conversing with him without the
slightest embarrassment.

But the duke seemed to be greatly interested, and his countenance expressed lively sympathy and kindliness.

"I believe that destiny has intrusted you with a great mission, Mr. Schiller," said the duke, when the poet had given
him a brief and terse account of the continuation and contents of his "Don Carlos."   "I believe that you are destined
to be the poet-preacher of the people; and to refresh the
hearts and enliven the imagination of the degenerate Ger-

mans; and I prophesy a great future for you! Your aim is a
noble one. You desire not only to assign to the purely
human, but also to the ideal, its proper sphere in this world;
and your 'Don Carlos' is an open combat between the purely
human and ideal, against materialism and custom. Through
it you will make many enemies among the higher classes, and
acquire many friends among the masses; and, although you
will not be the favorite of princes, you will certainly be beloved by the people. For the judgment of the people is good
and sound, and it will always give its sympathies to the champion of the purely human, as opposed to the ridiculous
assumptions of etiquette and prejudice. But I tell you beforehand, that, in so-called noble society, you will, with great
difficulty, have to fight your way step by step."

"I have been accustomed to such warfare since my earliest
youth," said Schiller, smiling. "Fate has not given me a bed
of roses, and Care has as yet been the only friend who stood
faithfully at my side."

"You forget the Muses," cried the duke, with vivacity.
"It seems to me that you have no right to complain of a want
of attention on the part of these ladies!"

"True, your highness," responded Schiller earnestly; "they
have at times been graciously inclined, and I am indebted to
them for some of the most delightful hours of my life."

"Nor has the favor of earthly goddesses and Muses been
wanting to the inspired poet's happiness," said the duke, and
he laughed loudly when he saw Schiller blush and cast his
eyes down.

"Oh, I see," he cried gayly, "you have earthly Muses also,
your ideal has become reality! Could there be any connection
between this and the songs of praise which Madame von Kalb
wrote me concerning you?"

"Your highness, I really do not understand your meaning."

"Or rather, will not understand it! But we will not examine the affair any closer. Madame von Kalb has certainly
made it my duty to interest myself for her poet, and I thank

her for having made me acquainted with you. And now I
should like to give a proof of my gratitude, and it would afford
me pleasure to have you tell me in what manner I can be useful to you."

"Your kind and gracious words have already been of great
benefit to me," said Schiller, heartily; "your goodness has
shed a ray of sunshine into my sometimes cold and cheerless
heart."

"Your heart is never cold, Schiller, for the fire of poetry
burns there. But in your little chamber it may sometimes be
cold and cheerless. That I can well believe, for when the
gods rain down blessings upon the poet they generally forget
but one thing, but that is the one thing needful, money!
The gods generally lay but one sort of capital in the cradle of
mortal man, either a capital in mind or one of more material
value; and truly he must be a great favorite to whom they
give both."

"Yes, a very great favorite," murmured Schiller, in a low
voice; and he read in the prince's countenance that he was
thinking of his favorite, Wolfgang Goethe, who had arisen
like a meteor before Schiller's gaze at the time he visited the
Charles School in Stuttgart, in company with the duke, to
witness the distribution of prizes to the scholars of this institution. While the scholar, Frederick Schiller, was receiving a prize which had been awarded him, the gaze of Goethe's
large eyes was fixed upon him, but only with the composed
expression of a great man who wished him well and con-
descended to evince sympathy. This look had sunk deep into
Schiller's heart, and he thought of it now as he stood before
the duke in the palace of Darmstadt—the duke, who could
be a friend to Goethe, but to him only a patron and an alms-
giver."

"I desire to be of service to you if I can," said the duke,
who, for some time, had been silently regarding Schiller,
whose eyes were cast down thoughtfully. "Have you any
wish, my dear Mr. Schiller, that I can perhaps gratify? I am

certainly not a mighty prince, and unfortunately not a rich one, but if I can help you in any way, I will gladly do so."

Schiller raised his head quickly, and his eye met the inquiring look of the duke with a proud gaze. Not for all the world would he have told the prince of his distress and want, would he have stood on the floor of that palace as an humble beggar, soliciting alms for the journey through life!

"Your highness, I repeat it, your friendly reception and your sympathy have already been a great assistance to me."

The duke's countenance brightened, and he breathed freer, as if a burden had fallen from his soul. "And this assistance shall never be wanting, of that you may be assured. Every one shall learn that Charles August, of Weimar, is happy to know the German poet, Frederick Schiller, and that he counts him among those who are dear to him. A German duke was your tyrant; a German prince drove you out into the world, therefore it is just and right that another German duke should show you friendship, and endeavor to make your path in life a little smoother. I will be ready to do so at all times, and to testify to my high opinion of yourself and your talents before the whole world, your tyrannical prince included. And a proof of it shall be given you before you leave Darmstadt! For the present, farewell, and if you should come to Weimar at any time, do not forget to pay your good friend, Charles August, a visit! You will not leave until to-morrow morning, I suppose?"

"No, your highness, not until to-morrow morning."

"Well, then, my dear Mr. Schiller, you will hear from me this evening."

Schiller returned to his hotel in a thoughtful mood. What could the duke's words mean? What token of esteem would Charles August give him? Perhaps even an appointment. Ah, and if ever so unimportant a one, it would still be an alleviation of relief. Perhaps the duke only intended to offer him the use of one of his unoccupied castles, in order that he might finish his "Don Carlos" in peaceful seclusion.

Well, that also would be a blessing, a benefit! The homeless one would then have a resting-place from which he could not be driven, where he would not be assailed by the cares and vexations of life. The hours dragged on sluggishly in the bare, uncomfortable little room at the hotel, and the poet tormented himself with suppositions and questions, while he listened attentively to hear the footstep of the expected messenger of the duke.

At last, after hours of waiting, a knock was heard at the door, and a ducal lackey handed Schiller a large sealed document. It seemed to regard him with a right official and solemn look with its great seal of state bearing the inscription, "Ducal private cabinet," and the poet's feelings were of the same nature when he opened it after the lackey's departure. What could it be that the duke offered him, an appointment or a retreat?

An expression of astonishment and surprise was depicted on Schiller's countenance as he read the document; his brow darkened, and he let the paper fall to the table. The duke offered him neither an appointment nor a retreat. He gave him a title, the title of a ducal counsellor. The secretary of the cabinet made known the generous determination of his master, and informed him that the document appointing him to this office would be made out in official form and forwarded to him on the duke's return to Weimar. Frederick Schiller should, however, be enabled to wear the title so graciously conferred, and call himself "ducal counsellor" from that hour.

While reading it for the second time, the poet laughed derisively. This was the solution of the riddle. He who had scarcely known how to counsel himself, was now the counsellor of a prince who would probably never desire his counsel. He who was tormented with cares, who had no home, had nothing he could call his own besides his manuscripts—he was now the possessor of a title.

How strange the contrast! The tragedy which waged war against princely prerogatives, etiquette, and ceremony, in favor of humanity, equality before the law, and nobility of soul—this tragedy was to bear, as its first fruit, the favor of a prince.

It was strange—it looked almost like irony, and yet!— He thought of Charlotte von Kalb—she would rejoice to see him thus honored by a German prince. He thought of his old parents, to whom it would undoubtedly be a great satisfaction to know that the former regimental-surgeon of the Duke of Wurtemberg had become so distinguished. It would prove to them that their Fritz, of whom the severe father had often despaired, had nevertheless attained honor and respectability in the eyes of the world.

Well, then, let it be so! A little appointment would certainly have been better, and some hunting-castle as a retreat would probably have furthered the completion of "Don Carlos." But one must be contented, nevertheless. The little was not to be despised, for it was an honor and a public acknowledgment, and would, perhaps, have the effect of infusing into the directors a little more respect for the poet, whose dramas they often maltreated and injured by poor and careless representation.

With a smile, Schiller folded the document and laid it aside. "Well," said he to himself, in a low voice, "I entertain the proud hope that I am a poet 'by the grace of God!' Moreover, I have now become a counsellor by the grace of a duke. All that I now wish is, that I may at last become a poet and a counsellor, by the grace of the people, and that they may approve my works, and hold me worthy of the title to their love and honor. To be the people's counsellor, is truly an honor above all honors. My soul longs for this holy and beautiful title. With all that I possess in mind and talent, in strength and energy, I will endeavor to deserve it, and to become that which is the poet's greatest and noblest recompense—the teacher and counsellor of the people!"

CHAPTER VII.

ADIEU TO MANNHEIM!

SCHILLER had returned to Mannheim as ducal counsellor of Weimar. Charlotte von Kalb received this intelligence with so much joy, that Schiller could not help feeling pleased himself. He threw his arms around her, and demanded a kiss as a condition of his retention of the title. Charlotte blushingly hid her face on his bosom, but he gently raised her head, and pressed an ardent kiss on the lips which uttered no refusal. But Charlotte now demanded that Schiller should leave her; and when he refused, and begged and implored that he might be permitted to remain, her eyes glistened, and a glowing color suffused itself over her cheeks.

"Oh, Schiller, you know not what you are doing and what you demand! Do you not see that an abyss lies between us?"

"I see it, Charlotte; but the arm of Love is strong and mighty, and he who truly loves, carries the loved woman over all abysses, or else precipitates himself with her into the yawning chasm?"

"There is another alternative, Schiller, and a terrible one. The abyss is crossed, and they are joined; and then afterward his illusion vanishes—he is undeceived. The ideal has been transformed into a very ordinary woman, whom he scorns, because her love was dearer and holier to her than her virtue. She feels his scorn, and the abyss over which he had borne her becomes the grave in which she voluntarily precipitates herself, in order to escape from him she had loved. Oh, Schiller, if the eye which has heretofore regarded me lovingly should ever cast upon me a glance of contempt! It would crush me, and I should die! Yet, in dying, my lips would denounce him who had known how to love, but had not kept faith; and would arraign him as a traitor and murderer before the judgment-seat of God! Oh, Schiller, I warn you once more not to enkindle a fire in my breast which can never be extinguished or repressed when once in flames, but will blaze upward grandly and proudly, setting aside all thought of the world and its rules and prejudices. We are now walking on the verge of the abyss; you on the one side, I on the other. But our voices reach each other; we can see each other's faces, and our glances can meet in loving friendship. You are free to go where you will; and if your path in life should lead you aside from the road on which I am journeying, I will look after you and weep, but I will make you no reproaches! Think of this, Schiller, and be contented that Charlotte should call you by the name of friend! Do not demand that she should give you another name, which you would now bless, but hereafter curse! Flee now, while it is yet time; and we shall still have the happy remembrance of the beautiful days of our friendship. Let us await the future in quiet resignation, and sustain ourselves with recollections of the past!"

"You are in a strange humor to-day, Charlotte," said Schiller, sadly. "Your eyes are so threatening, that I would almost be afraid of you, if I did not know that my Titaness is still a gentle, loving woman in spite of her fiery enthusiasm. No, Charlotte, you accuse yourself unjustly. No, you would never curse the man you had loved; in death you would bless him for the love he had once given you. You would not denounce, but pity and excuse him whom stern necessity compelled to separate from you—from what is dearest to him on earth. You would know that his path was bleak and lonely, and that, like the faces in Dante's 'Inferno,' he could only look back at the past with a tearful glance while wandering into the dreary future. This you would do, Charlotte. I know you better than you know yourself. The woman never curses the man she has truly loved; she pardons and still loves him when the stream of life surges in between, and forces him to leave her."

"For those who truly love, who have plighted troth, there

is no such compulsion," cried Charlotte, her countenance flushed with indignation. "If you say so, Schiller, you do not know what love is. You make light of the holiest feelings when you believe that it could ever be extinguished— that the necessities of life could ever separate two hearts eternally and indissolubly united in love."

"How strangely moved you are to-day, Charlotte!" answered Schiller, his countenance darkening. "I came here with a heart full of joy, and had so much to impart to you! I came as to a happy and peaceful retreat. But I now see that the time was badly chosen, and that Charlotte will not understand me to-day. Oh, why is it, my dear, that we human beings are all like Erostratus, who hurled the firebrand into the holy temple of the gods, and why do we all desire to unveil the mysterious picture in the temple of Isis!"

"Because we wish to look at the truth," she cried, passionately.

"The truth is death," sighed Schiller, "error is life; and woe to us if we are not satisfied with the beautiful illusion that adorns and disguises life, and casts a veil over death! I am going, Charlotte. It is better that I should, for you have saddened me, and awakened painful thoughts in my breast. Farewell for the present; and when I come again to-morrow, be kind and gracious to me, Charlotte, as you always are at heart!"

He took his hat, greeted her with a mournful smile, and left the room. Charlotte's eyes followed him with a glance of dismay.

"He does not love me," she cried in despair. "He does not love me! If he loved me, he would not have left me without plighting his eternal faith. All that I wished to hear was, that he desired an eternity of love; but he drew back in dismay and left me. He does not love me, and I, O my God, I love him!"

She sank down on her knees, covered her face with her hands, and cried bitterly.

And Schiller's thoughts were also of a bitter, and, at the same time, somewhat disquieting nature. He avoided seeing any one, and remained in his lonely room the entire day. He walked to and fro restlessly; from time to time, he seated himself at the table and wrote a few lines, and then arose, and, resuming his walking, either talked to himself or was lost in thought.

Charlotte also kept her chamber, and avoided all intercourse with others. Late in the evening, a knock was heard at her door, and her maid announced that a letter had arrived from the Counsellor Schiller.

Charlotte opened the door, took the letter, and ordered lights to be brought in. She then tore the cover from Schiller's letter; in it she found a little note on which the few words had been hastily written: "Dear Charlotte!—I have written down the thoughts which our conversation of to-day awakened in my bosom; and send them to you, for they belong to you. May we never share the fate of the poor youth in the temple of Sais! To seek the truth is to kill love, and yet love is the most beautiful truth; and true it is also that I love you, Charlotte! Believe this, and let us leave the great Isis veiled! FREDERICK SCHILLER."

After reading this, Charlotte unfolded the large sheet which was also contained in the cover. It was a poem, and bore the title, " The Veiled Picture at Sais."

Charlotte read it again and again, and her soul grew sadder and sadder. " He does not love me," she repeated, softly. " If he loved me he would not have written, but would have come to weep at my feet! That would have been a living poem! Oh, Schiller, I am the unhappy youth; I have seen the truth! My happiness is forever gone, and, like him, I will go to the grave in despair. I exclaim, with your youth, 'Woe to him who commits a crime in order to find the truth! It can never give him joy!'"

When Schiller returned on the following morning, Charlotte gave him a warm welcome, extended both hands, and regarded him with a tender smile, repeating the words from his letter, "Let us leave the great Isis veiled."

Schiller uttered a cry of joy, fell on his knees at Charlotte's feet, kissed her hands, and swore that he loved her and her only, and that he would remain true to her in spite of all abysses and chasms!

But the vows of mankind are swept away like the leaves of the forest; what to-day was green and blooming, to-morrow fades and dies!

Charlotte may have been right when she said that Schiller could love, but could not keep faith, for, after scarcely two months had elapsed since his return from Darmstadt, and the date of this interview with Charlotte, Schiller wrote to his new friend Körner, in Leipsic, as follows: "I can no longer remain in Mannheim. I write to you in unspeakable distress of heart. I can no longer remain here. I have carried this thought about with me for the past twelve days, like a determination to leave the world. Mankind, circumstances, heaven, and earth, are against me; and I am separated here from what might be dearer to me than all by the proprieties and observances of the world. Leipsic appears to me in my dreams like the rosy morning beyond the wooded mountain-range; and in my life I have entertained no thought with such prophetic distinctness as the one that I should be happy in Leipsic. Hitherto fate has obstructed my plans. My heart and muse were alike compelled to succumb to necessity. Just such a revolution of destiny is necessary to make me a new man, to make me begin to become a poet." And his distant friend in Leipsic responded to his cry of distress with a deed of true friendship. He invited Schiller to visit himself and his friends in Leipsic; and, in order that no moneyed embarrassments should delay Schiller's departure, Körner forwarded him a draft for a sum sufficient to defray his travelling-expenses and pay off his most pressing debts.

CHAPTER VIII.

PLANS FOR THE FUTURE.

THE preparations for his departure were soon made. Schiller had completely severed his connection with the theatre at Mannheim several weeks before. The actors were all inimical to him, because he had dared to take them to task in his journal, *The Thalia*, for having, as he said, " so badly maltreated his tragedy, " Intrigues and Love." The director, Mr. von Dalberg, had long since considered himself insulted and injured by the free and independent behavior of him who dared array his dignity and pride as a poet against the dignity of the director's office and the pride of aristocracy. This gentleman made no attempt whatever to retain Schiller in Mannheim. Schiller had to say farewell to but few acquaintances and friends, and it was soon over. He packed his little trunk, and was now ready to leave on the following morning. There were only two persons to whom he still wished to bid adieu, and these were Charlotte von Kalb and Andrew Streicher. He had agreed to spend the last hours of his stay with Streicher at his home, and as every thing was now in order, Schiller hurried to Charlotte's dwelling as evening approached.

She was sitting alone in her room when he entered; the noise of the closing door aroused her from her reverie, and she turned her head, but did not arise to meet him; she gave him no word of welcome, and gazed at him sadly. Schiller also said nothing, but walked slowly across the wide room to the sofa on which she was seated, and stood regarding her mournfully.

Neither of them spoke; deep silence reigned in the gloomy chamber, and yet their souls were communing, and one and the same wail was in both hearts, the wail ever approaching separation and parting.

" Schiller, you stand before me like the future," said Charlotte, after a long pause. "Yes, like the future—grand, gloomy, and cold—your countenance clouded."

"Clouded like my soul," sighed Schiller, as he slowly sank on his knees before Charlotte. She permitted him to do so, and offered no resistance when he took her hand and held it firmly within his own.

"Charlotte, my beloved, my dear Charlotte, I have come to take leave of you. I must leave Mannheim."

"Why?"

"My position here has become untenable. I am at enmity with the authorities of the theatre, and I no longer desire to waste my time and talents on such ungrateful showmen. Mr. von Dalberg's short-lived courtesy is long since ended, and he does not take my side in the difficulty with the presuming actors. I am tired of this petty warfare, and I am going."

"Why?" she repeated.

"You still ask, Charlotte; have I not just told you?"

"I have heard pretences, Schiller, but not the truth. I wish to know the truth, and I am entitled to demand the truth. The time has arrived to tear the veil from the statue of Isis! We must look the truth in the face, even if death should follow in its train! Schiller, why are you leaving Mannheim? Why are you leaving the place where I live?"

"Ah, Charlotte, this is a bitter necessity, but I must bear it. A mysterious power compels me to leave here. Who knows where the star of his destiny will lead him? We must follow its guiding light, although all is dark within and around us! True, I had thought that it would be the greatest delight of life to be ever at your side, to share with you all thought and feeling, our lives flowing together like two brooks united in one, and running its course through the bright sunshine with a gentle murmur! But these brooks have become rivers, and their waves, lashed into fury by passion, brook no control, and break through all restraints and barriers. Charlotte, I go, because I dare not stay! I will tell you all; you demand the truth, and you shall hear it! Charlotte, I go for your sake and for mine! You are married. I go! Your pure light has set fire to my soul; have I not reason to dread a future based on falsehood and deception? Your presence infused into my bosom an enthusiasm before unknown, but to this enthusiasm, peace was wanting."

"Oh, remain, Schiller, and, if we desire it, we can both find this peace—the peace of friendship!"

"No, Charlotte, our heart-strings are familiar with a greater harmony!"

"Well, if it be so, let the strings resound with the harmony of united souls! Oh, my friend, if we separate, we will no longer be to each other what we now are. I will not complain, and will not unveil the anguish of my soul before you; and yet, Schiller, remain, I implore you! When my candle is brought in, I will no longer enjoy its light; all will still be dark around me, for the evening will no longer bring you, my friend!"

"I can, and will be, your friend no longer, Charlotte, and therefore I am going! I will be all, or nothing! This suspension midway betwixt heaven and earth is destroying me! My soul glows with passion, and you inhale it with every breath of life. You have not the courage to face the truth!"

"I say, with you, I will be all, or nothing," she exclaimed, passionately. "Truth and falsehood cannot exist together; and it would be acting a falsehood if I gave my heart unlimited freedom, while my hands are in chains! All, or nothing! Only no hypocrisy! I will freely acknowledge my love to the whole world, or I will cover it with the veil of duty and resignation. But I will not sin under cover of this veil! Oh, Schiller, our life until now was a bond of truth, and you wish to sever it. Fate sent you to me; moments of the purest delight were vouchsafed us; and is the cup of happiness to be dashed from our lips now?"

Schiller did not reply at once, but bowed down over Charlotte's hand, and pressed it to his burning brow.

" Above all," he said, in a low voice, " above all, I know that it is in the bloom of youth only that we truly live and feel. In youth, the soul is illumined with light and glory; and my heart tells me that thou canst never dim its longing."

" 'Thou,' you say," she whisperd softly, " then I will also say 'thou!' Truthfulness knows no 'you!' The blessed are called 'thou!' * It is a seal which unites closely, and therefore we will impress it upon our holy and eternal union!"

She threw her arms around Schiller's neck—he was still kneeling at her feet—and pressed a kiss on his forehead. He embraced her yet more tenderly, and pressed impassioned kisses upon her brow, her cheeks, and her trembling lips.

" Farewell, thou only one, farewell!"

" Oh, Frederick," she sobbed, " was this thy parting kiss?"

" Yes, Charlotte, I must go! But you will be present with me in my every thought."

" And yet you go, Frederick?"

" Destiny so ordains, and I must obey! The world demands of me the use of my talent—I demand of the world its favor."

" And when you have achieved this favor," she said, plaintively, " then you will no longer care for love, or me!"

" You should not say so, Charlotte, for you do not believe it," said Schiller, angrily. " Why these painful words? I lose all in you, but you lose nothing in me! You are so wayward—ah, not like the woman I pictured to myself in the days of my youth."

" Oh, Frederick," she murmured, " do you not know that I love you, and you only?"

" I have hoped so in many moments of torment when you treated me coldly; but only for the last few days have I felt assured of it, and, on that account, loved, adored woman, the words must be spoken, therefore I flee from you!"

" You know that I love you," she cried, plaintively; " you know it, and yet you flee!"

---

* In Germany. the word "thou " is frequently used instead of "you " in families and among children, and intimate and dear friends.

"Yes, Charlotte, I do, because the waves of passion are surging high in my breast, and will destroy me if I remain. Peaceful love is the only atmosphere suited to the poet. Stormy passion distracts his thoughts and casts a shade on the mirror of his soul."

He arose and walked restlessly to and fro. It had grown dark in the mean while, and the figure of her friend flitted before Charlotte's vision like a shadow, but her eyes were fixed intently on the shadow which was nevertheless the only light of her being.

The figure now stopped before her, and when he laid his hand on her shoulder she felt the electric touch thrill her whole being. They could not see each other's faces on account of the darkness.

"Charlotte," said Schiller, deeply moved, "I owe you a great deal, and I can never forget it. My youth was dreary; I became familiar with error and sorrow at an early day, and this clouded my understanding and embittered my heart! And then my genius found your voice to utter my thoughts. You were my inspired Muse, and I loved you, and would be yours forever if I had the courage requisite for such a love!— the courage to permit myself to be absorbed in this passion; to desire nothing more, to be nothing more, than your creature, Charlotte; the vase only in which the boundless stream of your love empties itself. But this cannot remain so! My soul must be peaceful and independent of this power which terrifies and delights me at the same time. He only is free who elevates himself above passion, and the man who aspires to bend Nature to his will must be free."

"You are governed by pride," sighed Charlotte, "and pride has no confidence, no repose. You are not familiar with the sorrow and coldness of the world, or you would remain here with her who feels and sympathizes with you! Nothing is more terrible in its self-inflicted revenge than the determination to disregard the promptings of the heart in life."

"I do not disregard them, Charlotte, but the heart must not

be the only axis on which my life revolves, and it would be, if I remained near you, you divine woman, to whom my heart and soul will ever lovingly incline, forgetting all else, and yet —I desire your friendship only!"

As he said this he threw his arms around her, raised her up from the sofa, and covered her face with kisses.

"Oh, Frederick, you are crying! I feel your tears falling on my forehead!"

"Be still, Charlotte, be still, and—love me! For a single blissful moment love me, and let yourself be loved!"

"I love you, Frederick," she cried, passionately. "You fill my soul with anguish and delight, alternately. You love as I do! Only love alarms you; you will not accord to a mortal that which is divinely beautiful! Oh, Schiller, the essence of Divinity is within us; then wherefore should our love not be divinely beautiful, joyfully renouncing hope and desire in humility and resignation?"

He did not reply, but only drew her closer to his heart, bowed down his head on her shoulder, and sobbed.

The silence which now reigned in the dark room was unbroken save by the sobs of the weeping lovers.. After a long and painful pause, Schiller raised her head and withdrew his arms from Charlotte's figure.

"Let us have light," said he, and his voice now had a harsh sound—"light, that I may once more see your beloved countenance before I leave!"

"No, Frederick, when you leave, I will no longer require light; a cheerless life is more endurable in the dark. No light! Let us part in darkness, for in darkness I am doomed to grope my way hereafter, but the light of your countenance will always be reflected in my soul. Good-night, Frederick! You take with you all that is dear to me, even my beautiful dreams. The most lovely visions have heretofore surrounded my bed at night; but now they will follow you, for they came from you, and were the thoughts of your soul. Your thoughts fly from me, and my dreams follow them. You rob my day of its sun, and my night of its dream. Let us therefore separate in darkness!"

"Charlotte," said he, deeply agitated, "your words sound like tones from a spirit-world, and the past seems already to be leaving me! Oh, do not go; stay with me, sweet past, happy present! Stay with me, soul of my soul, beloved being! Where are you, Charlotte—where are you?"

She did not reply. Longingly he stretched out his arms toward her, but did not find her; he found empty space only.

"Charlotte, come for the last time to my heart! Come!— let me inhale from your lips the atmosphere of paradise!"

No reply. He seemed to see a shadow flit through the darkness, and then the words, "Good-night, Schiller!" struck his ear like the low, vibrating tones of an Æolian harp.

The noise of an opening and closing door could be heard, and then all was still.

A groan escaped Schiller's breast; he felt that Charlotte had left him—that he was alone.

For a moment he stood still and listened, hoping she would return; but the silence remained unbroken.

"Ah," murmured Schiller, "parting is like death! Ah, Charlotte, I have loved you dearly! I—be still, my heart, no more complaints! It must be so!"

He turned slowly and walked toward the door. "Farewell, Charlotte, farewell!"

No reply. It seemed to be only the echo which responded from out the dark space, "Farewell!"

Schiller opened the door and rushed out into the still night, and through the lonely streets, unconscious that he was bareheaded, oblivious of having left his hat in Charlotte's room. He rushed on, heedless of the raw night air and cutting wind.

At length he was aroused by the heavy drops of rain which were falling on his forehead. The cold rain awakened him from a last painful struggle with his passion, and cooled his head and heart at the same time.

"O God, I thank Thee for sending down the waters of heaven to cleanse my heart from passion and slavish love, and making me free again! And now I am free!—am once more myself! am free!"

Schiller entered Streicher's apartment with a cheerful countenance, and greeted his friend heartily; but Andrew regarded his wet clothing and dripping hair with dismay.

"Where in the world do you come from, Fritz? You look as if you had been paying the Maid of the Rhine a visit, and had just escaped from her moist embrace!"

"You are, perhaps, right, Andrew! I have just taken leave of the fair maid who had bewitched me."

"But what have you done with your hat, Fritz? Did you leave it with the maid as a souvenir?"

"You are, perhaps, right again, Andrew. I left my hat with the maid as a souvenir, and only succeeded in slipping my head out of the noose."

"Be kind enough to speak sensibly," said Streicher, "and tell me where your hat is."

"I have told you already I left it with the Maid of the Rhine as a souvenir."

"I wish you had not done so," said Andrew, in grumbling tones. "You had better have left her a lock of your yellow hair; that would have been cheaper, for hair grows again, but hats must be bought. Well, fortunately I happened to buy a new hat to-day, and that you must take, of course."

He handed Schiller a bran-new beaver hat, telling him to dry his disordered locks and try it on.

"Andrew," said Schiller, after having tried the hat on, and found that it fitted him perfectly. "Andrew, you bought this hat for yourself to-day?"

"Yes, for myself, of course, but you, wild fellow, come running here bareheaded, and no resource is left but to put my beaver on your head."

"Come here, Andrew," said Schiller, smiling, and when he

came up, Schiller placed the hat on the little bald head and pressed it down over his friend's eyes, making Streicher a very ludicrous object.

Schiller, however, did not laugh, but slowly lifted the hat up, and looked lovingly into the abashed and mortified countenance of his friend. " Andrew, I would never have believed that you knew how to tell an untruth!"

"And you see I acquitted myself badly enough," growled Streicher. " And bad enough it is that you should compel an honest man to tamper with the truth. Your hat had seen much service and well deserved a substitute, but if I had had the presumption to offer you a new one what a scene there would have been! So I thought I would exchange hats with you at the last moment, after you had entered the stage-coach. And I would have done so, had you not burst in upon me without a hat, and given me what I considered a fine opportunity to make you my trifling present."

" It is no trifling present, Andrew, but a magnificent one. I accept your hat, and I thank you. I will wear it for the present instead of the laurel-wreath which the German nation is on the point of twining for my brow, but which will probably not be quite ready until my head has long since been laid under the sod; for the manufacture of laurel-wreaths progresses but slowly in Germany; and I sometimes think my life is progressing very rapidly, Andrew, and that I have but little time left to work for immortality. But we must not make ourselves sad by such reflections. I thank you for your present, my friend, and am contented that you should adorn my head with a hat. Yes, when I consider the matter, Andrew, a hat is a far better and more respectable covering for a German head than a laurel-wreath. In our bleak, northern climate, laurels are only good to season carps with, and a sensible German had far better wish for a good hat than a laurel-wreath. Yes, far better, and we will drink a toast to this sentiment, Andrew. You invited me to a bowl of punch; out with your punch, you good, jolly fellow! We will raise

our glasses and drink to a future crowned with beaver hats!
Your punch, Andrew!"

Andrew hurried to bring from the warm stove the little,
covered bowl of punch, carefully prepared according to all
the rules of the art.

The two friends seated themselves at the little table on
which the steaming bowl had been placed, and filled their
glasses.

"Raise your glass, Andrew; 'Long live the beaver! destruction to the laurel!'"

"No, Fritz, I will not drink such a toast with you," said
Streicher, slowly setting his glass down. "It would be a sin
and a crime for Frederick Schiller to drink so unworthy, so
miserable a toast. You are in your desperate humor again
to-day, Fritz, and would like to invoke the very lightning
from heaven, and concoct with its aid a little tornado in your
own heaven."

"Yes, of course, you droll fellow!" cried Schiller, emptying
his glass at one draught. "Lightning purifies the atmosphere
and brings the sun out again. And you see my departure is a
mighty tornado, with showers of rain, with thunder and lightning, intended, no doubt, to cleanse and purify my life, that
it may afterward flow on through the sunshine, clear and
limpid. Andrew, I go from here to seek happiness and
peace."

"And, above all, renown," added Streicher, emptying his
glass.

"No," cried Schiller, vehemently, "no renown for me!
Translated into good German, renown means thorns, hunger,
want! I intend to have my portion of the viands with which
the table of life is richly provided. And do you know what
my purpose is?"

"No, but I should like to learn it."

"I intend to become a jurist," cried Schiller, emptying his
second glass. "Yes, that is it. I will begin a new life and
make a jurist of myself. My old life is ended, and when I

enter the stage-coach to-night to go to Leipsic, it will not
contain the poet Schiller, the author of 'The Robbers,' and
other absurdities, but the student, Frederick Schiller, on his
way to Leipsic to study jurisprudence at the university.
Don't shake your wise head and look so horrified, Andrew.
I tell you I will become a jurist; I am tired of journeying on
the thorny path of the poet, with bleeding feet and a hungry
stomach. All my illusions are vanished. My vision of a
golden meteor sparkling in the sun, proves to have been only
a soap-bubble; and this bubble called renown has now
bursted."

"You are again talking wildly and romantically, like
Charles Moor, in 'The Robbers,'" cried Streicher; "and yet
you are not in earnest!"

"But I am in earnest, my friend! The sad experience of
my past life has made me wise and practical. I will not discard poetry altogether, but will indulge in it at times only,
as one indulges in oysters and champagne on great and festive
occasions. My ordinary life will be that of a jurist. I have
given the matter much thought and consideration. Fortunately, I have a clear head and quick comprehension, I will,
therefore, with a firm will and untiring diligence, study and
learn as much in one year as others do in three. The university in Leipsic is rich in resources, and I will know how to
avail myself of them. If an ordinary head, by ordinary application, can acquire in three years sufficient knowledge to
enable a man to earn a comfortable living in the practice of
his profession, I can certainly attain the same end in a shorter
time. My attention has been directed to the study of systems
since my earliest youth; and in our Charles School, of blessed
memory, I have at least learned to express myself as fluently
in Latin as in German. Study, thought, and reflection, is a
delight to me, and the explication of difficult subjects a pleasure; and, therefore, I am convinced that I can become a good
jurist, and, with bold strides, swiftly overtake the snail-mov-
ing pace of others, and in a brief time attain that which the

most sanguine would scarcely imagine could be achieved in years."

"Then you, at least, admit that you are no ordinary man," said Andrew Streicher, shrugging his shoulders. "And, nevertheless, you propose to confine this extraordinary man in the strait-jacket of practical science. Truly, I lose my appetite, and even this punch seems sour, when I reflect that the poet of 'The Robbers' is to become an advocate!"

"You had rather he hungered, and wrote dramas, than he should lead a happy and comfortable life, and write deeds. Ah, my friend, the career of a poet is full of bitterness and humiliation. The wise and sensible shrug their shoulders when mention is made of him, as though he were a crazy fool; the so-called gentlefolk do not recognize him as their equal, and even the players on the stage act as though they conferred a favor on the poet when they render his dramas, and, as they say, give life to inanimate forms by their sublime impersonations. No, no, my mind is made up, I will write no more stage pieces, at least until I have achieved a respectable position in the world as a jurist. Man must always push on and possess the ambition which leads higher and higher. Are not you, too, ambitious, Andrew?"

"Of course, I am, and will strive with all my might to obtain my ideal, and become the leader of an orchestra."

"And I, Andrew, I will become a minister," cried Schiller, with enthusiasm. "Yes, that is my ideal!—minister of a little state—to devote my whole life, my thought, and being, to the happiness of mankind, to be a benefactor to the poor and oppressed, to advance men of talent and science, to promote the good and useful, to cultivate the beautiful. This, Andrew, is my ideal; and this is attained if I succeed in becoming a good jurist and a minister at one of our dear little Saxon courts. Yes, my friend, thus it shall be! You, an orchestra-leader—I, a minister! Let us arise with our foaming glasses, and shake hands over it. Let this be our last toast, and our final compact: 'We will neither write to, nor visit each other, until Andrew Streicher is the orchestra-leader, and Frederick Schiller the minister.' " *

"So let it be," cried Andrew, laughing. "Hurrah, the orchestra-leader! hurrah, the minister!"

They raised their glasses exultingly, and emptied them. They then gave each other one last embrace. The hour of departure and parting had come.

Andrew accompanied his friend in silence through the deserted streets of the slumbering city, to the post-office, where the coach stood awaiting the passengers. A last pressure of the hand, a last loving look, and the coach rolled on, and carried into the world the "new Cæsar and his fortunes!"

CHAPTER IX.

THE LAST RIDE.

YEARS, when we look back at them in the past, are but as fleeting moments; when we look forward to them in the future, they are eternities! How long was the year from the spring of 1785 to the spring of 1786 to be for young Frederick Schiller, who looked forward to it with so much hope and so many beautiful dreams!

How long was the same year to be for old Frederick, for the old philosopher of Sans-Souci, who grew day by day more hopeless, in whose ear was daily whispered the awful tidings, "You must die!"

He did not close his ear to thse mutterings of age and decrepitude, nor did he fear death. For him life had been a great battle—a continuous conflict. He had ever faced death bravely, and had fought gallantly against all sorts of enemies; and truly the worst and most dangerous among them were not those who opposed him with visible weapons, and on the real battle-field. It had been far more difficult to contend with

---

* Schiller's own words.—See "Schiller's Flight from Stuttgart," etc., p. 216.

folly, malice, envy, and prejudices—to pursue his conquering
course regardless of the cries of the foolish and the calumnies
of the ungrateful.

It is easier to conquer on the field of battle than to combat
prejudices, than to extirpate abuses. And, after the days of
real battles were over, Frederick was compelled to wage in-
cessant war against these evils. The one great and holy aim
of his life was to make his people happy and respected, rich
and powerful; and with all the energy and strength of which
he was capable he strove to accomplish these ends, never permitting himself to be confounded or dismayed by malice and
ingratitude. Commerce flourished under his rule—the fruits
of Prussian industry found a market in the most distant
lands. Barren lands had been made fertile. The soldiers of
war had become the soldiers of peace, who were now warring
for the prosperity of the people. This warfare was certainly
at times a little severe, and the good and useful had to be introduced by force. But what of that? Were potatoes less
nutritious, because the peasants of Silesia were driven into the
field by armed soldiers, and compelled to plant this vegetable?
Did it not become a great favorite with the people, notwithstanding their resistance to its introduction in the beginning?
Were not vast sums of money retained in the land by the cultivation of this vegetable, which would otherwise have been
used to purchase rice and other grains in foreign countries?
Had not the king succeeded in introducing the silkworm into
his dominions? Had not the manufacture of woollen goods
been greatly promoted by the adoption of a better system of
raising sheep?

But Frederick had not only fostered agriculture and industry, he had also evinced the liveliest sympathy for the arts
and sciences. Scholars and artists were called to his court,
and every assistance was rendered them. Universities and
academies were endowed.

But, while looking to the internal welfare of his kingdom,
his gaze was ever fastened on Austria, the hereditary enemy

of Prussia. He did not permit the house of Hapsburg to stretch out its rapacious hands after German lands. Looking to the future, and contemplating his death, he endeavored to secure his kingdom against the Hapsburgs beyond the time when he should be no more. This was evinced by Frederick's last political act—the formation of the " Union of Princes"— the Prussian king's last defiance to Austria. This " Union of Princes " was a confederation of German princes against rapacious, grasping Austria. It united all against one, and made the one the enemy of all. The intention and object of this union was to assist and protect each state against the common enemy, to tolerate no trespass on the rights of any one of them, to revenge a wrong done to the smallest member of the union, as if it had been perpetrated on the greatest. Moreover, the welfare of the German people was to be duly considered and promoted, the constitution maintained, and no violation of its requirements to be tolerated.

This " Union of Princes " was determined upon, and carried into effect, between Prussia and all the other German states, except Austria, and other states whose sovereigns were related to the Hapsburgs.

This union was Frederick's last political act! Against Austria he had first drawn his sword as a young king, and against Austria this, his last blow, was directed in uniting Germany, and making it strong in unity, and free in strength!

He had sown the seed destined to bear rich fruit, but he was not to be permitted to reap the harvest. His life was drawing to a close; and the poor, decrepit body reminded the strong and active mind that it would soon leave its prison, and soar to heaven, or into illimitable space!

But Frederick wished to serve his people to the last moment. As long as he could still move his hands, they should work for the welfare of his kingdom. As long as his intellect remained clear and active, he would continue to work. At times, however, bodily pain clouded his understanding, and made him peevish and irritable. To have occupied himself

with matters of state at such times would have been dangerous, as his physical condition might have affected the decisions
he was called upon to make.   In his paternal solicitude for
the welfare of his people, Frederick gave this subject due consideration, and endeavored to render his bodily afflictions harmless.   There were several hours in which he suffered but little
from the gout and the asthma, and these were in the early
morning, when he felt refreshed after having slept for one or
two hours.

One or two hours' sleep! This was all Nature accorded
the royal invalid, who had watched over Prussia's honor for
half a century, and whose eyes were now weary, and longed
for slumber and repose. But the king bore this affliction with
the patience of a sage—he could even jest about it.

"My dear duke," said he to the Duke of Courland, who
paid him a visit in June, 1786, "if, on your return to Courland, you should hear of a vacancy among the night-watch-
men, I beg of you to reserve the place for me, for, I assure
you, I have learned the art of watching at night thoroughly."

But he wished to employ his hours of wakefulness in the
night for the good of his people, and ordered that the members of his cabinet, who had been in the habit of coming to
his room with their reports at seven o'clock in the morning,
should now assemble there at four.

"My condition," said the king, when he acquainted the
three members of his cabinet with his desire, "my condition
necessitates my giving you this trouble, but it will be of short
duration.   My life is on the decline, and I must make the
most of the time which is still allotted me.   It does not belong to me, but to the state." *

Yes, his life was on the decline; but for a long time his
heroic mind found strength to overcome the weakness of the
body.   At times, when the physicians supposed his strength
was entirely exhausted, and that the poor, worn-out figure sitting out on the terrace under the burning July sun, and yet

* Zimmermann.—"Frederick the Great's Last Days," p. 163.

trembling with cold, would soon be nothing more than the empty tenement of the departed soul, he would gather the energies of his strong and fiery mind together, and contend successfully with the weakness of the body. Thus it was in the month of April, when his physicians believed him to be at the point of death. He suddenly recovered one morning, after a refreshing slumber, arose from his bed, dressed himself, and walked with a firm step down the stairway to the carriage, which he had ordered to be held in readiness to drive him out; he entered the carriage, but not with the intention of returning to the palace of Potsdam, but to drive to his dear Sans-Souci, to take up his residence there for the summer.

And thus it was to-day, on the fourth of July, when the king, who had passed the day before in great pain and distress, felt wonderfully refreshed and restored on awaking. He sent for the members of his cabinet at four o'clock in the morning, and worked with them until eight, dictating dispatches and lengthy administrative documents, which bore witness to the vigor of his mind. At eight o'clock he desired that his friends should pay him a visit, and conversed with them as gayly and wittily as in the long-gone-by days of unbroken health. He laughed and jested about his own weakness and decrepitude so amiably, that Count Lucchesini could not refrain from giving utterance to his delight, and hailing the king as a convalescent. "My dear count," said Frederick, shrugging his shoulders, "you are right; I will soon be well, but in another sense than the one you mean. You take the last flare of the lamp for a steady flame. My dear count, darkness will soon convince you that you are wrong. But I will profit by this transient light, and will persuade myself that I am well. Gentlemen, with your leave I will avail myself of the bright sunshine and take a ride. Order Condé to be saddled."

"But, sire!" cried Lucchesini, in dismay.

A glance from Frederick silenced the count.

"Sir," said he, severely, "while I still live, I must be addressed with no 'buts.'"

The count bowed in silence, and followed the other two gentlemen who were leaving the room. Frederick followed his favorite with a look of lively sympathy, and, as Lucchesini was about to cross the threshold, called him back. The count turned quickly, and walked back to the king.

Frederick raised his hand and pointed to the window through which the sunshine and green foliage of the trees could be seen.

"Look how beautiful that is, Lucchesini! Do you not consider this a fine summer day?"

"Yes, sire, a very fine summer day; but it is to be hoped we shall have many more such; and if your majesty would be quiet for the next few days, you would, with increased strength, be better able to enjoy them."

"And yet I will carry out my intention, you obstinate fellow," exclaimed the king, smiling. "But I tell you I will never recover, and I have a question to ask. If you had lived together with intimate friends for long years, and were compelled to take your departure and leave them, would you not desire to bid them adieu, and say to them, 'Farewell! I thank you!' Or would you leave your friends like a thief in the night, without a word of greeting?"

"No, sire, that I would certainly not do," replied Lucchesini. "I would throw my arms around my friend's neck, and take leave of him with tears and kisses."

"Now, you see," said Frederick, gently, "the trees of my garden are also my friends, and I wish to take leave of them. Be still, not a word! I am old, and the young must yield to the old. I have no fear of death. In order to understand life rightly, one must see men entering and leaving the world.* It is all only a change, and the sun shines at the same time on many cradles and many graves. Do not look at me so sadly, but believe me when I say that I am perfectly willing to leave the stage of life."

* Frederick's words a short time before his death.

And, raising his head, the king declaimed in a loud, firm voice:

> "Oui, finissons sans trouble et mourons sans regrets,
> En laissant l'univers comblé de nos bienfaits.
> Ainsi l'astre du jour au bout de sa carrière,
> Repand sur l'horizon une douce lumière,
> Et ses derniers rayons qu'il darde dans les airs
> Sont ses derniers soupirs qu'il donne à l'univers."

He extended his hand to the count with a smile, and, when the latter bowed down to kiss it, a tear fell from his eyes on Frederick's cold, bony hand.

The king felt this warm tear, and shook his head gently. "You are a strange man, and a very extravagant one. The idea of throwing away brilliants on an old man's hand! it would be far better to keep them for handsome young people. Now you may go, and I hope to find you well when I return from my ride."

Having intimated to the count, by a gesture of the hand, that he might withdraw, he turned slowly to his greyhound, Alkmene, which lay on a chair near the sofa, regarding the king with sleepy eyes.

"You are also growing old and weak, Alkmene," said the king, in a low voice; "and your days will not be much longer in the land. We must both be up and doing if we wish too enjoy another ray of sunshine. Come, Alkmene, let us go and take an airing! Come!"

The greyhound sprang down from the chair and followed the king, who walked slowly to his chamber to prepare himself for the ride.

A quarter of an hour later the king, assisted by his two valets, walked slowly through his apartments to the door which opened on the so-called Green Stairway, and at which his favorite horse, Condé, stood awaiting him. The equerry and the chamberlain of the day stood on either side of the door, and at a short distance two servants held the horses of these gentlemen.

The king's quick glance took in this scene at once, and

he shook his head with displeasure. "No foolishness, no pomp!" said he, imperiously. "My servants alone will accompany me."

The two gentlemen looked sadly at each other, but they dared make no opposition, and extended their hands to assist the king in mounting.

But it was a difficult and sorrowful task to seat the king on his horse. Deference prevented them from lifting him up, and the king's feebleness prevented him from mounting unaided. At last chairs and cushions were brought and piled up, until they formed a gradual ascent to the saddle-back, up which the two servants led the king, and succeeded in placing him on his horse. Condé, as if conscious that perfect quiet was necessary to the successful carrying out of this experiment, remained immovable.

But now that he was seated on the back of his favorite horse, Condé threw his head high in the air and neighed loudly, as if to proclaim his joy at being once more together with the king.

Alkmene did not seem to relish being behind Condé in manifesting joy, for she barked loudly and sprang gayly around the horse and rider, who had now taken the reins in his hand and started the sagacious animal by a slight pressure of the thigh.

The king rode slowly down the green stairway, that is, a succession of green terraces forming a gentle declivity in the direction of Sans-Souci. As the grooms were on the point of following him the chamberlain stepped up to them.

"Take care to keep as near the king as possible, in order that you may be at hand if any thing should happen to his majesty."

"His majesty's carriage shall be held in readiness at the Obelisk," said the equerry, in a low voice. "If any thing should happen to the king, bring him there, and one of you must ride in full gallop to the physician Sello!"

The two grooms now hurried on after the king, who had put spurs to his horse and was galloping down the avenue.

It was a beautiful day; a shower which had fallen the

night before had made the air pure and fragrant, and washed the grass till it looked as soft and smooth as velvet. The king slackened his speed. He looked sadly around at the natural beauties which surrounded him, at the foliage of the trees, and up at the blue sky, which seemed to smile down upon him in cloudless serenity. "I will soon soar up to thee, and view thy glories and wonders! But I will first take leave of the glories of earth!"

He slowly lowered his eyes and looked again at the earth, and inhaled its delicious atmosphere in deep draughts, feasted his eyes on nature, and listened to the music of the murmuring springs and plashing cascades, and of the birds singing in the dense foliage.

He rode on through the solitary park, a solitary king, no one near him; the two lackeys behind in the distance, the greyhound bounding before him; but above him his God and his renown, and within him the recollections of the long years which had been!

The friends who had wandered with him through these avenues, where were they? All dead and gone, and he would soon follow them!

He had often longed for death; had often said to himself that it would be a great relief to lie down and sleep the eternal sleep of the grave. And yet he was now saddened to his inmost being. It seemed to him that the skies had never before been so bright, the trees so fresh and green, or the flowers so fragrant! Why long for the peace of the grave! How delicious and refreshing was the peace of Nature! with what rapture did the soul drink in the sunshine and the fragrance of flowers!

"From the afflictions of the world I fly to thee, thou holy virgin, pure, chaste Nature," said he, softly to himself. "Men are but weak, miserable beings, and not worth living for; but, for thy sake, Nature, I would still desire to live. Thou hast been my only beloved on earth, and it is very painful to thy old lover to leave thee."

Yes, it was very painful. Nature seemed to have put on festive garments to-day, in order to show herself to the departing king in all her magnificence and beauty.

The king rode on slowly through the avenues of Sans-Souci, bidding adieu to each familiar scene. At times, when an opening in the trees offered a particularly fine view, he halted, and feasted his eyes on the lovely landscape, and then he would lower his gaze quickly again, because something hot had darkened his vision—it was perhaps a grain of sand thrown up by the wind, but certainly not a tear! No, certainly not! How could he weep, he who was so weary and sick of life?

"Yes, weary and sick of life," he said, in a loud voice. "Men are such miserable beings, and I am weary of ruling over slaves!—weary of playing the tyrant, when I would so gladly see freemen around me! No, no, I do not regret that I must die, I leave willingly, and my countenance will wear a smile when I am carried to the grave." *

It may be easy to take leave of men, but Nature is so beautiful, it smiles so sweetly on us! It is very hard to have to say to the sky, the earth, and to the trees and flowers: "Farewell! I will never see you more! Farewell!"

The trees and bushes rustle in the wind and seem to sigh, "Farewell!" The falling waters seem to murmur, "Nevermore!" Ah, there is yet a little corner in the king's and hero's heart, which is merely human; a little nook to which wisdom and experience have not penetrated, where natural feeling reigns supreme.

Yes, man tears himself from beautiful Nature reluctantly and sadly. He would like to gaze longer on the flowers, and trees, and shrubbery; to continue to breathe the fragrant air. But this man is also a hero and philosopher; and the hero whispers in his ear: "Courage, be strong! You have often looked death in the face without flinching—do so now!"

The philosopher whispers, "Reconcile yourself to that which

* The king's own words.

is inevitable. A town-clock is made of steel and iron, and yet it will not run more than twenty years. Is it surprising that your body should be worn out after seventy years? Rather rejoice that you are soon to read the great mysteries of creation, to know whether there is life beyond the grave, and whether we are again to be united with those who have gone before."

"These mysteries I will solve," cried the king, in a loud voice. "I greet you, O dead with whom I have wandered in these shady groves. We shall soon meet again in the Elysian fields, and I will bring you intelligence of this miserable earth and its miserable inhabitants. My mother, my sister, I greet you, and you Cicero, Cæsar, Voltaire! I am coming to join the immortals."

He raised his head and breathed freely, as if a heavy burden had fallen from his soul. His countenance was illumined with enthusiasm. He looked over toward Sans-Souci, which had just become visible through an opening in the trees; its windows shone lustrously in the bright sunshine, and the whole building glittered in the glorious light.

"It is my tomb," he said, smiling, "and yet the cradle of my renown. If I knew that I could escape death by not returning to my house, I would still do so. I am willing to yield my body to death, and am now going home to die!"

As he said this he slowly raised his arm and lifted his old three-cornered hat slightly, and bowed in every direction, as a king does when taking leave of his court.

He then slowly replaced the hat on his thin white hair, and pressed Condé so firmly with his knees, and drew in the reins so closely, that the animal galloped off rapidly. Alkmene could only manage to keep up with great difficulty. The terrified lackeys urged their horses to a greater speed.

This rapid ride did the king good, the keen wind seemed to strengthen his breast and dispel the clouds of melancholy from his soul. He had bidden his last adieu to Nature. Death was now vanquished, and the last painful sacrifice made.

When the king, after a two hours' ride through the park of Sans-Souci, galloped up the green stairway on his return, the chamberlain and equerry were astonished and delighted to find that he had met with no accident, and was positively looking better and stronger than he had done for a long time.

The king halted with a sudden jerk of the reins, and the lackeys rushed forward with chairs and cushions, to form a stairway for his easy descent, as before.

But with a quick movement Frederick waved them back. "Nothing of the kind," said he. "I can dismount with the aid of your arm. I will, however, first rest a moment."

He stroked Condé's smooth, tapering neck, and the intelligent animal turned his head around, as if to look at his master and thank him for the caress.

"Yes, you know the hand that strokes you," said the king, smiling. "We two have taken many a ride, and gone through rain and sunshine together. Farewell, my faithful Condé."

He had bowed down over the animal's neck to stroke its mane. When he raised his head, his quick, piercing eye observed a young officer coming over the terrace with an air of embarrassment; he hesitated and stood still, as if doubting whether he might be permitted to come nearer. "Who can that be?" asked the king, gayly. "What young officer have we here?—Come up, sir, and report."

The young man hurried forward, stepped close up to the king's horse, and saluted him by raising his right hand to his cap.

"I have the honor to report to your majesty," said he, in clear, joyous tones. "I have been ordered here at this hour, and punctuality is the first duty of the soldier."

"Well replied, sir," said the king. "Give me your arm and assist me to dismount."

The young officer hastened to obey the command, laid his hands on Condé's neck, and stretched his arms out as firmly as if they had been made of iron and were capable of standing any pressure. The king grasped these living supports and slowly lowered himself from the horse's back to the ground.

"Well done, my nephew, you have a strong arm, and, for your fifteen years, are quite powerful."

"Sixteen years, your majesty," cried the young man, eagerly; "in four weeks I shall be sixteen years old."

"Ah, sixteen already!" replied Frederick, smiling. "Then you are almost a man, and must be treated with due consideration. Mon prince, voulez-vous avoir la bonté de me donner votre bras?" *

"Sire, et mon roi," replied the prince, quickly, "vous me daignez d'un grand honneur, et je vous suis très reconnaissant!" † And after bowing deeply he offered his arm to the king.

"Just see how well he speaks French already!" said the king. "We will remain out here on the terrace for a few moments. The warm sunshine does an old man good! Lead me, my prince."

He pointed with his crutch to the arm-chair which stood near the open door of the saloon, and walked slowly across the terrace, supported by Frederick William's arm.

"Here," said he, as he sank slowly into the chair, breathing heavily, "here I will repose once more in the warm, bright sunshine before I enter the dark house."

He looked slowly around at the terraces and trees, and then his gaze fastened on the young prince, who stood near him with a stiff and formal military bearing.

"Lieutenant, forget for a few moments that you are before the king. You are at liberty to dispense with military etiquette. And now give me your hand, my son, and let your old uncle offer you a right hearty welcome."

The prince pressed the hand which he extended respectfully to his lips.

"Seat yourself," said the king, pointing to a stool which

---

* "Will you have the goodness to give me your arm, my prince?"
† "Sire and my king, you confer a great honor on me, and I am very grateful."

stood near his chair. And, when the prince had done as he bade him, he looked long and earnestly into his fresh, open face.

"I sent for you, my child," said Frederick, in a soft and tender tone, "because I wished to see you once more before I set out on my journey."

"Your majesty is then about to travel," said the prince naïvely.

"Yes, I am about to travel," replied Frederick, bowing his head gently.

"But, your majesty, I thought the grand manœuvres were to be held at Potsdam this time."

"Yes, the grand manœuvres will be held in Potsdam; and, at the grand review, I will have to report to Him who is the King of kings. Why do you look so awe-struck, my son? Perhaps it has never occurred to you that men are compelled to leave this paradise to die!"

"Your majesty, I had never thought seriously of death!"

"And you were perfectly right in not doing so, my child," said Frederick, and his voice had now regained its firmness. "Your attention must be firmly and immovably directed to life, for a great deal will be required of you on earth, and with your whole mind and strength you must endeavor to respond to these demands. You must study very diligently and make yourself familiar with the sciences. Which is your favorite study?"

"History, sire."

"That is well, Fritz. Impress upon your mind the great events of history, and learn, by studying the heroic deeds of kings, to be a hero yourself. Above all, your aims must be great, and you must struggle to attain them throughout your entire life. Who is your favorite hero in history?"

"Sire," replied the prince, after a little reflection, "my favorite hero is Cosmo de Medici."

The king looked at him in astonishment. "What do you know of him?" said he. "Who was this Cosmo de Medici?"

"He was a great general," replied the prince, "and a great lawgiver, and his sole endeavor was to make the people happy."

"Then you believe the chief aim of a great man, of a prince, should always be to make his people happy?"

"Yes, sire, his chief aim. Professor Behnisch once told me, in the history lesson of the great Cosmo de Medici, called by the people of Florence the 'benefactor of the people.' When he felt that his end was approaching, he commanded that he should be carried out in his chair to the largest square in Florence, 'For,' said he, ' I desire to die like a tender and happy father in the midst of his children.' But the children he spoke of were his subjects, who now poured into the square from all sides, and filled it so closely that it looked like a vast sea of humanity. When no more room could be found on the square, the people pressed into the houses, the doors of which had all been thrown open; and from the edifices which surrounded the square, thousands upon thousands looked down from the windows. Tens of thousands stood on the square, in the centre of which, and on an elevation, the chair, with the dying prince, had been placed. Yet, although so many inhabitants had assembled there, profound silence reigned. No one moved, and the eyes of all were fixed on the countenance of the dying prince. But he smiled, looked around at the vast concourse, and cried in a loud voice. 'As my last hour has come, I wish to make peace with God and men. Therefore, if there be any one among you to whom I have done injustice, or any one who can complain of any injustice done him under my rule, I beg that he will now step forward and call me to account, in order that I may mete out justice to him before I die! Speak, therefore, in the name of God. I command you to speak.' But no one came forward, and nothing was heard but the low sobs of the people. For the second time the prince asked: 'If there be any one among you to whom I have done injustice, let him come forward quickly, for death approaches!' And a loud voice from among the people cried: 'You have done nothing but good, you have been our benefactor and our father. You will cause us a pang, for the first time, when you leave us; we therefore implore, O father, do not leave your children!' And from the vast square and the windows of the circle of houses, resounded the imploring cry of thousands upon thousands: 'O father, do not leave your children!' The countenance of the prince was radiant with joy, as he listened to the imploring cry and the sobs of his people. 'This is a prince's sublimest requiem,' said he. 'Happy is that prince who can die in the midst of the tears and blessings of his people!' And when he had said this, he arose and extended his arms, as if to give them his benediction. The whole multitude sank, sobbing, on their knees. And Cosmo fell back into his chair. He had died in the midst of the tears and blessings of his people."

The prince's voice had faltered, and his eyes filled with tears, while concluding his narrative, and he now looked timidly at his uncle, who had regarded him intently throughout. The eyes of the venerable old man and the youth met, and their hearts seemed to commune with each other also, for they both smiled.

" And you would like to die such a death, my son?" asked Frederick in a soft voice. " Die like Cosmo de Medici, in the midst of the tears and blessings of his people?"

" Yes, sire, may such a death be mine!" replied the prince, earnestly; " and I swear to your majesty that if I should ever become king, my sole aim shall be the happiness of my people. I will always think of you, and remember your deeds and your words. Yesterday my new instructor, Mr. Leuchsenring, also told me something very beautiful. He told me that your majesty worked day and night for the welfare of your people, and that you had said: 'A king is only the first office-holder of his people!' And that pleased me so well that I have determined to make it the motto of my life."

" Very good," said the king, shaking his head, " keep this motto in your heart, but do not speak of it while you are not yet king, or it might cause you some inconvenience. Be careful how you speak of me when I am gone, and impress this lesson on your memory. A prince royal must never criticise the actions of the ruling king. He must be modest and silent, and give the people an example of an obedient and loyal subject, even if the king should do many things that do not please him. I repeat it,—a prince royal must observe and learn in silence. Never forget this, my son, and adopt this as another rule for your entire life. A good king must never devote too much of his attention to women and favorites, or allow them to influence him, for when he does, it is always to the prejudice of his people's interests, and to his own discredit. I desire to say nothing more on this subject, but remember my words."

"I will do so, sire," replied the prince, earnestly. "I will repeat these beautiful lessons daily, morning and evening, but noiselessly, that none may hear them."

"Well said, my nephew; but let us see how you stand in other respects. Put your hand in my coat-pocket, and take out a little book. I brought it with me in order that you might read something out of it for my benefit. Have you found it?"

"Yes, sire, I have. It is the 'Fables of La Fontaine.'"

"That is it! Now open the book at random. At what fable did you chance to open it?"

"Le Renard et le Corbeau."*

"Now first read the fable in French, and then let me hear you translate it."

The prince first read the fable with fluency and a correct pronunciation in the original language, and then rendered it with the same fluency and correctness in the German.

The king listened attentively, often inclining his head in commendation, and murmuring, at times, "Bravo, superb!"

He extended his hand to the prince when he had finished, and looked at him tenderly. "I am proud of you, Fritz," he cried, "and you shall be rewarded for your diligence. Re-

* The Fox and the Crow.

port to my chamberlain before you go, and he will give you ten Fredericks d'or. That is your reward for your impromptu translation."

"No, I thank you," said the prince; "I do not deserve this reward, and consequently cannot accept it."

"What! You do nòt deserve it? And why not?"

"Because it was not an impromptu translation; if it had been, it would not have been any thing like as good. By accident I opened the book at the same fable I had been translating yesterday and the day before with my instructor, and of course it was easily done the second time."

The king gazed long and thoughtfully at Frederick William's handsome and innocent young face, his countenance brightening and his eye glistening with pleasure.

He bowed down and stroked his cheek fondly with his trembling hand.

"Bravely said, my son; that pleases me. You have an honest and sincere heart. That is right. Never appear to be more than you are, but always be more than you seem to be.* The reward I promised you you shall have, nevertheless, for a king must always keep his promise. A king may never recall a favor once granted, however undeserving the recipient. But this is not the case with you, for you have really made great progress in your French. Continue to do so, and be very diligent, for you must speak the French language as readily as your own, and for this reason you should always speak French with your associates."

"And I do," cried the prince with alacrity. "My instructors always speak French with me, and are very angry when they hear my brother and myself speaking a word of German together. I often pass whole days without speaking a single word of German, and our valet speaks French only." †

* Frederick's own words.—See "Frederick William III.," von Eylert, vol. i., p. 455.

† To this habit of Frederick William may be attributed the fact that he was not able to express himself fluently in his own language in later years. When the king spoke French his conversation was vivacious and forcible; when he spoke German, however, he was stiff and embarrassed.

"I am glad to hear it, Fritz! The French language is the language of diplomacy throughout the world, and it is also best adapted to it on account of its flexibility. I love the French language, but not the French people. I think matters are taking a dangerous course in France, and that there will be trouble there before long. I will not live to see it, but the crater will open and cast its abominable streams of lava over all Europe. Prepare yourself for this time, my son. Arm and equip yourself! Be firm, and think of me. Guard our honor and renown! Perpetrate no wrongs, and tolerate none. Be just and mild with all your subjects, and severe with yourself only."

"I will be as severe with myself as Professor Behnisch is with me now," said the prince, earnestly. "I will give myself no immunity; but when I have done something wrong, I will prescribe a punishment for the offence."

"Is your professor so severe?" asked the king, smiling.

"Ah, yes, your majesty, very severe. A punishment follows in the train of every offence, and if I have only been the least bit rude or angry I must suffer for it at once."

"That is as it should be," said the king. "Your professor is entirely right. Above all things, a prince must be polite, and have control over himself. But in what do the punishments he inflicts consist?"

"Always in just such things as are most disagreeable: either, instead of taking a walk, I must stay at home and work, or my brother is left at home, and I am compelled to walk with the professor alone, and then we have nothing but learned conversations. Or, when I have not been diligent during the week, I am not permitted to visit my mother on Sunday and dine with her in the palace. Your majesty knows that we, my brother and myself, do not live in the palace, but with Professor Behnisch and Mr. Leuchsenring in Broad Street. Our table is, however, very bad, and for that reason I always look forward to the coming Sunday with pleasure, for then I eat, as it were, for the whole week. During the week, however, our fare is horrible; and when I dare to complain, the invariable rejoinder is, 'We have no money to keep a better table.'"

"And that is the truth," said Frederick, severely. "We should learn to stretch ourselves according to our cover at an early day, and to be economical with money. Moreover, that you do not suffer hunger is quite evident from your fresh, rosy cheeks, and vigorous body. You must eat your daily bread with a merry face, my son, and make no complaints. Young people should be entirely indifferent as to the quality of their food; the indulgences of the table are a solace of old age; youth should despise them; and a good apple ought to be as great a feast for a young man as a pineapple for an old fellow. In later years, when seated at a richly-laden table, you will certainly look back with pleasure to the time when you rejoiced in an approaching Sunday because you fared better on that day than on any other. My son, by suffering want, we first learn how to enjoy; and he only is wise who can find enjoyment in poverty. I hope that at some future day you will be a great, a wise, and an economical king, and for this reason I have instructed those who have charge of you to bring you up plainly, and to teach you, above all things, economy in money matters. For you must know that you have nothing of your own, and that the people are now supporting you; and, for the present, not on account of your services, but solely because you are a scion of your house."

"Sire," cried the prince, with vivacity, "sire, I am very young, and, of course, have not been able to do any service as yet; but I promise your majesty that I will become a useful man, and, above all, a fine soldier, and will make myself worthy of being the nephew of Frederick the Great."

"Do that, my son, make yourself worthy to be the king of your people; and bear in mind the beautiful history of the death of Cosmo de Medici, which you have just narrated. And now, my son, we must part. The sun is setting, and I feel a little tired, and will go to my apartments."

"Ah, every thing is so beautiful and magnificent here, and your majesty has made me so happy by permitting me to see you!"

"Yes," murmured the king, "the world is very beautiful." He looked longingly around over the terraces and trees, and his gaze was arrested by the peak of the obelisk, which stood at the entrance of the garden, and towered high above the trees. He raised his hand, and pointed to the peak.

"See, my son, how this peak overtops every thing else. Although high and slender, it stands firm in storm and tempest. This pyramid says to you, 'Ma force est ma droiture.' The culminating point of the pyramid overlooks and crowns the whole. It does not support, but is supported by all that lies under it, and chiefly by the invisible foundation, built far beneath. My son, thus it is also with the state. The supporting foundation is the people, and the peak of the obelisk is the king. Acquire the love and confidence of the people, this only will enable you to become powerful and happy. And now, my son, come to my heart and receive a parting kiss from your old king. Be good, and do only what is right! Make your people happy, in order that you may be happy yourself."

He drew the prince, who had knelt down before him, to his heart, pressed a kiss on his lips, and laid his cold, trembling hand on Frederick William's head for a moment, as if to bless him.

"And now arise, my child," said he lovingly. "Do not forget this hour."

"Sire it shall never be forgotten," whispered the prince, sobbing loudly, and covering the king's hand with tears and kisses.

"Call the lackeys," murmured the king, as he fell back in his chair, exhausted. "Let them carry me in."

The prince hurriedly summoned the servants; and they raised the chair in which Frederick lay with closed eyes.

For a moment only he opened his eyes to look at the prince,

and to wave him a last greeting with his hand. His eyelids closed again, and the king was carried into his "dark house" and into the library. After setting the chair down, the lackeys stepped noiselessly out of the room, believing the king to be asleep. Frederick opened his eyes, and looking around at the busts of his great ancestors, saluted them with a motion of the hand.

"All is finished," he said, loudly. "I have seen my garden for the last time, and have taken leave of Nature. When my body leaves this house again, it will be borne to eternal rest, but my spirit will fly to you, my friends, and roam with you in endless light and knowledge. I am coming soon. But," he continued, elevating his voiec, and speaking in firmer tones, "my sun has not yet set, and as long as it is still day I must and will work!"

He rang the bell, and told the servant to send Minister von Herzberg (who, at the king's request, had been sojourning at Sans-Souci for the last few weeks,) to his presence at once.

Frederick received the minister with a cordial smile, and worked with him, in erect composure of mind and clearness of intellect, for several hours, listened to his report, gave his decisions, and dictated in a firm voice several dispatches to the ambassadors of France and Russia.

"Herzberg, have these papers drawn up at once," said he, as he dismissed the minister. "The members of the cabinet must present them for my signature to-day, in order that they may be forwarded at the earliest moment. I must deal sparingly with my time, and employ each moment, for the next may not be mine."

"Oh, sire, it is to be hoped that you will still have years to devote to the happiness of your people, and—"

"Do you suppose I desire it?" exclaimed Frederick, interrupting him. "No, I am weary, and long to rest from the troubles and cares of life. You think I do not feel them, because I do not complain. But you must know that some things are only endurable when not complained of. My ac-

count with life is balanced, and, although it gave me some
laurels, yet the thorns predominated, and there was scarcely a
single rose among them. Be still! No complaints! But listen! I believe my end is approaching—already perhaps Death
lies in wait at my door—and I have something to say to you.
Madness and misrule will be the order of the day when I am
gone, mistresses and favorites will reign, and hypocrites and
impostors will practise iniquity under guise of piety. Well,
this you cannot prevent; and if the Lord should see fit to let
it come to pass, you must bear it as you best can. But when
the spendthrifts attack the treasury, when they begin to
squander the money I have saved with so much trouble, for
the amelioration of the country, on their mistresses and favorites, you must not tolerate it. You must speak to the king's
conscience in my name, and endeavor to persuade him, with
good and bad words, to consult his people's interests, and not
lavish on his favorites what belongs to the state. Will you
promise to do this?"

"Yes. I promise your majesty that I will do so," replied
Herzberg, solemnly. "I swear that I will faithfully and
fearlessly obey the commands of my great and beloved king;
that I will repeat to your successor the words your majesty
has just spoken, if occasion should require; and that I will
do all that lies in my power to prevent the expenditure of the
state treasure for any other purpose than that of the welfare
of the people and country."

"I thank you," said the king; "you have relieved my mind
of a great burden. Give me your hand, Herzberg, and let me
thank you once more. You have been a faithful servant to
your king, and you will continue to serve him when he has
long since passed away. And now, farewell for the present,
Herzberg; I desire to sleep a little. A cabinet meeting will
be held here at eight o'clock this evening."

"But, sire, would it not be better if your majesty rested
to-day, or else called the meeting at once, in order that you
might retire to your repose earlier?"

The king shrugged his shoulders. "There is no repose, except in the grave; and sleep is for the healthy only." And, even after they had left him, the king remained sitting at his writing-desk, and arranged his papers, and wrote a letter to his sister, the Duchess of Braunschweig.

The two lackeys stood in the antechamber, awaiting the summons of the king's bell, and whispering to each other that his majesty was again sitting up, and working at a very late hour, although his physician had expressly forbidden him to do so. And yet neither of them dared to enter and disturb him in his labors; they stood hesitating and casting anxious glances at the door.

But, behind this door, in the king's room, two eyes were regarding him intently; these were the eyes of his greyhound, Alkmene. Twice had the animal already jumped up from its bed, run to the king, and nestled caressingly at his side, and had then, when Frederick took no notice of it, hung its head and gone mournfully back to its cushion. It now raised its tapering head, and looked intelligently at the king, who sat writing at the table, his back turned toward the little dog. Suddenly it bounded across the room, sprang upon the king's chair, laid its slender forefeet on its master's shoulder, bent its graceful neck downward, snatched the king's pen from his hand, and jumped down to the floor with it.

"Be quiet, Alkmene," cried the king, without looking up from his work, in which he was entirely absorbed. "No nonsense, mademoiselle!" And the king took another pen from the stand.

Alkmene let the pen fall, and looked up at the king intently. When she saw that he continued writing, she uttered a low, plaintive whine. With one bound she was again on the back of the king's chair. Supporting her feet on his shoulder, she snatched the pen from his hand a second time, and jumped down with it. This time she did not let the pen fall, but held it in her mouth, and remained near the king's chair, looking up to him with her sparkling eyes.

Frederick looked down from his work at the little animal, and a smile flitted over his features.

"Really," said he, in a low voice, "I believe Alkmene wishes to remind me that it is time to go to bed. Well, come here, mademoiselle, I will grant your desire!"

As if understanding her master's words, Alkmene barked joyously, and jumped into the king's lap. The king pressed the little greyhound to his breast, and caressed it tenderly. "My friends have not all deserted me," he murmured. "I shall probably have a smiling heir, but, when my body is carried to the grave, my dog at least will remain there to weep over me."

He pressed the greyhound closer to his breast; deep silence reigned in the room. The wind howled dismally through the trees in the garden; a sudden blast dashed some fallen twigs against the low window, in front of which Frederick worked, and it sounded as if ghostly hands were knocking there. The wind whispered and murmured as if the voices of the night and the spirits of the flowers and the trees wished to bring the king a greeting.

Suddenly Alkmene uttered a long, distressful howl, and ran to the door, and scratched and whined until the servants took heart and entered the room.

The king lay groaning in his arm-chair, his eyes glazed, and blood flowing from his pale lips. His physician and a surgeon were summoned at once, and the king was bled and his forehead rubbed with strengthening salts. He awoke once more to life and its torments; and for a few weeks the heroic mind conquered death and bodily decrepitude. But the ride on Condé on the fourth of July was nevertheless his last. After that day Frederick never left his "dark house."

When the king of the desert, when the lion feels that his end is approaching, he goes to the forest, seeks the densest jungle and profoundest solitude, and lies down to die. Nature has ordained that no one shall desecrate by his presence the last death-agony of the king of the desert.

His Sans-Souci was the great king's holy and solitary re-treat; and there it was that the hero and king breathed his last sigh on earth, without murmur or complaint.

He died on the morning of the 17th August, in the year 1786.

A great man had ceased to live. There lay the inanimate form of him who had been called King Frederick the Second. But a star arose in the heavens, and wise men gave it the name Frederick's Honor. The same star still shines in the firmament, and seems to greet us and Prussia: Frederick's Honor!

BOOK II.

CHAPTER I.

AFTER THE KING'S DEATH.

"THE king is dead! Frederick the Second is no more! come, your majesty, to bring you this sad intelligence!"

These were the words with which the minister Herzberg, accompanied by the valet Rietz, walked up to the bed of the prince royal, Frederick William, on the night of the seventeenth of August, and aroused him from his slumber.

"What is it? Who speaks to me?" asked the prince royal, rising in bed, and staring at the two men who stood before him—the one with a sad, the other with a joyful expression of countenance.

"I ventured to speak to your majesty," answered Herzberg; "I, the former minister of King Frederick the Second. His majesty departed this life half an hour since, and I have come to bring the sad tidings in person. King Frederick the Second is dead!"

"Long live King Frederick William the Second!" cried the valet Rietz, as he busily assisted the king in dressing himself and finishing his toilet.

Frederick William remained silent. No words, either of sorrow or of joy, escaped his lips. Lost in thought, or perhaps painfully alive to the sublimity of the moment, or embarrassed as to what he should say, in order to satisfy two men so differently constituted, he silently submitted himself to his valet's attentions, while Von Herzberg had withdrawn to the alcove of the farthest window, and stood sadly awaiting the commands of the new king.

"Your majesty is attired," said Rietz, in low, submissive tones.

"Is the carriage in readiness?" demanded Frederick William, starting as if aroused from deep thought.

"Yes, your majesty, I ordered it to be ready at once."

"Come, then, Herzberg, let us go; Rietz, you will accompany us."

"But kings should not venture into the night air, without first breaking fast. The chocolate is already prepared. Will your majesty permit me to serve it up?"

"No, Rietz, every thing in its proper place," said the king. "My knees tremble; give me the support of your arm, Herzberg, and lead me."

He laid his hand heavily upon Herzberg's proffered arm, and walked out, leaning upon him. Rietz, who followed them, fastened his small gray eyes on the minister, and shook his fist at him behind his back. "You will not be the support of my king much longer," he muttered between his clinched teeth. "You and your whole pack shall soon be dismissed! We have stood in the background and looked on while you governed, long enough. Our time has at last come, and we will make the most of it." His manner had been threatening and hostile while muttering these words; but, as he now hurried forward to open the carriage door, he quickly changed it, and he not only assisted the king in entering, but also extended a helping hand to the minister. He then jumped up and took his seat beside the coachman, and the carriage rolled down the broad avenue that led to the palace of Sans-Souci. The drive was of short duration, the horses pushing forward as if aware that they were carrying a new king to his future. Not a word was spoken in the carriage; its occupants, the valet included, were lost in meditation. He also was fully aware that he was entering upon a new future, and he swore that it should not only be a brilliant but also a profitable one. He smiled complacently when he considered the pleasures and happiness life had in store for him.

Did not the king love him, and, still better, did not the king love his wife, the soi-disant Madame Rietz?

"A plain madame she will not remain much longer," said he to himself. "She is ambitious; I will place her at the head of the department of titles and orders, but I will superintend the department of finance and material profits. When such a good-natured couple as we are harness ourselves to a wagon, it will be strange indeed if we do not manage to pull it through the mire of life, and if it does not ultimately become transformed into a right regal equipage." At this moment the carriage turned the corner of the avenue, and there lay Sans-Souci, illumined by the first rays of the rising sun, bright and beautiful to look upon, although the corpse of a king lay within—the corpse of one, who but yesterday was the master and ruler of millions, to-day inanimate clay, a handful of dust from the dust of humanity.

The carriage halted, and, as no one came forward to open the door, Rietz reluctantly opened it himself. The king's house was the scene of confusion and sorrow, and could no longer be called the house Sans-Souci, "the house without care," since its royal occupant had closed his eyes.

The king entered the antechamber, and greeted with a kindly smile the two valets who stood near the door. Tears rushed to their eyes, and disregarding etiquette in their grief, they neglected to open the door that led to the inner apartments. Rietz hastened forward and opened it, and then followed the king and minister into the reception-room, which was still empty, as the princes and princesses, and the courtiers, had not yet been informed of the king's death.

"Le roi est mort! Vive le roi!" They will soon come with one weeping and one laughing eye; with a reluctant tear for the departed, and a fascinating smile for the living king, who had awakened this morning to find a crown on his brow, and a kingdom at his feet!

"Le roi est mort! Vive le roi!"

How desolate is the antechamber of the departed king to-day! Not a sound is heard! The portrait of the Marquise de Pompadour, which she had given Frederick as a mark of her favor, hangs on the wall, and smiles down upon this scene with its coquettish beauty. The king and the minister do not observe it, but Rietz, who follows close behind, looks up at the picture with a complacent smile, and thinks to himself that his wife will certainly become quite as celebrated and honored as the French king's flame. Why should not an empress also write to her some day—to her, the adored of the King of Prussia, and call her "ma cousine?" Why not?

It is only with the greatest difficulty that the valet can suppress his inclination to burst into laughter, when this thought occurs to him. As he follows his master into the king's study, he covers his face with his hand, and assumes an air of deep dejection. There are people in this room, and there might be observant eyes there also.

But no, there are no observant eyes in the king's study to-day. The men who are present are thinking only of their trouble and grief. There are no tears of etiquette and no sighs of assumed sorrow there. The king's four cabinet counsellors alone are present. In accordance with his request of the day before, they had come to his study at four o'clock in the morning, the accustomed hour. On the preceding day they had been admitted to his presence, and he had given them his instructions in a weak voice, and had even steadied his trembling hand sufficiently to affix his signature to a state document. To-day they had come, as usual, with the rising sun, but they now saw that their sun had set—nothing remained for them but to weep. The king did not see them, or did not seem to see them, but walked rapidly toward the open door, and the mourning group who had assembled in the adjoining apartment. On a blood-stained pillow in an armchair lay the countenance which was yesterday that of a king. A day had transformed it into a marble bust; it lay there with closed eyes, in peaceful serenity—a smile on the lips that had yesterday cried out to the sun, "Soon I will be with you!"

The great king was with the sun; that which lay in the chair was only the worthless casket of the flown soul.

Beside the body stood the physician Sello, in deep dejection. Behind the chair were the two lackeys, who had faithfully watched at the king's bedside during the preceding night; they were weeping bitterly, weeping because he had gone from them.

Deep silence reigned; and there was something in this silence which inspired even the valet Rietz with awe. He held his breath, and approached noiselessly to look at the corpse of King Frederick, whom he had never had an opportunity of viewing in such close proximity during his lifetime.

As the king approached the body, the servants sobbed audibly. The physician bowed his head deeper, to salute the rising star. The greyhound, which had remained quiet and motionless at the king's feet until now, jumped up, raised its slender head, and howled piteously, and then returned to its former position.

Deeply moved, his eyes filled with tears, the king stooped over the dead body, raised the cold hand to his lips, and kissed it; and then he laid his warm hand on the brow that had worn a crown, and had so often been entwined with laurel-wreaths.

"Give me, O God, Thy blessing, that I may be a worthy successor of this great king," said Frederick William, in a low voice, while tears trickled down his cheeks.—"You, my predecessor, made Prussia great; God grant that it may never be made weak through my instrumentality! Farewell, my king and uncle, and peace be with us all!"

"Amen!" said Herzberg, in a firm voice. "Last evening, when the shades of death were already gathering on his brow, his majesty King Frederick sent for me, and whispered these words, in faltering tones: 'On the morrow you will present my salutations to my successor beside my body.' Your majesty, King Frederick greets you through me!"

Frederick William inclined his head in response. "You

were with the king when he died, were you not, my dear
Sello?"

" Yes, sire, I was."

" At what hour did the king die?"

Sello raised his hand, and pointed solemnly to the large
clock which stood against the wall on a marble stand.   " Your
majesty, the hands of that clock stopped the moment the king
breathed his last sigh.   Sire, behold the first monument
erected to the memory of our great king!"

Frederick William looked both astonished and pleased.
" This is truly wonderful," he observed, in an undertone.
" They were then right!   We are surrounded by wonders.
The hand of a mysterious agency is visible in all things!"

He walked up to the clock, and a feeling of awe crept over
him as he regarded the dial.   To him the hands were ghostly
fingers pointing to the moment at which the king had died.

" Twenty minutes past two," said the king, softly.
" Strange, passing strange!"

He turned and beckoned to his valet to approach.

" Rietz, at what time did I call you last night, when I was
awakened by some fearful anxiety?"

" It was exactly twenty minutes past two, your majesty!   I
am certain of it, because you commanded me to consult your
watch at the time."

" Yes, that was the exact time," murmured the king to
himself.   " The spirits woke me, that I might greet the new
day that was dawning for me."

" Le roi est mort!   Vive le roi!"   The king, who gave enlightenment and freedom of thought to his people, is dead!
King Frederick is dead!   A shadow darkens the sun of this
first morning of the new era.   This shadow will soon become
a lowering cloud, and night and darkness will sink down over
Prussia.

" Le roi est mort!   Vive le roi!"

Frederick William had been gazing thoughtfully at the
clock.   With an effort he suddenly aroused himself.   The

hands of that clock proclaimed the cessation of the old and the beginning of the new era—of his era. He must be prepared to meet its requirements. For the second time he approached the corpse. "Where are the king's decorations?" he demanded of Strützki, the attendant, in whose arms the king had breathed his last.

Hastily drying his eyes, Strützki stepped softly to the little cabinet, and opened it.

"Leave the others," commanded the king, "and bring me only the ribbon of the Order of the Black Eagle."

Strützki speedily returned with the designated order. Holding the broad orange ribbon in his hand, the king now turned to the Minister von Herzberg.

"Count," said he, "bow your head, and receive, at my hands, the last souvenir of the great king who has cast off his mortal frame, in order that he may sojourn with us as an immortal spirit. The ribbon worn by Frederick the Great shall now adorn your breast, in order that the respect and esteem which I entertain for you be made manifest to the world. You will be as true and zealous a friend to me as you were to my great uncle. You will serve me, as you served him, in the capacity of minister of state; and you will be often called on for advice and counsel, Count Herzberg."

"Your majesty," murmured Herzberg, his voice tremulous with emotion, "your majesty rewards me beyond my deserts. I have done nothing but my duty, and—"

"Happy is that king," exclaimed Frederick William, interrupting him, "happy is that king who is surrounded by servants who take no credit to themselves for the good and great which they accomplish, considering that they have done no more than their duty. The obligation to acknowledge their services and show his gratitude, is on this account all the more incumbent upon him; there are very few people on earth who can say of themselves, in this exalted sense, that they have done their duty. But I am a very happy king; I have two such friends at my side on the very threshold of my career. You, my dear count, I have already rewarded for your services. Your patent as count shall be made out, and the insignia of the highest order of the Black Eagle presented you. You will still continue to administer the affairs of your foreign bureau. And now, you need rest, my dear count; I know that you have watched a great deal in the last few nights. *Au revoir!*"

After taking a last lingering look at the royal corpse, Herzberg retired; and King Frederick William turned to the valet, Rietz, who had stood, with his head bowed down, in order to hide the curiosity, and the indifference to the solemnity of the occasion, which were depicted in his countenance.

"And now, my dear Rietz," said the king, extending his hand to the valet, "now the time has at last come when I can reward you for your faithful services! I appoint you treasurer of my household, and keeper of my strong-box!" *

"Ah, your majesty, my beloved king," sobbed Rietz, as he pressed Frederick William's hand to his thick, swollen lips, "such grace, such favor, I have not deserved. I thank your majesty, however, from the bottom of my heart, and you shall always find in me a true and faithful servant! Oh, what will my wife say, and how happy she will be, over the new honor you have conferred upon me!"

The king withdrew his hand with a slight shudder, and looked almost timidly in the direction of the corpse, which lay there so grand and still. He did not see the quiet, stealthy glance which the treasurer fastened on his countenance.

If the corpse of the great Frederick had suddenly come to life again—if those closed eyes had opened once more—how withering a glance would they have bestowed upon the wanton valet! But even the corpse of a king hears no more, and the closed eyes open not again!

"Le roi est mort! Vive le roi!"

The king stepped slowly back, but his gaze still rested on

---

* The king's own words, uttered beside Frederick's corpse.

the countenance of the dead. Though closed, those eyes seemed to see into his heart.

"Rietz, send for the sculptor, in Potsdam, in order that a cast of the king's face may taken."

"Your majesty, it shall be attended to immediately."

He hurried toward the door, but a gesture of his royal master recalled him. Frederick William dreaded being left alone with the great dead and the weeping lackeys! For he well knew that the bodies of the departed were always watched over by the spirits of their ancestors. He knew that the spirits of those who had been dear to the departed in love and friendship, and the spirits of those who were his enemies while they trod the earth in the flesh, were now hovering over the body, and struggling for the possession of King Frederick's soul, even as they struggled for the soul of Moses. But a short time had elapsed since this had been communicated to him by the spirit of the great philosopher Leibnitz, whom the two believers, Bischofswerder and Wöllner, had conjured up to confirm the statements they had made to the unbelieving prince royal!

Yes, these hostile spirits are struggling over the body for the possession of the soul, and to remain, with this knowledge, alone with the dead and the contending spirits, inspires awe and terror.

"Rietz, my faithful follower, remain," said the king, almost anxiously. "But no! Call Lieutenant-Colonel Bischofswerder."

"Your majesty, he has ridden into the city to carry this sad intelligence to the present prince royal, and conduct him here to Sans-Souci."

"And the Councillor Wöllner?"

"Your majesty, I have dispatched a courier to Berlin to inform him of the king's death, and he will probably soon be here."

"Ah, Rietz, you are a faithful and considerate servant. Go before and open the doors. I will repair to the audience-chamber; the court will probably have assembled by this time!"

He waved the royal corpse a final adieu, bowed and walked backward to the door, as if retiring from an audience accorded him by the great Frederick. Profound silence reigned in the chamber for a moment, until Alkmene crept out from under the chair and again howled piteously.

CHAPTER II.

"LE ROI EST MORT! VIVE LE ROI!"

WHILE only two poor servants and a faithful dog remained with the dead king, the new king was receiving the congratulations of his court in the audience-chamber.

The court officials and ministers had already assembled; and now the princes of the royal family were coming in.

Rietz, who had remained in the antechamber, now entered and approached the king. "Your majesty, his royal highness the prince royal and Prince Louis have this moment arrived, and beg permission to tender their congratulations."

"Conduct the prince to the concert-hall," said the king, "I will join him there directly.—And Lieutenant-Colonel Bischofswerder?"

"Your majesty, he accompanied the prince royal."

The king bowed graciously. The word "majesty" sounded like sweet music in his ear, and drowned the wail of grief for the departed.

Bestowing a kindly smile upon the assembled court, the king left the audience-chamber in order to repair to the concert-hall, where the two princes awaited him.

Rietz went in advance, and, as he threw open the door of the concert-hall, cried in a loud voice, "His majesty the king!"

The two princes hastened forward, and pressed their father's extended hand to their lips.

"I take the liberty of tendering to my royal father my most humble congratulations." The prince uttered these words in a stiff and declamatory manner, merely repeating them as they had been taught him by his tutor, Professor Behnisch.

"I beg that your majesty will accord me your favor, and I assure my royal father that he will always find in me an affectionate son and his most obedient subject."

The king's countenance darkened as he gazed upon the prince, who would one day be his successor. Prince royal! An unpleasant word, truly; a gloomy and constant reminder of approaching death!—the prince royal, who is only waiting to be king, who, like the shadow of death, is ever at the monarch's side, reminding him of approaching dissolution. To love one's successor is certainly a hard task; but his existence may, at least, be forgiven, when he is the son of a loved wife, when the father loves his child. But when the prince royal is the fruit of a marriage of convenience, the son of an unloved wife—when the king has another and a cherished son, whose mother he has passionately loved!—Ah, how differently would this son have received his father! He would have thrown himself into his father's arms, and would have hugged and kissed him.

"Oh, my dear son Alexander, why are you not my successor? Why must you remain at a distance? why are you not permitted to stand at my side in this great hour? But all this shall be changed! My Alexander shall no longer remain in obscurity—no, he shall not!"

With his two sons the king had only exchanged a few words of ceremony. He responded but coldly to the formal congratulation of the prince royal; and replied with a mute gesture only to the embarrassed and stammering words of Prince Louis.

"And now go, my princes," said he; "go and look at the body of your great uncle, and impress the solemn scene upon your minds, that you may never forget it!"

"I shall never forget the great king," said the prince

royal, his countenance expressive of great tenderness and emotion. "No, your majesty, I shall never forget the great Frederick. He was always so gentle and gracious to me; and but a few days ago he spoke to me like a kind father, and that made me feel so proud and happy that I can never forget it, and never cease to be grateful while life lasts."

The long-repressed tears now rushed from the prince royal's eyes, and Prince Louis began to weep, too, when he saw his brother's tears, and murmured: "The great Frederick was also very gracious to me."

The king turned aside. His sons' tears were offensive. Who knows whether they will weep when their father also dies?

"Go, my sons, and pay a last tribute of tears to the past, and then turn your thoughts to the joyful realities of the present!"

The two princes bowed ceremoniously, and then left the room, retiring backward, as if in military drill.

The king's eyes followed them as they left the room, and his countenance darkened. "They are as stiff and awkward as puppets. And yet they have hearts, but not for their father!—Rietz!"

The chamberlain immediately appeared in the doorway, and stood awaiting his master's commands, his countenance beaming with humility.

"Rietz, go at once and inform my son Alexander of what has taken place! He must go to Charlottenburg with his tutor and await me there! Let him tell his mother that I will take tea with her this evening, and that she may expect me at six o'clock."

"Will your majesty pass the night in Charlottenburg?" asked the chamberlain, with his eyes cast down and the most innocent expression of countenance.

"I cannot say," replied the king; "I may go to Berlin, and—"

"Your majesty, perhaps, considers it necessary to pay a visit of condolence to the widowed queen at Schönhausen?"

Rietz had said this in an almost inaudible voice, but the king's attentive ear caught the words nevertheless, and his countenance beamed with joy.

"Yes, my friend and heart's interpreter, I will visit the widowed queen at Schönhausen. Take the fastest horse from my stable and ride there to announce my coming."

"To the widowed queen only, your majesty? To no one else?"

"You ask as if you did not know what my reply would be," said the king, smiling. "No, you may also present my compliments to the queen's beautiful maid of honor, Julie von Voss. Request her, in my name, to hold herself in readiness to receive me. I wish to speak with her on matters of great importance. Go, my friend!"

"To speak with her on matters of great importance," muttered Rietz, after he had left the room. "As if we did not all very well know what he has to say to this beautiful young lady; as if his love for her were not a public secret, well known to the queen, his wife, to the entire court, and to dear Madame Rietz, my wife! Very well, I will first ride to young Alexander, then I will speed to Schönhausen, and finally I will hie me to Madame Rietz in Charlottenburg, to make my report. My dear wife is so generous, and I can dispose of so much money! Life is so pleasant when one has money. And it is all the same who a man is and what he is! If he always has money, a goodly supply in his purse, he is a distinguished man, and is respected by all. Therefore the main thing is to become rich, for the world belongs to the rich; and I am quite willing that the world should belong to me. Oh, I will make the best use of my time; and those who suppose they can fool me by their flattery, and that I can be induced to intercede for them with the king, out of pure goodness of heart, will discover that they have calculated without their host. Money is the word, gentlemen! Pay up, and the influence of the mighty chamberlain shall be exerted in your behalf; but nothing gratis! Death only is gratis! No, I am wrong," said he, laughing derisively, as he gazed at a company of grenadiers, who were marching up the avenue toward the palace, where they were to be stationed as a guard of honor to the royal corpse. "The funeral costs a great deal of money."

The grenadiers passed on; and the subdued roll of the drums, which were draped in mourning, died away in the distance, while the winds wafted over from Potsdam the sounds of the tolling bells which proclaimed the king's death to the awakening city.   Rietz hurried off to send the son of the king to his mother in Charlottenburg, and then to ride to Schönhausen and deliver a loving greeting to Frederick William's new flame.   It was still silent and desolate in the chamber of the dead at Sans-Souci.   Strützki had once stepped softly out of the room to get some twigs from the elder-tree which stood on the terrace, to keep the flies from the face of the dead king.   And now the two lackeys were standing on either side of the chair, fanning away the miserable insects that had dared to light on this countenance since the hand of the artist Death had chiselled it into marble. Nothing was heard but the rustle of the twigs and the humming of the flies, ever returning, as if to mock man's vain efforts to drive them from what was justly their own.

The doors were softly opened, and the two princes glided in, and noiselessly approached the arm-chair in which Frederick lay, as if fearful of awakening him.

The prince royal looked at the body long and silently, and his countenance was expressive of deep and earnest feeling. "Stand aside, lackeys," said he, haughtily, "and you, too, my brother, I wish to be alone.   I wish to commune awhile with his majesty!"

The lackeys and Prince Louis retired; the former to the door, the latter to the distant window; and now the lad of sixteen was alone with the immortal Frederick.

He knelt down before the body, grasped the cold hand, and gazed on the marble features of the great dead with an expression of intense earnestness and determination.

"My great uncle and king," murmured he, "I swear to you that I will endeavor to do all that you recently enjoined upon me; and that I will ever strive to do honor to your great name. I swear to you that I will one day be a good and useful king, and endeavor to deserve the affection of the people. My dear uncle, I have a secret in my heart, and I must disclose it before you descend into the grave. It seems to me your sleep will be more peaceful when you learn it: I hate Madame Rietz and her husband. And if she is still living when I become king, I will punish her for her crimes, and will repay her for all the tears which she has caused my dear mother. No one knows of my determination except my mother, who recently told me what sorrow Madame Rietz had occasioned her, and then I was so angry that I wished to go immediately and kill her. But my mother exhorted me to silence and patience, and I promised that I would obey her. But when I am king, I will be no longer silent; then shall come the day of arraignment and punishment. This I swear to you, my dear, my great uncle and king; and this is the secret I longed to disclose. Yes, I will some day avenge my mother. Farewell, my king—sleep in peace! and—" A hand was laid upon his shoulder; he looked up and saw his young cousin Prince Louis, whose approach he had not noticed, standing beside him.

"I congratulate you, cousin," said Prince Louis, impressively, "and crave the continuance of your favor, prince royal of Prussia. His majesty the king sent me here to pay my respects to the royal corpse and the prince royal, but I propose to pay my respects to the latter first."

"No," said Frederick William, who had slowly arisen from his knees, "that you must not do, cousin Louis. I am not changed, and am no better because of our great king's death."

"But more powerful," said the prince; "you are now prince royal, and the greatest deference should be shown you. Oh, do not look at me so earnestly and angrily, cousin. You

think I am cold and indifferent; but no, I have only determined not to weep over the body of our dear uncle. My
mother tells me we shall also soon die, if we let fall a tear on
the countenance of the dead. And yet, Frederick, when I
reflect that the good uncle is dead who was always so kind to
me, and who was our pride and glory, I cannot help shedding
tears in spite of my mother's injunction. Oh, great Frederick, that you could have remained a few years longer on earth,
till that proud eye might have rested on a gallant prince and
brave soldier, instead of a foolish lad!"

"But, cousin, how can you speak so disparagingly of yourself, and so far forget your dignity as a prince?"

"Ah, a prince is no better than any one else," said Prince
Louis, shrugging his shoulders, "and while I have the greatest respect for your exalted rank, Mr. Prince Royal, I have
none whatever for my own little title; particularly at this
moment, when I see that the great Frederick, the hero and
king, was only a mortal. Oh, my dear uncle, why did you
leave us so soon! You were not yet so old—scarcely seventy-
four years, and there are so many who are older. A short
time since, as I was coming here to inquire after your health,
I saw an old man at the entrance of the park, warming himself in the sun; he sat with folded hands, and prayed aloud.
I approached and offered him a piece of money, which he rejected. I then asked him why he prayed and begged, if he
did not desire money. 'I am praying for the sick king,' said
he; 'I am entreating the sunbeams to warm and invigorate
the king's suffering body, and restore him to new life. The
king is so young! he should live much longer. I was a soldier when the king was baptized, and stood near by as a
sentinel; and now they say that he must die. That makes
me anxious. If so young a man must already die, my turn
will soon come; and I so much desire to live a little longer
and warm myself in the bright sunshine!' And the old man
of ninety is still sitting in the sunshine; while you, great
Frederick, were compelled to die! You have gone to the

sun, while we are still groping in darkness, and lamenting your loss, and—"

" Be still, cousin!" murmured the prince royal; " some one is coming! It is the sculptor who is to take a cast of the king's face. Come, let us go! Come!"

He extended his hand to Prince Louis, to lead him out of the room, but the prince drew back.

He knelt down before the body, and kissed the cold hand which had recently stroked his cheeks affectionately. Frederick had always loved Prince Louis, the son of his brother Ferdinand, and had often prophesied that he would live to accomplish something great and useful.

The young prince thought of this, as he pressed the cold hand to his lips in a last farewell. " I swear to you, my great uncle and king, that I will faithfully strive to fulfil your prophecy, and accomplish something good and useful, and to do honor to the name I bear. Let the kiss which I now press on your hand be the seal of my vow, and my last greeting!"

He arose, and his large dark eyes rested on the body with a lingering, tender look.

" Oh," sighed he, " why am I not a painter or an artist, that I might sketch this scene!"

" A happy suggestion," said the prince royal, eagerly. " I am certainly no artist, but I can draw a little nevertheless; and I intend to make for myself a memento of this day.— Mr. Eckstein, I beg you to wait a quarter of an hour, in order that I may make a sketch of this scene."

The sculptor, who had already approached the body with his apparatus, bowed respectfully, and stepped back. Prince Louis took a pencil and a sheet of paper from the king's writing-desk, and handed it to his brother the prince royal. The latter commenced to sketch the scene with hurried strokes.*
His brother stood at his side, looking on; behind the chair

* This drawing, which the prince royal had made of the body of Frederick the Great, was afterward framed, and hung for many years in his study, with this inscription, in his own handwriting: "1 sketched this on the 17th of August, 1786, between the hours of 9 and 10 P.M."

were the two lackeys, and the greyhound's head protruded from beneath the chair. The sculptor Eckstein had withdrawn to the farthest end of the room. Prince Louis had, however, noiselessly glided into the adjoining concert-room, where the instruments were kept. There were the flutes and violins in their cases, and there stood the magnificent piano, inlaid with ivory and mother-of-pearl, which the king's hands had so often touched.

The silence of the death-chamber was once more unbroken. The body lay there, so great and sublime in the two-fold majesty of death and renown, and the prince royal was absorbed in his work, when the silence was suddenly broken by subdued tones of plaintive music. These tones came from the concert-room, and filled the chamber of the dead with low and harmonious sighs and lamentations.

Alkmene crept out from under the arm-chair, and trotted slowly into the adjoining chamber, as if to see if her master, whose voice she had not heard since yesterday, had not called to her to come to him at the piano. The greyhound, however, returned to her former position, when she saw that it was another who sat at the piano.

No, it was not the king, but his nephew Louis, who was playing this requiem for the great departed, and tears were trickling down over his handsome and manly young face. Perhaps it was improper to break in upon the stillness of the sacred chamber in this manner. But what cared the young prince for that. He thought only of bringing the great dead a last love-offering, and none was there to prevent him. Etiquette had nothing more to do with the dead king. It had taken up its abode in the neighboring audience-chamber, with the living king. There, all was formality and ceremony. There, decorated excellencies and gold-embroidered uniforms were making profound obeisances. There, respectful congratulations were being made, and gracious smiles accorded by royal lips.

"Le roi est mort! Vive le roi!"

CHAPTER III.

THE FAVORITES.

KING FREDERICK WILLIAM stepped back into the little audience-chamber, and beckoned to his two friends Bischofswerder and Wöllner to follow him.

He embraced Bischofswerder, and pressed a kiss on his forehead. "My friend, you must never leave me, but always remain at my side."

"I will follow my royal master," said Bischofswerder, bowing profoundly, "as a faithful dog follows his master's footsteps, satisfied if he shall from time to time vouchsafe me a gracious look."

"I know you, my friend," said the king. "I know that you are disinterested, that you are not ambitious, and that the things of this world are of but little importance to your noble mind."

"Let it be my task to provide for your earthly as you have undertaken to provide for my spiritual welfare. My dear Bischofswerder, I appoint you colonel, and this shall be only the step from which you will be rapidly promoted to the rank of general; for you not only war bravely and daringly against visible men, but also against invisible spirits, and it is my holy duty and privilege to reward the brave."

"Your majesty," said Bischofswerder, gently, "the only reward I crave is your favor. I desire and solicit nothing more. The honors and dignities which you shower upon me, and of which I am so undeserving, only awaken anxiety by illumining my small merit, and making my unworthiness all the more conspicuous before the world. Nevertheless, I accept with thanks the promotion accorded me by the grace of my king, although I would rather decline the honor, and remain in obscurity in the shadow of your throne. But I dare not, for a higher one has commanded me to submit to your behests, and I must obey."

"A higher one?" asked the king. "Who is he? Who commands here besides myself?"

"Your majesty, the spirits of the great dead—the Invisible, whose power is greater than that of all the visible, however great and mighty they may be!"

The king had asked this question with a proud and haughty glance; suddenly his manner altered, his countenance assumed an humble, penitent look, his head sank down upon his breast, and he folded his hands as if in prayer. "I am a sinner and a criminal," he murmured. "In the pride of my new dignity I forgot my superiors; and the little visible creature dared to consider himself the equal of the Invisible! I now repent, beg for mercy, and am ready to yield obedience to my superiors.—They have then spoken to you again, these superior beings? They have imparted to you their wishes?"

"Your majesty," said Bischofswerder, in a mysterious whisper, "while sleeping last night, I was suddenly awakened by a wondrous radiance, and I sprang from my bed, believing that fire had broken out and enveloped my room in flames; but I felt that a gentle hand forced me back, and I now saw that the light which had terrified me came from a luminous countenance, which stood out in bold relief amid the surrounding darkness. The eyes of this countenance shone like two heavenly stars, shedding a soft light upon me. With a celestial smile on its lips, the spirit spoke to me: 'Your heart is humble and guileless. You have no craving after earthly honors, and are not attracted by grandeur and riches; but I command you to arise from your humility, and no longer to withdraw yourself from earthly honors, for those whom the Invisible love must also be recognized and elevated by the visible, that their favor be made manifest before men. You will be advanced to-morrow, and on the ensuing day you will receive a second advancement; and what your king offers you must accept. This is the will of the Invisible.' And after this wonderful spirit had spoken it vanished, and all was again enveloped in darkness. I, however, lit a candle, in order that I might have tangible proof, on arising the next morning, that this had been no dream; I wrote down on a sheet of paper the last words the spirit had spoken, and the hour at which it appeared. Your majesty, I have brought this paper with me to show it to my king. Here it is!"

The king took the writing, and read in a low voice: "You will be advanced to-morrow, and on the ensuing day you will receive a second advancement; and what the king offers you must accept. This is the will of the Invisible. Command of the radiant spirit, given in the night between the sixteenth and seventeenth of August, at twenty minutes past two."

"The hour at which the king died," exclaimed Frederick William, with astonishment, "and the hour at which I also suddenly awoke! Wonderful, wonderful indeed!"

"Your majesty, for those endowed with intuition there are no wonders," said Bischofswerder, quietly, "and your majesty belongs to this number."

"But only in a very slight degree," sighed the king. "I am still groping in the twilight; my eyes are yet dazzled by the splendor of the Invisible."

"But your majesty will advance steadily toward the source of light; and if the Invisible will permit me to conduct you into the holy temple of infinite knowledge, I will esteem it the greatest earthly blessing!"

"Yes," cried the king, in ecstasy; "yes, my friend, you shall conduct me; and, at the side of him upon whom this light has been shed, I will walk in safety over the slippery paths of life. Nothing can astonish me in the future, for the paper I hold in my hand is a miracle, and an evidence that the Invisible is omnipresent and omniscient. At the same moment in which King Frederick died I awoke with a cry, and at the same time the spirit announced to you that you would be advanced by your king—by me, who at that moment became king! My friend, I beg you to give me this paper, this evidence of the presence of the Invisible."

Bischofswerder bowed profoundly. "All that the king's

consecrating hand touches becomes his property, as I am his with all that is mine!"

"I thank you, colonel, I thank you. Ascend the step to honor which this day offers, and let it be my care that the prophecy for the ensuing day be also fulfilled. And now," continued the king, turning to Wöllner, who had stood with folded hands, his head bowed down, during this conversation; "and now, as to you, Councillor Wöllner, you are also deserving of thanks and reward."

"Far more deserving than I, poor unworthy man," exclaimed Bischofswerder; "for Chrysophorus, the effulgent, belongs to the chosen, and is the favorite of the Invisible. If your majesty empties the plenteous horn of your favor on the head of Chrysophorus, no drop will be lost, but all will fall on good and fertile soil."

The king greeted the noble, disinterested friend with a kindly smile, and then laid his hand gently on Wöllner's shoulder.

"Thus I will sustain myself on you, Wöllner, and as I now lay my right hand on you, so will I make you my right hand, as I make Bischofswerder my head, to think for me. You too shall be my head and my hand."

"But your heart, sire?" asked Wöllner, in his earnest and solemn voice. "Your heart you must be yourself, and no other human being must be your heart but the king himself."

Frederick William smiled. "My heart, that am I—I the king, but also I the man; and the head and hand which act for me, must also permit the heart to act, as it will and can! Councillor Wöllner, has the Invisible announced nothing to you? have you alone passed the night in quiet slumber?"

"Your majesty," replied Wöllner, with an air of self-reproach, "I have received no message from the Invisible; I must honor the truth, and acknowledge that I have rarely enjoyed such peaceful and unbroken slumber as in the past night."

"He slept the sleep of the just," said Bischofswerder, "and the spirits kept watch at the door of our Chrysophorus."

"Well, then, I will announce to you what the spirits did not announce," exclaimed the king, with vivacity, "Wöllner, I appoint you Privy Councillor of the Finances, and, at the same time, Intendant of the Royal Bureau of Construction."

"Oh, your majesty," cried Wöllner, his little gray eyes sparkling with joy, "that is more than I deserve, almost more than I can accept. I do not consider myself worthy of such high distinction; and this favor far exceeds my merit. And yet, notwithstanding the high honor my king has conferred upon me, I still dare prefer a request; one, however, which does not spring from any bold desire of my own, but one which the command of the Invisible compels me to utter. I am not actuated by earthly motives, but I must obey the behests of the spirits."

"What is this request, my dear privy councillor of the finances?" asked the king, with a smile. "I give you my royal word that your first request shall be granted."

"Your majesty, my request is only this: Give me your favor, your confidence, and your esteem, as long as I live."

"This I promise you, but as a matter of course I should have been compelled to do so, although you had not asked me. This, therefore, we cannot consider a compliance with your request. Speak, Wöllner, and prefer your other request."

"Well, then, your majesty, I beg to be permitted to arrange King Frederick's papers, and prepare this literary legacy for the press."

"I commission you not only to do so," said the king, "but, in order to remove all impediments and facilitate your labors, I make you a present of these papers, to have and to hold as your own property. You may print or suppress portions of them, as seems best to you. I make this one condition, however, that you do not destroy the king's writings, manuscripts, and papers, after you have examined and had them printed as your insight and judgment shall direct; but that you deposit them in the royal archives, set apart for the preservation of such documents."

"Your commands shall be obeyed in every particular," said
Wöllner, respectfully, "and that no doubts may arise on this
subject, I beg this favor of your majesty, that you make out
a written order to the effect that all the papers of the deceased king (whom I unhappily cannot call the blessed, because he lived in unbelief and darkness) be transferred to me
by the two privy cabinet councillors of the late king; they
taking a receipt for the exact number of sheets counted out
to me, and my written obligation to return each and every
one of them. And I will certainly make haste to accomplish
my task, for the Invisible has commanded me to complete the
great work with which I have been intrusted without delay."

"And are you permitted to acquaint me with the object of
this great work, my friend?" asked the king.

"Yes your majesty, I am not only permitted, but am commanded to do so! I am to impart to you the reasons why I
solicit the papers of the deceased king, and why I desire to
have them printed. The object is, that the eyes of your
majesty's subjects may be opened, and they be brought to the
knowledge that he, whom freethinkers and unbelievers called
a shining light, was a mocker at all religion, and an atheist
who scoffed at all that was holy, and did homage to himself,
the idol of renown and heathenish poetry, only. The Invisible has commanded me to unveil the scoffing mind of the unbelieving king, and make manifest to the world that such a
one may never hope to enter heaven and participate in bliss.
Listen, my dear king and master," continued Wöllner, in an
elevated voice, as the roll of drums announced the approach
of a body of troops; "listen to those drums proclaiming the
dawn of a new day! Hail the day which gives to millions of
misguided men a leader and a guide, destined to lead them
back to the right path; and to rear aloft the holy cross which
his predecessor trod under foot! Hail to your people, Frederick William, for you have come to rebuild the Church of God!
Hail to thee, thou favorite of the Invisible! hail, Frederick
William!"

And with a cry of enthusiasm, Bischofswerder repeated the words, "Hail to thee, thou favorite of the Invisible! hail, Frederick William!"

The king had listened to Wöllner with downcast eyes, and the joyful acclamations of his two friends seemed only to have given him disquiet and anxiety.

"I am an unworthy sinner," murmured the king, in a penitent voice, "and if you do not take pity on me and intercede for me with the Invisible, I am a lost man. I implore you both to sustain me with a helping hand, that I may not fall to the ground."

"The Invisible has commanded us to stay at your side and devote our lives to your welfare," said Wöllner, solemnly.

"And even if he had not," cried Bischofswerder, feelingly, "my own heart would have prompted me to do so, for I am my king's alone, and am ready to shed my blood for him. Tell us, therefore, what we are to do, and what is required to restore peace to your soul."

"Say, to my heart, my faithful friend," cried the king, "for it is my heart that needs peace. I love, love with glowing passion. And yet I have sworn in the holy lodge of the Invisible to dedicate my life to virtue. Oh, tell me, tell me, my friends, how can I keep my vow without giving my heart the death-blow! Do not let me sink in despair, but take pity on me. I feel sick and miserable; the torment of love and the conflict with duty rob me of all strength and courage. Oh, help me, help me! You, my friend Bischofswerder, let me drink once more of the elixir of life, which the great magician, Cagliostro, intrusted you with; give me once more life, health, and happiness!"

"Your majesty knows," replied Bischofswerder, "that I gave you the last drop of the precious elixir, given me by the great magician, to infuse new life and health into my veins, when the hour of death should draw near. I joyfully delivered myself over to death in order that my king might have new life; and I now learn, with the greatest sorrow, that it was not sufficient to accomplish its object. But what I would never do for myself, I will now do for my king. I will entreat the Invisible to impart to me the secret of the preparation of this elixir of life; I will address my thoughts to this magician with all the strength of my soul, and conjure him to appear and instruct me how to concoct the elixir of life for my king and master."

"Ah," sighed the king, sadly, "if it is necessary that the magician should appear here, personally, in order to impart to you this wonderful secret, my wish will probably never be gratified, for Cagliostro is at present, as my ambassador yesterday informed me, in London; and the believers are pouring into that city, from all parts of Europe, to see the sublime martyr, who languished in a French prison, on account of the unhappy necklace affair, until his innocence was proved, when he was restored to liberty, on condition that he should leave France at once and never recross its boundaries. Cagliostro then went to London, where he is now receiving the homage of his admirers; and there he expects to remain, as he informed our ambassador. How can your prayers and entreaties have sufficient power to call the magician here from so great a distance? His sublime spirit is united with the body, and is subject to finite laws."

"No, my king," replied Bischofswerder, quietly, "the sublime magician, Cagliostro is uncontrolled by these laws. The miraculous power of his spirit governs the body, and it must obey his behests. I read in your soul that you are in doubt, my king, and that you do not believe in the dominion of the spirit. But your majesty must learn to do so, for in this belief only are safety and eternal health to be found for you and for us all. I will invoke the Invisible in the coming night; and, if my prayer be heard, the magician of the North will appear in our midst this very night, to give ear to my entreaties."

"If this should occur," cried the king, "I am forever converted to this belief, and nothing can hereafter make me

waver in my trust and confidence in you, my Bischofswerder!"

"It will occur," said Bischofswerder, quietly. "I beg that
your majesty will call Chrysophorus and myself to your chamber at the next midnight hour, in order that we may invoke
the Invisible in your presence."

"At the next midnight hour?" repeated the king, in confusion. Bischofswerder's quick, piercing glance seemed to
read the king's inmost thoughts in his embarrassed manner.

"I know," said he, after a pause, "that your majesty intended to pass this night in Charlottenburg with your children and their mother; and if your majesty commands, we
will meet there at the midnight hour."

"Do so, my friends," said the king, hastily, "I will await
you in Charlottenburg, at the appointed time, although I
scarcely believe you will come; and doubt, very much,
whether Bischofswerder's incantations will have power to call
the great magician to my assistance. Oh, I am greatly in
need of help. If you are really my friends, and if the Invisible has anointed your eyes with the rays of knowledge, you
also must know what torments my soul is undergoing!"

"And we do know," said Bischofswerder. "It has been
announced to us."

"And we do know," repeated Wöllner, "the Invisible has
commanded me to implore his dearest son, King Frederick
William, not to burden his conscience with new sin, but to
renounce the passion which is burning in his heart."

"I cannot, no, I cannot!" exclaimed Frederick William;
and with a cry of anguish he buried his face in his
hands.

His two confidants exchanged a rapid glance; and Bischofswerder, as if answering an unspoken but well-understood
question of Wöllner's, shook his head dissentingly. He then
stooped down to the lamenting, moaning king.

"Your majesty," whispered he, "to-night we will also ask
the Invisible if he will not have indulgence with the king's

love; and permit the beautiful Fräulein von Voss to become the wife of the man she loves?"

"Oh, if this could be brought about!" cried the king, throwing his arms around his friend's neck, "I could be the happiest of mortals, and would gladly resign to you my whole kingdom to dispose of it as you see fit. Give me the woman I love, and I will give you my royal authority!"

Again the two confidants exchanged rapid glances, and Wöllner bowed his head in assent.

"We will entreat the Invisible to-night," said Bischofs-werder—"and I hope that he will grant what your majesty desires."

"But, if so, certain conditions will be exacted, and penance enjoined," said Wöllner.

"I am ready to consent to all his demands, and to do all he enjoins, if he will only give me this heavenly woman."

CHAPTER IV.

THE MAID OF HONOR.

No intelligence of the demise of the great king had as yet arrived at the palace of Schönhausen, the residence of Queen Elizabeth Christine, Frederick's wife. It was still early in the morning, and the queen, who was in the habit of sending a special courier to Potsdam every day, to inquire after the king's health, was now writing the customary morning letter to her husband.

She had just finished the letter, and was folding the sheet, when the door of the adjoining chamber was opened, and a tall and remarkably beautiful young lady appeared on the threshold. Her rich, light, and unpowdered hair fell in a profusion of little locks around her high-arched brow. Her large, almond-shaped eyes were of a clear, luminous blue, her delicately-curved nose gave her countenance an aristocratic expression; and from her slightly-pouting crimson lips, when she smiled, all the little Cupids of love and youth seemed to send their arrows into the hearts of the admirers of the lovely maid of honor, Julie von Voss. Her tall and slender figure showed the delicate outline and the rich fulness which we admire in the statues of Venus, and there was, at the same time, something of the dignified, severe, and chaste Juno in her whole appearance—something unapproachable, that demanded deference, and kept her worshippers at a distance, after they had been attracted by her alluring beauty.

The queen greeted her maid of honor, who bowed profoundly, with a gentle smile. " You have come for my letter, have you not, my child? The courier is waiting?"

" No, your majesty," replied the maid of honor, in a somewhat solemn voice. " No, it is not a question of dispatching a courier, but of receiving one who begs to be permitted to see you. The valet of your royal nephew Frederick William is in the antechamber, and desires to be admitted to your presence."

The queen arose from her sofa with a vivacity unusual in one of her age. " The valet of my nephew?" said Elizabeth Christine, with quivering lips—" and do you know what brings him here?"

" He will impart his mission to your majesty only," replied the maid of honor; and when the queen sank back on the sofa, and told her in faltering tones to admit the courier, she threw the door open, and summoned the valet with a proud wave of the hand. And straightway the broad, colossal figure of the royal privy chamberlain Rietz appeared on the threshold. With a smile on his thick lips, and his little gray eyes fixed intently on the pale old lady, who stared at him with an expression of breathless anxiety, the chamberlain entered, and walked across the wide room to the queen's sofa with the greatest composure, although she had expressed no desire that he should do so.

" Your majesty," said he, without waiting permission to

speak, "I have been sent by his majesty King Frederick William—"

The queen interrupted him with a cry of anguish. "By King Frederick William!" she repeated, in faltering tones. "He is then dead?"

"Yes," replied Rietz, inclining his head slightly. "Yes, King Frederick died last night; and he who was heretofore Prince of Prussia is now King of Prussia. His majesty sends the widowed queen his most gracious and devoted greeting; and orders me to inform her majesty that he will arrive here during the day to pay her a visit of condolence."

The queen paid no attention to the chamberlain's words; of all that he had spoken, she heard but this, that her husband, that Frederick the Great, was dead, that the man she had loved with such fidelity and resignation for the last fifty years was no longer among the living.

"He is dead! Oh, my God, he is dead!" she cried, in piercing accents. "How can life continue, how can the world exist, now that Frederick is no more! What is to become of unhappy Prussia, when the great king no longer reigns; what can it be without his wisdom and strength, and his enlightened mind?"

"Your majesty forgets that the king has a glorious successor," remarked Rietz, with cynical indifference.

A dark frown gathered on the brow of the maid of honor, Julie von Voss, when the chamberlain uttered these impertinent words; and she glanced haughtily at his broad, self-complacent countenance.

"Leave the room," said she, waving her hand imperiously toward the door; "wait in the antechamber till you are called to receive her majesty's reply and commands."

The chamberlain's countenance flushed with anger, but he quickly suppressed all outward manifestation of feeling, and assumed an humble and respectful manner.

"Your grace commands," said he, "and I am her zealous and obedient servant, ever ready to do her bidding. And herein I know that I am only fulfilling the desire of my royal master, who—"

"Leave the room at once!" cried the maid of honor, her cheeks flushing with anger.

"No," said the queen, awakening from her sad reverie; "no, let good Rietz remain, dear Julie. He must tell me of the great dead. I must know how he died, and how his last hours passed.—Speak, Rietz, tell me."

The chamberlain described the king's last hours in so ready and adroit a manner, managing to introduce the person of the new king so cleverly into his narrative, and accompanying his remarks with such intelligent and significant looks at the maid of honor, that she blushingly avoided his glances, and pressed her lips firmly together, as if to suppress the angry and resentful words her rosy lips longed to utter.

"I left his majesty King Frederick William in the death-chamber," said Rietz, as he finished his narrative. "But, even in the depth of his grief for his royal uncle, he thought of the living whom he loves so dearly, and commanded me to hasten to Schönhausen, to announce that he intended to gratify the longings of his heart by coming here, and that—"

"Will not your majesty dismiss the messenger?" interrupted the maid of honor in an angry voice.

"Yes, he may go," murmured Elizabeth Christine. "Tell the king my nephew that I await him, and feel highly honored by the consideration shown me."

"Your majesty, love and admiration draw him to Schönhausen," observed Rietz. "I can assure you of this, for the king confides every thing to me, and often calls me his—"

"Figaro," added the maid of honor, with a contemptuous curl of her proud lips.

"His friend," continued Rietz, without, as it seemed, having heard this cutting word. "I have the honor to know all my master's heart-secrets, and—"

"To be the husband of Wilhelmine Enke," exclaimed the

maid of honor, passionately. "Your majesty, will you not dismiss the messenger?"

"You may go, Rietz," said the queen, gently. But Rietz still hesitated, and fastened his gaze upon the young lady, with a smiling expression.

"Your majesty," said she, "I believe he is waiting for a gratuity; and we will not be rid of him until he receives it."

Rietz broke out into loud laughter, regardless of the presence of the mourning and weeping queen. "This is comical," he cried. "This I will relate to his majesty; it will amuse him to learn that this young lady offers his privy chamberlain and treasurer a gratuity. He will consider it quite bewitching on her part, for his majesty finds every thing she does bewitching. But I am not waiting for a gratuity, but for permission to deliver to Mademoiselle von Voss the messages which his majesty intrusted to me for her grace, and I therefore beg the young lady—"

"Go out of the room, and wait in the antechamber until I send for you!" said the maid of honor, imperiously.

"And will you soon do so?" asked Rietz, with unruffled composure. "I take the liberty to remark, that I have other commissions to execute for his majesty, and therefore I ask whether you will soon call me?"

"You have nothing to ask, but only to obey," said the young lady, proudly.

Rietz shrugged his shoulders; bowed profoundly to the queen, who was wholly occupied with her grief, and had heard nothing of this conversation, and then left the room with a firm step.

"She is very proud, very haughty," growled Rietz in a low voice, as he threw himself into a chair in the antechamber with such violence, that it cracked beneath him. "That she is, and it will require much trouble to tame her. But she shall be tamed nevertheless; and the day will come when I can repay her abuse with interest. Figaro she called me. I know very well what that means; my French education has not been thrown away. Yes, yes, Figaro! I understand! The ever-complaisant servant of Count Almaviva, and the negotiator in the affair with the beautiful Rosine. Oh, my young lady, take care! I am the Figaro, to-day, helping to capture the fair Rosine, in order to deliver her over to Count Almaviva. But I, too, have my beautiful Susanna; and some day, when Almaviva wearies of his divine Rosine, he will turn again to my Susanna; and you will then be thrown in the background. Figaro! Ah, my lovely maid of honor, I will give you cause to remember having called me this name! I will speak to my wife about this matter before the day is over!"

CHAPTER V.

FIGARO.

WHILE Rietz was sitting in the antechamber, in an angry and resentful frame of mind, the maid of honor was still at the queen's side, endeavoring to console her with tender words and entreaties.

"After all, your majesty is but suffering an imaginary loss," said the maid of honor finally, after she had exhausted all other grounds of consolation. "For you, all will be just as it was before, as it has been for many years; and it should be all the same to your majesty whether the king has died, or is still remaining in Sans-Souci, for you were widely separated in either case."

"But I was always with him in thought," lamented Elizabeth Christine. "I knew that he lived, that we breathed the same air; that the ray of sunshine which warmed me, fell also on his dear, noble head. I knew that the eyes of the country were directed toward Sans-Souci; and that the great king's every word found an echo throughout all Europe. It did me good, and was my consolation for all other wants, that this great hero and king, who was worshipped and admired by the world, sometimes thought of his poor wife, in his infinite goodness, and sometimes shed a ray of light on her dark and solitary life. I was permitted to be at his side on every New-Year's-Day, and hold with him the grand court-reception. And I always looked forward to this event with rejoicing throughout the entire year, for he was ever the first to congratulate me, although in silence; and then he looked at me so kindly and mildly with his wondrous eyes, that my heart overflowed with happiness and bliss."

"But he never spoke to your majesty, the cruel, unfeeling king!" said the maid of honor, shrugging her shoulders.

"Do not abuse him," said the queen, warmly. "He was not cruel, not unfeeling. For if he had been so, he would have sundered the tie which bound him to the unloved woman who had been forced upon him when he became king. But he was mild and gentle; he tolerated me, and I was permitted to love him and call myself his, although he was never mine. Instead of banishing me, as he might have done, he endured me, and accorded me the royal honors due his wife. True, I have not often seen him, and have very rarely spoken to him; but yet I heard and knew of him, and he never permitted my birthday to pass without writing me a letter of congratulation. Once, however—once he went so far in his goodness as to hold the New-Year's reception here in Schönhausen, because an accident which happened to my foot prevented my coming to Berlin. Oh, I shall never forget that day, for it was the only time the king visited me here; and since then it seems to me that the sun has never set, but still gilds the apartments through which Frederick had wandered. On that day," continued the queen, with a sad smile, absorbed in her recollections of the past, "on that day, something occurred which astonished the court, and was talked of in all Berlin. The king, who, on similar occasions in the city, had only looked at and saluted me from a distance, walked up to my side, extended his hand, and inquired after my health in the most kind and feeling manner. I was so confused and bewildered by this unexpected happiness, that I almost fainted. My heart beat wildly, and I found no strength to utter a single word in reply, that is, if my tears were not an answer.* But since that day the king has never spoken to me. The words, however, which he then uttered have always resounded in my ear like sweet music, and will lull me to sleep in the hour of death."

"Oh," exclaimed the maid of honor, in astonishment and indignation, "how can it be possible to love in such a manner?"

The queen, who had entirely forgotten that she was not speaking to herself, and that another listened to her plaintive wail, raised her head quickly, her blue eyes sparkling as if she had been but seventeen instead of seventy years old.

"How could it be possible not to love in such a manner, when one loved Frederick the Great?" said she, proudly. "I had made this love my life, my religion, my hope of immortality. I gave to this love my whole soul, my every thought and feeling; and it gave me, in return, joyful resignation and the strength to endure. Without this, my great, my beautiful love, I would have perished in the solitude and desolation of my being; but from it my life derived its support, its enthusiasm, and its perpetual youth. Years have whitened my hair and wrinkled my countenance, but in the poor, miserable body, in the breast of this old woman, throbs the heart of a young girl; and it bears me on with its youthful love, through and beyond all time and trouble, to those heights where I will once more behold him, and where he will, perhaps, requite the love he here despised. Love never grows old; when the heart is filled with it, years vanish like fleeting dreams, and it encircles mortality with the halo of undying youth! Therefore it must not surprise you, Julie, that the old woman you see before you can speak of her love. It was the love of my youth, and still makes me young. And now go, my child, and leave me alone with my recollections, and the great dead! I have much to say to him that God only

* See Preuss.—" Frederick the Great, a Biography," vol. iv.

may hear! Go, my child, and if, at some future day, you should love and suffer, think of this hour!"

She greeted the young lady with a gentle wave of the hand, and as the maid of honor left the room she saw the queen fall on her knees.

Slowly, and with her head bowed down, Julie von Voss walked through the adjoining rooms to her own apartments. "I will never love like this, and consequently never suffer like this," said she to herself. "I cannot comprehend how one can lose and forget one's self so completely in another, particularly when this other person does not love as ardently— as ardently as I am loved by—"

She stopped and blushed, and a slight tremor ran through her being. "I should like to know whether he loves me as passionately as this woman has loved her husband, whether— But," exclaimed she, interrupting her train of thought, "I had entirely forgotten that his valet is waiting to deliver a message."

Immediately on entering her parlor, she rang the bell, and ordered her chambermaid to show the valet, Rietz, who was waiting in the queen's antechamber, up to her apartments at once. She then walked slowly to and fro; she sighed profoundly, and her lips whispered in low tones, "I do not love him! No, I do not love him; and yet I will no longer be able to resist him, for they are all against me; even my own relatives are ready to sacrifice me. That they may become great, I am to be trodden in the dust; and that they may live in honor, I am to live in shame! But I will not!" she cried, in a loud voice; and she stood proudly erect, and held up her beautiful head. "No, I will not live in shame; every respectable woman shall not have the right to point the finger of scorn at me, and place me in the same category with the brazen-faced wife of the abominable Rietz! They shall not have the right to call Julie von Voss the king's mistress! No, they shall not, and—"

"The king's privy chamberlain," announced the maid, and behind her Rietz walked into the parlor.

"Poor Figaro has been compelled to wait a long time, my lady," said he, with a mocking smile. "You have treated Figaro's master, who longs for an answer, very cruelly."

"I did not ask your opinion of my conduct," said the maid of honor, haughtily. "You are the king's messenger; speak, therefore, and execute his majesty's commands."

"Ah, this is not a question of commands, but of entreaties only—the king's entreaties. His majesty begs that he may be permitted to see you after he has paid his visit of condolence to the widowed queen."

"Etiquette requires that I shall be present when her majesty, the widowed queen, receives his visit. And if his majesty desires to speak with me, I beg that he will graciously avail himself of that opportunity."

"Ah, but that will not answer," said Rietz, with a smile. "When his majesty expresses a desire to visit my lady here in her own apartments, he probably has something to say, not intended for the ears of other ladies. Perhaps his majesty wishes to speak with my lady about the widowed queen and her condition, and to ask your advice as to the proper arrangement of her household. I believe the king intends to place it on a far better footing, for he spoke a few days since with real indignation of the paltry salary received by Queen Elizabeth Christine's maids of honor—hardly sufficient to give them a decent support. The king will consider himself in duty bound to raise the salaries of these ladies; and you would certainly confer a great pleasure on his majesty by making known to him the amount you desire, and command for yourself. And you must not hesitate to mention a very considerable sum, for his majesty is generous, and will be happy to fulfil your wishes. It would, perhaps, be well for my lady to give me some hints in advance, in order that I may prepare his majesty. I shall be inexpressibly happy if my lady will permit me to be her most devoted servant, and it might also be of great advantage to her, for all Berlin and Potsdam —yes, all Prussia, knows that I am the king's factotum."

"Did his majesty commission you to utter all these impertinences?" asked Julie, coldly.

"How so,—impertinences?" asked Rietz, bewildered by the proud and inconsiderate manner of the lady, who regarded him, the almighty factotum, so contemptuously. "I have not, I certainly did not—"

"Silence! I listened to you out of respect for the king. And now, out of respect for myself, I command you to leave the room immediately. I will ask his majesty if he authorized his valet to tell me any thing else than that the king intended to honor me with a visit. Go!"

She proudly turned her back on the chamberlain, and walked through the room. She felt that she was suddenly held back. It was Rietz, who had caught hold of her dress, and he now sank on his knees, and looked up to her imploringly.

"Forgiveness, my lady, forgiveness! I have surely expressed myself badly, for otherwise my lady could not desire to leave the most devoted of her servants in anger. I only intended to say, that—"

"That you are the wedded husband of Wilhelmine Enke," cried the young lady with a mocking peal of laughter; and she withdrew her garment as violently as if a venomous serpent had touched it. She then left the room, still laughing, and without even once looking at the kneeling chamberlain.

Rietz arose from his knees; and his countenance, before all smiles, now assumed a dark and malignant expression. He shook his fist threateningly toward the door through which she had left the room, and his lips muttered imprecations. And now he smiled grimly. "Yes," said he, "I am Wilhelmine Enke's husband, and that will be your ruin at some future day! Threaten and mock me as you please; you are, nevertheless, nothing better than the bird that flies into the net to eat the alluring red berries placed there to entice it to inevitable destruction. The net is set, the red berries are scattered around; and you will not resist the temptation, my charming bird; you will be caught, and will perish!" And, laughing maliciously, he turned and left the room.

The maid of honor, Julie von Voss, had not heard his malignant words, and yet her heart was filled with anxiety and tormenting disquiet; and when the door opened, and her brother, the royal chamberlain, Charles von Voss, entered, she cried out in terror, and sank into a chair, covering her face with her hands.

"But, Julie," said her brother, angrily, "what does this childishness mean—what is the matter? Why does my presence terrify you?"

"I do not know," said she, "but when you appeared in the doorway, just now, it seemed to me that I saw the tempter coming to allure me to sin and shame!"

"Very flattering, indeed," observed her brother, "but there may be something in it. Only you forget to add that the tempter intends to offer you a world. What did Satan say to Christ when he had led Him up a mountain and showed Him the world at His feet? 'This will I give Thee if thou wilt fall down and worship me.' Julie, I also come to offer you a part of the world; to lay a kingdom, a crown, and a king at your feet."

"Have you seen the king? Has he spoken with you?" asked Julie, breathlessly.

"He sends me in advance, as *postillon d'amour*, and will soon be here himself."

"I will not see him," cried the maid of honor, stretching out both hands as if to ward off his approach. "No, never! He shall not visit me; I will lock my door, and not open it until he has gone, until he ceases to pursue and torment me!"

"My dear," said he, quietly, "I have come to speak with you seriously. You must now come to some decision; or rather, you must decide to do that which your family, which reason, policy, ambition, and pride counsel. You have bound the king in your toils with admirable ingenuity, and I congratulate you. No lion-tamer can tame the king of the desert more skilfully, and with greater success, than you have tamed your royal lion, who follows your footsteps like a lamb. This taming has been going on for three years, and your cruelty has only had the effect of making him more tender and affectionate. But there are limits to every thing, my discreet sister; and if the rope is drawn too tightly, it breaks."

"If it would only do so!" cried Julie, despairingly. "That is exactly my desire, my object. Oh, my brother, you and all my cruel relatives deceive yourselves about me; and what you consider the finesse of coquetry, is only the true and open expression of my feelings! For three years the king has pursued me with his love, and for three years I have met his advances with coldness and indifference. In every manner, by word, look, and gesture, have I given him to understand that his love was annoying, and his attentions offensive. Oh, that I could fly from this unendurable, fearful love, to the uttermost ends of the world! But I cannot go, for I am poor, and have not the means to live elsewhere, and free myself from the terrible fetters in which you are all endeavoring to bind me!"

"And besides, my dear sister, acknowledge that your own heart persuades you to remain. You love the king?"

"No," she cried, passionately, "no, I do not love him, although I must admit that I have seen no man I liked better. But I do not love him; my heart beats no quicker when he approaches, my soul does not long for him when he is at a distance; and at times, when the king is at my side, a terrible feeling of anxiety creeps over me, and I wish to flee, and cry out to the whole world—'Rescue me, rescue me from the king!' No, I do not love the king; and if I meet his advances coldly, it is not from policy, but because my heart prompts me to do so. Therefore, renounce all thought of winning me over to your plans. I will not become the associate of Wilhelmine Enke!"

"And truly you shall not," said her brother, earnestly. "On the contrary, my beautiful and discreet sister, you shall displace this unworthy person; you shall become the benefactress of Prussia, and, through you, virtue and morality shall once more stand in good repute at the court of our young and amiable king."

The eyes of the beautiful maid of honor sparkled, and a soft color suffused itself over her cheeks. "If that were possible," she cried, in joyous tones—"yes, if I could succeed in delivering the king from this unworthy bondage, if I could make this hateful person harmless, this indeed were an object for which much could be endured."

"You hate her, then, this Wilhelmine Rietz?"

"And who should not hate her?" asked Julie, passionately. "She is the disgrace of her sex; she heaps dishonor on the head of our noble and genial king; she has caused his wife so many tears, and—"

"And you, too, is it not so?" asked her brother, smiling. "My beautiful Julie, you have betrayed yourself, you are jealous. But one is jealous only when one loves. Do not longer deny it—you love the king."

"No, no, I do not, I will not love him," she cried, "for shame would kill me. Oh, my brother, I conjure you, do not demand of me that I deliver myself over to shame! Take pity on me, do not force me to abandon my quiet and peaceful life. I will be contented to remain here in this solitude at the side of the unhappy queen, to pass my days in *ennui* and loneliness. I am not ambitious, and do not crave splendor; permit me therefore to live in seclusion."

"No, my dear sister, we cannot permit you to do so," said the chamberlain, shrugging his shoulders. "If it concerned you alone, you could dispose of yourself as you thought fit. But behind you stands your family—your family, which has been brought down in the world by all sorts of misfortunes, and is far from occupying the position to which it is entitled, and to which I, above all things, wish to see it restored, for I acknowledge that I am ambitious, my dear sister, and I desire to achieve eminence. I am now on the highway to success, and I do not intend that you shall arrest, but rather that you shall promote, my progress. If you reject the king's addresses, of course the whole family will fall into disfavor, and that would not be agreeable, either to myself or to my dear uncle, the master of ceremonies of the widowed queen. He wishes to become the king's master of ceremonies, and I wish to become a cabinet minister. Apart from this, the family coffers are sadly in need of replenishment. Our ancestral castle is in a crumbling condition, the forests have been cut down, the land is badly cultivated, and the farmhouses and stables must be rebuilt, for they are only miserable ruins, in which the half-starved cattle find no protection from the weather; and it is your mission to restore the old family Von Voss to its former splendor."

"By my dishonor, by my criminality!" sighed Julia von Voss. "Oh, my mother, my dear mother, why did you leave me, and fly to heaven from all this degradation! If you were here, you would protect me, and not suffer me to be so cruelly tempted."

"You remind me of our dear mother at the right time, Julie. Do you remember what she told you on her deathbed?"

"Yes, my brother, I do," she replied, in a low voice. "She said: 'You will not be an orphan, for you have your brother to take care of and protect you. I transfer all my rights to him; for the future, he will be the head of the family, and you must love, honor, and obey him as such.'"

"'I transfer all my rights to him; for the future, he will be the head of the family, and you must love, honor, and obey him as such,'" repeated her brother, in an elevated voice. "Do not forget this, my sister. I, as the head of the family, demand of you that you become the benefactress of your family, of your queen, and of your whole country. A grand and holy task devolves upon you. You are to liberate the land, the queen, and the king himself, from the domination of sin and indecorum. In a word, you are to displace this Rietz and her abominable husband, and inaugurate the reign of virtue and morality in this court. Truly, this is a noble mission, and one well worthy of my beautiful sister."

"It will not succeed," said the maid of honor. "The king will never consent to banish this hateful Rietz."

"The greater would be the honor, if you succeeded in liberating the king from this scandalous woman, the queen from this serpent, and the country from these vampires. Ah, the whole royal family, yes, all Prussia, would bless you, if you could overthrow this Rietz and her self-styled husband!"

"Yes," said Julie, in a low voice, "it would be a sublime consummation; but I should have to purchase it with my own degradation. And that I will not—cannot do. Brother, my dear brother, be merciful, and do not demand of me what is impossible and horrible. The daughter of my mother can never become a king's mistress!"

"And who said that you should? Truly, I would be the last to require that of you. No, not the mistress, but the wife of the king. You shall become his wedded wife; and your rightful marriage shall be blessed by a minister of the Reformed Church!"

"But that is impossible!" exclaimed the maid of honor, whose eyes sparkled with joy, against her will, "that cannot be. The queen lives, and she is the king's wedded wife."

"Yes, the wedded wife of the right hand," said her brother, quietly; "but the king, like every other mortal, has two hands; and he has a privilege which other mortals have not—the privilege of wedding a wife on the left hand."

"Impossible, quite impossible, as long as the wife of the right hand lives!" exclaimed Julie.

"Of that, the consistory of church matters is alone competent to decide," replied her brother, with composure; "or rather, I expressed myself badly, the consistory has only a deliberative voice; and the decision rests with the king alone, who, in our country, represents the church, and is its head—the evangelical pope. It is his province to say whether such a marriage of the left hand is possible, notwithstanding a marriage of the right hand. Demand it of him; make it a condition. Remember the words which the beautiful Gabrielle said to Henry the Fourth, when he inspected her dwelling, and asked the lady he adored, 'Which is the way to your chamber?' 'Sire,' she replied, 'the way to my chamber goes through the church.' Remember this when you speak to the king."

"Be assured, I will remember it," cried Julie, with glowing cheeks, and a proud, joyous smile. "I will make my conditions; and only when the king fulfils them will I be his, and—"

"And, why do you pause, and why is your face crimsoned with blushes all at once? Ah! you hear an equipage rolling up the avenue, and your tender heart says the king, your future husband, is approaching. Yes, my beautiful sister," continued her brother, as he stepped to the window and looked out; "yes, it is the king. Now prepare yourself, my wise and discreet Julie; prepare to give your royal lover a worthy reception. For, of course, you will receive him? And I may tell—I may tell his majesty that you welcome his visit joyfully?"

"No, oh no," murmured the maid of honor, with trembling lips. "I am not prepared; I am not composed; I cannot receive the king now!"

"No childishness," said her brother, severely. "You will have sufficient time to compose yourself. The king must first pay his respects to the widowed queen, and the visit of condolence will last at least a quarter of an hour. I must now leave you; but remember that the fortunes of your family, and of the whole country, are in your hands, and act accordingly!"

He left the room hastily, without awaiting a reply, and went down to the grand audience-chamber, where the courtiers and cavaliers were assembled. The king had already retired with the widowed queen to her library.

On entering the chamber, he immediately walked up to his

intimate acquaintance, Bischofswerder, the newly-created colonel, who had accompanied the king to Schönhausen.

"It will succeed," said he, in a low voice, "our great ends will be attained; we will conquer our enemies, and secure dominion for ourselves and the invisible fathers. My sister loves the king, but she has been virtuously reared, and would rather renounce the king and her love, than sacrifice her moral principles."

"She is, therefore, the more worthy of the high mission to which she has been called by the will of the Invisible," said Bischofswerder, emphatically. "She shall rescue our loved master and king from the arms of sin, and lead him back to the path of virtue with the hand of love, sanctified and consecrated by these noble ends."

"But she demands another consecration. The consecration of a lawful marriage. If this can be procured, my sister will always be our obedient and devoted friend, and, through her instrumentality, we—that is, the Invisible—will establish our rule."

"Her desire is certainly a bold one," said Bischofswerder. "But we must endeavor to fulfil it. We will speak with our wise friend Wöllner on this subject; and will also lay the noble young lady's request at the feet of the sublime grand-kophta, and master of the invisible lodge."

"Is he here, the great grand-kophta?" asked Charles von Voss, eagerly. "Then what the circle-director announced yesterday in the assembly was really true, and the grand-kophta is in our midst."

"He was with us in that assembly, we were all enveloped in the atmosphere of his glory, but it is only given to the initiated of the first rank, to know when the Invisible is near. Oh, my friend, I pitied you yesterday, while in the assembly; lamented that you should still stand in the antechamber of the temple, and not yet have been permitted to enter the inner sanctuary."

"But what must I do before I am permitted to enter?"

asked Charles von Voss, in imploring tones. "Oh, tell me, my dear, my enviable, my illustrious friend, what must I do to advance myself and become a participant of the inestimable privilege of being permitted to enter the inner sanctuary, and belong to the band of the initiated?"

"You must belong to the band of the believing, the hopeful, and the obedient. You must prove to the Invisible, by unconditional submission, that you are an obedient instrument; and then you will be called!"

"And by what token will I know that such is the case?"

"You will receive a visible sign of the satisfaction of the Invisible. When you and we succeed, with his assistance, in establishing the dominion of the Invisible so firmly that he will rule Prussia; when Rietz and her whole faction of the unbelieving are made harmless and destroyed; when, through your sister's instrumentality, virtue and propriety once more regulate and sanctify the king's private life—then, my friend, the Invisible will give you a visible token of his satisfaction, and will make the Chamberlain von Voss, the Minister of State von Voss."

"Oh, my dear, my mighty friend!" cried the chamberlain joyfully; "I will do all that the superiors desire. I will have no will of my own. I will be an instrument in their hands in order that I may finally—"

"The king!" cried the chamberlain of the day, as he threw open the folding doors of the antechamber. "The king!"

And amid the profound silence of his courtiers, who bowed their proud heads respectfully, King Frederick William entered the audience chamber, on his return from the visit of condolence paid to the mourning widow of Frederick. He cast a quick glance around the chamber, and, observing the Chamberlain von Voss, beckoned him to approach.

In obedience to the king's command, the chamberlain walked forward. "Well," said the king in a low voice, "what does your sister say?"

"Your majesty, she said but little to me, but she will have a great deal to say to your majesty."

"She is then ready to receive me?" said the king, his countenance radiant with joy.

"Your majesty, my sister is awaiting you, and I will conduct you to her, if your majesty will graciously follow."

"Come," replied the king, and, without honoring his courtiers with a glance, the king followed the Chamberlain von Voss out of the audience-chamber.

CHAPTER VI.

THE ALLIANCE.

WILHELMINE RIETZ had passed the whole day in a state of great excitement. King Frederick was dead! Public rumor had communicated this intelligence; it had flown on the wings of the wind from Sans-Souci to Potsdam, from Potsdam to Charlottenburg and Berlin, and thence to all the towns and villages of the Prussian monarchy.

King Frederick the Great was dead! This report was uttered in wailing accents all over the country; and filled the eyes of millions of faithful subjects and admirers of Frederick with tears. This report also conveyed the tidings to the beloved of the prince royal, that she was now the beloved of a king.

But Wilhelmine would have much preferred to hear it from himself; to receive a visible proof that her image still filled the king's heart, and that the clouds of incense rising around the new monarchy had not dimmed the recollections of the past.

Long hours of anxious expectation passed, and when the clock struck the hour of noon and no messenger had arrived, she was seized with unutterable fear. At last at about two o'clock, her son Alexander arrived at Charlottenburg, with his tutor Mr. Von Chapuis, "at the king's command," as the

tutor announced. Nor could he give her any further infor-
mation, for he had not seen the king himself but had received
this command from the mouth of the valet, Rietz.

" That is a bad sign, a very bad sign!" murmured Wilhelmine to herself when she was again alone. " He sends my
son to a distance, in order to give no offence to his new court
at Potsdam. He does not love me; if he did, he would have
the courage to defy the prejudices of the world. Ah! he
loves me no longer, and henceforth I will be nothing more than
the despised, discarded mistress, to be greeted with derisive
laughter by every passer-by, and to have cause for congratulation if she can hide her shame in some obscure corner of
the earth, where she might escape the scornful looks and
stinging words of mankind. But this shall never be; no, I
will not be discarded—will not be trodden in the dust. And
now, Wilhelmine," she continued, with sparkling eyes and
glowing cheeks, " now prove that you are no weak, no ordinary creature; prove that you possess wisdom, courage and
energy. Fight for your existence, for your future, for your
love! For I do love him, and I cannot live without him.
And I will not live without him!" she cried loudly and emphatically. " He is the father of my children; he is my hope
and my future. Without him I am a despised creature; with
him I am a lady of distinction, who is flattered and courted
in the most devoted manner; and only abused and ridiculed
behind her back. But continue to abuse and ridicule me, my
triumph will be all the greater, when you must nevertheless
bend the knee and do homage to the hated person. I have
borne and endured a great deal for the poor prince-royal
Frederick William, and now I demand compensation and reward at the hands of the rich King Frederick William. No,
I will not be put aside! As long as I live, I will fight for my
existence, and fight with the weapons of strategy and force,
of intrigue and flattery. Ah, I rejoice in the prospect. Yes,
I really rejoice in it! At all events, it will lend an additional
charm to life, and be a change and a diversion!"

"The privy-chamberlain and treasurer of the king!" announced the servant, entering the room.

"Who is that?" asked Wilhelmine in astonishment. "I know no such gentleman."

"I am the gentleman, my dear wife, my adored Wilhelmine," said Rietz, laughing loudly, as he followed the servant into the room. "In me, my dear wife, you see the privy-chamberlain and treasurer, fresh as a newly-baked loaf from the oven of royal favor."

"Leave the room, Jean," said Wilhelmine, who, impelled perhaps by curiosity, gave himself the appearance of being busily occupied in arranging the room.

"No, my dear wife," said Rietz, beckoning to the servant, "have the goodness to permit Jean to remain a moment until I have given him my orders.—Jean, I am hungry, and feel an irresistible inclination to eat. Bring me something enjoyable, right away—for instance, a goose-liver pie, or a pheasant, or both. You can also bring some caviar and a piece of venison. And then have a bottle of champagne brought up and placed on ice; it is abominably warm to-day, and I need something cooling. Be quick, Jean."

The servant made no reply, but looked inquiringly at his mistress. Rietz caught this look, and laughed loudly. "I really believe this simpleton entertains the daring idea of not obeying me, his master!"

"Excuse me, sir," murmured the servant, timidly, "but my services were engaged by this lady."

"Yes, certainly; but you well know, you rascal, that I am the master, and that this lady is my wife, and—"

"Enough," interrupted Wilhelmine, gravely. "Set the table in the dining-room, Jean, and be quick!"

"Well spoken, Wilhelmine; let me kiss you for it, my treasure!" cried Rietz, walking with extended arms toward his wife, while the servant was opening the door. But the door had scarcely closed when he let his arms fall, and recoiled timidly from Wilhelmine, who stood before him with flashing eyes.

"Sir," said she, her voice trembling with anger; "sir, I forbid you to take such liberties, and use such familiar language in the presence of my servant."

"But, madame," replied Rietz, smiling, "it is only in the presence of your servant that I can use such language; and it seems to me that it suits my rôle very well. I have the honor to figure before the world as your husband, consequently I should play my rôle respectably before men, and prove that we are a happy and contented pair. The wickedness and malice of mankind are great; and if men should observe that I spoke to you with less tenderness, your enemies would certainly spread the report, that we were living together unhappily."

"I must inform you, sir, that I have no desire whatever to jest," cried Wilhelmine, impatiently. "Have the goodness to be serious. Now, that we are alone, I beg that you will not attempt to keep up the absurd farce of our so-called marriage."

"And bad enough it is for me that it is only a farce," sighed Rietz, impressively. "I would—"

The angry look which Wilhelmine bestowed upon him, repressed his words, and he quickly assumed a melancholy, submissive manner. "I am silent, madame, I am silent," said he, bowing profoundly, and with an air of deep pathos. "I am your most submissive servant, nothing else; and, having now paid my homage to the sun, I will retire, as its splendor has dazzled my eyes."

He crossed his arms before his breast, bowed to the earth before his mistress, as the slaves do in the east, and then arose and walked rapidly toward the door.

"Where are you going, sir?" asked Wilhelmine. "Why do you not remain here?"

"I cannot, mistress," said he, humbly. "The Moor has done his duty! The Moor can go! So it reads at least in Frederick Schiller's new piece, the one given at the theatre a short time ago."

"But you have not yet done your duty," said Wilhelmine,

smiling involuntarily. "You have not yet delivered your message."

"What message?" asked Rietz, with a pretence of astonishment.

"His majesty's message. For he it was, undoubtedly, who sent you here."

"You are right," said Rietz, with an air of indifference. "Yes, that is true. I had forgotten it. Good heavens! I have received so many commissions to-day, and been sent to so many ladies, that I forget the one in the other. I am now playing a very important rôle. I am the Figaro of my master Almaviva—the Figaro who has to help his master in carrying off his beautiful cousin. You know the piece, of course, the delightfully good-for-nothing piece, that created such a furor in France, and consequently here with us also?"

"Yes, I do, Rietz; and I beg you not to stretch me on the rack with your drollery! What did the king say? What messages did he entrust to you?"

"Oh, madame! You cannot require of me that I should betray Count Almaviva's confidence, and impart to you the messages entrusted to me?" cried Figaro Rietz, with noble indignation. "I have only to impart that which concerns my beautiful Susanna; and that is, his majesty is coming here this evening, and his rooms are to be held in readiness. He will first take tea, and then adjourn to the little laboratory to do some little cooking and brewing."

Wilhelmine's countenance, before bright and animated, darkened as the privy-chamberlain uttered these last words.

"The king intends to work in the laboratory? Then he is not coming alone?"

"He is coming alone, but I expect his assistants and teachers, the two great heroes of the invisible lodge, will follow at a later hour, in order to make a little 'hocus pocus' for his majesty—that is, I expressed myself badly—I wished to say, in order to work with his majesty in the secret sciences.

Yes, the two great luminaries are coming, and if I could be permitted to give you my advice—but no, so wise and enlightened a lady as yourself can have no need of the advice of so foolish and ridiculous a fellow as I am. I am therefore silent, and will now retire, in order to strengthen my body at least, as my mind is of so hopelessly weak a constitution, that all endeavors in that direction would be thrown away. My gracious queen, I beg that you will now kindly dismiss me!" He made a ceremonious bow, and then retired towards the door, walking backwards.

"Rietz, remain!" commanded Wilhelmine, imperiously.

"Impossible, my queen. My message is delivered; and the Moor not only can, but will go."

"Remain, Rietz; I beg you to do so," said Wilhelmine, advancing a step nearer.

"When the stomach commands," said Rietz, shrugging his shoulders, "the entreaties of the most beautiful of women are of no avail."

"Well, then go and eat," cried Wilhelmine, impatiently. "And when you have done eating, come back to my room!"

"Nor can I do that, my queen. I must then ride to Potsdam, where, by the king's command, I am to hold a secret and important conference with her majesty, the queen, that is, with her majesty of the right hand. I must, therefore, hoist anchor and sail again as soon as I have eaten, and—"

"Well then," said Wilhelmine, with determination, "I will accompany you to the dining-room, and we will converse while you are eating."

"Bravo! bravo! That was what I desired!" cried Rietz, laughing. "The servants shall see in how heavenly an understanding we live together; and how careful my wife is not to lose her husband's society for a moment. Give me your arm, madam, and lead me to the dining-room."

With a forced smile she took his arm, and permitted him to conduct her through the parlor to the dining-room. Jean had served up all manner of delicacies on a little table, and was now occupied, at the sideboard, in breaking ice for the champagne.

"Put a bottle of Rhine wine on the ice, too, Jean," cried Rietz, imperiously, as he seated himself comfortably in the chair, leaving his "wife" to find one for herself and bring it up to the table, at which he had already made an assault on a truffle-pie. "Magnificent!" said he, after eating a few morsels, "I must tell you, my dearest Wilhelmine, there is nothing better than a truffle-pie!"

Wilhelmine turned impatiently to the servant, who was turning the wine in the freezer: "You can now go, Jean, the gentleman will wait on himself."

"And my champagne!" exclaimed Rietz. But, with an imperious gesture, Wilhelmine dismissed the servant.

"Now we are alone," said Wilhelmine. "Now you can speak. You wished to give me your advice."

"Madam," rejoined Rietz, as he carried a savory morsel to his mouth; "madam, at this moment I can advise you to do but one thing, and that is, to try this truffle-pie, it is truly magnificent!"

"You are cruel," cried Wilhelmine, "you torture me!"

"Say rather, madam, that you are cruel," said Rietz, rising from the table to go after the champagne. "It is truly cruel to compel a man to arise, in the midst of the delights of the table, and wait on himself! Champagne loses its flavor when one has to pour it out himself!"

"I will wait on you, sir!" cried Wilhelmine, rising with vivacity, and taking the bottle in her hands.

Rietz nodded complacently. "That is right. That is piquant, and will season my repast. The almighty queen of the left hand waits on her submissive husband of the left hand. The mistress becomes the slave, the slave the master! This is a charming riddle, is it not? But I tell you, madame, it is not the last riddle we will propound! Oh, very many riddles will now be propounded; and some people would be very happy if they could find the right solution."

"You wished to give me good advice concerning the two favorites," said Wilhelmine, with a smile, that cost her proud heart much humiliation. "Speak, therefore, my dear Rietz! Give me your advice!"

Rietz held his glass up to the light, and gazed smilingly at the rising bubbles. "That reminds me of my old friend, the burgomaster of Stargard, the dear place of my nativity. The good Burgomaster Funk, was a true child of Pomerania, who despised High-German, and would have spoken Low-German, even with the king. Speaking Low-German, and eating dinner was his passion. And I have often thought, when I saw him sitting at the dinner-table, with so reverent and pious a countenance, that the old gentleman fancied himself in church, administering the sacrament as a priest. He applied himself with such heavenly tranquillity to the delights of the table, permitting nothing in the world to disturb him while so engaged."

"But I cannot comprehend what the recollections of your happy youth have to do with the advice you desired to give."

"You will soon do so, my queen," said Rietz, slowly emptying his glass. "And yet permit me to dwell a little longer on the recollections of my dear old master. For you must know that this good old gentleman was my master; under him I learned the arts of a valet, writer, and confidant, and all the little artifices and stratagems by which a valet makes himself his master's factotum. Truly the king is greatly indebted to the burgomaster; without him he would never have been the possessor of so excellent a factotum as the privy-chamberlain and treasurer Rietz. At the same time, I learned from my master how to become a gourmand; learned what precious knowledge, and how much practical study, were necessary to educate a man up to this sublime standard, and entitle him to the proud appellation of gourmand. My old master, who deservedly bore this title, inculcated in me the most beautiful and strict principles. In the midst of our conversation, and while the old gentleman was digesting, slowly imbibing his delicious mocha, and blowing clouds of smoke from his long pipe, it sometimes occurred that some one of the burghers of the little city would come, in his necessity, to his burgomaster to obtain advice or assistance. Then you should have seen his anger and rage. He would strike the table with his fist, and cry furiously: 'Vat, I give advice! After dinner, and for noting!'"

"Ah," exclaimed Wilhelmine, "now I begin to understand!"

"That is fortunate, indeed," said Rietz, laughing; and he held out his empty glass to Wilhelmine that she might fill it. "Then you begin to understand that the phrase 'after dinner, and for nothing,' is very beautiful and appropriate?"

"Yes, and I will give you a proof of it at once! Sir, what do you ask for your good advice?"

"Bravo, bravo!" cried Rietz. "Well sung, my prima donna! Now we shall understand each other; and with your permission we will proceed to talk seriously. Madame, will you form an offensive and defensive alliance with me? Do not reply yet! I have no desire whatever that you should buy the cat in the bag; first hear what I have to say, and then make up your mind. We are now at the beginning of a new era; and to most men the future is as a book written in mysterious and illegible characters. But I think I can decipher it, and I will tell you what it contains. I read in this book that Prussia is now governed by a king who can do anything but govern himself, and who is like soft wax in the hands of those who know how to manage him."

"How dare you speak so disrespectfully of your king?" cried Wilhelmine.

"Madame," said Rietz, shrugging his shoulders, "give yourself no trouble! To his valet and to his mistress—pardon me for this word, my queen—the greatest king is but an ordinary man; and when we two are alone, we need stand on no ceremony. The king, I say, will be ruled over. And the only question is, by whom? The question is, shall the valet and the mistress rule over the happy and prosperous kingdom of Prussia, or shall they leave this difficult but remunerative business to the Rosicrucians, to the Invisible Fathers, and to their visible sons, Bischofswerder and Wöllner."

"If they do that," cried Wilhelmine, with vivacity, "the mistress and the valet will be lost, they will be banished."

"That is also my opinion," said Rietz. "These dear Rosicrucians dread our influence. They know that we are both too wise to believe in the hocus pocus, and that it sometimes affords us pleasure to enlighten the king's mind on the subject of these mysterious fellows and their jugglery. I, for my part, hate these pious hypocrites, these wise fools. It is as impossible for me to live together with them in friendship, as it is for the honest dog and sneaking cat to sojourn harmoniously in one kennel. And I account it one of my greatest pleasures when I can sometimes give them a good blow, and tear out a piece of their sheepskin, in order to show the king that a wolf is disguised in sheep's clothing."

"I feel exactly as you do on this subject," cried Wilhelmine, laughing. "I find it impossible to accept their offers of friendship. They have frequently attempted to make me their ally, but I wish to have nothing to do with the Invisible Fathers of the inner temple; I prefer the visible sons in the outer halls, for we, at least, know what they are!"

"You are a divine woman," cried the chamberlain, in delight. "If you were not my wife I should certainly fall in love with you. It is fortunate, however, that you are my wife, for lovers are blind, and it behooves us both to keep our eyes open to avoid being caught in the snares which will be laid for us in great plenty by our pious fowlers. 'They or we;' this will be the watchword throughout the glorious reign of our king. The Pharisees and Rosicrucians, or—may I pronounce the word, my enchantress?"

"Yes, my friend, pronounce the word!"

"Well, then! The watchword is: 'The Pharisees and Rosicrucians, or the libertines and mistresses!' I cast my lot with the latter party, for with them good dinners and brilliant fêtes are the order of the day. With them pleasure reigns, and joy is queen."

"I am with you, my friend. Death and destruction to the Pharisees and Rosicrucians!"

"Long live the libertines and mistresses! They shall rule over Prussia! They shall guide the ship of state; and we, Wilhelmine Enke, we two will be the leaders and masters of this merry band! We will fight with each other and for each other; and the Pharisees and Rosicrucians are, and shall ever be, our common enemies! Give me your hand on this, my queen!"

"Here is my hand. Yes, the Pharisees and Rosicrucians are, and shall ever be, our common enemies!"

"You will aid me, and I you! We will protect and watch over each other. Our interests are identical, what furthers yours furthers mine. You, my beautiful Wilhelmine, are ambitious, and are not contented with my well-sounding name. You aim higher, and I do not blame you, for a crown would become you well, although it were only the crown of a countess."

"That would suffice," said Wilhelmine, smiling. "And you, my friend, what do you aspire to?"

"I am a very modest man, and decorations and titles have no charms for me. I do not wish ever to become more than I now am; but that, my queen, I would like to remain. I have no desire to be dispossessed of my situation; on the contrary, I desire to make of it a right warm and comfortable nest."

"And I will procure you the necessary down," cried Wilhelmine, laughing.

"Very well, but it must be eider-down, my love, for that is the softest. I love the exquisite and the excellent; I am a gourmand in all things. If there is one thing I could wish for, it would be that my whole life might consist of one long dinner, and I remain sitting at the savory, richly-laden table, until compelled to leave it for the grave. I am not ambitious, nor am I miserly; but money I must have, much money.   In order to lead a comfortable and agreeable life one must have money, a great deal of money, an immense quantity of money.   My motto is, therefore, 'My whole life one good dinner, and—after dinner, no advice for nothing!' "

"I consider this a wise motto, and, although I cannot make it my own, I will always respect it as yours, and act in accord. ance with it in your interest."

"That will be very agreeable," said Rietz.   "I will then be able to realize my ideal."

"And in what does your ideal consist, if I may ask the question?"

"My ideal is a house of my own, elegantly and luxuriously furnished, attentive and deferential servants, an exquisite cook, and the most choice dinners, with four covers always ready for agreeable, gay, and influential guests, who must be selected each day.   Do you know, my queen, what is essential to the realization of my ideal?   In the first place, the king must give me a house just large enough to make me a comfortable dwelling.   I know of such a house.   It stands at the entrance of the park of Sans-Souci.   It has only five chambers, a parlor, a cellar, a kitchen, and several servants' rooms. That is just the house for a modest man like myself; and I wish to have it.   And then rich clients are required, petitioners for decorations and titles, who come to me for counsel, supposing the king's confidential chamberlain can gratify their longings, if they only cajole him and show him some attentions.   For instance, if this nice new house were mine, I would furnish one room only, and that sparingly, letting all the others stand empty.   I would then show my visitors my dear little house, and it would be strange, indeed, if it were not soon handsomely furnished.   To accomplish this, nothing is wanted but your assistance, my gracious wife and queen."

"And in what manner shall I assist you, my dear philosopher?"

"In this manner, my adored: by sending the suitors who

come to you, to me—that is, those suitors who desire decorations, titles, or a noble coat-of-arms; for with politics I will have nothing to do. I only speculate on the foolishness of mankind. Therefore, let it be well understood, you are to send the foolish to me with their petitions—to tell them that decorations and titles are my specialty, and that I alone can effect anything with the king in such matters. In doing this, you not only send me clients who furnish my house, but you also enhance my respectability. You make an important person of me, to whom great deference must be shown, and who must be courted and flattered. The natural consequence will be, that I will have humble and devoted servants, and be able to secure agreeable and influential guests for my dinners. For I need scarcely inform you, that it would afford me no entertainment whatever simply to fill empty stomachs at my table. On the contrary, I desire to have guests to whom eating is a science, and who do not regard a good pasty merely as an article of food, but rather as a superior enjoyment. Will you help me to attain all this?"

"Yes, I will, my friend. But now tell me what services you propose to render in return!"

"I will be your obedient servant, your sincere and discreet friend, and your ally in life and death. When diplomatists and politicians apply to me for my good offices, I will refer them to you. I will always have your interests at heart. If Bischofswerder and Wöllner should ever succeed in poisoning the king's mind against you, or in depriving you of his favor, I will lend a helping hand in thrusting these pious lights into the shade, where they belong. You can depend on me in all things. I will represent your interests, as if they were my own, and as if I had the honor to be in reality what I, unfortunately, only appear to be, the husband of the beautiful and amiable Wilhelmine Rietz. But truly, the name sounds bad, and I will assist you in exchanging it for a longer and more harmonious one. The name Rietz is just long and good enough for me. It fits me snugly, like a comfortable, well-

worn dressing-gown; and I prefer it to a court-dress. But
for you, my fair one, we must certainly procure the title of a
baroness or countess. Moreover, as your disinterestedness and
improvidence in money matters is well known to me, I will
also consider it my sacred duty to look after your interests in
this particular, and call the king's attention to your necessities from time to time. For instance, you might require a
handsome palace in Berlin, or a larger villa here in Charlottenburg, or a magnificent set of jewelry, or an increase of
income."

"Ah, my friend, I will be very thankful for all this," said
Wilhelmine, with a bewitching smile. "But what is of para-
mount importance is, that the king should continue to love
me, or at least that he should never reject my love or discard
me. I love him. He is the father of my children; he was
the lover of my youth; and I can swear that I have never
loved another besides him. Even my worst enemies cannot
say of me that I was ever untrue to the love of my youth, or
that I ever had any liaison, except the one with the poor
prince royal, for whom I suffered want, rather than listen to
the addresses of rich and influential admirers."

"That is true," said Rietz, with an air of perfect gravity;
"they can make you no reproaches. Your life has been
altogether irreproachable; and the *chronique scandaleuse* has
had nothing to report concerning you."

"You are mocking me," sighed Wilhelmine. "Your words
are well understood. You wish to say that my whole life has
been one impropriety, and that I am the legitimate prey of
the *chronique scandaleuse*. Oh, do not deny it, you are
perfectly right. I am an outcast from society; and yet it
cannot be said of me, that I, like so many highly-respectable
ladies, have sold my heart and hand for an advantageous
marriage settlement. I only followed the dictates of my heart
and my love; and the world punishes me by erecting a barrier
between me and good society. But I have no intention
of submitting to this any longer. Why should the

king's beloved stand without the barrier, while many a countess, who has sold herself, and married an unloved man for his title and his wealth, and to whom faith is but an empty fancy, stands within on consecrated ground. This barrier shall crumble before me, and I will be received within the circle of this so-called good and exclusive society. To their hatred and contempt, I am quite indifferent, but they shall at least seem to esteem and respect me. They shall not leave me in perfect solitude in the midst of the world, as if I lived on a desert island, like Robinson Crusoe, and had great reason to be thankful when the king sometimes took the rôle of Friday and kept me company. I will be received in society; I will be the head of society; I will have parlors, where not only artists and men of intellect assemble, but to which the ladies of the best society must also come. This is my ambition; this is my dream of happiness. I will have a social position in defiance of all these so-called exclusive circles. Whenever I meet these people, and see them turn aside to avoid me with a contemptuous smile, I say to myself: 'Only wait, ye proud, ye virtuous! you shall yet fill Wilhelmine Rietz's parlors, and form the background of the brilliant picture of her power and magnificence. Only wait, ye noble gentlemen, you shall yet dance attendance in Wilhelmine Rietz's antechamber! Only wait, ye heroines of virtue, you shall one day walk arm in arm with Wilhelmine Rietz, and accord her the place of honor on your right hand!' You see I have consoled myself with these thoughts of the future for many years. But the future has now become the present, and the longed-for time has at last arrived when Wilhelmine Rietz will compel society to unbolt its portals and permit her to enter. Will you assist me in this matter?"

"I shall be delighted to do so," said Rietz, laughing. "I will be the locksmith, who furnishes the keys to open these doors with, and if keys will not suffice, he will provide picklocks and crowbars. But, enter you shall. It will be a difficult undertaking, to be sure, but it will amuse me all the more, on that account, to assist you, and help to pull down the pride of these arrogant people. Ah, I hate these people, and it will afford me immense satisfaction to see them compelled to humble themselves before you, and fawn and flatter in spite of their reluctance! Yes, I will help you to ascend this mountain, but I do not desire to rise with you, I prefer to remain below in the valley, and earn an honest livelihood, as the good old proverb says."

"And will become a rich man in the valley, while I will, perhaps, be struggling with debts and creditors on the heights above!"

"Yes," said Rietz, "there will certainly be struggles, and struggles of every variety. As for your debts, I will undertake to have them all paid; and in the future your income will be so considerably increased that you will no longer be under the necessity of making debts. But what I cannot take upon myself, unaided, is the struggle with your beautiful and high-born rival. That is woman's work; there, fists are of no avail, and delicate fingers can manipulate needles with far greater efficiency."

"You speak of my rival, the beautiful Julie von Voss."

"Yes, my adorable, I speak of her, and I will now prove to you that I am your friend. And I will tell what I have no right to tell. The privy-chamberlain breaks the inviolable seal of office. But what can I do? are you not my wife? And in the end, the most discreet man in the world can keep no secret from his wife! Now, listen!" And in a low, suppressed voice, as if fearing the walls might hear, he told her of his mission to Schönhausen, of the king's messages, and of his conversation with the beautiful maid of honor.

Wilhelmine listened with pallid cheeks and quivering lips, only interrupting him from time to time with a brief question, or an angry or threatening cry.

CHAPTER VII.

THE CONDITIONS.

WHILE this was occurring in the dining-room, Jean sat in the antechamber, holding himself in readiness to answer his mistress's bell, if it should ring. But no bell rang, and all was so still, the air so warm and sultry in the little chamber, and the soft twilight had so tranquillizing an effect, that Jean could no longer resist the temptation to close his eyes, and indulge in his dreams of the future. And perhaps he was dreaming, when a tall figure, completely enveloped in a black mantle, stood before him, laid his hand on his shoulder, and pronounced his name in a low voice. Perhaps it was only a dream when he saw this, and heard the veiled figure utter these words in a low voice:

"You belong to the third circle of the Invisible lodge?"

And he replied—whether in a dream or in reality, he was himself not perfectly satisfied—"Yes, I belong to that circle."

Furthermore, the veiled figure said: "You were sent here with orders to make an exact report of all that occurs, to the circle director, and to submit to his will, in all things. Do you bear this in mind?"

"I am the obedient servant of the Invisible," replied Jean, respectfully. "I will never forget my oath; if I did, punishment would overtake, and the just anger of the Invisible destroy me."

"Did the circle-director show you the symbol of the brotherhood?"

"Yes, he did."

"Behold the symbol," said the veiled figure, and for a moment a little triangular plate of metal shone in his open hand.

"I see it," replied Jean, rising, "and I know by this triangle that a brother of the higher degrees stands before me;

I therefore salute you with reverence, brother superior." He bowed profoundly, but the veiled figure merely nodded in return.

"Do you know the sign by which the master of the order, the grand kophta is recognized?" said he, in low and piercing tones.

"I do," replied Jean, his voice almost inaudible, from inward agitation.

The veiled figure thrust forth his hand from under the concealing mantle, and a large solitaire sparkled on his finger. "See, this is the sign," said he.

Jean uttered a cry of astonishment, and sank on his knees. "Command me, almighty one," he murmured, "your slave has no will but yours."

"Arise, and be my guide," commanded the veiled figure, and Jean stood up immediately.

"Where shall I lead, my exalted master?"

"Conduct me to the little room adjoining the laboratory of the present king, but by such a way that no human eye shall see, and no human ear hear me."

"Then, I must first beg permission," said Jean, hurrying towards the door, "to assure myself that no one is in the hall."

But the veiled figure followed, and held him back. "Why go that way?" he asked. "Why through the hall, when we can go through the door in the wall into the little passage that leads to the secret staircase?"

"That is true; I had forgotten that," said Jean, trembling, and looking with surprise and terror at his superior, who was so well acquainted with this strange house that he knew the secret doors and staircases.

"As my master pleases; here is the door." He pressed a small, almost imperceptible knob in the wall, and a little door sprang open.

"Go before, and lead me," said the veiled figure, pushing Jean through the entrance. "We must walk softly, and without uttering a word; the passage runs by the dining-room, where your mistress is conversing with the king's privy-chamberlain, and we might be heard. I will, therefore, give you my command here. You will lead me through the passage and down the staircase. With the key which you carry, you will then open the door and let me into the laboratory. You will then lock the door again, take the key from the lock, and hurry back to the antechamber. You will observe the most profound silence in regard to what has occurred; and, if life and your eternal welfare are dear to you, you will betray having seen me by neither word, look, nor gesture."

"Exalted master," whispered Jean, "I am nothing more than your slave and creature, and I know that my life is but dust in your hands. I fear the Invisible, and I adore you in your sublimity. Graciously permit me to embrace your feet, that the touch may impart to me eternal health and strength."

And he knelt down and kissed the feet of the veiled figure with impassioned tenderness.

The veiled figure bowed down to him and said: "Grace will be shed upon you; you are a good and obedient servant. At the next assembly you will learn that you have been elevated a degree, and have come a step nearer to the inner halls of the temple. Be silent, no word of thanks, but arise and conduct me!"

Jean arose and stepped forward, the veiled figure following him, and conducted him, as he had been directed, to the laboratory; he let him in, closed and locked the door again, and returned hastily to the antechamber.

Had this all really happened, or had Jean only been dreaming? He asked himself this question, and looked inquiringly and anxiously around in the little chamber. He was entirely alone; the secret door was closed. No one was with him, all was still around him, and profound silence seemed to reign in the dining-room also. Jean stepped softly to the door and listened. He could now hear a subdued murmur, and could even distinguish the voices of his mistress and the privy-chamberlain. They seemed to be conversing eagerly; but

they spoke in such low tones that it was impossible for Jean
to understand a single word.

And they were really engaged in a very earnest conversation; in a conversation which absorbed Wilhelmine's attention wholly. Rietz had not only related his interview with
the maid of honor, but had also given her a faithful account
of the king's visit to Schönhausen, and of the conversation
between Charles von Voss and his sister, in which he persuaded her to receive the king.

"How do you know this?" asked Wilhelmine, with a shrug
of her shoulders. "I imagine it could have needed no per-
suasion, that this young lady would have done so willingly
enough."

"There you are in error, my beautiful countess; I know
better, because I listened to the whole conversation between
the maid of honor and her brother."

"How? You were present?"

"Not exactly present, but I heard it, nevertheless. The
doors of the dilapidated old castle in Schönhausen are full of
cracks and crannies, and if you get near enough you can see
and hear very readily."

"And you were near the door of the maid of honor's
chamber?"

"So near that a sheet of paper could hardly have been
slipped in between us."

"And there was no one there to order the bold eavesdropper
to leave?"

"Yes, there was a human being in the little dressing-room
in which I stood, but this human being made no opposition
whatever to my listening at the door, for the simple reason
that I had paid well for the privilege. The young lady's
chambermaid loves money, and is of a speculative disposition.
She wishes to open a millinery establishment, and for that
money is necessary; and she takes it whenever she can get it.
I pay her in my gracious master's name for singing the king's
praise in her mistress's ear; and I pay her in my own name

for reporting to me the result of this singing, and permitting me to listen at the door when there is anything to be heard. To be sure, it cost me a considerable sum yesterday. This shrewd little kitten made me pay her twice: once for the conversation between the maid of honor and her brother, and the second time for the conversation between the king and the maid of honor."

Wilhelmine sprang up, and an exclamation of astonishment escaped her lips. "You have listened to the conversation between the king and the maid of honor, and now tell me of it for the first time. I conjure you, Rietz, my dear Rietz, my best friend, tell me of it. Speak—what did the king say, and what did she reply?"

"After dinner, and for nothing?" asked Rietz, as he stretched himself comfortably, poured the last few drops of champagne into his glass and carried it slowly to his lips.

"Speak, my dear Rietz. Say what I shall do. What will you have?"

"The little love of a house at the entrance of the park of Sans-Souci. It was built on speculation; that is to say, I had it built, hoping that the old king would be dead, and our Frederick William seated on the throne by the time of its completion. My hope is now realized, and I ask you, my adorable wife, will you use your influence to persuade the king to give me this house as a reward for my long and faithful services?"

"I will do so; I will storm the king with entreaties to give you this house."

"Then it is as good as mine already, and I thank my noble patroness. And now that I am paid in advance, I will impart to you the substance of that important conversation— that is, you will certainly not require me to repeat the king's protestations of love and vows of eternal fidelity."

"No, I do not require that of you," sighed Wilhelmine, with trembling lips; "that I can readily imagine. It can only have been a repetition of what he told me. Out upon men! They are a perfidious and faithless race!"

"Yes, they imbibe these qualities with their mother's milk; and King Frederick William also is only the son of his mother. Therefore, nothing of the king's protestations of love, and the noble indignation and conflict between love and virtue on the part of the young lady. To the king's intense gratification the young lady finally admitted, with many tears and sighs, that she would love him if he were not, unfortunately, already married, and if Madame Rietz were not in existence. If the king were no better than a poor nobleman, the young lady would esteem it perfect bliss to become his. She would joyfully undergo hardships and suffer want at his side; but she was not willing to occupy a position that would expose her to scorn and contempt. She could not cause the noble queen additional sorrow and pain; and finally, it would be quite impossible to tolerate a despised and hated rival like Wilhelmine Rietz at her side. But—good heavens! what is the matter with you? You turn pale, and wail and moan fearfully! Poor woman, if you are so sensitive, I must of course be silent."

"It is nothing—nothing at all," murmured Wilhelmine. "It was only a momentary pang, and it is now past. Speak on, I am quite composed. Speak! What did the king reply?"

"He begged her to name the conditions on which she could consent to be his; and the beautiful and wise maid of honor stated her conditions, assuring him that they were irrevocable—her ultimatum, as the diplomatists say. And truly these conditions were ridiculous. I almost burst out laughing when I heard them."

"And what were they? I pray you tell me," murmured Wilhelmine, clasping her hands tightly together to keep them from trembling.

"There were three conditions, and the maid of honor swore by the memory of her mother, who had died of grief caused by her love for the king's father, Prince August William, that she would neither see his majesty nor speak with him until he had promised to fulfill her conditions; and, that if he could or would not fulfil them, the young lady would leave the court forever, and retire into the deepest seclusion."

"She is cunning; oh, she is very cunning," murmured Wilhelmine, clasping her hands yet more firmly together. "And her three conditions?"

"Are as follows: firstly, the young lady exacts of the king that she be married formally and rightfully to his left hand, by a Protestant minister; secondly, she demands that, above all things, the consent of the queen, the wife of the right hand, be first obtained; and thirdly, and finally, she demands that Wilhelmine Rietz, together with her two children, be banished, and that an estate be given her in Lithuania, and she be compelled to remain there and never return to Berlin or Potsdam."

"And the king?" cried Wilhelmine, in piercing accents.

"The king stipulated for four weeks' time in which to consider the matter, kissed the proud lady's hand, and retired. Now, my queen, you know all, and it is also time for me to retire. I must ride to Potsdam at the king's command, and confer with the queen as to the conditions on which she would give her consent to this absurd marriage. But I cannot comprehend you, my beauty! You look as mournful as if you were on the point of starting for Lithuania already, and as if it were another than you who sways the king's heart and soul. I, for my part, place implicit confidence in your power, and am satisfied that the king will never give you up or desert you. Would I otherwise have courted your alliance? Would I have based my hopes of obtaining the little house at Sans-Souci on your intercession? No, my beauty; you are, and will remain, queen, in spite of all the wives of the right and the left hand. Only you must not be discouraged, and must not look so sad. For you well know that our good master cannot abide mournful faces, and invariably runs away from weeping women."

"It is true; you are right," said Wilhelmine. "I will wreathe my face in smiles. I will laugh."

And she burst out into a loud and vibrating peal of laughter, in which Rietz heartily joined.

"That is right," he cried; "now I admire you! You look like a lioness defending her young. That is right, my beauty! 'He who trusts in God, and strikes out boldly around him, will never come to grief,' my good old burgomaster Herr Funk used to say. Strike boldly, my queen, deal out heavy blows, and we shall never come to grief, and all will yet be well. And now, my charming wife, I must take leave of you, as I hear a carriage driving up that I wager brings no other than his majesty. It is not necessary that he should still find me here. I will, therefore, slip out of the back door and beat a retreat through the garden. Addio, carissima, addio!"

He bowed respectfully, threw her a kiss with the tips of his fingers, opened a window, and sprang out upon the terrace, from which a small stairway led down into the garden.

Wilhelmine frowned, and cast an angry look in the direction he had taken. "How degraded a soul! how base a character!" she murmured; "but yet I must cling to him, and be very friendly with him. He is my only support, my only friend; for without him I would be lost! And I will not be lost! I will maintain my position; while I live, I will bravely battle for it!"

"The king!" cried Jean, throwing the door open. "His majesty has arrived, and awaits my lady in her parlor."

"I am coming," said Wilhelmine, calmly. "Hurry down into the park, and tell my son and daughter that their father is here. They are down on the river; they must come at once to greet his majesty."

CHAPTER VIII

NEW LOVE.

THE king advanced to meet Wilhelmine with a gentle smile; and when, after a formal obeisance, she congratulated him in cold and ceremonious terms, Frederick William burst

out into laughter, caught her in his arms, and pressed a kiss
on her brow.

Wilhelmine trembled, and tears rushed to her eyes. She
felt like clasping him in her arms and conjuring him, with
tender reproaches and passionate words of love, not to abandon her, and not to drive herself and his children out into
the cold world. But she repressed her emotion—she knew
the king could not endure sad faces, and always fled from a
woman in tears.

She had the courage to smile, and seem to be gay; and her
countenance bore no trace of disquiet or anxiety. She conversed with perfect composure and indifference, as if no
change had taken or ever could take place in their relations
to each other.

Frederick William's joyousness had at first been assumed,
to hide his embarrassment; and he felt greatly relieved by
Wilhelmine's manner. He abandoned himself wholly to the
charming society of the beautiful and agreeable friend, who
had always so well understood how to enliven him and banish
all care from his breast. And when the two children entered
the parlor, and his favorite Alexander, a boy of ten years of
age, ran forward, looked wonderingly at his papa king, and
then threw his arms tenderly around his neck, and kissed and
hugged him, regardless of his royalty; when the lovely
daughter, in the bloom of sixteen summers, the charming
image of her young mother, walked forward, and seated herself on one of his knees opposite her brother, who sat on the
other; and when the still beautiful mother stepped up to
this group, her eyes beaming and her face wreathed in smiles,
and clasped father and children in one embrace, a feeling of
infinite comfort filled Frederick William's breast, and tears
rushed to his eyes.

He gently pushed the two children from his knees, and
arose. "Go down into the garden, my pets, and wait for me
in the rose-pavilion, when we will watch the sun set. But
now go, as I have something to say to your mother."

"But nothing unpleasant, I hope, papa?" said Alexander, anxiously. "You have nothing to say to my mamma that will make her sad?"

"And if I had," asked Frederick William, smiling, "what would you do to prevent it?"

"If you had," replied the boy, with a bold and defiant expression, "I know very well what I would do. I would not go away. I would remain here, even if my papa ordered me to go. But for this once I could not be obedient, although I should be scolded for it."

"And what effect would your remaining here have, Alexander?" asked the king.

"It would have this effect, your majesty," replied the boy, gravely. "My dear mamma would then hear nothing that would make her feel sad, or perhaps even make her cry."

"But if I should tell her something in your presence that would make her feel sad?"

"That you will not do, papa!" cried Alexander, erecting himself proudly. "No, while I am here you will certainly not make my mamma sad; for you know that I would cry too, if my mamma cried, and you certainly could not bear to see your poor little son and his mamma weeping bitterly."

"You love your mamma very much, I suppose?"

"Yes," exclaimed the boy, throwing his arms around his mother's neck, and laying his curly head on her bosom; "yes, I love my mamma very dearly; and my heart almost breaks when I see her cry. And she cries very often now, and—"

"Go, Alexander," said his mother, interrupting him. "You see your sister is an obedient daughter, and has already obeyed her father's command. Follow her now, my son; learn from your sister to obey your father without murmuring."

"Yes, my son, follow your sister," said the king, gently. "Fear nothing, my boy, I have no intention of making your mother feel sad."

"Then I will go, papa," cried Alexander, as he pressed his

father's hand tenderly to his lips. He then skipped joyfully
out of the room.

The king followed the handsome boy, with an affectionate
look, until the door closed behind him. He then turned to
Wilhelmine, who met his gaze with a gentle smile. "Wilhelmine, I have entered on a new life to-day. The poor
prince royal, who was harassed with debt, has become a rich
and mighty king. A young king's first and most sacred duty
is to prove his gratitude to those who were his loving and
faithful friends, while he was yet prince royal. And therefore, Wilhelmine, you were my first thought; therefore am I
come to you to prove that I have a grateful heart, and can
never forget the past. You have undergone hardships, and
suffered want for me; the hour of reward has now come.
Impart to me all your wishes freely, and without reservation,
and I swear to you that they shall be fulfilled. Will you
have a name, a proud title? will you have jewelry or treasures? will you have a magnificent landed estate? Speak out,
tell me what you desire, for I have come to reward you, and
I am king."

She looked at him proudly, with sparkling eyes. "You
have come to reward me," said she, "and you are king.
What care I for your royalty! The king has not the power
to grant my wishes!"

"What is it, then, that you wish?" he asked, in embarrassment.

"I wish what the king cannot, what only the man can
grant. I wish you to love me as dearly as the prince royal
loved me. I crave no riches and no treasures, no titles and
no estates. When we swore that we would love and be true
to each other until death, you did not dare to think that you
would some day reward me for my love. When we exchanged
our vows of love and fidelity, written with our blood, this was
the marriage contract of our hearts, and this contract con-
sisted of but one paragraph. It only secured to each of us
the love and fidelity of the other as a dower. Let me retain

this dower, Frederick William; keep your treasures, titles, and estates, for your favorites and flatterers. Such things are good enough for them, but not for me—not for the mother of your children! Leave me in possession of my dower of your love and fidelity!"

Frederick lowered his eyes in confusion, and did not seem to see her stretch out her arms imploringly. He turned away and walked slowly to and fro.

Wilhelmine's arms sank down, and a deep sigh escaped her lips. "The decisive hour has come," said she to herself. "It shall find me armed and prepared for the struggle!"

Suddenly the king stopped in front of her, and a ray of determination beamed in his genial, handsome countenance. "Wilhelmine," said he, "I stand on the threshold of a great and sublime future. I will not act a lie at such a time. Between us there must be perfect and entire truth. Are you ready to hear it?"

"I am ready," said she, gravely. "Truth and death are preferable to life and falsehood."

"Come, Wilhelmine," continued the king, extending his hand. "Let us seat ourselves on the sofa, where we have so often conversed in earnestness and sincerity. Let us converse in the same spirit to-day, and open our hearts to each other in honest sincerity." He conducted her to the sofa, and seated himself at her side. She laid her head on his shoulder, and subdued sobs escaped her breast.

"Do not speak yet," she whispered. "Let me rest a moment, and think of the beautiful past, now that your future looks so bright. I have not the courage to look at the future. It seems to me that I am like those unhappy beings, of whom Dante narrates, that they walk onward with their faces turned backward, and that they cannot see what is coming, but only that which has been and which lies behind them. Ah, like them I see only what has been. I see us two, young, happy, and joyous, for the star of our youthful love shone over us. I see you at my side as my teacher, instructing me, and endeavoring to cultivate my mind.—Frederick, do you remember the Italian lessons you gave me? With you I read Dante, you explained to me this awful picture of the reversed faces. Shall I now experience through you the dreadful reality of what you then explained in the poem? Shall I shudder at the aspect of the future, and only live on that which is past and gone? Tell me, Frederick, can it be true, can it be possible? Does love, with all its happiness and bliss, then really lie only behind us, and no longer before us? But no, no, do say so!" she cried, imploringly, as she saw that he was about to speak; "let us be still and dream on for a moment, as we are now on the threshold of a new era, as you say." She ceased speaking, and buried her head in Frederick William's bosom. He laid his hand on her neck and pressed her to his heart. A long pause ensued. A last ray of the setting sun shone in through the window, and illumined with its golden light the head of the poor woman who clung trembling to her lover's bosom.

The last ray of the setting sun! The spirits of the past danced and trembled in its luminous course; the days which had been, sparkled and glittered in its last ray, and then expired.

"Ah," sighed the king, after an interval of silence, "why is the human heart so weak? why does it not retain like the precious stone its brilliant tints and fiery lustre? why do the rainbow hues and fire of love vanish? Why has fate ordained that all things should be subject to change, even love?"

Wilhelmine raised her head—the hour of bitterness was past; she now had courage to face the future, to pass the threshold of the new era. What has the future in store for her? Will it be gloomy? Has the sun set for her whole life, as its last ray has set in the chamber where she now sits, in night and darkness, at the side of the man she once called the sun of her life?

"You no longer love me, Frederick William!"

"I do love you, Wilhelmine; certainly I do, right cordially and sincerely."

She uttered a loud cry and pressed her hand to her heart. How different was this tame assurance of love to the passionate protestations of former days!

"Speak on, Frederick William, speak on! I am prepared to hear all! You love me right cordially and sincerely, you say?"

"Yes, Wilhelmine, and God is my witness that this is the truth. I desire to do everything to contribute to your happiness?"

"Everything! everything, but love me as heretofore!"

"Ah, Wilhelmine, man is but man after all, and no God! Nothing in his nature is eternal and imperishable, not even love; not that ardent, passionate love which is only crowned by the possession of the loved and adored object. But possession it is, this longed-for possession, that kills love. We are only charmed with that for which we long; when once attained we become accustomed to it, and custom begets indifference. It is heart-rending that it should be so, but it is so! We cannot change human nature, and human we all are!"

"Words, words," she murmured. "Why not say it all at once. You do not love me? You love another? Answer these two questions; I conjure you, answer them!"

"I will, Wilhelmine. I no longer love you, you say. It is true, I no longer love you as I once loved you, but perhaps more, perhaps better, more purely! I no longer love you, but I entertain for you the dearest and most enduring friendship. Love is like the sun: it shines brightly in the morning, but sets when evening comes. Friendship is like the evening star, ever present, and only obscured at times by the greater brilliancy of the sun. Wilhelmine our sun has at last set after gladdening us with its rays for many long years. And you cannot justly complain of its departure; it was necessary that night should ultimately come. But the evening-star still shines in the heavens, and will ever shine there! I pray you, Wilhelmine, be no weak, no ordinary woman! Do not make useless complaints, but look at matters as they are. Be strong, and overcome the petty vanity of the woman who feels herself insulted when her lover's passion cools. I do not love you; and, as I am a man, and as the human heart is always susceptible to a new love, I am also ready to make this admission: I love another! Be composed, do not interrupt me with reproaches. This is unalterable, and we must have the courage to look the truth in the face! Yes, I love another, and love her as ardently as I once loved you, but—I now no longer believe in an eternity of passion; I know that it will decline, and I therefore no longer tell my new love as I once told you. I will love you as long as I live; but I only say, I will love you as long as my heart will permit! I know that a day will come when I will also weary of this love; but never, never will the day come, Wilhelmine, when the friendship I feel for you could grow cold, when I could become indifferent to her I once so passionately loved, and to whom I owe the happiest years of my life! Some day my heart will be callous to all love and all women, but it will ever beat warmly for you; the days of my youth will be reflected from your brow, and the recollections of happy years will bind me more firmly to you, than all the vows of love could bind me to other women. Be as strong, brave, and wise, as you have always been; forgive me this human weakness. Renounce my love, and accept my friendship—my true, lasting, and imperishable friendship."

"Friendship!" she repeated, with mocking laughter. "The word has a freezing sound. You promised me glowing wine, and now you offer to quench the thirst of my heart with cold water."

"Of wine we grow weary, Wilhelmine. Heavenly intoxication is followed by highly terrestrial headache; but pure water refreshes and revives without intoxicating; it gives health and tranquillizes the heart."

"Or turns it to ice," rejoined Wilhelmine.

"Not so, it gives new warmth! And thus it is with friendship also, Wilhelmine.'

"And all this means," said she, sobbing, "that you intend
to drive me from your side, to banish me? I am to be compelled to yield to a rival?"

"No, that you shall not do!" he cried with vivacity. "No,
you are only to consent to be my friend, to elevate yourself
above all petty jealousy, and to wisely and discreetly adapt
yourself to the unavoidable. If you should not be able to
do this, Wilhelmine, if you should attempt to play the *rôle* of
the jealous Orsina, instead of that of the discreet friend,
then only would I, to my own great sorrow, be compelled to
separate from you, to renounce the pleasure of associating
with my dear friend, and—"

"No," she cried in dismay, as she threw her arms around
him; "no, I cannot live without you, I will not go into exile
with my poor, dear children!"

"With your children!" repeated the king. "Who thinks
of sending these children into exile?"

"Do you not consider it possible that you will send me into
exile? And where I am, there my children will also be, of
course!"

"Where you are, Wilhelmine, there your daughter will be;
that is lawful and natural. But the son belongs to the father;
and, whatever may divide and separate us, my son Alexander
shall not leave me; my bright, handsome boy, remains with
his father."

It had grown dark, and he could not see the light of the
bold resolution Wilhelmine had formed, sparkling in her eyes.

She laid her hand on Frederick William's shoulder. "We
are standing on the threshold of a new era," said she, "my
son shall now decide between you and me. I lay my fate in
his hands, and will accept it as if it came from God. We
will have him called, and he shall choose between his father
and his mother. If he decides to leave me and remain with
you, I will bow my head in humility, and will remain, and
content myself with your friendship. I will stand in darkness, and view from afar my happy rival sunning herself in

your love. But if my son should decide to go with his mother, then, like Hagar, I will wander forth into the desert. But I will not complain, and will not feel unhappy; I will have at my side, my son, the image of his father; the son in whom I love the father!"

"So let it be," cried the king. "Our son shall decide. Go, and bring him in."

"No, I will only see him in your presence; you might otherwise suppose I had influenced his decision. Permit me to have him called."

She rang the bell, and ordered the servant to bring lights, and request his young master to come at once to his majesty's presence.

"We will soon learn the decision of fate," said Wilhelmine, when the servant had closed the door. "For fate will speak to me through the mouth of my son!"

CHAPTER IX.

THE DECISION.

A FEW minutes had hardly elapsed before the door of the parlor was opened, and Wilhelmine's son entered. With flushed cheeks and a displeased expression on his handsome face, the boy walked up to the king, who was gazing at him tenderly.

"My gracious father," said he, "you promised to join us in the rose-pavilion, down at the river side; and we waited and waited, but all in vain! The sunset was splendid; it was a beautiful sight to see the sun fall into the water all at once; but you would not come to tell the dear sun 'good-night.' Why not? I think a king should always keep his word, and you certainly promised to come!"

"Well, my severe young gentleman," said the king, smiling, "I beg your pardon. But I had to speak with your mother on matters of importance, and you must have the goodness to excuse me."

The boy turned and looked inquiringly at the face of his mother. "Was it necessary, mamma?"

The king burst into laughter. "Really," he cried, "you are a grand inquisitor, my little Alexander. I am almost afraid of you. But you have not yet answered his severity, mamma. Excuse me to this young gentleman by assuring him that we had matters of the gravest importance to discuss."

"Alexander knows that what the king says and does is above all blame," replied Wilhelmine, gravely; "and I beg that he may be excused for losing sight of the king and thinking only of the indulgent father. But now hear why your father sent for you, my son; and answer his questions as your little head and heart shall prompt."

"Shall I state the question?" asked the king, in some embarrassment. "I had rather you did it, Wilhelmine. However," he continued, as she shook her head in dissent, "It shall be as you desire. Listen, my little Alexander. Your mother thinks of going on a journey, and of leaving here for a few years. I intend to give your mother several estates in Prussia as a remembrance of this day, and she may conclude to make them her home for some years. Although such a life may be pleasant for ladies, it is very quiet and lonely, and not at all suitable for a young man who still has a great deal to learn, and who is ambitious of becoming a soldier, which he could not well accomplish in the country. I therefore, very naturally, desire that you should separate yourself from your mother for a few years, and remain with me, your father, who certainly loves you as much as she does. But we have determined to leave the decision to you, although you are still so young, and I now ask you, my son, will you go with your mother, or will you remain with your father? Do not reply at once, my child, but take time for consideration."

"Oh, my dear papa," said the boy, quickly, "there is

nothing to consider, I know at once what I ought to do. My dear mamma has always remained with me, she has never deserted me. And when I had the measles, a short time ago, she sat at my bedside, day and night, and played with me, and told me such beautiful stories. And I would never have got well if my mamma had not nursed me. Whenever she left my bed, if only for a few minutes, I grew worse and suffered much more, and when she returned I always felt relieved at once. And how could I now desert the dear mamma, who never deserted me?"

"Oh, my child, my darling child," cried Wilhelmine, her eyes filling with tears, "God bless you for these words! But yet this shall not be a decision. You must take some time for consideration, my son. I am going to live on my estates, as your father told you. It will be very quiet and lonely in the country; there will be no soldiers, no beautiful houses, no amusements, and no boys to play with. But if you remain here with your father, you will have all this, and be honored and respected as a prince. You will live with your tutor, in a splendid house, in the beautiful city of Berlin, you will take delightful rides and drives, and see the soldier's drill every day. Your father will give you all you desire."

"Then let him give me my mamma," cried the boy eagerly. "Yes, my papa, if I can live with my dear mamma in a fine house in Berlin, and if you will come right often to see us, I will have all I desire."

"But your mother will not remain in Berlin, Alexander, and, therefore, you must decide whether you will go with her, or stay here with your father."

"Well, then," said Alexander, gravely, "if I must choose between you, I will go with mamma, of course. To be sure, I am very sorry to leave my papa, but I cannot live without my mamma; she is so good to me and loves me so dearly, I am always afraid when she is not with me."

Speechless with emotion, Wilhelmine sank on her knees, her countenance radiant with delight, and extended her arms

toward her son, who threw himself on her breast with a loving cry.

The king turned away, his heart filled with unutterable
sadness. He covered his eyes with his hands, and stood in
the middle of the chamber, isolated and deserted in his grief,
while he could hear the kisses, sobs, and whispered words of
tenderness of the mother and her son. Suddenly he felt a
light touch on his shoulder and heard a mournful, trembling
voice murmur his name. The king withdrew his hands from
his countenance, and his eyes met Wilhelmine's. She stood
before the king, her right hand resting on the boy's shoulder,
who had thrown his arm around her waist and nestled closely
to her side.

"Farewell, Frederick William!" said she in a loud and
solemn voice. "Hagar is going forth into the desert of life!
The estates and treasures which you offer me, I reject; my
children must not suffer want, however, and the little that
has heretofore been mine, I will retain. As soon as I find a
place where I wish to remain, you will be informed of it, and
I desire that the furniture of this house be sent to me there.
The house shall be sold, and the proceeds will constitute my
fortune and the inheritance of my children. I leave here
with my children to-night. My thoughts and blessings will,
however, remain with the father of my children. Farewell,
your majesty, and may your happiness be complete! Farewell!" She bowed her head in a last greeting, and then turned
and walked slowly through the room, supported by her son.

The king looked after her in breathless suspense; with
every step she took his anxiety increased. And when she
opened the door, and mother and son were about to pass the
threshold, without even once turning to look at him, whose
eyes were filled with tears, and who was regarding them with
such fondness and such agony, he uttered a cry of dismay,
rushed after them, seized Wilhelmine's arm, and thrust her
back into the room with such violence that she fell helplessly
to the floor, and her son burst into tears.

His sobs seemed to arouse Wilhelmine from her insensibility. She arose, and turned with proud composure to the king, who stood before her almost breathless with passion.

"Send him out of the room," she murmured. "He should not see your majesty in this condition."

The king made no reply, but took the boy by the hand, kissed him tenderly, and then led him to the door, and locked it behind him. He then returned to Wilhelmine, who awaited him with pallid cheeks, although her manner was perfectly composed.

"Wilhelmine," said he, uttering each word with difficulty, "Wilhelmine, it is not possible. You cannot leave me. If you go, my youth, my happiness, my good star go with you! Have pity on me! See how I suffer! Be great, be good, be merciful! Stay with me!"

"Thou hearest him, O God," cried Wilhelmine, raising her arms toward heaven. "Thou hearest him, and Thou seest what I suffer! I have loved him from my youth. I have been true to him in every thought, with every breath of life. I have borne for his sake shame and disgrace, and the contempt of the world. I have bestowed upon him all the treasures of my soul and heart; and yet my sacrifices have not been great enough, I have not yet been sufficiently humiliated. He demands of the mother of his children a still greater sacrifice: that I renounce his love, and stand by and see him give to another the love he swore should be mine! O Thou Great, Thou Almighty God, have pity on me! Send down a flash of lightning to kill and save me! I cannot live without him, and I may not live with him."

"Wilhelmine," said the king, in a hollow voice, "you will not make this sacrifice? You will not remain with me as my best and dearest friend—the friend to whom I will give my whole confidence, who shall share my thoughts as my sister soul, and from whom I will conceal no secrets?"

She slowly shook her head. What did Cleopatra determine to do, rather than grace the triumph of her faithless lover and her hated rival, and pass under the yoke? She determined to die; she let loose the serpent which had been gnawing at her heart, that it might take her life. "I prefer to die like Cleopatra, rather than live like the Marquise de Pompadour."

"Well, then," said Frederick William, his voice trembling with emotion, and looking tenderly at Wilhelmine, "I will prove to you that the friendship I entertain for you is stronger than the love I have given to another. I sacrifice to you, the beloved of my youth and the friend of my soul, all the wishes and hopes of my heart. I will renounce my love for the maid of honor, Julie von Voss, and will see her no more. She shall leave the court, and I will never seek to recall her. Are you now contented, Wilhelmine? Will you remain with me, and not deprive me of my dear son, who was about to leave me on your account? Wilhelmine, will you try to forget, and—" The king's voice faltered, and tears rushed to his eyes, but with an effort he steadied his voice and continued: "and will you sincerely endeavor to compensate me for what I sacrifice?"

With a cry of joy, Wilhelmine threw her arms around the king's neck, and pressed a long and fervent kiss on his quivering lips.

"I thank you, Frederick William, I thank you! You promised me when you came that you would to-day reward me for my love and fidelity during the long years which have been. You have kept your promise, my beloved; you have rewarded me. You have made the greatest sacrifice one human being can make for another. You have sacrificed the passion of your heart, and are ready to keep the faith which you sealed with your blood. See here, Frederick William, see this scar on my hand! This wound I gave myself, in order that I might write for you in my own blood my vow of love and fidelity. You kissed the wound and drank of my blood, swearing that you would always love, and never desert me. You have kept your oath, Frederick William. You have conquered yourself; you have now sealed your faith with the greatest human sacrifice."

The king suppressed the sigh which trembled on his lips, and pressed Wilhelmine's head to his bosom. "Now you will remain, Wilhelmine? Now you will not go?"

She raised her head quickly, and looked at him with beaming eyes. "I will remain with you, Frederick William; I will remain. And, stronger in my love than Cleopatra was, I will pass under the yoke, and march quietly in the triumphal procession of my rival. Sacrifice for sacrifice! You were ready to sacrifice your passion, I will sacrifice to you my woman's pride and vanity! I, the discarded woman, will walk without murmuring behind your new love and be her trainbearer. Go, Frederick William, and woo this beautiful young lady; wed her, if your priests will permit; be happy with her, and love her as long as you can, and then return to your friend, who can never cease to love you—whose affection for you is the breath of her life."

"Oh, Wilhelmine, my dear, my generous Wilhelmine," cried the king, pressing her to his heart, "I can never forget this noble-hearted generosity; I can never cease to be grateful! I have told you already, and I now repeat it: the human heart is inconstant, and every love must at last die; but friendship lives forever. No earthly desires dim the pure flame of its holy affection. Oh, Wilhelmine, I will never desert you; never shall your enemies and rivals succeed in estranging my heart from you, my friend."

"Swear that they shall not!" cried Wilhelmine, raising her right hand. "Lay your fingers on this scar on my hand, and swear that you will be my dear friend throughout my whole life, that nothing shall separate us, and that nothing shall induce you to drive me from your side, but that I shall live where you live, and ever be your friend, your confidante, and your sister soul."

The king laid the fingers of his right hand on the scar, repeated the words she had spoken, and swore that he would be

her true and devoted friend until death, that he would never
drive her from his side, but that she should live where he
lived, and remain with him as his friend and confidante for
all time.*

"And now that we have come to an understanding," said
he with a joyous smile, "I may perhaps be permitted to reward my dear friend, and shed a ray of my newly-acquired
royalty on this humble dwelling! You said some time ago
that you desired to sell this house and live on the proceeds of
its sale. I approve of your plan. I will purchase this house
of you for five hundred thousand dollars. You will endeavor
to live on the interest of this sum; if there should be a hitch
now and then, and debts should arise, you need only inform
me of the fact and they shall be paid."

"Oh, my dear, my generous friend," cried Wilhelmine,
"how can I thank you, how—"

"Be still," said the king, interrupting her, "I have not
yet quite finished. The house is now mine; and the price
agreed upon shall be paid you to-morrow out of the royal
fund. As I can do what I please with my own property, I
intend to make a present of it to the mother of the Count and
Countess von der Mark. And it will be my first care to have
it enlarged and elegantly furnished, in order that it may be
a suitable dwelling for the Count and Countess von der Mark,
and particularly for their noble and beautiful mother!"

"The Count and Countess von der Mark?" repeated Wilhelmine with astonishment. "Who are they? Who is their
mother? I never heard of them!"

"You shall soon become acquainted with them, only wait,"
said the king smiling; and he went to the door, unlocked it,
and gave the bell-rope which hung beside it a violent pull.

"Where are the children?" asked the king, of the servant
who rushed forward to answer his summons.

"Your majesty, my young master and mistress are in the
dining-room."

_____

*This scene is accurate.—See "Mémoires de la Comtesse de Lichtenau."

"Send them to me immediately," said the king; and he remained standing at the door awaiting them. When they came running into the parlor with anxious, inquiring looks, the king took them by the hand and conducted them to their mother.

"Madame," said he, gravely, "I have the honor to introduce to you Countess Mariane and Count Alexander von der Mark."

"Count Alexander von der Mark?" repeated the boy, looking up wonderingly at his father. "Who is that?"

"That you are, my son," said the king, as he stooped down and raised the boy up in his arms. "You are the Count von der Mark, and your sister is the countess; and you shall have the Prussian eagle in your coat of arms, and shall be honored at my court as my dear, handsome son. All the proud courtiers shall bow their heads before you and your sister. The Count and Countess von der Mark shall have the precedence at my court over all the noble families; and their place shall immediately be behind the royal princesses."

"And that will be my dear mamma's place, too?" said Alexander. "She will always be where we are?"

"Yes," said the king hastily, "she will always remain with her dear children. Yes, and (as the young count once remarked that, if he could live in a splendid house 'under the Linden-trees' * with his mother, and if I would go to see them right often, he would have all he desired), I will make him a present of the most magnificent house 'under the Linden-trees' in Berlin, and the young count shall live there, and I will visit him right often in his new home."

"That will be splendid," cried the boy clapping his hands "You are delighted, too, are you not, Mariane?"

"Certainly I am," replied his sister, smiling, "and I thank his majesty for the great honor he confers in giving us such grand titles."

"I am glad to hear that you are pleased with your title, my

* "Unter den Linden," a street in Berlin.

dear daughter; but, as names and titles do not sustain life, a sufficient amount will be set apart for your use as pin-money. And when a suitable and agreeable gentleman demands your hand in marriage, you shall have a dowry of two hundred thousand dollars. When this becomes known you will certainly not fail to have a vast number of admirers from which to make your selection. No more thanks, if you please! We will now go to dinner. Count von der Mark, give your mother your arm, I will escort the young countess."

"Your majesty," announced the servant, who entered at this moment, "Colonel von Bischofswerder and Privy-Chamberlain von Wöllner have just arrived, and beg to be admitted to your majesty's presence!"

"True, indeed," murmured the king, "I had altogether forgotten them. Madame, you will please excuse me for withdrawing from your society. I must not keep these gentlemen waiting, as I directed them to meet me here on important business. When this business is transacted I must however return to Potsdam. Farewell, and await me at breakfast to-morrow morning."

CHAPTER X.

THE INVOCATION.

"You have then really come, my friends," said the king. "You have really determined to attempt to invoke the Invisible?"

"God is mighty in the weak," said Wöllner, folding his hands piously; "and we men are merely the vessels into which He pours His anger and His love, and in which He makes Himself manifest. By fasting and prayer I have made myself worthy to commune with spirits."

"The longing after the Invisible Fathers throbs in my heart and brain; and, if in the heat of this longing I invoke them, they will lend an ear to my entreaties, and approach to answer the questions of your majesty, their best-beloved son."

"Nor have I a doubt on the subject," said Bischofswerder, complacently. "I will entreat the spirit of the grand-kophta with the whole strength of my soul, and with all the means which the holy secret sciences place at my disposal. The hour has come in which will be determined whether the immortal spirit controls the mortal body, compelling it to obey its behests in spite of time and space."

"Then you really consider it possible, my friend? You are yet of the opinion that the grand-kophta will appear in answer to your invocations?"

"Yes, sire, I am of that opinion!"

"That is to say, his spirit will come amongst us in some intangible shape. You cannot be in earnest when you assert that he will answer your call in the body, as I have already told you that the grand-kophta is in London. Our ambassador not only saw him there, but spoke with him the very day he dispatched the courier, who arrived here yesterday."

"Your majesty, the secret sciences teach me that the spirit controls the body; and we will now test the truth of this lesson. If the grand-kophta does not appear in flesh and blood, and give to your majesty, with his own hand, the elixir of life for which your soul thirsts, science lies, and the sublime spirits consider me unworthy of their confidence! In that event, I will renounce my right to enter the inner temple; it will be evident that I am not one of the enlightened. I will bow submissively to the anger and contempt of the Invisible, and return voluntarily to the outer temple to begin my apprenticeship anew."

The king shook his head thoughtfully. "Your faith is heroic; and I only hope you are not doomed to be disappointed. And now, let us begin our work!"

"His majesty's will be done," replied the two Rosicrucians, respectfully. "Will your majesty permit us to go to the laboratory in order to make our preparations?"

" I will accompany you, and render assistance as an inferior brother. You know that no one besides us three is permitted to enter this laboratory; and I therefore keep the key in a secret drawer of my writing-desk, which I alone can open!"

" Permit us to withdraw, in order that we may not see from what place your majesty takes the key."

The two Rosicrucians walked toward the door, and turned their faces so that they could not see what was done behind them.

" I have the key," said the king, after a short interval. "Come, my brothers. I am now ready!"

He walked rapidly to the door, unlocked it, and entered the laboratory, followed by Bischofswerder and Wöllner.

But hardly had the king stepped into the room before he uttered a cry of terror, and staggered back, pale with fright.

"The Invisibles! the Invisibles!" he murmured. "See! See! They knew we were coming, and have made all the preparations!"

" All hail, the Invisible Fathers," cried Wöllner, with enthusiasm. "They have prepared the altar."

" The Invisibles are awaiting us; they approve of our purpose," shouted Bischofswerder, exultingly. " Oh, behold, my king! Oh, see, my brother!"

He drew the king eagerly to the large furnace which occupied one entire side of the laboratory; and it really looked as if invisible hands had been at work in this chamber. A bright fire was burning in the furnace, jets of flame darted forth through the openings, and licked the pans and retorts in which liquids and mixtures of various colors boiled and simmered.

" All is prepared," said Bischofswerder, who had been examining the retorts closely. " It seems the Invisibles are concocting a secret mixture. But my eyes are blinded, and my brain is still in darkness; these substances and elixirs are unknown to me; I only feel that their fragrance fills me with wondrous delight. Oh, come, your majesty, and inhale this blessed aroma—this atmosphere of invisible worlds!"

The king timidly stepped up close to the furnace, and inclined his head over the retort pointed out by Bischofswerder. Dense vapors arose from the bubbling mass and enveloped the king's head.

"It is true," said the king, inhaling deep draughts of the vapor. "It creates a wondrous sensation of delight and ecstasy!"

"It is the fragrance of the spirit-world," said Wöllner, impressively.—"Oh, I feel, I know that my prayers have been heard. They are coming! Lo, the Invisibles are approaching! Look, my king, look up there!"

The king turned eagerly to Wöllner, whose right arm was raised, and pointed to the opposite wall.

"See, see these heavenly forms waving their hands and greeting us!"

"I see nothing," murmured the king, sadly. "The visions which bless the eye of the anointed are invisible to me. I see nothing!"

No, the king saw nothing! To him the chamber was empty. He saw no spirits, nor did he see Bischofswerder throw a handful of white powder into the large retort at this moment. But he saw the white clouds which now ascended from the furnace; he saw the flames which burst forth from the retorts, and, in the explosions and detonations which ensued, he heard the roar of invisible musketry.

"The Invisibles are contending fiercely," exclaimed Wöllner. "The good and bad spirits are warring with each other, and struggling for the possession of our noble king. The holy ones and the Rosicrucians are battling with the freethinkers and scoffers, and the so-called enlightened. Give the former the victory, Almighty God! Incline Thyself to the believers and Rosicrucians, and deal out destruction to the unbelievers and scoffers! On my knees I entreat thee, Thou Ruler of all things! have pity on the king, have pity on us, and—"

A loud and fearful detonation—a whistling, howling roar—

drowned his voice. Dense white clouds, through which tongues of flame darted in every direction, ascended from the furnace and gradually filled the room.

The king had staggered back, and would have fallen to the ground, but for Bischofswerder, who had supported him and conducted him to an arm-chair, into which he sank back helplessly. His eyes closed, and for a few moments he was in an unconscious condition.

Suddenly the king's name resounded in his ear and aroused him from this trance. "Awake, Frederick William, awake! Ours is the victory! The holy cross of love and of roses is victorious! The evil spirits have flown! Awake, Frederick William, awake! The Invisibles are ready to answer your questions!"

The king opened his eyes and looked around. He saw nothing at first but the clouds which encircled him. But suddenly a face seemed to arise in their midst—a face of deathly pallor? Long brown hair fell down on either side of the broad, but low forehead. Its widely-opened glassy eyes seemed to stare at the king, who shuddered, and would have turned away had not some invisible power compelled him to continue gazing at this death-like countenance. By degrees the vision grew more distinct, and stood out from the surrounding vapor in bolder relief. The neck and shoulders now appeared, and gradually the entire body of a man of a powerful build was disclosed. He wore a tightly-fitting jerkin of leather; his neck was encircled with a broad, double lace collar. A golden star glittered on his breast, and a richly-embroidered velvet mantle, bordered with ermine, hung down over his broad shoulders. This mighty, princely figure stood immovable in the midst of the white clouds, which enveloped it like a winding-sheet. But its large, proud eyes seemed fixed on Frederick William with a cold, hard look. The king shuddered, and uttered low entreaties for mercy.

"Fear nothing, Frederick William," said the vision, which spoke without opening its lips. These tones struck on the king's ear like a voice from the grave. "Fear nothing, Frederick William; I have not come to alarm, but to console you. The Invisibles have sent me to soothe your heart, and give peace and consolation to your soul. Do you not know who I am, Frederick William?"

"No," replied the king, in a low voice, "I do not."

"I am Philip of Hesse," rejoined the closed lips. "Philip of Hesse, called, by foolish and short-sighted men, 'The Magnanimous.'"

"Ah, now I know who you are, my prince," cried the king. "You, it was, who overthrew the rebellious peasants in battle, who overcame Franz von Sickingen, and introduced the reformation into Germany. You were the prince who submitted to the Emperor Charles the Fifth, after the unfortunate battle of Mühlberg; were taken prisoner by him, and held in captivity until released by the treaty of Passau. Tell me, sublime spirit, are you not the spirit of that noble prince, of Philip the Magnanimous?"

"I am! My whole life was a struggle, and I had many enemies to contend with. But my most formidable enemy was my own heart. This enemy was love, passionate love. Wedded since my sixteenth year with Christina of Saxony, selected as my wife for state reasons; my heart became inflamed with love for the beautiful Margaret von Saale, and my one great desire was to win her and call her my wife. But her virtue withstood my entreaties; and, although she loved me, she was nevertheless determined to fly from me unless our union could be consummated by the blessing of a priest. It was in vain that I besought her to become mine. These were days of agony, and this struggle was harder than any I had maintained on the field of battle. I then suffered and wept as though I were a puling boy, and not a warrior and prince."

"You are recounting the history of my own sufferings," murmured the king, in a low voice. "You are describing my own struggles!"

"I know it," replied the apparition. "My eye sees your heart, and your sufferings, and therefore have I come to console you, to tell you that I have suffered as you suffer, and that your wounds shall be healed as mine were. The maiden you love is as virtuous as Margaret von Saale was. Like Margaret von Saale she demands that she be made your wedded wife. In my distress and misery I addressed myself to the great reformer, whom I had patronized with pious zeal. I asked Luther if the church could bless a marriage of the left hand, when a marriage of the right hand already existed; and Luther, the man of justice and of truth, replied: 'It stands in the Bible that the left hand shall not know what the right does; and, consequently, it is not necessary that the right hand should know what the left does. The wife of the left hand has nothing to do with the wife of the right, forced upon you for reasons of state. The former is the wife of the prince, the latter will be the wife of the man. And, as two persons are united in you, the prince and the man, these persons can contract two marriages, the one for the prince and the other for the man, and the blessing of the church is admissible for both.' But the sensitive conscience of my beautiful Margaret was not yet satisfied. I now turned to Philip Melanchthon, the great scholar, the strictly moral and virtuous man, and demanded his opinion, telling him that the decision should rest in his hands. But Philip Melanchthon decided as Luther had done, and proved by Holy Writ that such a marriage was possible and admissible. He, however, added the condition that the consent of the wife of the right hand must be obtained before the marriage of the left hand could be consummated. My generous wife gave her consent. Margaret von Saale became my wedded wife, and the mother of seven children, who were the joy and pride of their parents. To tell you this, I left the peaceful grave. Such were the commands of the sublime spirits, who are greater than I, and who rule over the living and the dead. Learn by my example how virtue can be reconciled to love. Put away from you the unchaste woman with whom you live; turn your countenance from her forever—and seek and find your happiness at the side of the noble young woman to whom you shall be united by priestly blessings. Farewell! My time has expired, I must go."

The apparition seemed to melt away; it grew darker and fainter. For a while its dim and uncertain outlines could be seen when the clouds lifted, and then it disappeared entirely. The clouds also slowly vanished; and now they were gone, the fire could once more be seen burning brightly in the furnace. The king looked around, and observed his two friends kneeling and praying on either side of his chair.

"Have you been listening, my friends? Did you hear the utterances of the blessed spirits?"

"We have heard nothing but mutterings and shrieks, and therefore we have been entreating the sublime spirits to mitigate their anger," said Wöllner, shaking his head. "But I saw a vision, a heavenly vision," cried Bischofswerder. "I saw my beloved king and master, standing between two noblewomen. They both regarded him tenderly. They stood, the one on the right, the other on the left hand; on the extended right hand of both glittered a golden ring, the precious symbol of marriage. The countenance of my royal master was radiant with delight; and above him shone the star of pure and chaste love. And it seemed to me that I heard a heavenly voice cry: 'Find your happiness at the side of the noble young woman to whom you will be joined by priestly blessings.'"

"These were the last words of the sublime spirit that appeared to me," said the king, joyfully. "You heard them, my faithful friend, while wrestling in prayer at my side. Oh, I thank you both; and while I live, I will reward your fidelity. But, alas," continued the king, with a deep-drawn sigh, "I only fear that my life will be of short duration! I feel weak and exhausted, and upon you and your influence, my friend, I depend for the life-restoring elixir."

"I will procure it, you shall have it," cried Bischofswerder, rising from his knees with youthful vivacity, in spite of his corpulence. "The invocation shall now begin. I will command my spirit to leave the body, and fly through time and space to the grand-kophta, to entreat him to give to the doubting, unbelieving king a visible sign of his heavenly power, to convince him that the mind rules over the body."

"Do not attempt it, my dear friend; do not, I solemnly conjure you," implored Wöllner. "It is tempting God, to seek to set at naught the laws of Nature. It is possible that your mighty spirit has power to tear itself from the body, and transport itself from place to place with the rapidity of thought; but consider the difficulty of returning, consider whether the cold, dead body can be a fitting receptacle and abode for the spirit on its return."

"I know that this is the great danger to which I shall be exposed," replied Bischofswerder. "But I will dare all for my king, and no danger shall terrify me when his health and happiness are at stake.—Be still, my king! No thanks whatever! I love you! That suffices, that explains all! And now let me take my departure! Now let me invoke the grand-kophta, the dispenser of life and health!—But listen, Wöllner, listen to these last words! If the Invisibles assist me, and enable my spirit to leave its earthly tenement, my body will grow cold and assume a death-like appearance. But this must not lead you to suppose that I am dead. Only when this condition shall have lasted more than half an hour, I beg that you will kneel down beside my body and entreat the Invisibles to command my spirit to return to its earthly abode. Truly I would not wish to remain in a bodiless state, when the king needs my services. And now, my king and master, permit me to kiss your hand before I go."

"No, my true, my generous friend, come to my heart!" cried the king, as he embraced Bischofswerder, and pressed a kiss on his forehead.

"And now, hear me, ye Invisibles! Lend an ear to my

prayer! Give wings to my spirit that it may fly through time and space!—Here, Wöllner! hold my body!"

Wöllner rushed forward in answer to this call, and caught Bischofswerder in his arms as he was on the point of falling to the floor. He rested the head on his breast, covered the face with his hand, and gently stroked his cheeks and brow. The king, who stood behind him in breathless suspense, did not comprehend what was going on, and did not see the little bottle which Wöllner held under his friend's nose, nor did he see him slip it adroitly into his coat-sleeve when he arose. But when Wöllner stepped back, and pointed solemnly to the tranquil body, the king saw that Bischofswerder's spirit had flown. He saw that the pallid, inanimate object, which lay in the chair, was nothing more than the empty tenement, once the abode of Bischofswerder's spirit. Of this, the widely-extended, glassy eyes, and the stiffened features, were sufficient evidence.

The king shuddered, and turned away. "It is fearful to look upon the lifeless body of a friend who dies in an endeavor to save and prolong our life. How fearful, if death should be the stronger, and prevent the spirit from returning to its dwelling! Not only would we mourn the loss of a friend, but his death would have been in vain, and the elixir of life unattained! We must observe the time closely and count the minutes, in order that the prayers may begin when the half-hour has elapsed." With trembling hands the king drew his richly-jewelled watch from his pocket, and watched the creeping hands in breathless anxiety. His alarm increased as time progressed, and now, when only five minutes were wanting to complete the half-hour, the king turned pale and trembled with terror. "Only one minute more, then—"

"He moves," whispered Wöllner. "See, your majesty! Oh, see! There is life in his eye, his mouth closes, the hue of life returns to his cheek. A miracle, a miracle has taken place! The spirit has returned to the earthly tabernacle!"

Bischofswerder is once more among the living; he arises.

His eyes seek the king and find him. With unsteady gait, a smile on his lips, he approached the king. "Sire, my spirit greets you, my heart shouts for joy. I bring you glad tidings! The grand-kophta has yielded to my entreaties. He approaches to give my king life and health, and above all things to remove his unbelief!"

"He is then really coming? He approaches?" cried the king, joyfully.

"Call him, your majesty! Call the grand-kophta, but do so with a believing and confident heart."

"Grand-kophta! Sublimest of the sublime! Lend an ear to my entreaties! Appear Divo Cagliostro! Appear, my lord and master!"

A flash, a detonation, proceeding from the furnace, near which Wöllner stands, and all is once more concealed by the clouds of vapor which fill the room. When they at last rise and pass away, a tall figure, enveloped in a long black mantle, is seen standing in the middle of the room. The head only is uncovered, and this head is surrounded with waving black hair, in the midst of which a precious stone shines and sparkles with the lustre of a star. And the large black eyes, which are fastened on the king's countenance, with a mild and tender look, also shine like stars.

Carried away with rapture and enthusiasm, the king falls on his knees, and raises his hands in adoration.

But the grand-kophta advanced noiselessly to the kneeling king, begged him to rise, and helped him to do so with his own hand. "Yes, you are really my sublime master," cried the enraptured king. "I feel the warm, living body, the loving pressure of the blessing-dispensing hand. Hail, master! hail Cagliostro!"

"You appealed to me for assistance," said Cagliostro, in solemn tones. "I heard the call of the noble messenger you sent me as I was about to enter the St. James's Palace in London. King George of England had received another visitation from the demons who confuse his brain and darken his intellect. I was sent for and urged to come at once and drive out the demons from the head of the sick king. But it is of more importance that the healthy should not become sick, than that the sick man's condition should be somewhat improved. The spirit Althotas cried out to me, saying: 'Hasten to King Frederick William of Prussia; without your assistance he must languish and die. Hasten to preserve his health and strengthen his noble soul with the breath of immortality.' At first I was uncertain of whom Althotas spoke, for I had not yet heard of king Frederick's death. But before my eyes there suddenly arose the vision of an old man reclining in an arm-chair. He was on the threshold of the grave; his lips quivered and his eye grew dim, and the blood refused to flow from the open vein. Two weeping servants stood at his side; a greyhound lay at his feet. Above him in the air I saw the demons of unbelief struggling for the soul which had just left the body; but the good angels turned away in anger. And I interpreted this vision aright; I now knew that the unbelieving king was dead, and that Frederick William, the favorite of the Invisible Fathers, was now king of Prussia. Althotas then cried out, for the second time: 'Hasten, Frederick William needs you sorely. Hasten, that he may not die. I impart to the mortal the strength of immortality!' I turned my back on St. James's Palace, and immediately repaired to the holy laboratory of the spirits, to procure the necessary remedies. I then arose and flew to my suffering king on the wings of the Invisible."

"It is then true, it is really possible!" cried the enraptured king. "You are really the great Cagliostro! You have accomplished this miracle, have compelled the body to subject itself to the will of the spirit, and fly through time and space at its command! Oh, let me fall down and embrace your knees! Infuse the heavenly breath of thy lips into my enfeebled body!"

And he sank on his knees before the grand-kophta, and looked up to him in supplication.

"Arise, Frederick William; favorite of the Invisible, arise from your knees! I have not come to humble you, but to raise you up. The king who rules over millions of human beings, must not bend the knee to mortal man, and worship that which is visible and perishable. Humble your immortal spirit before the immortal, and lift up your soul in adoration to the unseen and imperishable. Be the ruler of men, and the humble subject of the Invisible. Arise, Frederick William, and listen to what I have to say, for my time is short, and Althotas awaits me on the threshold of St James's Palace, in London."

In obedience to this command the king arose from his knees, and stood before the magician, whose luminous eyes were still fixed intently on his countenance.

"You are not ill, Frederick William," said he, "nor are you well; your spirit lacks buoyancy, its wings are drooping, and your pulse is feeble. Death is slowly but surely approaching, and you would languish and die, if there were no means of driving off this grim monster."

"Oh, have pity on me! Give me the life-preserving elixir! Save me! I swear that my gratitude shall be unbounded, and that I am ready to bestow any reward that the Invisible Fathers may demand."

"They, indeed, demand no sacrifice and accept no reward, as men do. Their actions are influenced by higher laws. Love, honor, and obedience, are the rewards they exact."

"And from the depths of my heart, I promise them love, honor, and obedience."

"The Invisibles know you to be an obedient servant, and therefore am I here to restore health and strength to your body. But hear me, Frederick William, and lay my words to heart! In order that death may obtain no power over you, your heart must regain its joyousness, and your soul its buoyancy. A passionate love, which you are too weak to overcome, has filled your heart, and therefore its joyousness is dimmed. Then, gratify this passion, Frederick William!

The Invisibles give their consent! Let your whole being be imbued with this pure, this noble love; renounce all ignoble passions and desires. Make the fair maiden you love your wife, and peace, joy, and tranquillity, will once more abide in your heart, and your spirit will regain its buoyancy, and bear you aloft to the heights of enthusiasm. But your body shall also be restored to health; we will drive from it all weakness and disease. I bring you the elixir of life, of health, and of strength!"

"Oh, thanks, unspeakable thanks!" cried Frederick William, seizing the little bottle which Cagliostro held in his hand, and carrying it eagerly to his lips.

"Let me drink, sublime master! Let me drink of this heavenly elixir at once!"

"No! Save this precious medicine for a time when you will need it, when I will no longer be with you. For the present I am here, and I will infuse strength and health into your body! Receive these blessings, Frederick William! In the name of the Invisible, I anoint you king of the world and of life!"

As he uttered these words, he poured a few drops of some fluid on the king's head from a bottle which he held in his hand. A delicious fragrance instantly filled the room. The king raised his head with an exclamation of delight, and inhaled, in long draughts, the fragrant atmosphere.

"A wondrous sensation thrills my being; I feel so happy, so buoyant! I am leaving earth; and now I seem to see the portals of Paradise!"

"Take this, and these portals will open to your view," said Cagliostro, handing the king a little pill of some grayish substance. "Eat this, and all the bliss of Paradise will be yours!"

The king took the pill from Cagliostro's extended hand, carried it to his lips, and slowly swallowed it. Instantly a tremor seized his whole body, his cheeks turned deathly pale; he tottered and sank back into the chair which Wöllner had noiselessly rolled forward.

Cagliostro stooped down over him, and regarded the shadows which passed across and darkened the king's countenance. By degrees these shadows disappeared. His features brightened, and at last his countenance shone with joy and happiness, and was radiant with smiles.

"He is in Paradise," said Cagliostro, stepping back from the chair. "His spirit revels in heavenly delights. An hour will elapse before he returns from Paradise to this earth, and the remembrance of what he has seen and enjoyed in this hour will be a sunbeam in his existence for a long time to come. He will long for a renewal of this bliss, and you must console him with the promise, that I will either appear to him in person, or else send him, by a messenger, at the expiration of each year, one of these wonderful pills, which condenses the delights of a whole life into one hour, provided he is an humble and obedient servant, and does the will of the Invisible in all things. His soul is lost in rapture, and his ear is closed to all earthly sounds!—And now, my friends, come nearer, and listen to my words."

The two Rosicrucians, Wöllner and Bischofswerder, approached, in obedience to his command; and when Cagliostro laid his hands on their shoulders, their countenances beamed with delight.

"Speak to us, sublime master! Your utterances fall on our souls like heavenly dew. Speak, and command your servants to do your will!"

"You must continue the course marked out for you by the Fathers through me. You must aid in building up the kingdom of the Church and the Invisible on this earth. The Invisible Church, and her visible priests and representatives, shall alone rule on earth in the future, and, therefore, thrones must be overturned, crowns trodden in the dust, and the names of the kings and princes of earth uprooted like weeds and cast in the oven. An era of terror is drawing nigh when the sword and firebrand will go hand in hand through the land, and rapine and slaughter be the order of the day. The demons of insurrection and rebellion are already at work, threatening princes, and greeting the people with these words of promise: Liberty and Fraternity. We, the Invisible, the Sacred Fathers of the holy Church, have sent them out to carry terror to the hearts of princes. The king who has just died devoted his whole life to the enfranchisement of the spirit of the people; our chief endeavor must be to fetter this spirit, and restore the people and their rulers to their former humility and submission. They must do penance in sackcloth and ashes, and be made aware that the priests of the holy Church and the pious brothers of the order, can alone save them, and reduce their rebellious subjects to obedience and submission. The knife and burning fire are sometimes necessary to heal wounds and diseases. And these remedies we will apply. The revolution can be made a mighty and sublime weapon in the hands of the Invisible, and the bloodiest paths may lead to the greatest good! Alas, that we should be compelled to tread such paths!"

"Alas! alas!" cried the two Rosicrucians, pale with terror. The countenance of the slumbering king, however, still wore the same enraptured expression.

"But," continued Cagliostro, "of these evils, good will come. The proud flesh shall be cut out with the knife, and the wound burned with fire, in order that it may heal the more rapidly. The storm of the revolution will shake the earth. Thrones will tremble, and princes fall down in the dust. The people will be lashed to fury, like the waves of the storm-tossed sea. But the holy Church will be the little vessel that bids the sea be still, and stems the tide of the people's wrath by leading them back to humility and belief. Anger makes blind, and in their blindness they can the more readily be fettered. We, the Invisible Fathers, use the people to terrify the rulers. In all parts of Europe, the fathers and brothers of our order are preparing this work of destruction and overthrow, in order that the noble and sublime may be built up anew out of the débris. Oh, my brothers, perform diligently your allotted task! In the name of the Invisible Fathers, I deliver over to you this kingdom and this king! Govern him, and make him serviceable to the holy order and the holy Church. You shall rule in Prussia. Build up the good, destroy the evil! But the greatest good is, belief; the greatest evil, unbelief! Root out the king's unbelief! You will be justified in using any means, for the end sanctifies the means; and even that which is in itself vile, becomes a holy weapon in the hands of the chosen!—And now, my brothers, I bid you a final adieu; my time has expired, I must go!"

"Oh, master, do not leave us!" cried Bischofswerder. "Stay with us, and promote our holy ends."

"Stay with us, and assist us in leading the king back to the right path," exclaimed Wöllner.

"You can accomplish it without my assistance. Your will is strong, and his resistance will be but feeble! You shall be the kings of Prussia; you shall reign in the land! But do not forget that as rulers you will still be servants!"

"That we will never forget! We will ever obey the commands of the Invisibles, and faithfully execute their will as announced to us by your sublime lips!"

"Who knows that my lips will never speak to you again," said Cagliostro, in a sad voice. "I wander through the world on the verge of an abyss, and the storm and revolution are my companions. From the murder and bloodshed of the revolution, the Church will blossom afresh. Remember these words, ye brothers of the cross and of the roses! Remember them, and farewell forever!"

CHAPTER XI.

THE WILL.

THE solemn ceremony was over. The body of the great king had been borne forth from the apartments in which he had governed Prussia for so many years; from the house which had been his chief delight on earth, and which was thenceforth to stand as a monument of his life. But the deceased king's commands and wishes were disregarded in the very beginning. And it was made manifest to the world that his successor did not intend to walk in his footsteps, and did not share his independent views on religious subjects, and his freedom from all prejudices. Frederick had caused a burial vault to be built for himself on the terraces. He desired that his body should find a last resting-place in the garden which he had made, and near the house in which he had lived with his friends, and in which he had been so happy!

But his successor considered such a resting-place, in the temple of Nature, and under the dome erected by the hand of the Almighty, an unfit abode for the remains of a king. He considered the temple of brick and mortar erected by the hand of man a far more worthy receptacle for the dead monarch.

The philosopher of Sans-Souci had not attended church for many years; and now, as if to proclaim to the world that a revolution had taken place in Prussia, the king's body was deposited in the church. To the Garrison Church in Potsdam, where the plain and unadorned coffin of King Frederick William the First had been placed in the vault under the altar, the gloomy funeral procession of the dead ruler wended its way on the evening of the eighteenth of August. His generals and officers, the magistrate of Potsdam, and the members of his household, followed the funeral car. But his successor, King Frederick William, and the princes and princesses, were not present. In solitude, as he had lived, King Frederick descended into the dark vault in which the coffin of his father awaited him. In life, they had kept at a distance from each other; death now brought them together, and their mortal remains lay side by side in peace and tranquillity. Death reconciles all things; in his hands even kings are but as the dust of the earth.

On the morning after Frederick's interment, King Frederick William repaired to Sans-Souci, where the opening and reading of the monarch's will was to take place. The royal princes, who had not accompanied the king's body to its last resting-place, were by no means absent on this momentous occasion, and Princes Henry and Ferdinand, and even the Princess Amelia, Frederick's sister, who was decrepit from age, and deformed by the mental and bodily anguish she had undergone, had come to Sans-Souci to be present at the reading of the will. These three were standing in an alcove, conversing eagerly, but in an undertone. Their manner was expressive of resentment and anger, and the glances which they from time to time cast toward the door through which the king was expected to enter, were full of hatred and derision.

"Bischofswerder has been made colonel; and Wöllner, privy-councillor," murmured Prince Henry, bitterly; "even that abominable fellow, Rietz, has received a title. But he never thought of his family; for us there are no favors."

"And how could there be?" rejoined Princess Amelia, in her sharp, scornful voice. "The favorites stand where the golden shower falls, and you do not desire that we should do likewise, I hope? I, for my part, shall certainly decline the honor of standing at Wilhelmine Enke's side; nor have I any desire to share the royal favor with the king's new flame, the maid of honor, Von Voss."

"She will soon hold an important position," whispered Prince Ferdinand. "The king intends to make her his wife."

"Impossible!" exclaimed the hoarse voice of the princess. "That is, unless our dear nephew first manages to put his legitimate wife out of the way with the aid of his sorcerers."

"Perhaps he intends to take King Solomon as his model," said Prince Henry, derisively. "He also was an archprofligate, although he was accounted a most holy and worthy king."

"Let him pronounce a Solomon's judgment on himself," screeched the princess; "let him cut himself in three pieces:

one for the queen, a second for Wilhelmine Enke, and the third for the new favorite."

"The last must, however, be spoken of with the greatest deference," whispered Prince Ferdinand. "The king will have it so. The maid of honor, Von Voss, is exceedingly virtuous, and insists on a marriage. The king had an interview with the young lady on the day of Frederick's death; and she then imposed three conditions: She demands that the queen's consent be first obtained, then a church marriage, and finally the king's separation from Madame Rietz."

"The queen will not give her consent," said Princess Amelia.

"She has already done so! The Privy-Chamberlain Rietz, accomplished this masterpiece of diplomacy. The king pays his wife's debts, and doubles her pin-money; and for this consideration she consents to the marriage of the left hand." *

"They are all mercenary creatures, these women," muttered Prince Henry. "They are like dissembling cats, that are always ready to scratch and betray their best friends. In this respect a queen is no better than a beggar-woman! For money, a queen compromises her honor and her rights; and permits a virtuous mantle to be thrown over vice. But this time it will be of no avail, since no priest can be found to consummate this unlawful marriage."

"You are mistaken, my dear brother," said Prince Ferdinand, smiling. "One has already been found. The king asked advice of his newly-appointed Privy-Councillor Wöllner. This fellow was formerly a preacher, as you well know, and is therefore well acquainted with priestly stratagems. He proved to the king, by historical references, that such double marriages were possible, and that even Luther had permitted the landgrave Philip to contract a marriage of this kind. Moreover, he called the king's attention to the fact, that he was an ordained preacher himself, and, as such, entitled to exercise the functions of that calling, and offered to perform the ceremony himself."

* Historical.

"They are all mercenary creatures, these men,' said Princess Amelia, with a malicious side glance at her brother,
Prince Henry.

"I am surprised to hear that, my dear sister," remarked
Prince Henry. "It seems you have changed your opinion of
men very materially."

"No," she rejoined, angrily, "no, I have always known
that men were miserable creatures. There were only two ex-
ceptions: the one was my brother Frederick, and the other
was the man whom even the great King Frederick could not
keep in fetters—he who broke the heaviest bars and strongest
chains with the strength of his invincible spirit, and liberated
himself in defiance of all kings and jailers. I thank you,
Henry, for reminding me of him! My heart has been envenomed by mankind, and is old and withered, but it grows
warm and young again when I think of him for whom I suffered so much, and who made of me the old hag I now am.—
But here comes the king, our dear nephew." And Amelia,
whose countenance had been illumined for a moment with a
ray of youth, resumed her spiteful and gloomy look, and hob-
bled toward her dear nephew, who was just entering the
chamber, followed by Count von Herzberg and the newly-
appoined minister of state, Von Voss. "How handsome your
majesty looks!" cried Princess Amelia, in her hoarse voice;
"how young and handsome! If it were not for the thin hair,
the embonpoint, and the dear wife, one might take your majesty for a youthful Adonis, going a wooing, and—"

"And who has the misfortune to meet a bad fairy * on the
road. But it makes no difference, custom has robbed your
evil glance of its terrors, and we will never cease to love and
esteem you. I beg leave to assure my dear aunt Amelia, as
well as my two uncles, that I will always remain their affectionate and devoted nephew, and that it will afford me the
greatest pleasure to gratify their wishes. However, we will
speak of this hereafter, but now let us consider the grave pur-

* A nickname given the princess at court.

pose for which we have come together. Count von Herzberg, I beg you to conduct the ambassador of the Duke of Brunswick to our presence."

The king seated himself on the sofa which stood in the middle of the room. Princess Amelia and the two princes seated themselves in chairs, in his immediate vicinity. In front of them, and near the window, stood a table covered with green cloth, and beside it three elegantly carved chairs. This was Frederick the Great's writing-desk, the desk at which he had thought and labored so much for the welfare and honor of his kingdom and subjects.

"Baron von Hardenberg, minister, and extraordinary ambassador of his highness, the Duke of Brunswick," cried Count Herzberg as he entered and presented this gentleman to the king. Baron von Hardenberg bowed with the grace of a courtier and an elegant man of the world, and then looked up at the king, expectantly, with an air of perfect ease and composure.

"Speak, Baron von Hardenberg," said the king, with some little embarrassment, after a short pause. "My uncle, the Duke of Brunswick, sends you. What message does the baron bring?"

"Sir, I bring, at the command of my gracious master, the duke, the last will and testament of King Frederick the second, of blessed memory—with unbroken seals, and in exactly the same condition as when years ago delivered by his deceased majesty to the duke, and by him deposited in the state archives at Brunswick, where it has remained until now."

The baron handed the sealed document to the king, and begged him, and the princes, and ministers, to examine the seals, to assure themselves that they had not been tampered with, and requested his majesty to break them, and open the will, after having satisfied himself of that fact. After this had been done, and after Herzberg had testified to Frederick's handwriting, the king returned the document to Baron von Hardenberg.

"You brought us these last greetings and injunctions of the great king, and it is therefore but just and proper that you, as the representative of the duke, should make us acquainted with the contents of the will. I authorize you to read it aloud. Seat yourself at that table between my two ministers. And now read."

Count von Hardenberg spread the document out on the table, and commenced to read in a loud and sonorous voice, as follows:

"Life is but a fleeting transition from birth to death. Man's destiny is to labor for the welfare of society, of which he is a member, during this brief period. Since the duty of managing the affairs of state first devolved upon me, I have endeavored, with all the powers given me by Nature, to make the state which I had the honor to govern happy and prosperous. I have caused justice to be administered, I have brought order and exactitude into the finances, and I have introduced that discipline into the army, which makes it superior to the other troops of Europe. After having done my duty to the state, in this manner, it would be a subject of unceasing self-reproach, if I neglected that which concerns my family. Therefore, in order to avoid the dissensions which might arise among the members of my family in regard to the inheritance, I herewith declare to them this my last will and testament:

"(1.) I willingly, and without regret, return the breath of life which animates me to beneficent Nature, which honored me with its bestowal, and this body to the elements of which it is composed. I have lived a philosopher, and I desire to be buried as such, without pomp, show, or splendor. I desire neither to be dissected nor embalmed. I desire to be buried in Sans-Souci, on the terrace and in the vault which I have had prepared for the reception of my body. In this manner the Prince of Nassau was laid to rest in a wood near Cleve. Should I die in time of war, or on a journey, my body must be conveyed to the most convenient place, and afterwards to Sans-Souci in the winter, and deposited as above directed.

"(2.) I bequeath to my dear nephew, Frederick William, my successor to the crown, the kingdom of Prussia, provinces, states, castles, fortifications, places, munitions, and arsenals, lands which are mine by right of conquest or inheritance, all the crown jewels which are in the hands of the queen, my wife, the gold and silver plate in Berlin, my villas, libraries, collections of medals, picture galleries, gardens, etc., etc. Moreover, I leave him the state treasure as he may find it at my death, in trust. It belongs to the state, and must only be used in defending or assisting the people.

"(3.) If death compels me to leave unpaid some small debts, my nephew shall pay them. Such is my will.

"(4.) I bequeath to the queen, my wife, the revenue she now draws, with the addition of ten thousand dollars per annum, two tuns of wine each year, free wood, and game for her table. Under this condition, the queen has consented to make my nephew her heir. Moreover, as there is no suitable dwelling that can be set apart as her residence, I content myself with mentioning, for form's sake, Stettin as an appropriate place. At the same time, I request of my nephew that he hold suitable lodgings in readiness for her in the palace in Berlin, and that he show a proper consideration for the widow of his uncle, and for a princess whose virtue is above all reproach.

"(5.) And now, we come to the Allodial estate. I have never been either miserly or rich, nor have I ever had much to dispose of. I have considered the state revenues as the ark of the covenant, which none but consecrated hands might touch. I have never appropriated the public revenues to my own use. My own expenses have never exceeded the sum of two hundred thousand dollars; and my administration leaves me in perfect quietude of conscience, and I do not fear to give the public a strict account of it.

"(6.) I appoint my nephew Frederick William residuary legatee of my Allodial estate, after having paid out the following legacies."

After the king, in twenty-four additional clauses, had named a legacy for all of his relatives, either in money, jewels, or something else, and after he had determined the pensions for the invalid officers and soldiers of his army, and for his servants, the testament continued:

"I recommend to my successor that he honor and esteem his blood, in the persons of his uncles, aunts, and all other relatives. Accident, which determines the destiny of man, also regulates the succession. But the one, because he becomes king, is no better than the others. I, therefore, recommend to all my relatives that they live in a good understanding with each other; and that they, if it be necessary, sacrifice their personal interests to the welfare of the fatherland and the advantage of the state.

"My last wishes when I die will be for the happiness of this kingdom. May it ever be governed with justice, wisdom, and strength! May it be the happiest of states, through the mildness of its laws; may its administration in respect to finance ever be good and just; may it ever be most gallantly defended by an army that breathes only for honor and fair renown; and may it last and flourish to the end of all centuries!"

"Amen! amen!" exclaimed the king, folding his hands piously, when Baron von Hardenberg had concluded. "Amen! The intentions of my great and exalted uncle shall be carried out in all things! God bless Prussia, and give me strength to govern it and make it happy! I thank you, baron, and promise myself the pleasure of a confidential interview with you to-morrow morning before you take your departure."

His ministers having retired with the ambassador, in compliance with an intimation from the king that they might do so, Frederick William now turned with a gracious and genial smile to Princess Amelia and her two brothers, who, like the king, had arisen from their seats.

"My exalted uncle particularly recommended that I should consider the welfare of my uncles and aunts," said Frederick. "I assure you, however, that this recommendation was unnecessary; without it, I would have been only too happy to contribute to your happiness and welfare, to the extent of my ability. I beg each of you, therefore, to prefer some request, the gratification of which will serve as a remembrance of this solemn occasion.—Speak, Prince Henry; speak, my dear uncle; name some favor that I can grant."

The prince started, and a glowing color flitted over the countenance that was an exact copy of the deceased king's. The word "favor," which Frederick's smiling lips had uttered, pierced the prince's heart like a poisoned arrow.

"Sire," said he, sharply, "I crave no favor whatever at your hands, unless it might be considered a favor that my rights be protected, and justice be shown me, in the matter of my claims to a certain succession."

"To exercise justice is no favor, but a duty," replied the king, mildly; "and my dear uncle Henry will certainly be protected in all his rightful claims."

"In my claims to the succession in the Margraviate Schwedt?" inquired Prince Henry, hurriedly; and his eyes, which were large, luminous, and keen, like Frederick's, fastened a piercing glance on his nephew's countenance.

Frederick William shrugged his shoulders. "That is a political question, which must be decided in a ministerial council, and not in a family conference."

"That is to say, in other words," screeched Amelia, with mocking laughter, "Prince Henry will always belong to the dear family, but never to the number of the king's ministers and councillors."

The king, actuated perhaps by a desire to turn the conversation, now addressed Prince Ferdinand: "And you, my dear uncle, have you no particular wish to impart?"

The prince smiled. "I am not ambitious, and my finances are fortunately in good order. I recommend myself and family to the king's good-will. I should be particularly pleased if my oldest son Louis could be honored with the protection of his royal uncle."

"He shall stand on the same footing with my son," said the king. "I desire him to be the friend and companion of my son Frederick William; and I trust that he will infuse some of his spirit and fire into the latter. The young princes are made to complete each other, and I shall be glad to see them become close friends.—And now, my dear aunt and princess," continued the king, as he turned to Amelia, "will you be kind enough to name your wishes."

The princess shrugged her shoulders. "I am not ambitious, like brother Henry, and I have no children to care for, like brother Ferdinand. My own wants are few, and I am not fond enough of mankind to desire to collect riches in order that I may fill empty pockets and feast those who are in want. Life has not been a bed of roses for me, why should I make it pleasant for others? There is but one I desire to make happy; he, like myself, has lived through long years of misery, and can sing a mournful song of the hard-heartedness and cruelty of mankind. Sire, I crave nothing for myself, but I crave a ray of sunshine for him who was buried in the darkness of a prison, who was robbed of his sun for so many long years. I crave for an old man the ray of happiness of which his youth and manhood were wickedly deprived. Sire, in my opinion, there is but one shadow on the memory of my exalted brother. This shadow is Frederick Trenck.[*] Let justice prevail. Restore to Von Trenck the estates of which he was unjustly deprived; restore the title and military rank of which he was robbed. Sire, do this, and I, whom misery has made a bad fairy, will hereafter be nothing more than a good-natured and withered old mummy, who will fold her hands and pray with her last breath for the good and generous king who made Frederick von Trenck happy."

"It shall be as my dear aunt desires," said the king, with emotion. "Frederick von Trenck shall be put in possession of his estates, and restored to his military and civic honors. We

[*] Frederick von Trenck suffered long years of imprisonment on Princess Amelia's account.—See "Frederick the Great and his Family," by L. Mühlbach.

will also invite him to our court, and he shall not have to fear being again thrown into the gloomy dungeons of Magdeburg, although Princess Amelia should smile graciously upon him."

The princess distorted the poor old face, which was so completely disfigured with scars, in an attempt at a smile, which was only a grimace; and she was herself unaware that the veil which had suddenly dimmed her eyes was a tear. For long years she had neither wept nor smiled, and shed tears to-day for the first time again. For the first time in many years she thanked God, on retiring, for having been permitted to see the light of this day. She no longer desired to die, but prayed that she might live until she had seen Frederick von Trenck—until she had received his forgiveness for the misery she had caused him! To-day, for the first time, the embittered mind of the princess was touched with a feeling of thankfulness and joy. And it came from the bottom of her heart, when she said to Frederick William, on taking leave of him after the reading of the will: "I wish I were not a bad, but rather a good fairy, for I could then give you the receipt for making your people and yourself happy!"

The king smiled at this. He had that receipt already! He had received it in the elixir of life which Cagliostro had given him. These drops were the receipt for his personal happiness; and, as for making the people happy, Bischofswerder and Wöllner must know the receipts necessary to effect that object. In their hands the king will confidently place the helm of state. They are the favorites of the Invisible Fathers; the chosen, the powerful. And they shall rule Prussia, they, the Rosicrucians!

This thought filled the king's heart with joy, but it filled the hearts of the opponents of the pious brotherhood, of the enemies of Bischofswerder and Wöllner, with dismay and anxiety. And the number of their enemies was great, and many of them were men of high rank and standing.

There was also at the court a party which entertained bitter but secret enmity to the Rosicrucians.

CHAPTER XII.

LEUCHSENRING.

At the head of the opposition party at court stood Franz Michael Leuchsenring, the prince royal's instructor, Goethe's friend, and a member of the former Hain association. He had been called to Berlin by Frederick the Great to assume the position of French tutor to the future King of Prussia, and impart to him a thorough knowledge of French literature.

Baron von Hardenberg sought out the tutor, whom he had known and loved for many years, on the morning after the reading of the will. The meeting of these long-separated friends was hearty and cordial, and yet the keen glance of the ambassador did not fail to detect the cloud which rested on Leuchsenring's countenance. After they had shaken hands, and exchanged a few questions and remarks relative to each other's health and circumstances, the baron raised his delicate white hand and pointed to Leuchsenring's brow.

"I see a shadow there," said he, smiling; "a shadow which I never before observed on my friend's forehead. Is the handsome Leuchsenring no longer the favorite of the ladies, and consequently of the muses also? Or have we again some detestable rival, who dares to contend with you for a fair maid's favor? I know what that is; I saw you in the rôle of Orlando Furioso more than once, when we were together in the Elysian Fields of Naples, where we first met and joined hands in friendship. My friend, why did we not remain in bella Italia! Why has the prose of life sobered us down, and made of you the teacher, and of me the servant of a prince!— But enough of this; and now answer this question: Who is the rival? Am I to be your second here in Berlin, as I was on three occasions in Naples?"

Leuchsenring smiled: "I observe, with pleasure, my dear baron, that your ministerial rank has not changed you. You are still the same merry, thoughtless cavalier; while I, really, I can no longer deny it, have become a misanthrope. With me gayety and love are things of the past; and, unfortunately, women have nothing to do with the shadow which your keen glance detected."

"And more unfortunately still, you have become a politician," exclaimed the baron, smiling. "What I have heard is then true; you no longer write love-letters, but occupy yourself with learned treatises. You have joined a political party?"

"It is true," said Leuchsenring, emphatically. "I am filled with anger and hatred when I see these advocates of darkness, that is, these Rosicrucians, or, in other words, these Jesuits, attempting to cast their vast tissue of falsehood over mankind. I feel it to be my duty to tear asunder its meshes and lay bare the toils in which they hoped to involve mankind."

"Bravo, bravo!" cried Hardenberg. "I am delighted to hear you declare your views in this manner. I now perceive that you are in earnest. And I will give you a proof of my confidence by asking your advice in my personal affairs. King Frederick William has honored me with an audience, and I have just left his presence. It seems his majesty has taken a fancy to me; some effeminate feature in my countenance has found the highest appreciation. To be brief, the king has graciously proposed to me to enter his service; he offers me a ministerial position."

"And what reply did you make to this proposition?" asked Leuchsenring, eagerly.

"I begged some little time for consideration. I was not sufficiently acquainted with the political phase, and I desired to discuss the matter with you, my friend, before coming to a decision. And now, give me your opinion. Shall I accept?"

"First tell me what you are, and then I will reply. Tell me whether you are a Rosicrucian, that is, a Jesuit, or whether you have remained a faithful brother of our society? Give me your hand, let me touch it with the secret sign; and now tell me if you are still a brother."

"I am," said Hardenberg, his jovial face assuming an earnest expression, and he touched Leuchsenring's extended hand in a peculiar manner. "The grasp of this hand proclaims to you that I have remained true to the society; and that I am still a brother of the order and a zealous freemason."

"Thanks be to God that you are my friend!" cried Leuchsenring. "Then you are with me, with those who are preparing for the future, and erecting a barrier in the minds of mankind to the present tide of evil. And now I will answer your question. Do not accept the offer which has been made you, but save yourself for the future, for the coming generation. Gloomy days are in store for Prussia, and the good genius of the German fatherland must veil its head and weep over the impending horrors. The demons of darkness are at work in the land. Superstition, hypocrisy, Jesuitism, and lasciviousness, have combined to fetter the understanding and the hearts of men. A period of darkness such as usually precedes the great convulsions and epochs of history will soon come for Prussia. Believe me, we are standing on a crater. The royal favorites are covering it with flowers and garlands; the royal Rosicrucians are administering elixirs and wonder-working potions, to obscure the eye and shut out the fearful vision. They are, however, not arresting the progress of the chariot of fate, but are urging it on in its destructive career. As good springs from evil, so will freedom spring from slavery. The oppression which rulers have been exercising on their subjects for centuries, will now bear its avenging fruits. The slaves will break their fetters, and make freemen of themselves."

"Ah, my friend," exclaimed Hardenberg, shrugging his shoulders; "you see the realization of unattainable ideals; unfortunately, I cannot believe in it. Tell me, by what means are these poor, enslaved nations to break their fetters and make freemen of themselves?"

"I will tell you, and make your soul shudder. The slaves, the down-trodden nations, will free themselves by the fearful means of revolution. It already agitates every soul, and throbs in every heart. The time of peace and tranquillity is at end; the storm no longer rages in the heads and hearts of poets only, but in every human heart. The thoughts and songs of the poets have pierced the heart of nations, and fermented a storm that will soon burst forth; as it sweeps along it will destroy the old and build up the new. With his 'Robbers,' Schiller hurled the firebrand into the mind of youth, and princes and rulers are feeding and nourishing the enkindled flame with the trumpery of their gold-glittering rags, and their vices. This flame will blaze up until it becomes a mighty conflagration. The vices of princes are the scourges chosen by God, to chastise the nations, in order that they may rise up from the dust, and that slaves may become men! Louis the Fifteenth of France, with all his crimes and vices, was an instrument in the hands of the Almighty. And Marie Antoinette, with her love of pleasure, her frivolity, and her extravagance, is such an instrument, as is also Frederick William of Prussia, with all his thoughtlessness, his good-nature, and his indolence. Even this hypocritical generation of vipers, this lying, deceiving brotherhood, these Rosicrucians and Jesuits, must serve God's purposes. Falsehood exists only to make truth manifest; and bondage, only to promote liberty. Therefore I will not complain, although vice should be triumphant for a while. The greater the success of evil now, the greater the triumph of good hereafter. The greater the number of Jesuits who execute their dark deeds now, the greater the number who will be destroyed."

"They exist only in your imagination, my exalted friend," said Hardenberg, smiling. "There are not any Jesuits in Prussia."

"They are everywhere," said Leuchsenring, interrupting him, and grasping his friend's arm in his earnestness. "Yes, there are Jesuits. They go about with us, they sit with us at table, they grasp our hands as friends, they flatter us as our admirers, they smile on us in the persons of the women we love, they leave no means untried to fetter our hearts and understanding. The Rosicrucians, what are they, one and all, but disguised Jesuits! They wish to impose Catholicism on us, and drive out Protestantism. They wish to mystify the mind, and make the soul grovel in sin and vice, from which condition the victims around whom they have woven their toils will only be permitted to escape by flying to the bosom of the Catholic Church. To the bosom of that Church which offers an asylum to all restless consciences, and dispenses blessings and forgiveness for all vices and crimes. For this reason, these Rosicrucians tempt the good-natured, thoughtless king to luxury and debauchery; for this reason they terrify his mind with apparitions and ghosts! In his terror he is to seek and find safety in the Catholic Church! I see through their disguise; and they know it. For this reason, they hate me; and they cry out against me because I have exposed their wiles and stratagems, and proclaimed that these vile Rosicrucians are Jesuits in disguise, whose object is the expansion of Catholicism over the earth. This I proclaimed in a treatise, which aroused the sleeping, and convinced the doubting, and excited the wrath of the Rosicrucians against me."

"I have heard of it," said Hardenberg, thoughtfully. "I heard of your having hurled a defiant article at the secret societies, through the medium of the 'Berlin Monthly Magazine;' * but, unfortunately, I could never obtain a copy."

"That I can readily believe," said Leuchsenring, laughing; "the dear Rosicrucians bought up the whole edition of the monthly magazine. When the new one is published, they will buy that up, too, in order to suppress the truth. But they will not succeed. Truth is mighty, and will prevail; and we freemasons and brothers of the order of the Illuminati, will help to make truth victorious. We freemasons are the champions of freedom and enlightenment. Many of the most in-

---

* This article appeared in the August number of 1786, and created a great sensation in all classes of society.

fluential and distinguished men of Berlin have joined our order, and are battling with us against the advocates of darkness and ignorance—against the Jesuits and Rosicrucians. We call ourselves Illuminati, because we intend to illumine the darkness of the Rosicrucians, and manifest truth, in annihilating falsehood! My friend, the struggle for which we are preparing will be a hard one, for the number of Rosicrucians and Jesuits is vast, and a king is their protector. The number of the Illuminati is comparatively small; and only the kings of intellect and science, not, however, of power and wealth, belong to our brotherhood. But we shall overthrow the Jesuits, nevertheless. We stand on the watch-tower of Prussia, and our Protestant watchword is Luther's word, 'The Word they shall not touch.'"

"Well said, my gallant friend," cried Hardenberg. "Your ardor inspires me, your enthusiasm is contagious. I will take part in this great and noble struggle. Admit me into your order!"

"You shall become one of us! A meeting of our brotherhood takes place this evening at the house of our chieftain Nicolai. You must accompany me, and I will see that you are admitted."

"And then, when I have become a member of your order, and am enrolled among the number of the enemies of the Jesuits and Rosicrucians, you will no doubt consider it advisable for me to accept the king's proposition?"

"No, my friend, I cannot approve of it; I cannot advise you to do so."

"How? You do not desire me to remain and fight at your side? You despise my assistance?"

"I do not despise your assistance; I only wish to spare you for better times. I have a high opinion of your capacities, and it would be a pity if your usefulness should be prematurely destroyed. But this would be the case if you remained here at present. The Rosicrucians are not only mighty, but are also cunning. They would soon recognize an enemy in the

Minister of State, and would not be slow in relieving him of his office and power. They would pursue the same course with you that they have pursued with me."

"What course have they pursued with you? In what can the instructor of the prince royal have offended—the instructor appointed by Frederick the Great? What harm can the Rosicrucians do him?"

Leuchsenring took up an open letter which lay on the writing-desk, and smiled as he handed it to Hardenberg. "Read this," said he, "it will answer your question."

Hardenberg glanced quickly over the few lines which the letter contained, and then let it fall on the table again with an air of dejection.

"Dismissed!" he murmured. "The body of the late king is hardly under ground, and they already dare to disregard his will, and send you your dismissal."

"They go further," said Leuchsenring, angrily. "They not only dismiss me, but what is still worse, they have appointed a Rosicrucian to fill my position. General Count Brühl has been selected to give the finishing touch to the education of the young prince."

"And you will now leave Berlin, I suppose?" said Hardenberg. "Well, then, my friend, I make you a proposition. You do not desire me to remain here; I now propose to you to accompany me to Brunswick. Save yourself and your ability for better times, save yourself for the future!"

"No, I will remain," cried Leuchsenring, with determination. "I will not afford the Rosicrucians the pleasure of seeing me desert my post; I will defend it to the last drop of my blood. I will remain, and the Jesuits and Rosicrucians shall ever find in me a watchful and relentless enemy. All those brave men to whom God has given the sword of intellect, will battle at my side. The Rosicrucians will bring gloom and darkness over Prussia, but we, the Illuminati, will dissipate this darkness. The vicious and the weak belong to the former, but the virtuous and strong, and the youth of the nation, will join the ranks of the Illuminati. Oh, my friend, this will be a spirit-warfare, protracted beyond death, like the struggles of the grim Huns. The spirits of falsehood must, however, eventually succumb to the heavenly might of truth; and darkness must, at last, yield to light! This is my hope, this is my banner of faith; and therefore do I remain here in defiance of my enemies, the Rosicrucians. This struggle, this spirit-warfare, is my delight—it excites, elevates, and re-freshes me. But when the victory is ours, when the new era begins, when the old has been torn down, and the new Prussia is to be built up, then your time will come, my friend; you shall be the architect selected to erect this stately edifice. For the dark days of the Rosicrucians and King Frederick William, your services are not available. But after these will come the bright days of the young king, and at his side you shall stand as friend and councillor! For, believe me, King Frederick William the Second will only pass over the horizon of Prussia, and darken the existence of the people, like a storm-cloud, with its thunder and lightning. But cloud and darkness will be dissipated, and after this, day will dawn again, and the sun will once more shine. You have come to Berlin to see Prussia's unhappiness, but you shall now see something else. I will show you Prussia's hope, and Prussia's future!—Come!"

He took his friend's arm and led him to the window, which commanded a fine view of the adjoining garden. It was only a plain garden, with walks of yellow sand, and beds of or-dinary flowers. A bench stood under an apple-tree, covered with fruit, on the main walk, and between two flower-beds. On this bench, two boys, or rather two youths, were sitting, attired in plain, civil dress. The one was very handsome, and well-made; his large, bright eyes were turned upward, the loud tones of his voice could be heard at the window, and his animated gestures seemed to indicate that he was reciting some poem, and was carried away with enthusiasm. The other, a tall youth of sixteen, with the soft, blue eyes, the mild countenance, and good-natured expression, was listening attentively to his companion's declamation.

It was the latter whom Leuchsenring pointed out to his friend. "See," said he, "that is the future King of Prussia, King Frederick William the Third, that is to be. At his side you are to stand as councillor; and he will need your advice and assistance. He will reap the bitter harvest which will spring from the seed the Jesuits and Rosicrucians are now sowing. Save yourself for Frederick William the Third, Baron Hardenberg, and do not waste your talents and energies in the unfruitful service of Frederick William the Second."

"The one you point out, the one with the fair hair, and the mild, diffident expression, is then the Prince Royal of Prussia. I wish you had shown me the other, that handsome lad, that youthful Apollo, with the proud smile and piercing eye. I wish he were the future King of Prussia."

"That is Prince Louis, the present king's nephew. You are right, he looks like a youthful Apollo. If he were the future king, he would either lift Prussia up to the skies, or else hurl it into an abyss, for he is a genius, and he will not tread the beaten track of life. No, it is better that his gentle young friend should some day wear the crown of Prussia. They have increased his natural timidity by severe treatment. He has no confidence in himself, but he has good, strong sense and an honest heart, and these qualities are of more importance for a king than genius and enthusiasm. I do not know why it is, my friend, but I love this poor, reserved boy, who has suffered and endured so much in his youth. I love this prince, who has so warm a heart, but can never find words to express his feelings. I pity him, for I know that his youthful heart is burdened with a secret sorrow. I have divined the cause, in an occasional word which escapes his lips unawares, and in his manner at times. It is the sorrow of an affectionate and tender-hearted son, who wishes to love and esteem his father, but dares not look at him, for fear of seeing the spots and shadows which darken that father's countenance."

"Poor, poor lad!" said Hardenberg, moved with sympathy. "So young, and yet such bitter experience! But, perhaps, it is well that such should be the case; if he has received the baptism of tears, and has been anointed with affliction, he may become a king by the grace of God! I will do as you say, Leuchsenring; I will save myself for the future, and, if such be the will of God, I will one day serve your young king of the future."

"And something tells me that God will permit you to do so," cried Leuchsenring, joyously. "It may be that I will not live to see the day. My enemies, the Rosicrucians, may have destroyed, or the storm-wind of the revolution have swept me away by that time; but you will remain, and at some future day you will remember the hour in which I showed you the young prince royal, Frederick William the Third. He is the future of Prussia, and, in the dark day which is now dawning, we are in sore need of a guiding light. Fix your eye on the Prince Royal of Prussia, and on his genial friend, Prince Louis Ferdinand!"

BOOK III.

CHAPTER I.

SCHILLER IN DRESDEN.

"THAT is false, I say; false!" cried Schiller, with glowing cheeks and sparkling eyes, as he walked to and fro in his little room. "It is all slander, vile slander!"

The two friends, the young councillor of the consistory, Körner, and the bookseller, Göschen, stood together in the window recess, gazing sadly and sympathetically at the poet, who rushed to and fro, almost breathless with rage, hurling an angry glance at his friends, whenever he approached them. Suddenly he stopped, and fastened his gaze on them, intently. "Why do you not reply?" asked he, in loud and wrathful tones. "Why do you allow me to accuse you both of a falsehood, without even attempting to justify yourselves?"

"Because we wish to give your just anger time to expend itself," said Körner, in his soft, mild voice. "To our own great sorrow we have been compelled to wound our friend's feelings, and it is quite natural that this wound should smart."

"And we do not justify ourselves against these reproaches, because they do not apply to us," added Göschen, "and because they are only the utterance of your just indignation. Believe me, my friend, we would gladly have spared you this hour, but our friendship was greater than our pity."

"Yes, yes, the old story," cried Schiller, with mocking laughter. "Out of friendship, you are pitiless; out of friendship you give the death-blow to my heart! And what the most cruel enemy would hardly have the courage to whisper in my ear, merciful friendship boldly declares!"

"Schiller, you are deceived! Schiller, the girl you love is a cold-hearted coquette, who does not love you, who only keeps you in leading-strings, in order to extort presents from you, and to be able to say that a poet adores her!"

"But I will give no credit to such unworthy insinuations! My love shall not be regarded as a mere mockery. You shall not have the pitiful triumph of tearing me from the girl I love. I declare to you and the whole world, I love her, I love the beautiful, the admired, the courted Marie von Arnim. To her belong my thoughts, my wishes, and my hopes. She is my ideal of beauty, of youth, and of female loveliness. I exult in this love; it will raise me from the dust of earth to the sphere of the eternal and immortal gods!"

"My poor friend!" sighed Körner, "like your love, the gods only exist in your poetical fancy. Listen to reason, Schiller!"

"Reason!" cried he, stamping the floor, wrathfully. "That means the dry insipidity of every-day life, instead of life's festival, wreathed with flowers. No, I will not listen to reason; for you call it reason to consider it possible that the most divine creature on earth could be a base coquette!"

"Now you go too far, Schiller," said Göschen, eagerly, "no one made such grave accusations against the daughter. We only said of the mother that she misused your love for her daughter, and that she would never consent to your union. We said that the beautiful young lady was aware of this, and continued to receive your attentions, although she knew the gentleman selected by her mother as her future husband, and would finally consent to marry him. As friends, we conceived it to be our duty to tell you this, in order that you might no longer be deceived in your noblest impulses, and continue to throw away your love, your confidence, and your money, on unworthy objects."

"That is the word," cried Schiller, with mocking laughter, "now you have uttered the right word! My money, or rather *your* money, you would say! You tremble for your vile

dross! You made me advances, and Don Carlos is not yet
completed. You now fear that my love might distract my
attention, and draw me from my work, and that the two hundred dollars which—"

"Frederick Schiller!" cried Körner, interrupting him,
while Göschen turned away, his lips trembling, and his eyes
filled with tears; "Frederick Schiller, now you are unjust;
and that, a friend must not be, even in his deepest grief.
Vile dross has nothing to do with this sacrifice of friendship,
and it was not for its sake that we undertook the thankless
office of making the blind see. You well know that Göschen
is a noble and disinterested friend, who rejoiced in being permitted to help the poet of Don Carlos out of his difficulties,
but it is, of course, painful to him to see the loving, confiding
man, squander what the poet earns."

"It is true, it is true!" cried Schiller, "I am unjust! I
reproach you instead of reproaching myself, and myself only.
Oh, my friends, forgive these utterances of my anguish, consider what I endure! You are both so happy; you have all
that can lend a charm to life, and adorn it. You are wealthy,
you do not know what it is to have to contend with want, and
to struggle for existence, nor have you any knowledge of that
more painful struggle, the warfare of life without love, without some being who loves you, and is wholly yours. You, my
friends, have loved and loving wives, who are yours with every
fibre of their being. You have also well-appointed house-
holds, and are provided with all that is requisite to enable you
to exercise a generous hospitality. But, look at me, the solitary, homeless beggar, who calls nothing on earth his own
but that spark of enthusiasm which burns in his heart, who
must flee to the ideal, in order to escape the too rude grasp of
reality. Why must I alone rise from the richly-laden table
of life with unsatisfied hunger? Why are the stars, for me,
merely candles of the night, that give me light in my labors,
and the sun only an economical heating apparatus, to which I
am only in so far indebted as it saves me expensive fuel for

my stove in winter. Grant me my portion of the repast
which the gods have prepared for all mortals, let me also partake of the golden Hesperian fruit. My friends, have pity
on the poor wanderer, who has been journeying through the
desert of life, and would now recline on the green oasis and
rest his weary limbs!" He sank down into a chair, and
covered his quivering face with his trembling hands.

His two friends stood at his side regarding him sorrowfully. Neither of them had the cruel courage to break in
upon this paroxysm of anguish with a word of encouragement
or consolation.

A pause ensued, in which the silence was interrupted only
by Schiller's deep-drawn sighs, and the few indistinct words,
which he from time to time murmured to himself. But suddenly he arose, and when he withdrew his hands from his
face its expression was completely changed. His countenance
was no longer quivering with pain and flushed with anger,
but was pale, and his glance defiant. And when he now
shook back the long yellow hair which shaded his brow, with
a quick movement of the head, he looked like a lion shaking
his mane, and preparing to do battle with an approaching
enemy.

"Enough of these lamentations and womanish complaints,"
said he, in a resolute, hoarse voice. "I will be a man who
has the courage to listen to the worst and defy the greatest
agony. Repeat all that you have said. I will not interrupt
you again, either with complaints or reproaches. I know
that you are actuated by the kindest intentions, and that,
like the good surgeon, you only desire to apply the knife and
fire to my wounded heart in order to heal it. And now,
speak, my friends! Repeat what you have said!"

He walked hastily across the room to the little window,
stood there with his back turned to the room, and beat the
window-panes impatiently with his cold hands.

"Frederick, why repeat what is already burning in your
head and heart?" said Körner, gently. "Why turn the knife

once more in the wound, and tell you that your noble, generous love is not appreciated, not honored? The best and fairest princess of the world would have reason to consider herself happy and blessed, if the poet by the grace of God loved her; and yet his noble, generous love is misused by a cold, calculating woman, and made the means of adorning its object for richer suitors."

"Proofs!" cried Schiller, imperiously, and he drummed away at the window-panes till they fairly rang.

"It is difficult for others to give proofs in such cases," replied Körner, in a low voice. "You cannot prove to the man who is walking onward with closed eyes, that he is on the verge of a precipice; you can only warn him and entreat him to open his eyes, that he may see the danger which menaces. We have only considered it our duty to repeat to you what is known by all Dresden, and what all your acquaintances and friends say: that this Madame von Arnim has come to Dresden to seek a husband of rank and fortune for her daughter, and that she only encourages Frederick Schiller's attentions, because the poet's homage makes the beautiful young lady appear all the more desirable in the eyes of her other suitors."

"An infernal speculation, truly!" said Schiller, with derisive laughter. "But where are the proofs? Until they are furnished, I must be permitted to doubt. I attach no importance whatever to the tattle of the good city of Dresden; to the malicious suppositions and remarks of persons with whom I am but slightly acquainted, I am also quite indifferent. But who are the *friends* who believe in this fable, and who have commissioned you to relate it to me? At least, give me the name of one of them."

"I will at least give you the name of a lady friend," said Göschen, sadly; "her name is Sophie Albrecht, my wife's sister."

Schiller turned hastily to his friends, and his countenance now wore an alarmed expression.

"Sophie Albrecht!" said he, "the sensitive artist—she in

whose house I first saw Marie. Is it possible that she can have uttered so unworthy a suspicion?"

"She it was who charged me to warn you," replied Göschen, with a sigh. "For this very reason, that you first met Madame von Arnim and her daughter in her house, does she consider it her duty to warn you and show you the abyss at your feet. At this first interview, she noticed with alarm how deep an impression the rare beauty of Miss von Arnim made on you, and how you afterwards ran blindly into the net which the old spider, the speculative mother, had set for you. This Madame von Arnim is the widow of a Saxon officer, who left her nothing but his name and his debts. She lives on a small pension given her by the king, and has, it seems, obtained a few thousand dollars from some rich relative; with this sum she has come to Dresden, where she proposes to carry out her speculation—that is, to keep house here for some little time, and to entertain society, and, above all, rich young cavaliers, among whom she hopes to find an eligible suitor for her daughter. This at least is no calumny, but Madame von Arnim very naively admitted as much to my sister-in-law, Sophie Albrecht, calling her attention to the droll circumstance, that the first candidate who presented himself was no other than a poor poet, who could offer her daughter neither rank, title, nor fortune. When Sophie reminded her that Frederick Schiller could give her daughter the high rank and title of a poet, and adorn her brow with the diamond crown of immortal renown, the sagacious lady shrugged her shoulders, and remarked that a crown of real diamonds would be far more acceptable, and that she had far rather see her daughter crowned with the coronet of a countess than with the most radiant poet's crown conceivable. And she already had the prospect of obtaining such a one for her daughter; the poet's admiration for her beautiful daughter had already made her quite a celebrity."

"You are still speaking of the mother, and of the mother only," murmured Schiller. "I know that this woman is sordid, and that she would, at any time, sell her daughter for wealth and rank, although purchased with her child's happiness. But what do I care for the mother! Speak to me of the daughter, for she it is whom I love—she is my hope, my future."

"My poor friend," sighed Körner, as he stepped forward and laid his hand on Schiller's shoulder. This touch and these words of sympathy startled Schiller.

"Do not lament over me, but make your accusations," cried Schiller, and he shook his golden lion's mane angrily. "Speak, what charges can you prefer against Marie von Arnim? But I already know what your reply would be. You would say that she has been infected by the pitiful worldly wisdom of her scheming mother, and that I am nothing more to her than the ornament with which she adorns herself for another suitor."

"You have said so, Frederick Schiller, and it is so," replied Körner, in a low voice. "Yes, the worldly-wise and scheming mother has achieved the victory over her nobler daughter, and, although her heart may suffer, she will nevertheless follow the teachings of her mother, and make a speculation of your love."

"That is not true, that is calumny!" cried Schiller, violently. "No, no, I do not believe you! Say what you please of the mother, but do not defile her innocent daughter with such vile, unsubstantiated calumny!"

"What proofs do you demand?" asked Göschen, shrugging his shoulders. "I repeated to you what Madam von Arnim told Sophie Albrecht, namely, that a rich suitor had already been found for her daughter."

"Yes, that the mother had found one. But who told you that the daughter would accept him; that Marie was a party to this disgraceful intrigue?"

"Of that you can certainly best assure yourself," said Körner, slowly.

"How can I do that?" asked Schiller, shuddering slightly.

"Does not Miss Marie permit you to visit her in the evening?"

"Yes, she does."

"Only when you see a light at the window of her chamber—the signal agreed upon between you—only then you are not permitted to come. Is it not so?"

"Yes, it is so, and that you may well know, as I told you of it myself. When Marie places a light at that window it is a sign that begs me not to come, because then only the intimate family circle is assembled, to which I certainly do not as yet belong."

"You can, perhaps, assure yourself whether the young lady was strictly accurate in her statement. You intend paying her a visit this evening, do you not?"

"Yes, I do," cried Schiller, joyfully, "and I will fall down on my knees before her, and mentally beg her pardon for the unjust suspicions which have been uttered concerning her."

"I do not believe that she will receive you to-day," said Körner, in a low voice. "This so-called family circle will have assembled again; in all probability you will see a light in the designated window!"

"Why do you believe that?"

"Well, because I happened to converse with several young officers to-day, who are invited to Madam von Arnim's for this evening. They asked if they might not, at last, hope to meet you there, regretting, as Madam von Arnim had told them, that your bashfulness and misanthropy made it impossible for you to appear in strange society. I denied this, of course, and assured them that Madam von Arnim had only been jesting; but they said her daughter had also often told them that Frederick Schiller was very diffident, and always avoided the larger social gatherings. 'If that were not the case,' said these young gentlemen, 'Schiller would certainly appear at Madam von Arnim's the dansante this evening, that is, unless the feelings awakened in his bosom by the presence of Count Kunheim might be of too disagreeable a nature.'"

Schiller shuddered, and a dark cloud gathered on his brow. "Who is this Count Kunheim?"

"I asked them this question also, and the young officers replied that Count Kunheim was the wealthy owner of a large landed estate in Prussia, who had intended remaining a few days in Dresden in passing through the city on his way to the baths of Teplitz. He had, however, made the acquaintance of Miss von Arnim at a party, and had been so captivated by her grace and beauty that he had now sojourned here for weeks, and was a daily visitor at Madam von Arnim's house."

"And she never even mentioned his name," murmured Schiller, with trembling lips, the cold perspiration standing on his forehead in great drops.

"No, she told you nothing about him," repeated Körner. "And this evening Count Kunheim will be with her again, while the little taper will burn for you at the window, announcing that the impenetrable family circle has once more closed around the fair maid and her mother."

"If that were true—oh, my God, if that were true!" cried Schiller, looking wildly around him, his breast heaving with agitation. "If this beautiful, this divine being could really have the cruel courage to—"

He had not the courage to pronounce the bitter word which made his soul shudder, but covered his face with his hands, and stood immovable for a long time; wrestling with his grief and anguish. His two friends did not disturb him with any attempts at consolation. They understood the poet well; they knew that his heart was firm, although easily moved. They knew that after Frederick Schiller had wept and lamented like a child, he would once more be the strong, courageous man, ready to look sorrow boldly in the face. And now but a short time elapsed before the manly breast had regained sufficient strength to bear the burden of its grief. Schiller withdrew his hands from his face, threw his head back proudly, and shook his golden mane.

"You are right, all doubt must be removed," said he; "I will see if the light has been placed at the window!"

He looked at his large silver watch—a present from his father. Its old-fashioned form, and the plain hair-guard with which it was provided, instead of a gold chain, made it any thing but an appropriate ornament for a suitor of Marie von Arnim. "It is eight o'clock," said he—"that is, the hour of reprieve or of execution has come. Go, my friends, I will dress myself, and then—"

"But will you not permit us to accompany you to the house?" asked Körner. "Will you not permit your friends to remain at your side, to console you when the sad conviction dawns on your mind, or to witness your triumph, if it appears (what I sincerely hope may be the case) that we have been misinformed?"

Schiller shook his head. "No," said he, solemnly, "there are great moments in which man can only subdue the demons when he is entirely alone, and battles against them with his own strength of soul. For me, such a moment is at hand; pray leave me, my friends!"

CHAPTER II.

GILDED POVERTY.

THE chandelier in the large reception-room had been already lighted; and in the adjoining room, the door of which was thrown open, the servant hired for the occasion was occupied in lighting the candles in the plated candlesticks, while at a side table a second servant was busily engaged in arranging the cups and saucers, and providing each with a spoon; but he now discontinued his work, and turned to the elderly lady, who stood at his side, and was endeavoring to cut a moderately-sized cake into the thinnest possible slices.

"My lady," said the servant, humbly, "ten spoons are still wanting. Will you be kind enough to give them to me?"

"Ah, it is true," replied the lady, "I have only given you the dozen we have in daily use, and must fetch the others from the closet. You shall have them directly."

"My lady," remarked the first servant, "there are not candles enough. Each of the branched candlesticks requires six candles, and I have only six in all."

"Then you will have to double the number by cutting them in two," rejoined her ladyship, who was counting the slices of cake, to see if she had not already cut a sufficient number.

"Thirty-three," she murmured, letting her finger rest on the last slice. "That ought to be enough. There will be twenty persons, and many of them will not take cake a second time. A good piece will be left for to-morrow, and we can invite Schiller to breakfast with us on the remainder."

At this moment, a red-faced maid, whose attire was far from being tidy, appeared at a side door.

"My lady," said she, "I have just been to the grocer's to get the butter and sugar, but he would not let me have any."

"He wouldn't let you have any?" repeated Madame von Arnim. "What do you mean?"

"My lady," continued the cook, in a whispering voice, and with downcast eyes, "the grocer said he would furnish nothing more until you paid his bill."

"He is an insolent fellow, from whom you must buy nothing more, Lisette," cried Madame von Arnim, very angrily. "I will pay this impertinent fellow to-morrow morning, when I have had my money changed, but my custom I withdraw from him forever. I wish you to understand, Lisette, in the future you are to buy nothing whatever from this man. Go to the new grocer on the corner of Market Square, give him my compliments, and tell him that I have heard his wares so highly praised that I intend to give him my patronage. He is to keep an account of all I purchase, and I will settle with him at the end of each month."

"My lady," said the cook, "as I have to go out again, anyhow, wouldn't it be better for me to run over to the game dealers, in Wilsdruffer Street, and buy another turkey? One will certainly not be enough, my lady."

" But, Lisette," rejoined her ladyship, angrily, " what nonsense is this? When we talked over the supper together you said yourself that one turkey would be quite sufficient."

" Yes, my lady, but you then said that only twelve persons were to be invited, and now there are twenty!"

" That makes no difference, whatever, Lisette! What will well satisfy twelve, will satisfy twenty; moreover, it is not necessary that they should be exactly satisfied. I was invited to a supper, a few evenings since, where they had nothing but a roast turkey, and a pie afterwards. There were twenty-two persons, and although each plate was provided with a respectable piece of the roast, I distinctly observed that half of the turkey was left over. Go, therefore, and get the butter and sugar, but *one* turkey is entirely sufficient.—Every thing depends, however, on the carving," continued her ladyship, when the cook had taken her departure, " and I charge you, Leonhard, to make the carving-knife very sharp, and to cut the slices as thin and delicate as possible. Nothing is more vulgar than to serve up great thick pieces of meat. It makes it look as if one was not in good society, but in some restaurant where people go to eat all they desire."

" My lady knows what my performances are in that line," said the elder servant, simpering; " my lady has tried me before. Without boasting, I can make the impossible, possible. For instance, I carved yesterday, at Countess von Versen's, for a company of twenty-four people, and as a roast, a single hare, but I cut it into pieces that gladdened the heart. I divided the back into as many pieces as there were joints. Eighteen joints made eighteen pieces, I divided the quarters into twenty pieces, making in all thirty-eight, and so much still remained that my lady, the countess, afterward remarked that she would perhaps have another little party this evening, and gave me two groschens extra for my services."

" Carve the turkey so that half of it shall remain," said her ladyship, with dignity, "and I will also give you two groschens extra."

The servant smiled faintly and bowed in acknowledgment of this magnanimous offer. He then turned to the table at which the young servant was occupied in folding up the napkins into graceful figures. "Here are three bottles of white wine, my lady," said Leonhard, thoughtfully. "I very much fear that it will not go round twice, even if I fill the glasses only half full."

"Unfortunately I have no further supply of this variety," said her ladyship, with dignity, "it will therefore be better to take a lighter wine, of which I have several varieties in my pantry. I will take these three bottles back and bring you others." With a bold grasp she seized them and vanished through the side door.

"Do you know what her ladyship is now doing?" asked the experienced servant, Leonhard, his mouth expanded into a broad grin, as he danced through the room in his pumps, and placed the chairs in position.

"She has gone after a lighter wine," replied the younger and inexperienced, who, with commendable zeal, was at this moment transforming the peak of a napkin into a swan's neck.

"After a lighter wine," repeated Leonhard, derisively. "That is, she is on her way to the pantry with her three bottles of wine, a pitcher of water, a funnel, and an empty bottle. When she enters the pantry she will lock the door, and when she opens the door and marches forth, she will have four full bottles instead of three, and only the pitcher will be empty."

The other servant looked up in dismay, heedless of the fact that his swan's neck was collapsing into an ordinary napkin again. "Mr. Leonhard, do you mean to say that her ladyship is diluting the wine with water?"

"Young man, that is not called diluting, but simply 'baptizing,' and, indeed, it is very appropriate that, in Christian society, where every body has been baptized, the wine should also receive baptism. Bear this in mind, my successor."

" Your successor? How so, your successor?" asked the other, eagerly, as he pushed a piece of bread under a napkin, which he had just converted into a melon. " Do you propose to retire to private life, and resign your custom to me, Mr. Leonhard?"

" Such custom as this, willingly," growled Leonhard, " that is, when I have received my money—when her ladyship pays the last penny she owes me!"

" Then she has not paid you for your services?" said the younger, in a faint voice.

" She has been in my debt since I first served her; she owes me for four dinners and eight soirées. She promised to pay each time, and has never kept her word; and I would certainly have discontinued coming, long ago, if I had not known that my money would then certainly be lost. As it is, I now and then receive a paltry instalment of a few groschens. To-day," he continued, " she went so far as to promise me two groschens extra. Promised! yes, but will she keep her word? And it is very evident to me what the end of all this is to be. Her ladyship wishes to be rid of me; and I am to be set aside, little by little, and by you, my friend. To-day, we are to wait on the table together; but the next time she drums a company of matrimonial candidates together, you alone will be summoned. Therefore, I call you my successor. I hope you will profit by my example. It is a fearful thing to say, but nevertheless true, I stand before you as a living example of how her ladyship cheats a noble servant out of his well-earned wages. But patience, patience! I will not leave this field of my renown without having at least avenged myself! I intend to beg her ladyship to pay me; and if she refuses to do so, I will exercise vengeance, twofold, fearful vengeance. Before the company assembles, I will be so awkward as to fall down and break the four bottles of baptized wine—before the company is assembled, because if I did it afterwards, the guests would hear the crash, and know that she had had wine; but if I do it beforehand, nobody will believe that I broke the bottles."

"That is a splendid idea," observed the younger servant, grinning. "I will bear this in mind, and follow your example."

"I told you I was a living example, my successor," said Leonhard, impressively. "You can learn of me how to suffer, and how to avenge your wrongs."

"But you spoke of twofold vengeance. In what will your second act of vengeance consist?"

"The second act of vengeance will be this: in spite of the promised—mark the words of your unfortunate living example—in spite of the promised two groschens, I will not cut the unhappy turkey (which, to judge by the length of her spurs, must have been torn from her family as an aged grandmother) into little, transparent slices, leaving half of it for the next day; but I will cut the whole turkey into pieces, and such great thick pieces, that it will not go round once, and nothing but the neck and drumsticks will be left when her ladyship's turn comes. Bear this in mind for the future, my successor! I am now going to her ladyship with a flag of truce before the battle. If she rejects the conditions on which I consent to make peace, the result will be made known to you by its crashing consequences. I am now going, my successor; and I repeat it, for the last time, I am your living example!"

Gravely nodding his well-dressed and powdered head, the servant glided through the room on his inaudible dancing-shoes, and vanished through the side door, which opened into a small room, connected with the kitchen by a passage. Her ladyship was neither in this room nor in the kitchen, but, as Leonhard had prophesied, had repaired to the pantry and locked herself in. The living example smiled triumphantly, and knocked gently at the door.

"What is it?" asked her ladyship from within. "Who knocks?"

"Only Leonhard, my lady, who has come after the four bottles of wine."

"You shall have them directly," replied his mistress; and Leonhard, whose ear was applied to the keyhole, heard for a moment a sound as of water gurgling through a funnel. Then all was still, and he hurriedly withdrew from the keyhole.

The door was now opened, and Madame von Arnim looked out. "Come in and take the wine; there it stands."

Leonhard danced up the two steps and into the pantry, and laid hold of the bottles, two in each hand.

"And now, my lady," said he, bowing profoundly, and waving his arms slowly to and fro with the bottles, like a juggler who first throws himself into the proper position before beginning his performances; "and now, my lady, I beg that you will graciously accord your humble servant a few moments' conversation."

Her ladyship inclined her head haughtily. "Speak, Leonhard, but be brief; my company will soon arrive."

The younger servant was still at work preparing for the supper; and, while so engaged, was at the same time reflecting on the dangers and uncertainties of life, and particularly on those attending a career so open to the caprices of fortune as that of a valet de place. Suddenly the silence was broken by a loud crash; and the servant rushed to the side door to listen. He could now distinctly hear the angry, scolding voice of her ladyship, and the humble, apologetic murmurs of the cunning Leonhard.

"Yes," said the younger servant, grinning with delight, "he has broken the four bottles of wine! Consequently," he quickly added, his voice subdued to a low murmur, "her ladyship has not paid him, and will probably not pay me either! That is sad, for I bought a pair of new cotton gloves especially for this occasion," said he, surveying his hands.

No, her ladyship had not paid Leonhard; as usual, she had endeavored to console him with promises for the future, and the servant had taken his revenge. With unspeakable satisfaction, he was now engaged in picking up the fragments of glass which covered the floor, perfectly indifferent to the volleys of wrath which her ladyship thundered down upon him from the threshold of the pantry.

"What am I to do now? what can I do?" asked his mistress, finally. "To give a supper without wine is impossible!"

Having cleared the wreck away, Leonhard now arose.

"My lady," said he, with an air of profound deference, "I deeply regret this unfortunate occurrence, and I humbly beg you to deduct the value of these four bottles of wine when you pay me my wages for the four dinners and eight soirées, not including to-day's!"

"That I will do, as a matter of course," rejoined her ladyship; "but what am I to do now!"

"I take the liberty of making a suggestion," murmured the living example, submissively. "In the first instance, your ladyship took from me the three bottles of strong wine, giving me four bottles of a lighter variety instead. Now, as I have had the misfortune to break these four bottles, how would it do to fall back on the original three bottles of strong wine? As I pour out the wine in the pantry, I could baptize it a little, and add some water to each glass. What does your ladyship think of this plan?"

Her only reply was an annihilating glance, which Leonhard received with an air of perfect composure, as her ladyship rustled past him and descended into the kitchen.

CHAPTER III.

MARIE VON ARNIM.

WITH glowing cheeks and sparkling eyes her ladyship passed on, not to the parlor, but through a side door and into a small chamber. It was a plainly-furnished bedroom. It contained two uncurtained beds and a bureau, which stood in front of

the only window through which but little light penetrated
the room from the narrow side street into which it opened.
A young girl of extraordinary beauty was sitting before the
bureau, on which a single candle burned. Her small, lovely
oval head was that of a Venus; the tall, slender and graceful
figure, that of a Juno. In conformity with the fashion of
that day, her dark-brown and shining hair was arranged in
hundreds of little curls, encompassed with a golden band,
which terminated on her forehead in a serpent's head. Her
eyes—the large blue eyes which contrasted so wondrously with
the dark hair—were gazing at the mirror. A sad smile played
about her beautiful, crimson lips, as she looked at the reflection of her own figure, at the lovely, rosy countenance, the
full and rounded shoulders, the arms of dazzling whiteness,
and at the tapering waist, brought out to great advantage by
the closely-fitting blue silk bodice. She wore no ornament
but the golden band in her hair; her jewels were her youth
and her beauty; the tears which trembled on her eyelashes
were more precious gems than were ever mined for in the
depths of the earth, for these came unsought from the depths
of her heart.

She was so completely absorbed in her sadly-sweet dreams
that her mother's entrance was unobserved; and not until
now, when her mother stood at her side, was she awakened
from her reverie.

"What do you wish, mamma?" she asked quickly. "Have
our guests arrived? Am I to go down?" She was about to
rise, but her mother motioned her back with an imperious
gesture.

"Remain where you are, no one has come yet. Lisette
will announce the arrivals as they come. I desire to speak
with you."

Her daughter sighed, folded her hands on her lap, and let
her head fall on her bosom in mute resignation. "I think I
know what you wish to speak about, mother," she whispered.

"That I can readily believe, nor is it at all surprising that

you should," said her corpulent ladyship, as she seated herself
at her daughter's side. "I wish to speak to you of our future
and of your duties. This state of things can continue no
longer! I can no longer endure this life of plated poverty.
I must no longer be exposed to the humiliations I am compelled to suffer at the hands of shoemakers and tailors, grocers
and servants, and the host of others who are dunning me for
a few paltry groschens. My creditors have compelled me to
run the gantlet again to-day, and I have been so annoyed
and harassed that I feel like crying."

"Poor mother!" sighed Marie. "Ah, why did we not remain in quiet, little Pillnitz, where we were doing so well,
where our modest means were sufficient for our support, and
where we were not compelled to gild and burnish our poverty!"

"For the hundredth time I will tell you why we did so,"
rejoined her mother, impatiently. "I left Pillnitz, and
brought you to Dresden, because in Pillnitz there were only
pensioned revenue officials, invalid officers, and a few gray-
headed lawyers and judges, but no young gentlemen, and,
least of all, no marriageable, wealthy gentlemen, for you."

"For me, mamma? Have I ever expressed any longing to
be married?"

"Perhaps not, for you are a simple-minded, foolish dreamer;
but I desired it. I recognized the necessity of making a
wealthy and a suitable match for you."

"If you had recognized this necessity, mother," cried
Marie, bursting into tears, "it was very cruel of you to let any
other than such wealthy, marriageable gentlemen come to our
house. If this is really a matrimonial bureau, we should have
permitted only those to register themselves who possessed the
necessary qualifications."

"I see you are becoming quite sarcastic and bitter," said
her ladyship, shrugging her shoulders. "You have profited
somewhat by your interview with Schiller."

Marie drew back with a quick, convulsive movement, and a
sigh escaped her lips. "You should not have mentioned the

name of this noble man at such a time, at a time when I am again compelled to deceive him."

"Enough of this sentimentalism, Marie," rejoined her mother. "Monsieur Schiller is a very pleasant and agreeable man; he may be a great poet besides, but a suitable husband for you, he is not! He can scarcely earn enough for his own support, and his clothing is not respectable. How did he look when he came here yesterday? You will admit that it is impossible to bring him into the society of rich cavaliers and elegant officers, in his disorderly costume."

"He looked just as he did when we first met him at Madame Albrecht's, and yet you then begged him to visit us. And you it was who afterwards encouraged his visits."

"Nor do I regret having done so," remarked Madame von Arnim, quietly. "Councillor Schiller is a man of high respectability and eminence. Our intimacy with him is of great advantage to us. It proves to the world that we are wise and intellectual ourselves, for otherwise, so intellectual a man would not have selected us as associates. Believe me, this intimacy has greatly advanced our social position; it has called great attention to us, and placed your youth and beauty in the proper light. Gentlemen of the highest standing and greatest wealth now consider it a great honor to be permitted to visit at our house, since they know that Frederick Schiller adores you, each one of them is anxious to achieve the renown of supplanting the celebrated poet in your favor and making you his wife. You have a great many suitors, Marie, and you owe them, in a great measure, to your intimacy with Schiller."

"But that is wrong, that is criminal!" cried Marie, bursting into tears.

"Why so?" rejoined Madame von Arnim, laughing. "He was the alluring bait we used to catch our gold-fishes with; I can see nothing criminal in that. Why was this wise man foolish enough to fall in love with you, as he must have known that a union between you and him is impossible?"

"Why impossible?" asked Marie, quickly; she dried her eyes, and looked defiantly into her mother's complacent, smiling countenance.

"Why impossible? Because you are of too good, too noble a family to ally yourself with a man who is not a nobleman, who has no preëminent rank."

"Mother, Frederick Schiller's rank is higher and more illustrious than that of counts and barons. There are hundreds of princes, counts, and barons, in the German empire, and but one poet, Frederick Schiller. Happy and highly honored throughout all Germany will the woman be to whom Frederick Schiller gives his name, whom he makes his wife."

"Well, that may be," said Madame von Arnim, contemptuously, "but one thing is certain, and that is, that you will never be this woman."

"And why not?" asked Marie, passionately. "If Schiller really loves me, and offers me his hand, why shall I not accept it? Because he is not wealthy? He will know how to convert the treasures of his intellect into millions of money. Until then I can practice economy. My wants are few, and you well know, mother, that I can make a little go a long way. Then, permit me to be happy in my own way. I will tell you the whole truth, mother, I love Frederick Schiller, and, if he asks me to be his wife, I shall be the happiest of God's creatures."

"Nonsense!" rejoined her ladyship. "You will be kind enough to give up all thought of this foolish love, and make up your mind to marry the noble and wealthy gentleman selected for you by your mother."

"Mother," cried Marie, imploringly, "do not be so cruel, have pity on me! Do not compel me to destroy my own happiness, for I tell you that I can only be happy at Schiller's side."

"And why should you be happy?" asked her mother, coldly. "What right have you to happiness above the rest of mankind? Do you suppose I am happy? *I* have never been, and have never imagined I had a *right* to be. Life is a pretty hard nut; in attempting to crack it we break our teeth, and when we at last succeed, we find that it is empty, after all. Whether we are personally happy or not, is a matter of small moment—the one thing is to do our duty to others; and your duty it is, to repay your mother for her sacrifices for yourself and your brother. At your father's death you were both young children, and of course his lieutenant's paltry pension was not sufficient for our support. But I could not let you starve, and it was my duty to give you an education that would qualify you to take the position in society to which your rank entitles you. I did not hesitate for a moment, and, although I was still young, and might have made a second and an advantageous marriage, I gave up all such plans, sold my handsome and costly trousseau, and retired with you to the little town of Pillnitz, where I devoted myself wholly to the education of my children. You know that this is so, do you not?"

"I do," replied Marie, as she grasped her mother's hand and carried it to her lips. "You sacrificed yourself for your children, and they are indebted to you for all that they are."

"Unfortunately, that is not a great deal as yet," said her mother. "Your brother is only a poor second-lieutenant, whose salary is not sufficient for his support, and you are only an indigent young lady of noble birth, who must either become a governess or marry a fortune. My means are now entirely exhausted. Little by little I have sold all the valuables I possessed, my diamonds, my jewelry, and my silverware. I finally parted with my last jewel, the necklace inherited from my mother, in order that we might live in Dresden a year on the proceeds. But the year is almost at an end, and my money also. We cannot maintain ourselves here more than four weeks longer, and then the artistic structure of our social position will crumble over our heads, and all will be over. You will be compelled to earn your own bread, your poor brother will be reduced to the greatest extremities, and your mother will have to take up her abode in a debtors' prison, as, after her well-considered plans have failed, she will have no means to meet the demands of her numerous creditors. All this will be your work, the responsibility rests with you."

"O my God, have pity on me!" sobbed Marie. "Show me the result of all this trouble!"

"The result is, governess or countess," said Madam von Arnim, quietly. "In your weakness you may suppose there could be a third alternative, that of becoming Councillor Schiller's wife. Yet I will never give my consent to such a misalliance; a misalliance is only excusable when gilded over with extraordinary wealth. But Councillor Schiller is poor, and will always remain poor; he is an idealist, and not a practical man. I should like to know what advantage I should derive from having the poet Schiller as a son-in-law. Can he compensate me for my sacrifices? can he replace my jewels, my trousseau, and my silver-ware? You know that he cannot, and never will be able to do so. It is your sacred and imperative duty to compensate and reward me for the sacrifices which I have made for you, and to secure to me in my old age the comfortable existence of which care and solicitude for yourself and your brother have hitherto deprived me. You will marry the rich Count Kunheim. You will receive his attentions in such a manner as to encourage him to offer you his hand, which you will then accept. I command you to do so!"

"But, mother, this is impossible, I do not love the count, I cannot marry him! Have pity on me, mother!" she sank down on her knees, and raised her hands imploringly. "I repeat it; I love Frederick Schiller!"

"Well, then, love Frederick Schiller, if you will," said her ladyship, with a shrug of her shoulders, "but marry Count Kunheim. It is given to no woman to marry the object of her first love, to make the ideal of her heart her husband. You will only share the common lot of woman; you will have to renounce your first love and make a sensible marriage. I can tell you, however, for your consolation, that marriages of the latter sort generally prove much happier in the sequel than these moneyless love-marriages. When hunger stalks in at the door love flies out at the window. On the other hand, the most lovelorn and desolate heart will finally recover, when given a daily airing in a carriage-and-four. Drive in your carriage, and accord me a seat in it; I am weary. I have been travelling life-long on the stony streets, and my feet are wounded! Marie, I entreat you, my child, take pity on the poor mother, who has suffered so much, take pity on the brother, who must give up his career in life, unless we can give him some assistance. He would be compelled to leave the army, and perhaps his only resource would be to hire himself out as a copyist to some lawyer, in order to earn a subsistence. Marie, dear Marie, I entreat you, take pity on your family! Our happiness is in your hands!"

She made no reply, she was still on her knees, had covered her countenance with her hands, and was weeping bitterly. Her mother gazed down upon her without an emotion of pity, her broad, fleshy face and little gray eyes expressed no sympathy whatever.

"Be reasonable, Marie," said her ladyship, after a short interval, "consider the happiness of your mother and brother, rather than the momentary caprice of your heart. Cast aside these dreams, this sensitiveness, and seek your own happiness in that of your family."

"It shall be as you say," said Marie, rising slowly from her knees. "I will sacrifice my own happiness for your sake, but I make one condition."

"And that is—?"

"That all these little mysteries and intrigues be discontinued, and Schiller be told the whole truth. No more signs are to be given requesting him not to come; he is no longer to be made use of and yet denied at the same time. He must not be permitted to hope that his addresses will be accepted; he must learn that they will be rejected. If he should then still desire to visit us, our door must be open to him at all times, and the light must never be placed in my window again to warn him off. This is my condition. Accept it, and I am ready to cover my face with a mask, and play the rôle which the necessities of life compel me to assume."

"I will accept it," replied Madame von Arnim, "although I consider it very impolitic. Schiller's nature is violent, easily excited, and deficient in that aristocratic cultivation which represses all the movements of natural impulse. For instance, if he should come here this evening, a very disagreeable scene might ensue; he would be capable of reproaching me or yourself quite regardless of the presence of others."

"And he could reproach us with justice," sighed Marie, "I am resolved rather to bear his anger than to deceive him any longer."

"But I am not," rejoined her ladyship, "I have a perfect horror of these *scènes dramatiques*. But you will have it so, you made it your condition, and nothing remains for me but to accept it. And now, be discreet, be sensible; induce Count Kunheim to declare himself this evening, if possible, in order that Schiller may hear of your betrothal as a *fait accompli*."

"I will do your bidding," said Marie, with a sad and yet proud smile. "Give yourself no further care, the sweet dream is at end, I have awakened. It is a sad awakening, and I will have to weep a great deal, but my tears shall not accuse you; if I am unhappy, I will not say that you were the cause of my unhappiness. It was God's will, this shall be my consolation; God wills it and I submit!"

"And you do well, and will live to thank me for having prevented you from becoming the wife of a poor German poet. And now, that we have disposed of this disagreeable affair, come to my heart, my daughter, and give me a kiss of reconciliation."

But, instead of throwing herself into her mother's extended arms, Marie drew back. "No," said she, "do not kiss me now, mother; we could only exchange a Judas kiss. Come, give me your hand, mother, and let us go to the parlor to receive our guests. Let us, however, first extinguish this candle."

"Yes, we will, or rather I will carry it with me to the kitchen, where a little more light would not be amiss," said her ladyship, taking the candle from the bureau. "Go to the parlor, my daughter, and receive our guests, I must first go to the kitchen to see if every thing is in order."

They both left the chamber; Marie repaired to the parlor, and her mother passed on to the kitchen, to see if the new grocer had furnished the butter and sugar. To her great relief, she learned that he had, and, elated by this success, she determined to send to the accommodating grocer for a few bottles of wine to replace the broken ones. Nothing more was now wanting for the completion of her soirée! She hastily gave the cook a few instructions, and then returned to the bedchamber with the candle.

"He must not come this evening," said her ladyship to herself; "he might frustrate the whole plan, for Marie is transformed into another being in his presence, and Count Kunheim would not fail to observe that she did not love him. No, the light must be burning—Schiller must be kept away. As the rich Countess Kunheim, Marie will some day thank me for not having kept my promise. Yes, she certainly will!"

She hastened forward to the window and placed the light in a conspicuous place. But what was that! At this moment, a loud peal of laughter resounded in the narrow street beneath the window—a peal of laughter that was so bitter, so mocking, that it startled even her ladyship's fearless heart; it seemed almost like a threat.

Her ladyship now repaired to the parlor to receive her guests, who had begun to arrive, and this disagreeable sensation was soon forgotten. Madame von Arnim greeted each

one of her guests with the same stereotyped smile—the same
polite phrases. She quietly conducted the few old ladies, who
had been invited to give dignity to the occasion, into the
adjoining boudoir, and recruited an invalid major to play
whist with them. And now, after having satisfactorily disposed of these guests, and rendered their gossiping tongues
harmless, she returned to the parlor, and displayed to the
assembled officers and cavaliers the smiling, pleasant countenance of a lady who is ready to become a loving and tender
mother-in-law.—For propriety's sake, a few young women
had also been invited, having small pretensions to good looks,
and of modest attire; such ladies as are commonly termed
friends, and who are nothing more than the setting which
gives additional lustre to the gem. To entertain these friends
was the mission of the second-lieutenants, while the officers
of higher rank and the wealthy cavaliers congregated around
the goddess of their adoration—the lovely Marie von Arnim.

She was now once more the radiant beauty; her countenance was rosy and joyous, her blue eyes were bright and
clear, and bore no evidence of the tears which had flowed back
to her heart. A smile played about her rosy lips, and merry,
jesting words escaped the mouth which but now had uttered
wails and lamentations. Count Ehrhard von Kunheim was
completely captivated by her grace and beauty; his gaze was
fastened immovably on her lovely countenance. The homage
she received from all sides was a flattering tribute to the lady
of his choice—the lady he now firmly resolved to make his
bride. It was very pleasant to see his future wife the object
of so much adoration. He would gladly have seen the whole
world at her feet, for then his triumph would have been so
much greater in seeing himself favored above all the world.

He gazed proudly at the array of rank by which his love
was surrounded; the expressions of admiration were sweet
music in his ear. He mentally determined to address her
this very evening; in a few brief hours it would be in his
power to cry out to his rivals: "The lovely Marie von Arnim

is mine! She is my bride!" How great, how glorious a triumph would that be! It was a pity that *he* was not present! To have carried off this prize before him would have crowned his triumph.

"Miss Marie," asked the count, interrupting the joyous conversation which she was carrying on with several officers, "you have graciously promised to make me acquainted with your protégé, Mr. Schiller? Is he likely to come this evening?"

The smile faded from her lips, the lustre of her eyes was dimmed, and she looked anxiously around, as if seeking help. Her eyes met the keen, threatening glance of her mother, who at once came forward to her assistance; she felt that escape was no longer possible—the hand of fate had fallen upon her.

"I fear Councillor Schiller is not coming," said her ladyship, in her complacent manner.

"No, he is not coming," repeated Marie, mechanically. Regrets, and many praises of the genial poet they so much admired, and whose latest poems were so charming, now resounded from all sides.

"It is really a pity that you have never been able to gratify us by producing this celebrated poet," said Count Kunheim to the beautiful Marie.

With a forced smile, she replied, "Yes, it is really a pity."

"And why is he not coming?" asked several gentlemen of Madame von Arnim. "Pray tell us, why is it this councillor only comes when you are alone, and is certain of meeting no company here?"

"He avoids mankind, as the owl does the light," replied her ladyship, smiling. "We gave him our solemn promise that we would not receive other visitors when he is with us; we promised, moreover, that we would let him know when we had company in the evening by giving him a signal."

"And do you really give him the signal, my lady?" asked Count Kunheim.

"Yes, we do," replied Marie, in a low voice.

"And may I ask in what the signal consists that announces to the man-fearing poet that other mortals have approached his goddess?"

"It is no secret," said Madame von Arnim. "I will tell you, count. The signal is a lighted candle placed at the window of our dressing-room. When he sees this light, he beats a retreat, and turns his back on our house."

"Will he come if no light is burning for him?" inquired Count Kunheim, quickly.

"He will," replied Madame von Arnim, laughing.

"Therefore, if no light should burn in the window, he would come this evening?"

"Certainly he would. He vows that he only lives and thinks when in my daughter's presence; and he would undoubtedly have come this evening if I had not given him the signal."

"But, mother," exclaimed Marie, "you are mistaken; we did not give the signal to-day."

"Then, as you gave no signal, he has simply declined to avail himself of your invitation for this evening," remarked Count Kunheim.

"No, no, count, he has not come, because I gave the signal."

"Not so, my lady," observed a cold, quiet voice behind her; "true, you gave the signal, but he has come nevertheless."

"Schiller!" exclaimed Marie, turning pale, and yet she smiled and her eyes sparkled. She was on the point of hastening forward with extended hands to meet him, but her mother had already interposed her colossal figure between her and the poet, and was gazing at him defiantly, as if to signify her readiness to take up the gauntlet if he should meditate warfare.

"You are heartily welcome, Councillor Schiller," said she, in dulcet tones. "We feel highly honored and are partic-

ularly pleased to have you join us at last on an evening when
we have company. These gentlemen will all be delighted to
make your acquaintance. We were speaking of you when you
entered, and all were regretting that you were not here, and—"

"Of that I am aware," said Schiller, interrupting her. "I
had been standing in the doorway for some time, but you
were conversing so eagerly that no one noticed my presence.
I saw and heard all."

Schiller's voice trembled while uttering these words, and
his countenance was deathly pale.

"Then you heard us all express an ardent desire to make
your acquaintance," said Count Kunheim, stepping forward.
"I esteem myself highly fortunate in being able to gratify
this desire. Permit me to introduce myself. I am Count
von Kunheim."

Schiller did not seem to observe the count's extended hand,
and bowed stiffly; he then looked over toward the window-
niche, to which Marie had withdrawn, and where she stood
trembling, her heart throbbing wildly. How angry, reproachful, and contemptuous, was the glance he fastened on her
countenance! But his lips were mute, and as he now withdrew his gaze, he erected his head proudly, and a derisive
smile quivered on his thin, compressed lips. With this smile
he turned to the gentlemen again, and greeted them with a
haughty inclination of his head, like a king who is receiving
the homage of his subjects. "You expressed a desire to see
me, gentlemen, I am here. The conversation which I overheard, compelled me to show myself for a moment, in order to
correct a little error imparted to you by Madame von Arnim."

"An error?" said her ladyship, in some confusion.
"Really, Mr. Schiller, I am at a loss to understand exactly
your meaning."

"I will make myself understood, Madame von Arnim.
You told these gentlemen that I avoided mankind as the owl
avoids the light. But this is not the case, and I beg these
gentlemen not to credit this statement. I do not avoid man-

kind, and I do not hate my fellow-creatures, but I love them. I love and revere the human countenance, for the spirit of God is reflected in the human eye. I love my fellow-creatures, and although they have sometimes caused me pain, and rudely awakened me from my dreams of happiness, yet, my faith in humanity is unshaken, and—"

"Oh, Schiller," cried Marie, stepping forward from the window-niche, and no longer able to conceal her agitation, "Schiller, give me your hand, tell me—"

"Miss von Arnim," said he, interrupting her, "I have nothing to say to you, I only desire to speak to these gentlemen! I do not wish you to consider me a foolish misanthrope, gentlemen, and therefore, I take the liberty of correcting a second erroneous statement made by Madame von Arnim. She told you that I had exacted of her the promise, to warn me by a signal-light when the ladies were entertaining company, because social intercourse was burdensome and repugnant to me. This is, however, not the case, but exactly the reverse. These ladies, and particularly Miss Marie von Arnim requested me to come here only when the window was dark, and on the other hand never to visit them when I saw a light in the window. Miss von Arnim—"

"Schiller," said she, interrupting him, in a loud and trembling voice, and laying her hand on his arm, "Schiller, I conjure you, go no further!"

"Miss von Arnim also explained to me why she desired this," continued Schiller, as though he had not heard Marie's imploring voice, as though he did not feel the pressure of her trembling hand. "Miss von Arnim told me that on the evenings in which the signal would be given the circle of her mother's nearest relatives would be assembled in the house, in which circle it was impossible to introduce a stranger. Gentlemen, it affords me great pleasure to recognize in you the dear cousins and uncles of this young lady, and I congratulate her on her brilliant and exclusive family party. And now permit me to explain why I dared to enter this house, although the light displayed in the window proclaimed the presence of the family."

"But there was no light at the window," exclaimed Marie, eagerly; "this is an error! I desired that you should come this evening, and on that account it was expressly understood between my mother and myself that no—"

"The light was there," said her ladyship, interrupting her; "I had placed it there! Be still, do not interrupt the councillor; he said he had something to explain.—Continue, sir! Why did you come, although the light was displayed in the window?"

"Because I wished to know what it really meant," replied Schiller, with composure and dignity. "You see, my lady, I am not afraid of the light, and I seek the truth, although I must admit that it is a painful and bitter truth that I have learned to-day. But man must have the courage to look facts in the face, even if it were the head of the Medusa. I have seen the truth, and am almost inclined to believe that the eternal gods must have imparted to me some of the strength of Perseus, for, as you see, I have not been transformed into stone, but am still suffering. And now that I have corrected her ladyship's errors, I humbly beg pardon for having cast a shadow over the gayety of this assembly. It will certainly be for the last time! Farewell, ladies!"

He inclined his head slightly, but did not cast a single glance at the lovely Marie von Arnim; he did not see her faint, and fall into Count Kunheim's arms, who lifted her tenderly and carried her to the sofa, where he gently deposited his precious burden. Nor did he see the friends rush forward to restore the insensible young lady to consciousness with their smelling-bottles and salts. No, Frederick Schiller observed nothing of all this; he walked through the parlor and antechamber toward the hall-door. Near the door stood the 'living example,' looking up with an expression of unspeakable admiration at the tall figure of the poet, who had written his two favorite pieces, "The Robbers," and "Fiesco."

He was so grateful to the poet for having put her ladyship to shame, that he would gladly have knelt down and kissed his feet.

"Oh, Mr. Schiller, great Mr. Schiller," murmured Leonhard, hastening forward to open the door, "you are not the only one whom she has deceived. She has deceived me also; I, too, am a wretched victim of her cunning. But only wait, sublime poet, only wait; I will not only avenge myself, but you also, Mr. Schiller. I will cut the pieces still larger, and the turkey shall not go half around, not half around! I will avenge both myself and Schiller!"

He did not hear a word of what Leonhard had said, for he hurried past him, down the steps, and out into the street. There he stood still for a moment gazing at the lighted windows, until a veil of unbidden tears darkened his vision. The burning tears trickling down his cheeks aroused him. He shook his head angrily, and pressed his clinched hands against his eyes to drive them back; not another tear would he shed. Away! Away from this house! Away!

CHAPTER IV.

SOULS IN PURGATORY.

As if pursued by the Furies, with uncovered head, his yellow locks fluttering in the wind, he rushed onward through the streets, over the long Elbe bridge, past the golden crucifix, which towered in the moonlight, and now along the river bank beneath the Brühl Terrace, following the river, and listening to the rippling waves, that murmur of peace and eternal rest.

The moon threw golden streaks of light on the river, and a long shadow on its bank, the shadow of the poet, who was hurrying on in grief and agony. Where? He did not know, he was not conscious that he was walking on the verge of an open grave; he was only instinctively seeking a solitude, a retreat where the ear of man could not hear, nor the eye of man see him. He wished to be alone with his grief, alone in the trying hour when he would be compelled to tear the fair blossom from his heart, and tread it under foot as though it were a poisonous weed. He wished to be alone with the tears which were gushing from his soul, with the cries of agony that escaped his quivering lips—alone in the great and solemn hour when the poet was once more to receive the baptism of tears, that his poetic children, his poems, might be nourished with the blood that flowed from his wounded breast.

He had now entered the little wood which at that time skirted the river bank a few hundred yards below the terrace. Its darkness and silence was what he had sought, and what he needed. Alone! Alone with his God and his grief! A loud cry of anguish escaped his breast and must have awakened the slumbering birds. The foliage of the trees was agitated by a plaintive whispering and murmuring, as though the birds were saying to the moonbeams: "Here is a man who is suffering, who is wrestling with his agony! Console him with your golden rays, good moon; give him of your peace, starry summer eve!"

Perhaps the moon heard the plaintive appeal of the birds and the spirits of the night, for at this moment it broke forth from the concealing clouds and showed its mild, luminous countenance, and pierced the forest with its golden beams, seeking him who had disturbed the peace of slumbering Nature with the agonized cry of his wakeful, tormenting grief.

There he lies, stretched out like a corpse, or like one in a trance. But the moon sees that he is not dead, not unconscious, and sadly witnesses the tears trickling down his countenance, and hears his sobs and wails, the wails of the genius suffering after the manner of humanity; and yet the spirit of God dwells in his exalted mind, and will give him strength to overcome this grief.

The night sheds a soft light on his tearful countenance, as though it greeted him with a heavenly smile; and the stars stand still and twinkle their greetings to the poet. The mel-

ody of the birds is hushed, and they listen in the foliage, as
though they understood his lamentations.　Schiller had now
raised his head; the stillness and solitude of the night had
cooled the burning fever of his soul.

"Is it then true, am I destined only to suffer and to be deceived?　Years roll on and I have not yet enjoyed the golden
fruits that life promises to man, the golden fruits of Arcadia.
My heart was filled with such joyous anticipations, my soul
longed for these fruits.　Although the spring-time of my life
has hardly begun, its blossoms have already withered.　All is
vanity and illusion!　Falsehood alone can make men happy,
truth kills them like God's lightning!　I have looked thee in
the face again to-day, Truth, thou relentless divinity, and my
heart burns in pain, and my soul is filled with agony.　The
poet is a prophet, my present condition proves it; what the
poet in me sung, the poor child of humanity now experi-
ences; my sufferings are boundless."

He buried his face in his hands, and the moon saw the tears
which trickled out from between his fingers, and heard the
poet's plaintive, trembling voice break in upon the stillness
of the night like the soft tones of an Æolian harp:

> "Ich zahle Dir in einem andren Leben,
> Gieb Deine Jugend mir!
> Nichts kann ich Dir als diese Weisung geben.
> Ich nahm die Weisung auf das andre Leben
> Und meiner Jugend Freuden gab ich ihr!
>
> Gieb mir das Weib, so theuer Deinem Herzen!
> Gieb Deine Laura mir!
> Jenseit des Grabes wuchern Deine Schmerzen!
> Ich riss sie blutend aus dem wunden Herzen,
> Ich weinte laut und gab sie ihr!" *

> * "I will repay thee in a holier land—
> Give thou to me thy youth;
> All I can grant thee lies in this command.
> I heard, and, trusting in a holier land,
> Gave my young joys to Truth.
>
> Give me thy Laura—Give me her whom love
> To thy heart's core endears;
> The usurer bliss pays every grief—above!
> I tore the fond shape from the bleeding love
> And gave—albeit with tears."
>
> 　　　　　　　　　*Sir E. B. Lytton's Schiller.*

"And gave—albeit with tears!" repeated Schiller once more, and a cry of anguish escaped his breast. "Is it then inevitable? Is man born only to suffer, and are those right who assert that life is only a vale of sorrow, and not worth enduring?"

He seemed to be painfully meditating on this question. Nature held its breath, awaiting his answer; even the birds had ceased chirping, and the wind no longer dared to rustle in the tree-tops. In what tones will the Æolian harp of the soul respond? What reply will the poet make to the question propounded by the man?

He looks up at the bright firmament shedding its peaceful beams upon his head; he looks at the stars, and they smile on him. There is something in him that bids defiance to all sorrow and melancholy. A soft, heavenly, and yet strong voice resounds in his soul like the mysterious manifestation of the Divinity itself. He listens to this voice; the pinions of his soul no longer droop; he rises, stretches out his arms towards the moon and the stars, and his soul soars heavenward and revels in the glories of the universe.

"No," he exclaimed, in loud and joyous tones, "no, the earth is no vale of sorrow, it is the garden of the Almighty. No, life is no bauble to be lightly thrown away; the sufferings life entails must be endured and overcome. Give me strength to overcome them, thou indwelling spirit; illumine the darkness of my human soul, thou flame of God, holy poetry! No, it were unworthy the dignity, unworthy the honor of manhood, to bow the head under the yoke of sorrow, and become the slave of melancholy for the sake of a faithless woman. A greeting to you, you golden lights of the heavens! you shall not look down on me with pity, but with proud sympathy! I am a part of the great spirit who created you, am spirit of the spirit of God, am lord of the earth. Down with you, sorrows of earth! down with you, scorpions! I will set my foot on your head, and triumph over you. You shall have no power over me. I am a man; who is more so?"

And exultantly and triumphantly he once more cried out to the night and the heavens: "I am a man!"

It was not the sky which now illumined his countenance, it was the proud smile of victory; the light in his eyes was not the reflection of the stars, but the brave courage of the soul which had elevated itself above the dust of the earth.

"The struggle is over, grief is overcome! I greet thee, thou peaceful tranquil night, thou hast applied the healing balsam to my wounded breast: and all pain will soon have vanished!"

He turned homeward, and walked rapidly through the wood and along the river bank, which was here and there skirted with clumps of bushes and shrubbery.

Suddenly he stood still and listened. It seemed to him that he had heard the despairing cry of a human voice behind some bushes, close to the river bank. Yes, he had not been mistaken, he could now hear the voice distinctly.

Schiller slowly and noiselessly approached the clump of bushes from behind which the voice had seemed to proceed; he bent the twigs aside, and, peering through the foliage, listened.

He beheld a strange sight. He saw before him the river with its rippling waves, and, on its narrow bank, kneeling in the full moonlight, a human form—a youth whose countenance was pale and emaciated, and whose long black hair fluttered in the breeze. His features were distorted with anguish, and the tears which poured down his hollow cheeks sparkled in the light like diamonds. He was partially undressed, and his coat, hat, and a book, which, to judge from its size and shape, appeared to be a Bible, lay at his side on the sand. The youth had raised his bare arms toward heaven, his hands were clasped together convulsively, and in his agony his voice trembled as he uttered these words:

"I can no longer endure life. Forgive me, O God in heaven, but I cannot! Thou knowest what my struggles have been! Thou knowest that I have tried to live—tried to bid defiance to the torments which lacerate my soul! Thou knowest how many nights I have passed on my knees, entreating Thee to send down a ray of mercy on my head, to show me an issue out of this night of despair! But it was not Thy will, Almighty Father! Thou hast not taken pity on the poor worm that writhed in the dust, on the beggar who stretched out his hands to Thee, imploring alms! Then, pardon me at least, and receive me in Thy mercy! I am about to return to Thee; O God, receive me graciously! And thou, thou hard, cruel, joyless world, thou vale of affliction, a curse upon thee—the curse of a dying mortal who has received nothing but torment at thy hands! Farewell, and—"

He arose from his knees, and rushed forward with extended arms toward the deep, silent grave that lay there ready to receive him. Suddenly a strong hand held him as in a vice, he was drawn back and hurled to the ground at the water's edge. It seemed to him that a giant stood before him—a giant whose golden locks were surrounded by a halo, whose eyes sparkled, and whose countenance glowed with noble anger.

"Suicide," thundered a mighty voice, "who gives you the right to murder him whom God has created! Felon, murderer, fall on your knees in the dust and pray to God for mercy and forgiveness!"

"I have prayed to God for weeks and months," murmured the trembling youth, writhing in the dust, and not daring to look up at the luminous apparition that hovered over him like God's avenging angel. "It was all in vain. No ray of light illumined the night of my sufferings. I wish to die, because I can no longer endure life! I flee to death to seek relief from the hunger that has been gnawing at my vitals for four days, and has made of the man a wild animal! I—"

His wailing voice was silent, his limbs no longer quivered; when Schiller knelt down at his side, he saw that his features were stiffened and that his eyes were widely extended and glassy.

Schiller laid his ear on the unfortunate man's breast and felt his pulse. His heart was not beating; his pulse no longer throbbed.

"It is only a swoon, nothing else; death cannot ensue so quickly unless preceded by spasms. Poor unfortunate, forgive me for calling you back to the torment of existence; but we are men, and must not violate the laws of Nature. I must awaken you, poor youth!"

He stretched out his hands to the river, filled them with water, and poured it on his pale forehead, and, as he still lay motionless, he rubbed his forehead and breast with his hands, and breathed his own breath into his open mouth.

Slowly life dawned again, a ray of consciousness returned to the glassy eyes, and the trembling lips murmured a low wail, which filled the poet's soul with sadness, and his eyes with tears of sympathy.

There lay the image of God, quivering in agony; the most pitiful complaint of the human creature was the anxious cry of the awakening human soul, " I am hungry! I am hungry!"

"And I have nothing to allay his hunger with," said Schiller, anxiously; "nothing with which to make a man of this animal."

"Woe is me," groaned the youth, "this torment is fearful! Why did you call me back to my sufferings? Who gave you the right to forbid me to die?"

"Who gave you the right to die?" asked Schiller, with severity.

"Hunger," groaned the youth, "hunger, with its scorpion teeth! If you compel me to live, then give me the bread of life! Bread! Give me bread! See, I beg for bread! I preferred to die rather than beg, but you have conquered me and bowed my head in the dust, and now I am a beggar! Give me bread! Do not let me starve!"

"I will bring you bread," said Schiller, mildly. "But, no, you might avail yourself of my absence to accomplish your dark purpose. Swear that you will remain here until I return."

The unfortunate youth did not reply; when Schiller again knelt down at his side, he saw that he was again in a swoon.

"When he awakens, I will have returned," murmured Schiller. He arose, and ran rapidly to the little inn that stood at the foot of Brühls's Terrace. To his great joy, a light was still burning in the main room, and, when he entered, several guests were still sitting at the table enjoying their pipes and beer. Schiller stepped up to the counter, purchased a loaf of bread and a bottle of wine, and returned with all possible haste to the unfortunate youth, who had resumed consciousness, and was, at the moment of his arrival, painfully endeavoring to raise his head.

Schiller knelt down, and rested the poor youth's head on his knees. "Be patient, my poor friend, I bring relief, I bring bread!"

How hastily did his trembling hands clutch the loaf, and how eagerly did they carry it to his mouth! How radiant was his countenance when he had taken a long draught from the bottle which Schiller held to his pale lips.

The poet turned away, he could not endure this painful sight. Sadly and reproachfully he looked upward.

"O God, Thou hast made Thy world so rich! There is enough to provide a bounteous repast for all! The trees are laden with fruits, and man may not pluck them; the bakeries are filled with the bread of life, and man may not take, although he is starving. He sinks down in the death agony while the rich usurer drives by in his splendid equipage, and looks down proudly and contemptuously upon the unhappy man whose only crime is that he is poor. O eternal, divine Justice, it is in vain that I seek thee behind the clouds. I look for thee in vain in the palaces of the rich, and in the huts of the poor!"

"Ah, how refreshing, how delightful was this bread and wine!" sighed the unfortunate youth. "You are my saviour, you have freed me from torment. I thank you! Let me kiss this merciful hand!—You will not permit me, you withdraw it? You despise me, the suicide, the coward? You have a right to do so!"

"No," said Schiller, gently, "I do not despise, I pity you. I also have suffered, I also have felt the scorpion stings of poverty. No, I do not despise you. All men are brothers, and must aid one another. All cares are sisters, and must console one another. Speak my brother, tell me, how can I aid you? Unburden your bosom to my sister soul, and I will try to console you."

"You are an angel-messenger from God," sobbed the young man. "Your lips speak the first words of sympathy I have heard for long months. I could bathe your feet in tears of gratitude. Yes, my brother, you shall hear the sad history of my life, and then you will perhaps justify, perhaps pardon, the crime I was about to commit. Oh, my brother!"

Schiller seated himself at his side on the river bank, and the pale youth rested his head on the poet's proffered shoulder. A pause ensued. While he who had but just returned from the gates of death, was endeavoring to collect his confused and wandering thoughts, the voice of pity was resounding in the heart of him who had been stronger than his brother in the hour of trial, who had bid defiance to misfortune, and with manly fortitude had overcome grief. His heart was filled with sympathy for his weaker and less courageous brother, who had desired to flee from life because his soul lacked the pinions which had borne the poet aloft, above the dust and misery of earth.

"How can he fly to whom the Almighty, the Omnipresent, has not given the pinions of enthusiasm? He must crawl in the dust, his only thought is the gratification of his animal instincts, and like an animal he must live and perish. For him from whom God withholds this heavenly ray, all is night and darkness—no stars shine for him; it were well he sought safety in the silence of the grave, in a cessation of torment! I thank Thee, O God, for the strength Thou hast given, for the ray of light Thou hast sent down to illumine my dark path in life!"

These words did not pass Schiller's lips, they were only uttered in the depths of his soul. He looked up at the moon and stars, journeying in unchangeable serenity on their heavenly course. "Smile on, smile on! You know nothing of man's sufferings. The eternal laws have marked out your course. Why not ours, too? Why not man's? Why must we wander in the desert of life, seeking happiness, and finding pain only! We conceive ourselves to be godlike, and yet we are no more than the worm that writhes in the dust, and is trodden under foot by the careless passer-by."

These were the thoughts that passed through Schiller's mind, while the pale youth at his side was narrating, in a voice often interrupted by sobs and tears, the history of his sufferings.

It was a simple, unvarnished story of that suffering and want altogether too proud to seek sympathy or relief. A story such as we might daily hear, if our ears were open to the mute pleadings that so often speak to us in the pale, care-worn countenances of our fellow-travellers in the journey of life. Why repeat what is as old as the world! A shipwrecked life, a shipwrecked calling! There was that in this son of poverty which urged him to the acquisition of knowledge; he believed his mind endowed with treasures, and his ambitious heart whispered: "You will one day be a renowned preacher! God gave you inspiration; inspiration will give you the words with which to move the hearts of men!" He was the son of a poor tailor, but his father looked with pride on the boy who always brought home the best testimonials from his school, and who was held up to the other scholars as a model of diligence. It would be an honor for the whole family if the tailor's son should become a learned man and a pastor. All that the parents could save and earn by hard work they willingly devoted to the education of their son, that he might become a scholar, and the pride of his family.

What is there, that is glorious and beautiful, which parental love does not hope for, and prophesy for the darling son?

Young Theophilus had passed his examination with honor, and had repaired to the university in Leipsic to continue his studies when the sad intelligence of his father's death reached him, summoning him back to Dresden, to his mother's assistance. He now learned, what he, the student who had lived only in his books, had hitherto had no knowledge of whatever. He learned that his affectionate father had contracted debts, and pawned all that he possessed, in order that his son's studies might be promoted. When the father found it no longer possible to assist his son, he had died of grief. And now the usurers and creditors came and took possession of every thing, regardless of the distressful cries of the unhappy mother, and the protestations of her despairing son. The law awarded them all, and they took all! Theophilus had reason to esteem it almost a blessing when his mother followed her husband to the grave a short time afterward. In the hospital of the Ursuline Sisters, he had at least found shelter for her, and six days afterward she found rest in her last abode in the narrow coffin accorded her by charity.

But where was a refuge to be found for the poor son who had so suddenly been driven from the study into the desert of life, where he could find no oasis in which to refresh himself and rest his wearied limbs? At first he refused to be discouraged, and struggled bravely. So little is needed to sustain life! and for this little he was willing to give all the knowledge acquired by honest diligence. He applied to the rich, to the learned, to artists; he offered his services, he wished to give instruction, to teach children. But, where were his recommendations? What guaranties had he to offer? The man who sought work was taken for a beggar, and the persons to whom he applied either turned their backs on him, or else offered a petty gratuity! This he invariably rejected; he wished to work, he was not a beggar. His unseasonable pride was ridiculed, his indignation called beggar insolence! Long

days of struggling, of hunger, and of humiliations; long
nights without shelter, rest, or refreshment! This little
wood, on the river bank, had been his bedchamber for a long
time. Here, on the bed of moss, accorded him by Nature,
he had struggled with despair, feeling that it was gradually
entwining him in its icy grasp! Finally, it held him as in a
vice, and he felt that escape was no longer possible. Hunger
had then spoken to him in the tempter's voice, and whispered
to his anxious soul that crime might still save him; it whispered that he could not be blamed for a theft committed
under such circumstances, and hard-hearted society would
alone bear the responsibility. Then, in his anguish, he had
determined to seek refuge, from the tempter's voice, in death,
in the silent bed of the river.

Theophilus narrated this sad history of his sufferings with
many sighs and groans. He painted a very gloomy picture
of his life, and Schiller was deeply moved. He laid his hand
on the poor youth's pale brow and looked upwards, an expression of deep devotion and solemn earnestness depicted in his
countenance.

"Thou hast listened to the wails of two mortals to-day,
thou Spirit of the Universe. The one spoke to Thee in the
anger of a man, the other in the despairing cry of a youth.
Impart, to both of them, of Thy peace, and of Thy strength!
Give to the man the resignation which teaches him that his
mission on earth is not to be happy, but to struggle; teach
the youth that the darkest night is but the harbinger of coming day, and that he must not despair while in darkness and
gloom, but ever look forward hopefully to the coming light."

> "Thou hast had Hope—in thy belief thy prize—
> Thy life was centred in it,"

murmured Theophilus, smiling sadly.

Schiller started and looked inquiringly at the youth, who,
in so strange a coincidence of thought, had given expression
to his despair in lines taken from the same poem from which
the poet had repeated a verse in his hour of trial.

"Are the lines you have just uttered your own?" asked
Schiller.

"No," replied the youth, softly, "from whence should such
inspiration come to me. The lines are from Schiller's poem,
'To Resignation,' from the pen of the poet who is the favorite
of the gods and muses, the poet who is adored by all Germany."

"Do you know this Frederick Schiller, of whom you speak
with such admiration?"

"No, I have never seen him, nor do I desire to see him! I
love and adore him as a sublime spirit, as a disembodied
genius. I would, perhaps, envy him if he should appear before me in human form."

"Envy him, and why?"

"Because he is the chosen, the happy one! I do not wish
to see the poet in bodily form; I do not wish to know that he
eats and drinks like other men!"

"And suffers like other men, too," said Schiller, softly.

"No, that is impossible!" cried Theophilus, with vivacity.
"His soul is filled with Heaven and the smiles of the Divinity; he cannot suffer, he cannot be unhappy!"

Schiller did not reply. His head was thrown back, and he
was gazing up at the heavens; the moon again shone on his
countenance, and the starlight sparkled in the tears that
rolled slowly down his cheeks. "He cannot suffer, he cannot
be unhappy!" he repeated in a low voice. It seemed to him
that a transformation was going on within himself, that he
was growing larger and stronger, and that his heart had laid
on a coat of armor. He sprang from the ground, stood
proudly erect, and shook his arms aloft. "Here truly is
manly strength, the sinews are tightly drawn, the muscles are
firm; a genius has selected this breast as its abode, to give it
strength to shake off the burden of sorrow." He felt that his
good genius had conducted him to this unhappy man, that he
might be taught that the strong alone can bear pain, and that
the weak must succumb under the rod of affliction. His

heart was filled with pity for the weak brother at his side. "It was God's will that I should save you from death; in so doing, I however contracted the obligation to preserve your life. I will meet this obligation. Tell me, what were your plans before your father's death?"

"I hoped, when I should have finished my course at the university, to enter some family as teacher, where I could, in time, earn enough to enable me to go to the Catholic Seminary in Cologne, and maintain me there, while completing my studies."

"You are a Catholic?"

"My father was from the Rhine, and my mother was of Polish extraction. Both were Catholics, and it was their fond hope that their son might some day receive ordination and become a priest of the Catholic Church. It seems, however, that I have only been ordained to misery, and I could veil my head and die in shame and remorse!"

"Young man, this is blasphemy, you forfeit God's grace when you speak in this manner. He sent me here to save you, and with his aid I will not leave my task uncompleted. How much will enable you to prepare yourself for your future career?"

"The sum that I require is so great that I scarcely dare mention it."

"Would one hundred dollars be sufficient?"

"That is far more than I need, more than I ever possessed!" cried Theophilus, almost terrified.

"If I should promise to give you this amount—to give it to you here, at this same place, and at this hour, in a week from to-day, would you swear to wait patiently and hopefully until then, and to make no further wicked attempt on your life?"

"I would swear to do so," replied Theophilus, in a trembling and tearful voice.

"By the memory of your father and mother?"

"By the memory of my father and mother!"

"Well, then, my brother, with God's help I will bring you the money in a week from to-day. I would say to-morrow, if I had the money; but I am poor, like you, my brother. No, this is hardly true. I am rich, for I have friends, and these friends will furnish the money you require, if I entreat them to do so."

"You will narrate my history to your friends?" said Theophilus, blushing.

"That I will have to do, in order to awaken sympathy, but I will not mention your name, nor will I so closely narrate the circumstances that they can possibly divine of whom I am speaking. Moreover, you told me that you had no friends or acquaintances in Dresden?"

"True," sighed Theophilus, letting his head sink on his breast, "misfortune knows itself only, and cares are its only friends. It conceals its wounds, and hides itself in darkness. But I have no longer the right to be proud; I bow my head in humility. Plead my cause, my noble, generous friend, my saviour! God's mercy will give you eloquence, and the consciousness of having saved a human being from disgrace and crime will make your words irresistible. My heart is filled with the joyful conviction that God has sent you as a messenger of peace and reconciliation. I will believe in, and confide in you; I will live, because you tell me to live!"

"Live, my brother, and hope!" said Schiller, gently. "Await me at this place, and at this hour, a week from to-day; I hope to bring you the money. But you must have something with which to purchase the necessaries of life until then. Here, my brother, take all that I have in my purse. I have only four dollars, but that sum will suffice to provide you with food and lodging."

Theophilus took the money, and kissed the giver's hand. "I have proudly rejected the gifts offered me by the rich, preferring to die rather than receive their heartless charity. But from you, brother Samaritan, I humbly accept the gift of love. I willingly burden myself with this debt of gratitude."

"Let us now separate," said Schiller. "In a week we meet again. But *one* request I desire to make of you."

"You have but to command, and I will obey you implicitly."

"I beg you not to attempt to find me out, or to learn who I am? We have seen each other's countenances in the moonlight, but they were covered with a golden veil. Do not attempt to remove this veil in the light of day, and to learn my name. I feel assured that you will make no mention of this incident of to-night, but I also desire to avoid meeting you in future. I therefore beg you not to go out much in Dresden, and not to frequent the main streets of the city. If we should meet, my heart would prompt me to extend my hand and speak to you, and that would not be desirable."

"Further down on the Elbe there is a little inn where I can board cheaply. From here I will go to this inn and there remain till the appointed hour. I will not go near the city."

"Good-night, brother!" said Schiller, extending his hand. "Here we shall meet again. And now, turn you to the left, and I will turn to the right. May good spirits watch over us till our return!"

CHAPTER V.

SEPARATION.

SCHILLER walked homeward with rapid strides. The streets of the city were silent and deserted, and the houses enveloped in darkness. He passed by the house in which she lived for whom he had suffered so much. He did not look up, but his head sank lower on his breast, and a feeling of unutterable sadness came over him; but he had no pity for himself, not a single sigh or complaint escaped his breast.

A sensation of chilliness crept over him as he now entered his solitary dwelling. No one was there to extend the hand of sympathy and bid him welcome. His two friends had awaited his return for a long time, but had finally gone home. They knew their friend's disposition, they knew that Schiller always avoided men when his passions were aroused, and sought out some solitude where no eye could witness his struggle to subdue them.

"He very probably has gone to Loschwitz, to spend a few days in the pavilion in which he wrote 'Don Carlos,'" said Körner. "His genius always directs the poet aright, and he possesses the healing balsam for his wounds in his own breast. I will go to Loschwitz myself, to-morrow, to see if he is there, and to make a few inquiries as to his condition. If I find him there I shall leave him to himself till his agitation and passion have subsided, and he voluntarily returns to his friends."

"But if he is not there?" said Göschen, anxiously, as they stepped out into the street. "I never before saw Schiller in so violent a state of excitement. If this fearful awakening from his delusion should overcome him—if in his despair he should—"

"Do not conclude your sentence," said Körner, interrupting him, "do not utter that terrible word. Do not insult your absent friend; remember that he is a genius. He will not yield to despair like an ordinary man; his soul will soon recover its buoyancy."

But for this night, at least, Körner's prophecy was not destined to be fulfilled. True, Schiller had overcome despair, but the pain still rankled in his breast. The bed on which he threw himself in his physical exhaustion was a bed of pain. His thoughts and remembrances were the thorns that pierced his heart, and drove sleep from his couch.

He arose the next morning at a late hour in a state of feverish excitement, entered his plainly-furnished parlor, and looked gloomily around him. But yesterday his parlor had looked so cosey and comfortable, to-day it seemed so bare and desolate. Those flowers in the little vase were but yesterday so bright and fragrant, to-day they were faded. The books and papers on his table were in the greatest disorder. The appearance of the room awakened in Schiller the sensation of sadness and desolation we experience on entering the deserted room of a dear friend who has suddenly left us.

Yes, joy, love, hope, and enthusiasm, had departed from this room; it now looked dreary and desolate. How can we work, how can we write poetry, without enthusiasm, without joy?

"Elegies on a faithless sweetheart," said Schiller, in loud, mocking tones. "A tearful poem, with the title: 'When last I saw her in the circle of her suitors;' or 'The amorous swain outwitted!'"

He burst into laughter, stepped to the window, and commenced tapping on the panes with his fingers, as he had done when Körner and Göschen first aroused his suspicions concerning his love. He was now reminded of this; he hastily withdrew his hands and walked back into the room. But he suddenly recoiled, and uttered a cry of dismay, as though he had seen a ghost. Marie von Arnim stood in the doorway, pale but composed, her large blue eyes fastened with an imploring expression on Schiller's countenance.

She gave him no time to recover from his surprise, but locked the door behind her, threw her bonnet and shawl on a chair, and walked forward into the the room.

"Schiller," said she, in a soft, trembling voice, "I have come because I do not wish you to despise me, because I do not wish the thought of me to leave a shadow on your memory."

He had now recovered his composure; a feeling of anger raged in him and demanded utterance.

"What is there surprising in your coming? Why should you not have come? Ladies of rank go in person to their tailors and shoemakers when they desire to make purchases or leave orders, why should you not come to a poet to order a nuptial poem. I am right in supposing that the young lady

wishes me to write a poem in honor of her approaching nup-
tials with Count Kunheim, am I not? I am also right, I
believe, as regards the name of that favored member of the
exclusive family circle of yesterday, who is destined to become
that young lady's husband?"

"Yes, you are," she replied, softly. "You see, Schiller, I
have not interrupted you, but have received your words as the
penitent receives the blows of the rod, without complaint or
murmur, although blood is streaming from her wounds. But
now be merciful, Schiller! let this punishment suffice, and
listen to me!"

"I know what the substance of the poem is to be," observed
Schiller, in the same threatening voice. "Undoubtedly you
desire a sort of illustration of the courtship, from the first
meeting down to the avowal, and then the golden honeymoon
is to be painted in brilliant colors. Probably it would meet
your wishes if a comical feature were also introduced; for instance: a poor poet, who, in his absurd conceit, had dared to
consider himself Count Kunheim's equal, and who, acting on
this belief, had even dared to fall in love with the beautiful
young lady, who, of course, only laughed at his presumption."

"No, Schiller, who would have been the proudest and happiest of women if circumstances had permitted her to avow
her love freely and openly."

"Yes," cried Schiller, gruffly, "circumstances are always
the scapegoats of the weak and faithless. I, however, admit
the difficulties arising from the circumstances by which you
were surrounded in this instance. You were making use of
the poet's love to allure richer suitors into your toils, a game
requiring some finesse. My rôle was neither a flattering nor
a grateful one, but yet it was a rôle, and a dramatic poet cannot expect to have good ones only. But enough of this! Let
us speak of the poem. When must it be ready?"

"Schiller," she cried, almost frantic, tears streaming from
her eyes, "Schiller, will you have no pity on me?"

"Did you have pity on me?" asked he, with a sudden

transition from his mocking to an angry tone of voice, and regarding Marie, who had folded her hands humbly, and was looking up at him entreatingly, with glances that grew darker and angrier as he spoke. " I ask you, did you have pity on me? Did it never occur to you, while engaged in your shrewd calculation, that you were preparing to give me a wound for which there is no cure? When two loving hearts are torn asunder by death or the hand of fate, the pain can be borne, and time may heal the wound; when the cruel laws of human society compel us to separate from those we love, a consolation still remains. The sacred, the undimmed remembrance of past hours of bliss, and the hope that time, the great equalizer, may remove all obstacles, still remains. But what consolation remains to him who has been cheated of his love, his enthusiasm, and his ideal?—to me, over whose heart the remembrance of this deception lies like a pall? From whence am I to derive faith, hope, and confidence, now that you, whom I loved, have deceived me? You have not only destroyed my happiness, but you have also offended the genius of poetry within me. Henceforth all will seem cold and insipid. The word 'enthusiasm' will ring in my ear like a mockery. I will even mistrust the vows of fidelity uttered by the lips of my dramatic creations; for, now that you have so shamefully deceived me, there is no longer any thing noble, pure, and beautiful."

He hurled a last angry glance at her, and then turned away, walked to the window and looked out into the street. Marie von Arnim followed him and laid her cold, trembling hand on his arm.

" Schiller, if I were really the woman you take me to be, would I have come to you at the risk of being observed by others—at the risk of its becoming known throughout the city that I had visited you? I have come, Schiller, because I was unwilling that the most beautiful music of my life should end in discord, because I was unwilling that you should remember me with anger, when I only deserve commiseration."

"Commiseration!" repeated Schiller, shrugging his shoulders.

"Yes," she continued, in a soft voice, "yes, I deserve it. I am not bad, not faithless, and not false. I am only a poor girl whose heart and hands have been fettered by fate. A poor girl who cannot do what she would, but must obey God's command and submit to her mother's will. Do not require me to acquaint you with all the misery which afflicts my family, with the cares and humiliations which those must suffer who cover their want with a veil of wealth, and polish and plate iron poverty till it has the appearance of golden plenty. Believe me, Schiller, we are so poor that we do not know how we are to escape from our importunate creditors."

"And yet, you gave agreeable dinners, and entertained the exclusive family circle at delightful suppers," observed Schiller, jeeringly, and without even turning to look at Marie, who stood behind him.

"My mother would have it so, Schiller. She had sold her last jewels in order that she might be able to come to Dresden, where she hoped to marry her daughter to a fortune. Schiller, you will believe me when I swear that I knew nothing of this, and that my first and greatest joy on coming to Dresden was experienced when I made your acquaintance, and when you honored me with your notice! Schiller, I have dreamed a sweet, a blissful dream."

"And the light in the window was the night-lamp in this dream," he observed, in mocking tones.

"I make no attempt to justify myself," said she, gently. "My mother gave me her commands, and I was compelled to obey. When she yesterday declared to me that the only issue out of all her troubles was for me to accept Count Kunheim's addresses, and begged me to do so, I only consented after a long and fruitless struggle, after many tears and entreaties. I yielded to my mother's commands, but I exacted this condition: Schiller must now learn the whole truth, these little mysteries must cease, and no light shall be placed at the window this evening, requesting him not to come. This, my mother promised, but she was cruel enough to break her promise."

"So that I should still wander about, a deluded and credulous simpleton, if I had not broken through the barriers of the exclusive family circle in defiance of the warning light."

"I am thankful that fate willed otherwise, and frustrated my mother's intentions," said Marie, gently. "When we are compelled to deny any one the happiness we would so willingly accord, it is our duty to tell him the truth, although it may be painful. Truth is a two-edged sword; it not only wounds him who hears, but him also who imparts it. I have come, Schiller," continued Marie in an agitated voice, after a short pause, "to take leave of you—to say to you: Schiller, we shall never meet again in life, let us part in peace!"

"Never again!" murmured he, slowly turning his countenance toward the woman, who had heretofore looked so bright and joyous, so radiant with youth and beauty, and who now stood at his side so humble and submissive, her tearful eyes raised imploringly to his.

"Never again!" sighed Marie. "Our paths in life will henceforth be widely separated. I intend to marry the man whose wealth will save my mother and brother. I will be to him a faithful and grateful wife, although I may not be a loving one. I am to be affianced to Count Kunheim at noon to-day, and I have employed the last hour of my liberty in coming here to take leave of you, Schiller, and to beg forgiveness for the pain inflicted on you, of which I am the innocent cause."

"The innocent cause!" cried Schiller, turning around and staring at her with his large, flaming eyes. "How can you say that you are the innocent cause of the pain which you inflicted on me? You knew that I loved you. I told you so, and you listened to my avowal. You gave me hope, although you must have known that my love was hopeless."

"You speak of yourself only," rejoined Marie, in low and

trembling tones. "You are not thinking of me at all; it does not occur to you that I also have suffered, that I also have hoped. Yes, Schiller, I did suppose that my mother would yield to my prayers and entreaties; even yesterday I conjured her on my knees to permit me to seek my own happiness in my own way, as my heart prompted. At that time I was not aware that my mother's circumstances were so desperate. I knew not that her honor and even her liberty were endangered. When she admitted that such was the case, when she disclosed the whole sorrowful truth, I felt as though my heart would break, as though all the blossoms of my future had suddenly faded. The conviction forced itself upon me that it was my duty to sacrifice, to my mother's welfare, my own wishes and hopes. I did my duty; I gave up my own happiness to save my mother—to secure, at least, a ray of sunshine in the evening of her life. I have submitted. I will become the wife of Count Kunheim."

"And will say to him that you joyfully accept and reciprocate his generous love!"

"No, I will not tell this noble man a falsehood, nor have I done so. When he yesterday evening offered me his hand, I told him honestly and openly that I esteemed and confided in him, and would be a very thankful and faithful wife, but that my heart was no longer free—a love dwelt therein that could never die, for it was Schiller whom I loved!"

"You told him that?" asked Schiller, with emotion. "And he—"

"He agreed with me that the heart which loved Schiller could never forget him, but added that he would only esteem me the more, and could never be jealous on account of this love. He said that my love for Schiller should be the altar of our married life and of our house—the altar to which we would bring the fruits of our noblest thoughts and feelings."

"Noble, generous man!" cried Schiller, "Yes, he deserves to be happy and to possess you. Be his wife, Marie, and do your duty. Let the early blossom of your heart fade, and let the full summer-rose of your love bloom for your husband. You can do so, Marie, for—I say it without anger or ill-will—you have never loved me! No, do not contradict, do not attempt to assure me that such is not the case. In this hour, when my soul is elevated above all selfish wishes and desires—in this hour, I rejoice in recognizing the fact, *you have never loved me.* I know that a kind Providence has thus spared you the pain I now endure; I know you will be happy at the side of the noble and high-souled man who demands your hand in marriage. I do not mean to say that you will soon forget me; I think too well of myself to believe this. No, you will yet shed tears when you think of him who loved you, but the bridegroom will be there to dry these tears. With tender sympathy he will speak to you of your love, as of a beautiful dream of the spring-time, and you will find that the awakening from this dream on a bright, flowery summer day, is also beautiful, and that will console you. Some day, after many years, when my pain has long since vanished, and I have gone home to the unknown land from whence no traveller returns—some day, when your weeping children and grandchildren surround your couch, and you feel your last hour approaching, you will once more remember this dream of the spring-time. It will greet you like a ray of sunshine from the new life that is dawning. With a smile on your lips, you will turn to your children and say: 'I leave you gold and treasures, a brilliant name and high rank. But I leave you a more precious legacy. Schiller loved me, and a poet's love is a blessing that is inherited from generation to generation. Your father's name gives you rank and honor before men, but the love which the poet consecrated to your mother gives you renown and immortality. Strive to be worthy of this love. Go to the grave of the poet who died in solitude and poverty, and pray for him!'"

"No, Schiller, that will not be all that I say to those who will some day surround my death-bed," said Marie, drying her tears, in order that her large, luminous eyes might gaze at his sad countenance more fully and firmly. "I will say to them: 'I am now returning to God, and to my first, my imperishable love. In death I may proudly and joyfully confess I have loved Schiller! I still love him!'"

The poet, as if irresistibly attracted by her enthusiasm and her glowing countenance—hardly knowing what he did—extended his arms toward Marie. She threw herself on his breast; he pressed her gently to his heart, and let his hand rest lovingly on her head.

It was a silent and solemn moment, a last blissful and sorrowful embrace. Their lips were dumb, but their hearts communed in holy thought and prayer.

After a pause, Schiller gently raised up between his hands the head that was still resting on his breast; he gazed long and lovingly into the fair girl's countenance. The tears that flowed from his eyes fell on hers like glowing pearls, mingling with her own tears and trickling down her cheeks. Schiller bowed his head, and kissed the lips that responded warmly to his own. He then pressed her hands to his eyes and released her from his embrace.

She turned slowly, walked toward the door, and put on her shawl and bonnet. "Farewell, Schiller!"

"Farewell, Marie!"

And now she stood in the doorway, her eyes fastened on him in a last lingering look. He stood silently regarding her.

A grating noise broke in upon the silence; it was the closing door behind which Marie had vanished. Schiller remained standing at the same place, his eyes fixed on the door. Had it suddenly grown so dark? was the sun overcast? or was it only the tears in his eyes that made the room look so gloomy? Had a storm suddenly arisen? did an earthquake make the ground tremble beneath him? or was it only the storm of passion that was passing over his head? Why was it that his knees trembled, and that he would have fallen to the ground had not a chair stood near by, into which he sank, groaning?

The hour in which a man wrestles with his agony—the hour of renunciation and conquest, is sacred; the eye of God only may witness it, but no tongue must attempt to describe it, unless indeed that of the poet whose pain is surrounded by the halo of poetry—the poet to whom the hour of renunciation has also become the hour of enthusiasm.

Some one is weeping and lamenting behind that door. Is it Marie?

Some one is speaking in loud and earnest tones behind this door. Is it the poet composing an inscription for the gravestone of his love?

> " Give me thy Laura—give me her whom love
> To thy heart's core endears;
> I tore the fond shape from the bleeding love,
> And gave—albeit with tears!"

A loud knock is heard at the door, and then a second, and a third, in quick succession. Schiller shakes back the hair from his countenance, and hastens forward to see who is clamoring for admission.

CHAPTER VI.

THE SONG "TO JOY."

It was the postman, who brought the poet a rosy, perfumed letter from Weimar.

With eager hands, Schiller opened and unfolded the missive. His countenance beamed with joy as he recognized Madame von Kalb's handwriting. " Good and noble woman, you have not forgotten me! Do you still think of me lovingly?"

No, she had not forgotten him; she still loved him, and begged him, with tender and eloquent entreaties, to come to her.

" Schiller, the world is a solitude without you; you are the thought of my inmost thoughts, the soul of my soul! Frederick, separation from you has disclosed the holy mystery of your heart and of mine. It is this: We are the two halves that were one in heaven, and our mission on earth is to strive to come together, in order that our eternal indivisibility and unity of spirit may be restored. Schiller, when we are once more united, hand in hand, and are gazing in each other's eyes, we shall feel as if we had left the earth and were once more in heaven. Frederick, come to your Charlotte!"

"Yes, I am coming to my Charlotte, I am coming!" cried Schiller, in a loud voice, as he pressed the letter to his lips. "You have saved me, you have made me myself again, Charlotte! I am no longer lonely, no longer unloved. Your heart calls me, your spirit longs for me. I feel as though my soul's wings, destined to bear me aloft above the misery of earth, were growing stronger. They will bear me to you, Charlotte—to you, the dearest friend of my life! You shall console, you shall restore me, your friendship shall be the balsam for the wounds of my heart. Eternal Fate, I thank thee for having permitted me to hear this call of friendship in this my hour of trial. I thank thee that there is still one soul that I can call mine; I praise thee that I am not compelled to stand aside in shame and tears, like an unloved, friendless beggar, while the happy are feasting at the richly-laden table of life. One soul I can at least call my own, and I will keep her holy, and love and thank her all the days of my life. Away with tears! away with this sorrowing over a dream of happiness! Farewell, Marie! Be forgiven. I will think of you without anger, and rejoice when you become a happy countess! Farewell, Marie! * A greeting to you, Charlotte! I am coming to you! I am coming!"

He walked slowly to and fro; the cloud of sorrow that had

---

* Marie von Arnim married Count von Kunheim, and retired with him to his estates in Prussia. She never saw Schiller again, nor did she ever forget him. A fine portrait of Schiller hung over her bed until her death. After the death of her husband, in the year 1814, Countess Kunheim returned to Dresden, and lived there in retirement until her death, in the year 1847. But she died without issue, and could not fulfil Schiller's prophecy, and speak to weeping children and grandchildren assembled around her death-bed.

rested on his brow gradually lifted, and his countenance grew clearer and clearer. The man had conquered—the poet was once more himself.

"I will go to Körner! I must see my friend!" He took down his hat, and walked out into the street. His mind had freed itself of its fetters, his step was elastic, and he bore himself proudly, his blue eyes turned heavenward, and a joyous smile rested on his thin and delicate lips.

Thus he entered Körner's dwelling, and found his friend on the point of starting to Loschwitz, to see what had become of the poet. Schiller extended both hands and greeted him with a loving glance.

"Here I am again, my friend. The prodigal son returns from his wanderings, and begs to be permitted to take up his abode in your heart once more. Will you receive him, friend Körner?"

"I will not only receive him, but will kill the fatted calf in honor of his return. I will give a festival, to which all our friends shall be invited, in order that they may rejoice with me, and exclaim, 'The wanderer has returned! Blessed be the hour of his return!'"

Schiller threw himself into his friend's arms, and pressed him to his heart. "I have caused you much sorrow and trouble. I have been a wild and stubborn fellow. Why should beautiful women be blamed for not loving this ungainly and unmannerly fellow, when there are so many handsomer, richer, and happier men in the world? Marie von Arnim is right in marrying the rich and handsome Count Kunheim; and you must not blame her on this account, or say of her that she deceived me. She has only done what we all must do on earth: she has done her duty, and God will bless her and give her His peace in the hour of death for so doing.—But let us speak no more of this."

"No, my friend, we will speak of it no more," said Körner, heartily; "let us only rejoice that you have returned to your friends; that you once more believe in us and our friendship.

How happy my wife will be when her dear friend is restored
to her again! how glad Göschen will be when you once more
extend your hand to him in a loving greeting!"

"Poor, generous Göschen!" said Schiller, thoughtfully.
"I was cruel and unjust to him yesterday, I imputed ignoble
motives to my friend!"

"He thinks of it no longer," said Körner; "he has no
memory for the words spoken by your anguish. He will be
only too happy when you once more greet him with a loving
smile."

"How good and patient you all are with me!" said Schiller,
softly; "and how little have I deserved such treatment at
your hands! In truth, I feel as though I had now returned
to you after along separation—as though I had only seen you of
late through a cloud that had arisen between us, and in which
a single star shone, and— Be still, no more of this! The
cloud has been dissipated; I now see you again, and will rejoice with you as long as we are together."

"Schiller, you do not contemplate leaving us?" said Körner, sadly.

"I am a poor wanderer, my friend, whose stay at any one
place is but brief. At last, a time will come even for me,
when I can lay down my staff and knapsack, and exclaim,
'Here I will rest! This is my home!' But the gods only
know whether this home will be in the grave or in the heart
of a woman!"

"No sad thoughts now, my friend, if you please, now that
I am ready to exult and rejoice over your return!"

"You are right, no sad thoughts at this time! Let us turn
our thoughts to joy. The first song I write shall be in praise
of joy. I will no longer avoid mankind, no longer seek solitude! As you said, Körner, so shall it be! Give the prodigal son a festival, call our friends together, let us once more
assemble around the festive board and partake of the repast
of friendship and joy. This festival shall be in honor of my
return and of my departure."

Körner gave this festival. The lost one, who had of late withdrawn himself from his friends in the violence of his love, had now returned, and this was a fitting occasion for joy and festivity. He called his friends together; he had for each a kind word and a tender greeting. Göschen was richly rewarded when Schiller gave him the manuscript of his Don Carlos, that was now to be given to the world, and to entwine the halo of immortality around the poet's brow, and to enkindle and fan the flame of enthusiasm in thousands and thousands of hearts!

Six days after Schiller's "return," the festival which Körner had promised took place. Körner and his beautiful young wife, Theresa Huber, Göschen, and the artist Sophie Albrecht, were present; a few friends in Leipsic had also joyfully availed themselves of Körner's invitation, and had come to Dresden to see the poet once more.

There he sat at the festive board, his arm thrown around Körner's neck? in his right hand he held the goblet filled with sparkling Rhine wine. His eyes beamed and his countenance shone with enthusiasm. His glance was directed upward, and, perhaps, he saw the heavens open and the countenance of the blessed, for a soft and joyous smile played about his lips.

"Look at this favorite of the muses," cried Körner. "One might suppose they held him in their embrace, and were whispering words of inspiration into his poet's heart."

"Perhaps they are whispering a song of joy in my ear, my friend, in order that I may repeat it to you, the favorite of the gods! But before I do so, I will narrate a history—a history that will touch your hearts and open your purses, unless you are cold-hearted egotists, and then you deserve to share the fate of King Midas, whose very food and wine were turned into gold because he was a hard-hearted miser. I condemn you to this punishment if you have the courage to listen to my story without being moved to tears and generosity!"

With deep pathos and eloquence Schiller recounted to his

listening friends his midnight adventure, his conversation with the poor youth who had attempted to take his own life. So graphic was his representation of the unfortunate youth's distress and vain struggles, that the hearts of his hearers were deeply touched, and no eye remained dry.

When he had concluded his narrative and told his friends of the promise he had made to poor Theophilus, Schiller arose from his seat, took the plate which lay before him, and walked around the table, halting at each seat and extending his plate like a beggar, with soft words of entreaty. When the ready hands opened and dollars and gold-pieces rang out on the plate, Schiller inclined his head and smiled, thanking the givers with looks of tenderness.

Now he had returned to his seat and was counting the money. "Seventeen gold-pieces and thirty dollars. I thank you, my friends! You have saved a human life; you have redeemed a soul from purgatory! To-morrow night I will take this love-offering to the poor youth; the blessing of a good man will then rest on your closed eyelids, and you will be rewarded with sweet dreams and a happy awakening. Now, my dear friends, you shall receive from the poet's lips the thanks that are glowing in my heart. Now, you shall hear the exulting song to joy which Körner supposed the Muses were whispering in my ear. Raise your glasses and listen; when I incline my head repeat the words last spoken."

Schiller arose, drew a small, folded sheet of paper from his pocket, opened it, glanced over it hastily, and then let it fall on the table. He did not require it; his song resounded in his mind and brain; it was written on the tablets of his heart, and his lips now uttered it exultantly:

> "Joy, thou brightest heaven-lit spark,
> Daughter from the Elysian choir,
> On thy holy ground we walk,
> Reeling with ecstatic fire!"

His eyes shone with enthusiasm, his cheeks glowed, and a heavenly smile illumined his whole countenance, while reciting his song "To Joy."   His friends caught the inspiration of his poem, arose with one accord from their seats, clasped hands and gazed into each other's eyes—into the eyes that shone lustrously, although they were filled with tears.   Now, at the culminating point of his rapture, Schiller's countenance suddenly quivered with pain as he recited a second verse of his song:

> "Yea—who calls *one* soul his own,
> *One* on all earth's ample round:—
> Who cannot, may steal alone,
> Weeping from our holy ground."

"Who cannot, may steal alone, weeping from our holy ground," repeated his friends.   The tears gushed from their eyes; they clasped hands more firmly, and listened breathlessly to the words of the poet, whose voice now rose again to the high tones of enthusiasm.   It was almost like an adoration of joy, friendship, and love.   Their hearts beat higher, mightier and mightier the waves of rapture surged in their kindred souls.

> "Myriads join the fond embrace!
> 'Tis the world's inspiring kiss.
> Friends, yon dome of starry bliss
> Is a loving father's place."

They embraced each other; they wept, but with rapture, with enthusiasm.   The kiss that passed from mouth to mouth was given to the whole world; for all that the world could offer of love, of friendship, and of happiness, the friends found combined at the happy festival to which Schiller had dedicated his song "To Joy."

CHAPTER VII.

TOGETHER ONCE MORE.

Night had come, a dark, gloomy night.   The moonlight that had played so beautifully, on the rippling waters of the Elbe, a week before, was wanting on this night.   The sky was overcast, and the clouds that were being driven through the

heavens by the wind, cast on the river dark shadows that
looked like yawning graves.

Theophilus stood on the river bank at the same place where
he had knelt and prayed a week before. He stood there gazing at the dark river and looking up from time to time at the
driving clouds.

"If he should not respect his word, if he should not be able
to keep his promise, because no generous hearts responded to
his entreaties! What then? Will this river be my grave?
Are the waves murmuring my death-song? No, no! be brave,
Theophilus; wait patiently, be strong in hope! His voice
was so gentle, so full of conviction, when he promised to meet
me here to-night, to bring me help! He appeared before me
like the angel Gabriel; I will believe that God sent him in
human form, and that he will also send him a second time.
Hope, my heart, and be strong in faith!"

He folded his hands in silent prayer, and listened anxiously
to every slight noise other than the murmuring of the waves
on the shore, and the rustling of the wind in the trees, that
broke in upon the stillness of the night. Some distance
up the river, on its opposite bank, lay the city with its many
lights. On the Elbe bridge, towering conspicuously above
all other objects, stood the gilded crucifix, surrounded by a
circle of lighted lamps, placed there by pious hands.

Theophilus saw this crucifix, and it awakened pious
thoughts and brave resolutions in his breast. "I will endure
all that may befall me in patience and hope. By resignation
and pious devotion, I will endeavor to atone for the sins committed in my despair. My whole life belongs to Thee, my
God, and shall be dedicated to Thy service! I will serve the
poor and the unfortunate. Every man who suffers shall be
my brother, to every man who stumbles will I extend a helping hand. I will strive to dry the tears of the weeping, and,
if I can do nothing else, I will, at least, pray with them.
This, I swear to Thee, my God!—this I swear by yon luminous crucifix!"

The great bell resounded from the tower of the Catholic Church, striking the eleventh hour. Theophilus shuddered; he remembered that he had heard this bell at the moment when he was on the point of plunging into his watery grave, and that it had then resounded on his ear like a death-knell.

"Never will I hear this hour strike without fear and trembling. It will always sound to me like the knell of the doomed criminal. Grant, O God, that in such an hour I may prove myself a repentant sinner, and make atonement for my crime! I resolve that I will do so," cried he, in a loud voice. "I swear that this eleventh hour shall each day remind me of my crime, and find me ready to devote to the welfare of mankind the life I was about to sacrifice to despair."

"In the name of God and humanity I accept your vow!" said a solemn voice behind him. "Here I am, my brother. Forgive me for having kept you waiting, but important business prevented my coming earlier, and I found it difficult to steal away from the friends who were with me, without attracting observation. While awaiting me, you have formed good resolutions, and made your peace with God and your conscience. Hold fast to them, my brother; be firm and brave. Elevate your thoughts above things perishable, let your soul soar above the vanities of earthly existence, and you will find that spiritual joys will amply console you for the sorrows of earth. Here is the money I have brought you, here are one hundred and twenty dollars. According to your calculation it will suffice to enable you to complete your studies, and give you a start in your career. Take the money, my friend, and let us part."

"Part! without giving me the name of my benefactor and saviour?" asked Theophilus, holding the hand, that had given him the money, firmly clasped in his own. "Part! and may I never hope to see and thank you in the light of day?"

"Thank me, my brother, by being happy. Bear the light

of day within you, and then I shall be rewarded, then my memory will live in your heart. Why should I tell you my name? I am your brother, let that suffice. Go on your way, be just, and do good to others who are suffering and who are unhappy, as you were. This shall be my thanks: I say to you, with Christ: 'What you do to the least of these my brethren, that you have done unto me.' Bear this in mind!"

The voice was silent; Theophilus knew that he was again alone. He folded his hands, bowed his head, and prayerfully repeated the words, that, in the stillness of the night, and amid the rustling of the wind, had resounded on his ear like the solemn tones of an organ. "What you do to the least of these my brethren, that you have done unto me. Bear this in mind!"

"I will bear this in mind! I will endeavor to atone for the evil I have done! I dedicate myself to God's service. The holy crucifix, that illumines the surrounding darkness, has also illumined the darkness of my soul. I will go to Cologne, and enter the seminary, in order that I may become a priest—a pious, humble priest of the Church of God. Farewell! earthly vanity, earthly pride, and earthly hope! I will be a priest of mercy, for God has shown me mercy, and sent an angel-messenger to save me. I will bear this in mind!"

While Theophilus was wending his way to Dresden, Schiller was journeying toward Weimar in the stage-coach. After giving Theophilus the money collected for him, Schiller had hurried to the post-office, where his friends were waiting to take leave of him, and bid the traveller a last farewell.

"Farewell! We shall soon meet again; I will soon return!" cried Schiller from the stage-coach, as it rolled out of the court-yard on through the city gate into the soft summer night.

"Charlotte is awaiting me!" murmured Schiller, as he sank back on the hard cushions. "Charlotte is awaiting me. She is the friend of my soul. Our spirits belong to each other, and I will show my friend the wounds of my heart, in order that she may heal them with the balsam of tender friendship."

But, strange to say, the nearer he came to his journey's end, the more joyfully his heart throbbed, the less painful its wounds became.

" Charlotte, dear Charlotte, if I were but already with you! I feel that the fire which drove me from Mannheim is not yet extinguished; a breath from your lips will suffice to kindle the spark into a conflagration."

There is Weimar! Now the stage-coach has entered the city. Schiller is on classic ground! On the ground where Germany's greatest poets and intellects dwell. Wieland and Herder, Bertuch and Bode, dwell here; here are also many artists and actors of eminence, and here lives the genial Duke Charles August! And yet Weimar is desolate, for Goethe is not here; he left more than a year ago.

Schiller knew this, but what did he care now! He had so longed to tread this classic ground that his heart throbbed with joy at the prospect of seeing and becoming acquainted with the celebrated men whose works he had read with so much enthusiasm—whom he could now meet with the feeling that he was not unworthy of them, and that he also now filled a place in the republic of intellect.

He had been occupied with these thoughts during the whole journey; but now they suddenly vanished. He thought only of Madame von Kalb, the friend he had not seen for two years—the friend whose dear lips had called him to her side in the hour of his deepest distress.

He had taken lodgings in the chief hotel of the city; it was already quite late in the evening, so late that it seemed hardly proper to call on a lady. He would not remain in his solitary chamber, but would walk out, and at least look at the house in which she lived. If the lights had, however, not yet been extinguished, if she should still be awake— He did not complete this thought, but sprang down the steps, ordered the servant, who was walking to and fro in the hall, to accompany him and show him the house in which Madame von Kalb lived, and rushed down the designated street with such long and rapid strides that the servant could scarcely follow him.

There is the house in which Madame von Kalb lives, a modest little house at the entrance of the park. A light is still burning behind the basement windows, and he sees the shadow of a tall woman pass across the closed curtains. "That is her figure, I would recognize it among thousands! That is Charlotte!"

"I intend to enjoy this beautiful summer night in the park," said Schiller, turning to the servant, with a hasty movement. "You may return, I will be able to find my way back, alone."

As soon as the servant had vanished around the next corner, he walked up to the door and opened it very softly, in order that the bell above it might not betray his entrance. "I will take her by surprise," murmured he to himself; "I will see what effect my unexpected coming will have on my dear friend."

The bell rang in such low tones that it could certainly not have been heard in the room. But a servant came forward from the back end of the hall.

"I call at Madame von Kalb's request. She is in this room, is she not?"

"Madame von Kalb is in. May I have the honor of announcing you?"

"It is unnecessary, she is awaiting me. I can enter unannounced."

He had uttered these words in subdued tones; Charlotte must not hear him, must know nothing of his arrival until he stood before her. He opened the door noiselessly, closed it gently behind him, and now stood between the door and the heavy velvet curtain that hung over the entrance. He could, however, see his friend through an opening in the curtain. She sat reclining on the sofa, her beautiful eyes gazing dreamingly into empty space. Her cheeks were pale with inward agitation, and a soft smile played about her lips. Of whom was she thinking? Of whom was she dreaming?

"Charlotte! dear Charlotte!"

She uttered a cry and sprang up from her seat.

"Charlotte, you called me to your side, and here I am! Will you not welcome me?"

She stood as though incapable of utterance, but the beautiful, the loved countenance, with its proud and noble expression, its rosy lips, and soft smile, was before him. Before her stood Schiller, whom she had yearned for since they last parted, whom she had loved ardently and faithfully for two long, long years, without having seen him. But, now he was there, he stood before her with extended arms. She thought nothing, she felt nothing more than that Schiller had returned, and was once more at her side. Happy, blissful reunion!

"Welcome, my Schiller! welcome, friend of my soul!" She threw herself on his bosom, and he entwined his arms around her, as though they were two chains with which he intended to bind, and hold her forever. Yes, forever!

"Tell me, Charlotte, that you love me! utter the word which your lips refused to confess in Mannheim. Do not again drive me out into the darkness of life, as you did in Mannheim. I am weary of wandering, and am disgusted with the world. You alone are true, in you only can I confide. Accord me a home where I may lay down my head and rest. Tell me, Charlotte, that this is my heart's home. Tell me that you love me? You do not reply, Charlotte? Why are you silent?" He opened his arms to release her, that he might look at her. But she did not raise her head, she still lay on his breast. She had fainted! He lifted her in his arms, carried her to the sofa, and knelt down beside her. As she lay there with closed eyelids, and pale lips, he bowed down over her and pressed his glowing lips to hers, entreating her to return to life. "Charlotte, friend, awaken! Forgive me for having dared to surprise you in the wilfulness of

my happiness. Return to me, friend of my soul! I will be
quiet and gentle, will sit at your feet like a child, and be
contented to look up at your dear countenance, and read in
your eyes that you love me. Open these dear eyes! Soul of
my soul, heart of my heart, let me hear your loved voice!
Give me a word of consolation, of hope, of love!"

And Charlotte, called by the voice she had longed to hear
for two long years, awoke, and looked up lovingly into the
countenance of him who was the sun of her existence. She
entwined her arms around his neck and kissed his lips and his
eyes. "I greet you, I kiss you, proclaimer of my happiness."

"You must tell me that indeed you love me. My heart
thirsts for these words; it is wounded and bleeding, and you
must heal it. I will drink that oblivion from your lips,
Charlotte, that will make me forget all, save that you love
me. It is disconsolate to be alone and unloved! I cling to
your heart as the shipwrecked mariner clings to the flower
thrown up before him by the waves, hoping thereby to save
himself. Charlotte, do not let me sink, save me! Let me
seek safety from the storm in the haven of your love! Say
that you will let me seek and find peace, enthusiasm, and
happiness, in this longed-for haven."

She threw her arms around his neck, and pressed a kiss on
his forehead. "I love you, Schiller, I love you; I have the
courage to tell you so, and to break through all barriers, and
place myself at your side. I have the courage to testify before the whole world, and even to confess to my husband: 'I
love Frederick Schiller. Our souls and hearts are bound together. Tear them asunder, if you can!' I love you, and
with that I have said all—have said, that I will be yours before God and man, and that nothing shall longer separate us."

"And your husband?" asked Schiller, anxiously.

"He is a good and generous man," said Charlotte, smiling.
"He will not desire to hold me fettered to himself against my
wish. Our union was based on convenience and interest, and
was never a happy one. We have lived together but little;

our natures were entirely different. I have lived in retirement, while my husband has passed his time in luxury and amusements at the court of Queen Marie Antoinette, where he is a welcome guest. We respect and esteem, but we do not love each other. When I confess my love and plead for a divorce, my husband will certainly give his consent. Then I can belong wholly to the man I not only love, but so highly esteem that I joyfully dedicate myself to him until death, and even beyond the grave."

"It shall be as you say, my friend," cried Schiller, raising her hand to his lips. "Nothing shall separate us, and even the king of terrors shall have no terrors for us; in the joyousness of our union of souls we will defy him. Yes, we will defy death, and the whole world!"

They kept their promises; they defied the whole world; they made no secret of their union of hearts; they denied to none that they were one and indivisible. Charlotte had the heroism to defy the world and acknowledge her love freely. She had the courage to remain whole days alone with Schiller in her little house. She held herself aloof from society, in order that Schiller might read to her his two new novels, and, above all, his 'Don Carlos.' Nor did she avoid being seen with him in public. How could she deny him before men, when she was so proud of him and of his love! She helped to adorn and make comfortable the little apartments he had rented; she sent him carpets, flower-vases, chairs, and many other things. She felt that she was his mother, his sister, his sweetheart, and his friend. In the ardor of her passion, she endeavored to combine the duties of these four persons in herself; she felt that the divine strength of her love would enable her to do so. In her confidence and guilelessness of heart, she never even asked herself this question: Will the man I love be willing to rise with me in this whirlwind of passion, to soar with me from heaven to heaven, and to revel in ever-youthful, celestial thought and feeling, regardless of earthly mutability?

Together, they visited the heroes of art and literature in Weimar, and, together, they drove out to Tiefurt, where the Duchess Amelia and taken up her summer residence.

The duchess gave the poet of "Don Carlos" and "Fiesco" a cordial welcome. "I was angry with you on account of your 'Robbers,' Mr. Councillor," said she, "nor was 'Louise Müllerin' entirely to my taste. But 'Fiesco,' and, above all, 'Don Carlos,' have reconciled me to you. You are, in truth, a great poet, and I prophesy a brilliant future for you. Remain here with us in Weimar!"

"Yes, Mr. Schiller," cried the little maid of honor Von Göckhausen, as she stepped forward, courtesied gracefully, and handed him a rose, "remain in Weimar. The muses have commanded me to give you their favorite, this rose, and to tell you, *sub rosa*, that Weimar is the abode of the gods, and that the nine maidens would be well contented to remain here."

"Göckhausen, take care," said the Duchess, laughing. "I will tell Goethe what a fickle, faithless little thing you are. While he was here, my Thusnelda's roses bloomed for him only, and for Goethe only was she the messenger of the gods and muses. Now, the faithless creature is already receiving messages from the muses for Frederick Schiller! But she is not to be blamed; the poet of 'Don Carlos' deserves homage; and, when even the muses worship Goethe and Schiller, why should not Göckhausen do it also? Do you know Goethe?"

"No, not personally," replied Schiller, softly; "but I admire him as a poet, and I shall be happy if I can some day admire and love him as a man also."

"You should have come earlier," sighed the duchess. "You should have made his acquaintance during the early days of his stay in Mannheim. Then, you would indeed have loved him. At that time, he was in the youthful vigor of his enthusiasm. It was a beautiful era when Goethe stood among us, like the genius of poetry, descended from heaven, enflaming our hearts with heavenly rapture. He is still a great poet, but he has now become a man of rank—a privy-councillor! Beware, my dear Councillor Schiller, lest our court atmosphere stiffen you, too, and rob your heart of its youthful freshness of enthusiasm. Goethe was a very god Apollo before he became a privy-councillor, and was entitled to a seat and voice in the state council. By all means avoid becoming a minister; the poet and the minister cannot be combined in one man. Of this, Goethe is an example."

"No, he is not," cried Göckhausen, eagerly; "Goethe can be all that it pleases him to be. He will never indeed cease to be a poet; he is one in his whole being. Poetic blood courses through his veins; the minister he can shake off at any time, and be himself again. This he proved some eighteen months ago, when he suddenly took leave of our court and all its glories, and fled from the state council, and all his dignities and honors, to Italy. He cast all this trumpery of ducal grace behind him, and fled to Italy, to be the poet by the grace of God only!"

"See, my Thusnelda has returned to her old enthusiasm!" cried the duchess, laughing. "That was all I desired; I only wished to arouse her indignation, and make her love for Goethe apparent.—Now, Mr. Schiller, you see what my Thusnelda's real sentiments are, and how true she is to her distant favorite."

"Much truer, probably, than he is to his former favorites, ' said Göckhausen, smiling. "Men cannot be true; and I am satisfied that Werther, if he had not shot himself prematurely, would subsequently have consoled himself, although the adored Lotte was married, and could never be his. Laugh on, duchess! I am right, nevertheless. Is not Goethe himself an example of this? Did he not love Charlotte von Kästner? If he had shot himself at that time, he could not have consoled himself afterwards with Charlotte von Stein, to become desperate once more, and finally to take a pleasant and consolatory trip to Italy, instead of leaving the world. Truly, the Charlottes are very dangerous to poets; but I would, however, advise each and every one of them to beware of falling in love with a poet, for—how forgetful I am! I beg your pardon, Madame von Kalb!"

"Why, my dear young lady?"

"Because I did not remember that you, too, were a Charlotte," murmured the malicious maid of honor, meekly.

Von Kalb laughed, but she was more subdued and thoughtful after this visit than usual. Her eyes often rested on Schiller with a peculiar, inquiring look, and when he sat at her side on the sofa that evening, she laid her hands gently on his shoulders and gazed intently into his countenance.

"You love me, Schiller, do you not?"

"I love you, although you are a Charlotte. That is the question you intended to ask, is it not?"

She smiled and laid her head on his shoulder. "Schiller, I would that our union of heart and soul had already received its indissoluble consecration. I would that my husband had already given his consent to a separation and I were wholly yours."

"Are you not truly and wholly mine? Is not our union indissoluble? Does not God, does not the whole world know that we are one and inseparable? Does not society respect and treat our relation to each other with consideration for both of us? The people with whom we come in contact have the discretion to leave us when they observe that we wish to be alone. Did not Von Einsiedel, who called on you this evening, leave again when the servant told him that I was with you? Was not even the Duchess Amelia so considerate as to invite us together yesterday; for that she did so out of consideration for the relation existing between us, Wieland told me.* You see, therefore, my dearest friend, that no one doubts, or ignores our union."

"Why do you call me your dearest friend?" asked she, anxiously.

"Why? Because you are. Is it not your opinion, also, that friendship is the highest power of love?"

---

* Schiller's own words.—See his correspondence with Körner.

She said yes, but she was very thoughtful after Schiller had gone. "I would that my husband were here, and that the word of separation had already been spoken!" she murmured.

Several months passed before her husband arrived in Weimar. Madame had not been able to endure this uncertainty, this continued hypocrisy. She had written to her husband, confessing her love and her relation to Schiller, and begging him, as her best friend, to give her his advice and to promote her happiness.

Her husband had replied at once as follows: "My dear friend, for the very reason that I am, as you say, your best friend, I will treat your letter as though I had not received it. It is obliterated from my memory, and I only know that I love and esteem you as the mother of my little boy, and that the dearest wish of my heart is your happiness. Let us leave these little afflictions of the heart to time, the great healer. I am coming to Weimar in a few months, and we shall then see if time has not exercised its healing properties on yourself and on the heart of an easily-excited poet. If this should not be the case, however, and you should then repeat the words written in your letter, it will still be time to see whether the desires of your heart can be gratified without detriment to our son's interests. Let us, therefore, postpone the decision for a few months."

He had also written to Schiller, but without any reference to Charlotte's communications. His letter was full of quite hearty sympathy, profound admiration for the poet, and earnest assurances of friendship. He concluded by announcing that he would come to Weimar in a few months, and that Schiller would find him ready to do him any service, and to make any sacrifice for him that the poet could expect at the hands of a friend.

Schiller folded the letter thoughtfully, and a glowing color suffused itself over his cheeks. "He will come," said he to himself, in a low voice. "It will be a strange meeting for me, I already blush with shame when I think of it. He loves me,

he calls me his friend, and yet he knows all! Will I really
have the courage to demand this sacrifice of a friend, and—"
asked he in a low voice—"and do I really so ardently desire
this sacrifice? I came here to seek consolation from a dear
friend, and I found love—love that has drawn me into the
whirlpool of passion. We are both being driven around in
its eddying circles, and who knows but that marriage is the
sunken reef on which our hearts will ultimately be shipwrecked. Save us from a violent end, thou Spirit of the
Universe; save me from such an end, thou genius of poetry;
let me fly to some peaceful haven where I can find safety from
the storms of life! There is a mystery in every human
breast; it is given to God only and to time, to solve it. Let
us, therefore, wait and hope!"

When her husband arrived in Weimar a few months afterward, this mystery seemed to have sunk deeper in Charlotte
and Schiller's hearts; neither of them had the courage to lift
the veil and speak the decisive word. Charlotte was paler
and quieter than usual, and her eyes were often stained with
tears, but she did not complain and made no attempt to bring
her husband to an explanation.

Only once, when she held her little boy, who had just recovered from an attack of illness, lovingly in her arms, her
husband stepped up to her, and gave her a kind, inquiring
look:

"Could you ever make up your mind to leave this child,
Charlotte—to deliver it over to the care of a stranger."

"Never, no, never!" cried she, folding her arms tenderly
around her delicate little boy. "No, not for all the treasures—for all the happiness earth can offer, could I part with
my darling child!"

"And yet you would be compelled to do so, if you should
lay aside the name your child's father bears," said her husband, gently.

He made no explanation of his words, but his wife had well
understood him, and also understood his intention when,

after a short interval, he smilingly observed that he would now go to see Schiller, and take a walk with his dear friend.

When her husband had left the room she looked down at the pale child, who was slumbering in her arms. Tears gushed from her eyes, and she folded her hands over her boy's head:

"Give us all peace, Thou who art the Spirit of Eternal Love! Give us wisdom to discern truth and strength, to make any sacrifice in its behalf!"

On the evening of this day, after a long walk which Schiller had taken with Charlotte's husband, and during which they had conversed on the highest intellectual topics only, Schiller wrote to his bosom friend Körner, in Dresden: "Can you believe me when I assert, that I find it almost impossible to write anything concerning Charlotte? Nor can I even tell you why! The relation existing between us, like revealed religion, is based on faith. The results of the long experience and slow progress of the human mind are announced in the latter in a mystical manner, because reason would have taken too long a time to attain this end. The same is the case with Charlotte and myself. We commenced with a premonition of the result, and must now study and confirm our religion by the aid of reason. In the latter, as in the former case, all the intervals of fanaticism, skepticism, and superstition, have arisen, and it is to be hoped that we will ultimately arrive at that reasonable faith that is the only assurance of bliss. I think it likely that the germ of an enduring friendship exists in us both, but it is still awaiting its development. There is more unity in Charlotte's mind than in my own, although she is more changeable in her humors and caprices. Solitude and a peculiar tendency of her being have imprinted my image more firmly in her soul, than her image could ever be imprinted in mine. Her husband treats me precisely as of yore, although he is well aware of the relation existing between us. I do not know that his presence will leave me as I

am.   I feel that a change has taken place within me that may
be still further developed." *

CHAPTER VIII.

GOETHE AND MORITZ.

"CHEER up, my friend!   Grumble no longer!   Rejoice in
life and throw off the burden of your cares!   Open your eyes
and behold the beauties of the world created by the Almighty
Spirit of the Universe!   We have studied and worshipped the
immortal gods and immortal arts in Rome—we have been
living with the ancients; now let us live for a few days with
eternal youth, with ever-fading, ever-blossoming Nature!
Let us live like God's children in His glorious world!"

It was Goethe who spoke these words—not Goethe, the
secretary of legation, who, at the end of the year 1786, had
secretly withdrawn from his friends, and even from his beloved Madame von Stein, and fled to Italy, the land he so
ardently desired to visit.   No, it was not that Goethe, who,
during the last months of his sojourn in Weimar, had es-
chewed his youthful exuberance of feeling, his exaggerated
manner, and his Werther costume, and had assumed the grave
dignified air which he deemed becoming in a high official!
No, he who spoke these words, was the poet Johann Wolfgang Von Goethe, the poet who was once more himself, now
that he sojourned under Italy's glorious skies—the poet whose
soul glowed with enthusiasm, and on whose lips inspiration
trembled—the poet who sought the essence of the Divinity in
the least flower, and who saw the glory of his Maker reflected
in the countenance of each human being.

This Goethe it was who spoke these cheering, encouraging
words.   He addressed them to Philip Moritz, with whom he
had been living in Rome, and other parts of Italy, for the last
two years, and with whom he had rejoiced and sorrowed in

* Schiller and his Times, by Johannes Scherr.—Vol. ii., p. 89.

many pleasures and vicissitudes. They had both come to Italy to make new men of themselves. Goethe, to become himself again—to become the original, creative genius. Moritz, to heal his heart-wounds, and refresh his mind with the wonders of art and nature that abound for every man, who has eyes to see, in Italy—this land of art and poetry. Philip Moritz had eyes to see, and the woman he loved had begged him not to close them, not to shut out from his vision the treasures which the God of creation and the gods of art had so plentifully bestowed upon this favored land.

Marie von Leuthen was the woman of his love, and she it was who had entreated him to go to Italy, that he might recover from the wounds life had inflicted, his grief be healed, and hope restored to his heart.

"Go," she had said to him, "Italy and art will be a healing balm for your wounds. Recover from them, and return after two years, renewed in mind and constant in heart, and I will give you a joyful answer if you then ask me if I love you."

Philip Moritz had journeyed to Italy as she bade him. On arriving in Rome he learned that Goethe had been in the city for some time. Moritz at once sought out his adored poet, and since then they had been close comrades. He admired and worshipped Goethe, who tenderly loved the friend (who was often so gloomy, and whose merriment was often exaggerated), in spite of his peculiarities. Together they visited the treasures of art in Rome; together they made excursions to the neighboring villages and places of interest, on foot or on horseback, as the case might be. On an excursion of this kind to Frascati, Moritz had been thrown from his horse, and had his arm broken. Goethe had nursed him like a brother; for long days and weeks he had been the sufferer's only consoler and associate.

"I have just left Moritz," he wrote on one occasion to Madame von Stein. "The bandages were to-day removed from his arm, and it appears to be doing well. What I have experienced and learned at the bedside of this sufferer, in the last two weeks, may be of benefit to us both in the future. During this period he was perpetually alternating between the greatest misery and the highest delight." *

This "greatest misery" the poor hypochondriac had borne in silence. The "highest delight," he had shared with his happier friend, with Goethe, the favorite of the gods.

In the autumn they had both left Rome, and gone out to Castel Gandolfo, to pay a visit to the house of a hospitable friend. Many eminent poets and artists were sojourning at this charming place at that time. Gayety and merriment was the order of the day. It was in vain that Goethe endeavored to draw his friend Moritz into this magic circle of enjoyment. It grieved him deeply to see his friend brooding over his studies, to see the sad and gloomy expression that rested on his features. Goethe's entreaties and exhortations were at times successful in arousing him from this condition; but, after a short interval of forced gayety and mocking merriment, he would relapse into his ordinary state of silent melancholy.

" Let us live as God's children in His glorious world!"

Moritz raised his pale countenance from the book over which he had been brooding, and looked tenderly, and yet sadly, at Goethe.

" Happy, enviable man," said he. " But who can feel and think as you do?"

" You can, Moritz, if you only try," cried Goethe. " But, above all, tell me what burden is resting on your soul, and what these wrinkles on my friend's brow mean."

" They mean that I have a sad presentiment," replied Moritz, with a sigh, as he threw his book aside and rose from his seat. " I am angry with myself on this account, and I have sought to dispel this presentiment, but all to no purpose! The skies of Italy are no longer serene, the whole world seems like a huge grave; of late, even Rome's works of art have appealed to me in vain; my ear has been deaf to their sublime language."

* " Trip to Italy."—Goethe's Works.

"But, speak out, growler, monster," cried Goethe, impatiently, "what northern spleen has again penetrated your northern heart? what is the matter with you? What imps have taken up their abode in your brain? What crickets are fiddling in your ears, and transforming the author, the linguist, and the sage into a miserable, grief-stricken old woman, who shuffles along through God's beautiful world, and burrows in the ground like a mole, instead of soaring upwards to the sun like an eagle?"

"Corpo di Bacco!" cried Moritz, striking the table so furiously with his fists that he sent the books flying in every direction, and upset the ink-bottle, flooding his papers with its black contents. "Corpo di Bacco! Enough of your ridicule and abuse! How dare you call me a miserable old woman, how dare you compare me with a mole? How dare you make yourself merry over my northern heart? You, above all, whose heart is a lump of ice, an extinguished coal, that even the breath of a goddess would fail to enkindle! If one of us is an iceberg, it is you, Mr. Johann Wolfgang Goethe! You are an iceberg, and your heart can never thaw again, but will remain coffined in an eternal winter. What do you know of the sufferings of a man who loves the fairest, the best, and the noblest of women, and who, tormented by terrible forebodings of her death, tears his own flesh with the serpent's tooth of care, and who is blinded by his grief to all the beauties of God's world!"

"That is it," said Goethe, heartily, "then I have attained my object. With the iron hammer of my abuse I have beaten on the anvil of your obdurate temperament until I have made the sparks fly and kindle a fire. That was all I desired, you overgrown, harmless child; I only called you an old woman in order to awaken the man in you, and I now beg your pardon a thousand times for this abuse. He who has seen the old shrews that infest the neighborhood of St. Peter's, and has suffered from their visitations in the Chiesa Maria della Pace, knows how terrible a creature such an old fright is, and how offensive it is to be compared to such a personage. I humbly beg your pardon, Philip Moritz, professor, sage, connoisseur of art, and first-class etymologist. But as for your presentiments and your fears that some evil may have befallen your sweetheart, permit me to say that they are only the vagaries of a lover who blows soap-bubbles into the air, and afterward trembles lest they should fall on his head as cannonballs. Why, in the name of all the saints, do you give vent to your yearnings in trumpet tones, and afterward consider them the death-song of your love? Was it not agreed upon between you two lovesick children of affliction that these two years of your sojourn in Italy should be a trial of your love and fidelity? Was it not understood that you were not to exchange a single letter during this period?"

"Yes, that was our agreement," replied Moritz. "Marie would have it so; she wished to try me, to see whether I would remain faithful and constant in love, even among the glories of Italy."

"Well, then! What is it that oppresses you? What do these lamentations signify? What are you afraid of?"

"Do not laugh, Goethe," murmured Philip Moritz. "I will tell you, a dream has tormented and alarmed me; a dream that has returned to me for three successive nights. I see Marie lying on her couch at the point of death, her cheeks pale and hollow, her eyes dim and fixed; old Trude kneels at her side wringing her hands, and a voice cries in my ear in heart-rending tones: 'Philip, my beloved Philip, come! Let me die in your arms.' This is the dream that has haunted me for three nights; these are the words that have each time awakened me from sleep, and they still resound in my ear when I am fully aroused."

"Dreams amount to nothing," said Goethe, shrugging his shoulders, "and your faith in them proves only that Cupid transforms even the most sensible men into foolish children, and that the wanton god can make even sages irrational."

"I would he made you so, you mocker at love and marriage," rejoined Moritz, grimly. "I would like to see you a victim of this divine madness. I trust that Cupid, whom you deride, will send an arrow into your icy heart and melt it in the flames of infinite love-pains and heaven-storming longings! I hope to see you, the sage who has fled from all the living beauties, from all the living women here in Italy, as though they were serpents of Eden—I hope to see you compelled by one of them to eat of the apple, and experience the dire consequences! I hope—"

"Hold, rash mortal!" said Goethe, interrupting him, with a smile. "You know that children and fools often speak the truth, and that their prophecies often become realities. It is to be hoped an all-kind Providence will preserve me from a new love, from new flames. No, the fires of love have been extinguished in my heart; in the warm ashes of friendship that still remain, a spark may sometimes glimmer sufficiently to enable me to read the name of my beloved friend, Charlotte von Stein, engraven therein."

"Warm ashes of friendship, indeed!" osberved Moritz, in mocking tones. "A sorry tenant for the heart of the poet of Werther."

"Really," cried Goethe, "I believe this fellow would be capable of imploring the gods to visit a 'Werthercade' upon me."

"I not only would be capable of doing so, but I really will do so," rejoined Moritz. "I entreat the gods to bless and curse you with a heaven-storming, bliss-conferring and annihilating love, for that is all that is wanting to drive the last vestiges of humanity out of you, and make of you a demi-god with a halo of love-flames around your semi-divine head. Yes, Wolfgang Goethe, poet by the grace of God, to whom the immortal have vouchsafed the honor of creating an 'Iphigenia' and an 'Egmont'—yes, I hope that a glowing, flaming, and distracting love, may be visited upon you!"

"That you should not do," said Goethe, gently, "let me make a confession, Moritz: I believe that I am not capable of such a love—am not capable of losing my own individuality in that of another. I am not capable of subjecting all other thoughts, wishes, and cravings, to the one thought, wish, and craving of love. Perhaps this was at one time my condition, perhaps my Werther spoke of my own life, and perhaps this tragedy was written with the blood of my heart, then bleeding for Charlotte Kästner. But you perceive that I did not shoot myself like Werther. I have steeled my heart since then to enable it to rely on its own strength, and to prevent its ever being carried away by the storm of passion. I am proof against this, and will ever be so!"

"To be in Rome!" exclaimed Moritz, "in Rome, with a heart void of all save the ashes of friendship for Charlotte von Stein, and to remain cold and indifferent to the most beautiful women in the world!"

"That is not true, that is calumny!" said Goethe, smiling. "My heart is not cold, but glows with admiration and love for the noblest and loveliest woman, for the goddess of beauty, chastity, and virtue. She was my first love in Rome, and will be my only love. I yearned for her until she at last yielded to my entreaties, and took up her abode in my poor house. Yes, I possess her, she is mine! No words can give an idea of her, she is like one of Homer's songs!" *

"I would like to know," cried Moritz, in astonishment, "yes, really, I would like to know of whom you are speaking!"

"I am speaking of her," said Goethe, pointing to a colossal bust of the Juno Ludovisi, that stood on a high pedestal in a corner of the room. He approached the pedestal, looked up into the proud and noble countenance of the chaste goddess, and greeted her with a radiant smile.

"I greet you, mysterious goddess, on whose brow love and chastity are enthroned! When I behold you I seem to hear words of revelation, and I then know that you reflect all that the fancy of the poets, the researches of the learned, and the piety of priests, ever thought or depicted that is sublime and

* Goethe's own words.—See "Trip to Italy," Goethe's works, vol. xxiii., p. 159.

beautiful. You are the blessing-dispensing Isis of the Egyptians, the Venus Aphrodite, and Mother Mary, all in one, and I stand before you in pious awe, adoring, loving and—"

"Holy Mary! Holy Januarius!" screamed a voice from the doorway, and a woman, in the picturesque dress of an Italian peasant, rushed into the room. "Signori, signori, a wonder, a miracle!"

"What do you mean, Signora Abazza?" asked Goethe, laughing, as Moritz, alarmed by the old woman's screeching, withdrew hastily to the window recess.

"What do I mean?" repeated the old woman, as she sank breathlessly into a chair. "A miracle has occurred, Signori! My cat is praying to God the Father!"

"How so, signora?" asked Goethe, while Moritz had abandoned his retreat and was slowly approaching the old woman, curiosity depicted in his countenanec.

"I mean just what I say, signori! I went to your bedchamber to make up the bed, and the cat accompanied me as usual. Suddenly I heard a whining and mewing, and when I looked around, supposing she had hurt herself in some way, I saw her—but come and look yourselves. It is a miracle, signori! A miracle!" She sprang up, rushed to the door of the bedchamber, opened it, looked in, and beckoned to the two friends to approach. "Softly, softly, signori; do not disturb her!"

Goethe and Moritz walked noiselessly to the door, and looked into the adjoining room. There, on the antiquated wardrobe, opposite Schiller's bed, and illumined by the sunlight that poured in through the broad window, stood the colossal bust of the almighty Jupiter. In front of this bust, full of beauty and regal composure, stood Madame Abazza's gray cat, upright on her hind feet. She had laid her forepaws on the god's broad breast, and stretched her neck so that she could gaze into his majestic countenance, and touch with her tongue the lips with their godlike smile, and the beard with its curling locks. She kissed his divine lips

ardently, and zealously licked his curly beard, stopping now and
then to gaze for a moment at his royal countenance, and to
utter a tender, plaintive mew, and then renewing her attention to beard and lips.

Goethe and Moritz looked on with smiling astonishment,
the old woman with pious dismay.

"Come to me, pussy," cried the signora at last; "come to
me, my little pet, I will give you some milk and sugar;
come!"

But call and entreat as she would, the cat would not allow
herself to be disturbed in her devotions, not even when
Goethe walked heavily through the room and stepped up to
the wardrobe. She continued to kiss the god's lips and
beard, and to utter her plaintive mews. Signora Abazza,
who was standing in the door-way, with folded hands, now
protested that the cat sang exactly like Father Ambrose when
he officiated at the morning mass, and that her heart, the
signora's, was filled with pious devotion.

"I must, however, bring this cat-mass to an end," cried
Goethe, laughing, "for if the cat continues her devotions
much longer, another miracle will take place: the divine
locks will dissolve, and the lips, so expressive of wisdom and
majesty, will be nothing more than shapeless plaster. Halloo!
father cat, away with you! You shall not transform the god
into a lump of plaster!" With threatening tones and gestures
he frightened the cat down from the wardrobe, and drove her
out of the room. Goethe and his friend then returned to the
parlor.

"Wonders are the order of the day," said Moritz, thoughtfully, "and we are surrounded by a mysterious atmosphere of
dreams and tokens."

"Only when we are dreamers," cried Goethe, laughing.
"To the unbiassed there is nothing miraculous, to them all
things seem natural."

"How can you explain the cat's rapturous devotion?"

"In a very prosaic, pitiful manner," replied Goethe, smiling. "You know, exalted dreamer, that this bust was moulded but a few days ago, and you also know that grease was used to prevent the plaster from adhering to the form. Some of this grease remained in the cavities of the beard and lips; the cat's fine sense of smell detected its presence, and she was endavoring to lick it off." *

Philip Moritz raised his arms, and looked upward with comic pathos: "Hear this mocker, this cold-hearted materialist, ye eternal, ye sublime gods! punish the blasphemer who mocks at his own poetic genius; punish him by filling his cold heart with a lost passionate love! Cast down this proud poet in the dust, in order that he be made aware that he is still a mortal in spite of his poetic renown, and that he dare not attempt to hold himself aloof from human love and human suffering!—Venus Aphrodite, pour out the lava streams of your passion on this presumptuous poet, and—"

"Hold, hold!" cried Goethe, laughing, as he seized his friend's arms, and forcibly drew them down. "You remind me of Thetis invoking the wrath of the great Zeus upon the head of the son he believed to be guilty, and to whom the god granted his cruel prayer."

"Signori, signori!" cried Signora Abazza from the outside.

"Come in, come in, signora! What is the matter this time?"

"Signore Zucchi has arrived from Rome with his divine signora," said the old woman, appearing in the doorway, "they inquired at the post-office for your letters and papers, as they promised to do, and here is the mail Signora Angelica has brought you."

Goethe hastily opened and examined the sealed package which she had handed him. "Newspapers! newspapers!" exclaimed he, throwing the folded papers on the table. "I am surrounded by living Nature, what care I for lifeless newspapers."

"You will not read them?" said Moritz. "You have no

---

* This cat story Goethe relates precisely as above, in his "Italian Trip."—See Goethe's Works, vol. xxiii.. p. 181.

desire to learn what is taking place in the German empire, to learn whether the emperor has undertaken another campaign against presumptuous Prussia or not?"

"No, I wish to know nothing of war," said Goethe, softly. "I am a child of peace. I wish eternal peace to the whole world, now that I am at peace with myself." *

"Then permit me, at least, to interest myself in these matters," said Moritz, taking one of the papers from the table and opening it. With a cry of joy Goethe picked up the three letters that fell to the floor.

"Two letters for me! A letter from my Charlotte, and one from my dear friend, Herder! And here is a letter for you, friend Moritz."

"A letter for me!" said Moritz, clutching and hastily opening the letter Goethe held in his extended hand. "Who can have written to me?"

"Read, my friend, and you will see. I will first read Herder's letter, it probably contains his opinion of my 'Egmont,' which I sent him some time ago."

He seated himself at the little table, opposite Moritz. Both were soon busily reading, and Goethe was so completely absorbed in his letter that he did not notice how pale Moritz had become, and how the letter trembled in his hands; nor did he hear the deep sighs that escaped his lips.

"I knew these fault-finders would not understand my Clärchen; they demand another scene, explaining her relation to Egmont. Another scene! Where am I to introduce it? Where?"

"Goethe," said Moritz, rising and handing the letter, which he had read again and again, to his friend, "Goethe, read this, and then laugh at my dreams and presentiments, if you can."

"What is it?" asked Goethe, looking up. "But what is the matter with you, my friend? How pale you are, and how you tremble! Tears in your eyes, too! Have you received bad news?"

---

* Goethe's own words.—See "Italian Trip," vol. xxiv., p. 146.

"I have," groaned Moritz. "Marie is ill. Read!"

Goethe took the letter and hastily glanced over it. It was from Professor Gedicke in Berlin; he announced that Marie Leuthen had been ill for some time; that she had, at first, concealed her illness, but now admitted it, and expressed an ardent desire to see Moritz. The physician had given it as his opinion that a reunion with her lover after so long a separation would have a beneficial effect on his patient, and infuse new life into her being; it was therefore considered desirable that Moritz should speedily return to Germany and Berlin, to restore health and happiness to his beloved. "Strange, truly strange!" said Goethe. "Your dream is being fulfilled, your presentiment has become reality."

"Fearful reality!" groaned Moritz. "Marie will die, I shall not see her again!"

"No, oh no," said Goethe, endeavoring to console him. "You take too gloomy a view of things; your fancy conjures up horrible visions. You will see her again. The magical influence of your presence, the heavenly fire of your love, will save her. Women are generally such sensitively constituted beings that all ordinary laws are set at defiance when they love. They die of love, and they live on love. Marie is ill because she longs to be with you; she will recover when she once more beholds you, and reads love and fidelity in your countenance."

"Marie will die!" groaned Moritz. "God grant that I may, at least, arrive in time to kiss the last death-sigh from her lips!"

"You are then about to take your departure? You will leave Italy and return to Germany?"

Moritz shrugged his shoulders. "Truly, Goethe, in this question I see that your heart is cold and loveless. I leave here within an hour!"

Goethe extended both hands, and his eyes shone with deep sympathy, as he gazed lovingly into his friend's pale countenance. "Moritz, I am not cold and not loveless. I understand you. I appreciate your grief. I know that you must leave me, and must answer this call. Do not misunderstand me, my friend, and when I subdue the holy flames, that glow in your soul and my own, with the prose of every-day life, remember that I have eaten much bitter fruit from the tree of knowledge, and that I anxiously avoid being poisoned in that manner again. But a blasphemer I am not, and be it far from me to desire to shake your resolution. Love is the holy god who often determines our thoughts and actions, and love it is that calls you! Go, my friend, answer this call, and may love console and give you heavenly delight. Go! I will assist you in getting ready! We will go to work at once! The stage leaves here for Rome in a few hours, and you will arrive there in time to take the mail-coach for Milan this evening."

Goethe assisted his friend in preparing for his departure with such tender solicitude that Moritz's eyes filled with tears at the thought of separation from his dear companion.

Angelica Kaufmann, the celebrated painter, who had now been married to the artist, Tucchi, for some months, sent twice to her friend Goethe inviting him to take a walk, but in vain. It was in vain that a merry party of artists, who were sojourning in Castel Gandolfo, sang beneath Goethe's window, and entreated him to join them in an excursion to the mountains, where they proposed to draw, paint, and amuse themselves till evening.

Goethe let them go without him and remained with his friend, endeavoring to console and encourage him. When the trunk was entirely packed, Goethe quietly slipped a well-filled purse into the tray, hastily locked the trunk, and handed the key to Moritz. "All is now ready, my friend. Listen how our friend, the stage-driver, is cracking his whip and giving vent to his impatience, at the delay we have caused, in his charming Italian oaths. We will promise him a gratuity, as an incentive to make him drive rapidly, to ensure your arriving in Rome in time for the mail-coach."

"May heaven grant that I arrive in Berlin in time to find Marie still living! this is all I crave! You see life has made me humble and modest; my life has been rich in misfortunes and poor in joys. I found two beautiful blossoms on my journey: Marie's love and Goethe's friendship. But I will lose them both; death will tread the one of these blossoms under foot, and life the other."

Goethe laid his hand gently on Moritz's shoulder, and gazed into his countenance in deep emotion. "What fate has determined concerning the blossom of your love, that we must await with composure and resignation, for death is an almighty king, before whom the haughtiest head must bow in reverence. But the blossom of friendship which we have so tenderly nurtured, and which has so often cheered and refreshed our hearts—that blossom we will preserve and protect from all the storms of life. You may be right in asserting that the flames of love are extinguished in my heart, but the light of friendship is still burning brightly there, and will only expire with my death. Be ever mindful of this, and, although you suppose me to be a cold lover, you shall never have cause to consider me a cold friend. Let this be our farewell; ever bear this in mind."

"This thought will console and encourage," said Moritz, his eyes filling with tears. "All that I have enjoyed in these last few years that was good and beautiful, I owe to you, and have enjoyed with you alone! Farewell, my Pylades! I feel that, like Orestes, I am being pursued by Furies, and driven out into the world, to death and to despair! Farewell, Goethe!"

They clasped each other in a long embrace, and then Goethe led his friend down to the stage in silence. He gave the angry driver a gratuity, and pressed his friend's hand warmly in a last farewell.

CHAPTER IX.

LEONORA.

GOETHE stood for a long time on the steps in front of the house, following with his gaze the departing stage, and listening to the jingling of the little bells with which the horses were adorned. When this also had finally become inaudible, Goethe turned slowly, a deep sigh escaping his lips, and reëntered the house.

But his apartments seemed bare and solitary, and even the drawings and paintings which had usually afforded him so much pleasure, were now distasteful.

He impatiently threw brush and palette aside and arose. "This solitude is unendurable," he murmured to himself, "I must seek company. I wish I knew where my merry friends have gone, I would like to follow them and take part in their merrymakings. But they will all have gone, not one of them will have been misanthropical enough to remain at home. I shall probably have to content myself with the society of Signora Abazza and her cat."

With rapid strides he passed down the broad marble steps and out into the garden. Here all was still and solitary. No human forms could be seen in the long avenues, bordered on either side with dense evergreen. No laughter or merry conversation resounded from the myrtle arbors. In vain the wind shook down the ripe fruit from the orange trees, the merry artists were not there who were in the habit of playing ball with the golden fruit. In great dejection Goethe moved leisurely down the avenue which led to the large pavilion, built on a little hill at the end of the garden, and commanding a magnificent view of Lake Albano and its wooded shores. Goethe walked slowly toward this point, regardless of his surroundings of the marble statues that stood here and there in niches hewn out of the dense evergreen, and of the murmur-

ing of the neighboring cascades. The study of Nature in all
its details usually afforded him great enjoyment. He sought
out its mysteries as well in mosses, flowers, and insects, as in
the tall cypress, the eagle, and the clouds. But to-day, Nature with all its beauties was unheeded by the poet, he was
thinking of his absent friend; the words of separation still
resounded in his ear. His mind was burdened with an anxious
feeling like a presentiment of coming evil.

But Goethe was not the man to allow himself to be weighed
down by sadness. He suddenly stood still, threw back the
brown locks from his brow with a violent movement of the
head, and looked around defiantly.

"What misery do you wish to inflict on me, hollow-eyed
Melancholy," cried he, angrily. "Where do you lie concealed? from behind which hedge have you fastened your
stony gaze on me? Away with you! I will have nothing to
do with you; you shall not lay your cold, damp hand on my
warm human heart. I will—"

He suddenly ceased speaking, and looked up at the pavilion,
astonishment depicted in his countenance. In the doorway
of the pavilion, facing the garden, stood two girlish figures.
A ray of sunshine penetrated the open window at the other
end of the hall and illumined this door-way, surrounding these
figures as with a frame of transparent gold, and encircling
their heads with a halo of light. The one was tall and slender; the dark complexion, the brown cheeks, slightly tinged
with crimson, the purple lips, the delicately-curved nose, the
large, sparkling black eyes, the glossy black hair, and an inexpressible something in her whole appearance and expression,
betrayed the Roman maiden, the proud daughter of the
Cæsars. The young girl who stood at her side was entirely
different in appearance. She was not so tall, and yet she was
as symmetrical in form as the goddess ascending from the
waves. Her light hair fell in a profusion of ringlets around
the brow of transparent whiteness, and down over the delicate
shoulders that were modestly veiled by her white muslin dress.

Her large black eyes were milder than, but not so luminous as, those of her companion; her delicately-formed cheeks were of a rosier hue; an innocent smile played about her purple lips, and illumined her whole countenance. Her lovely head rested on her companion's shoulder, and when she raised her right arm and laid it around her neck, the loose sleeve fell back and disclosed an arm of dazzling whiteness and rare beauty. They stood there in silence, surrounded by a halo of sunshine, looking dreamily around at the garden with its variegated autumnal hues.

At the foot of the hill on which the pavilion was situated, stood Goethe, his countenance radiant with delight, feasting his eyes on this charming picture.

"Apollo himself must have sent me this divine picture. I will engrave it deeply on my heart, that it may some day find utterance in living, breathing poetry. Ye are the fair ones of whom my soul has of late been dreaming, whenever Torquato Tasso's image arose before my imagination. I will make you both immortal, at least in so far as it is given to the poet to make aught immortal. Apollo, I thank thee for this apparition! These are my two princesses, my two Leonoras, and here stands Tasso, looking up to them with enraptured adoration! But, O ye gods, harden my heart against the flames of love, preserve me from Tasso's fate!"

"Signor Goethe!" exclaimed the Roman maiden, who had just perceived the poet standing at the foot of the hill, as she stepped forward to the head of the stone stairway that led up to the pavilion. She stood there bowing her head in greeting, and beckoning to him to come up, while the fair-haired girl remained in the door, smiling at her friend's eager gestures.

"Come up, Signore; mother is in the pavilion, and a party of friends will soon join us here; we shall then play and be merry."

"Yes, we shall play and be merry," cried Goethe, as he rushed up the steps, and extended his hand to the fair friend who awaited him.

"A greeting to you, beautiful Amarilla, and many thanks for your kind invitation." Signora Amarilla grasped his hand cordially, and then turned to her friend, "Leonora—"

"Leonora!" repeated Goethe, startled, "the signora's name is Leonora?"

Signora Amarilla looked at him with astonishment. "Yes, Leonora. And why not? Is this name so remarkable, so unheard of?"

"No, not exactly that, and yet it is a remarkable coincidence that—"

In her animation, Amarilla took no notice of the words Schiller had murmured, but ran to the door, grasped her friend's hand, and led her forward. The young girl seemed to follow her almost reluctantly; her lovely eyes were cast down, and a brighter color diffused itself over her cheeks.

"Leonora, this is the Signore Goethe, about whom I told you so much this morning—the signore who lives in Rome, in the house adjoining ours, on the Corso—the one to whom the artists recently gave the magnificent serenade that was the talk of all Rome for three days. We supposed the signore to be a rich Inglese, because he indulged in so costly a pleasure, but he tells us that he is only a poor German poet; this, however, I do not believe. But look up, Leonora! look at the gentleman! He is an intimate acquaintance of mine, and I have already told you so much about him."

While Signora Amarilla was laughing and speaking, with the unceasing fluency of tongue peculiar to the ladies of Rome, Leonora stood at her side, her eyes still cast down. Goethe's gaze was fixed immovably on the beautiful vision before him. Did his ardent gaze, or his glowing thoughts, exercise a magical influence over her? Slowly she raised her head, and opened the large timid eyes, shaded with long black lashes, and looked at Goethe. Their glances met, and both started; the hearts of both beat higher. Her cheeks glowed, his turned pale. He felt as though a whirlwind had arisen in his heart, and was carrying him he knew not where, either

heavenward or into an abyss. His head swam, and he staggered back a step; she grasped her friend's hand, as if to sustain herself.

Signora Amarilla had observed nothing of this mute
greeting and interchange of thought; she chatted away
merrily.

"Now, Signore Goethe, permit me to introduce this young
lady; you will have great cause to be thankful for the honor
conferred on you. This is my dear friend Signora Leonora
Bandetto. Her brother is the confidential clerk in the business establishment of Mr. Jenkins. He was very homesick,
and longed to be with his family in Milan. As he could not
conveniently leave Rome, he begged that his sister Leonora
might be permitted to come on to live with him and take
charge of his household. The most beautiful daughter of
Milan came to Rome in answer to this appeal. I made her
acquaintance at a party at Mr. Jenkins's, and we became
friends. We love each other tenderly, and I stormed Signore Bandetto with entreaties until he consented to lend me
his sister for a few weeks. Leonora came to Castel Gandolfo
to-day, and will spend two weeks with us, two heavenly weeks.
This is the whole story, and now let us go into the pavilion."

She tripped gayly toward the door, leading her friend by
the hand; Goethe followed them slowly, his breast filled with
strange emotions.

At the entrance they were received by Signora Amarilla's
mother, who was surrounded by a number of young ladies
who had just arrived. Several young gentlemen, artists and
poets, soon joined the party; the little pavilion was now the
scene of great gayety. Laughter and jesting resounded on
all sides; and, finally, the game of lotto, the favorite game of
the Romans, and the occasion of this little gathering, was
commenced.

Poor Moritz, poor friend, who is journeying toward Rome
in sadness, it is well that you cannot look back at this scene!
It is well that you cannot see the friend for whom your heart

is sorrowing, seated between the two lovely women, between Amarilla and Leonora, laughing and jesting with the former, but having eyes and thoughts for Leonora only! It is well, poor Moritz, that you cannot see Goethe's eyes kindling with rapture, and his countenance radiant with enthusiasm, as he laughs and jests, the youngest among the young, the gayest among the gay!

It is now Signora Amarilla's turn to keep the bank. Goethe is her partner; he divides his money and winnings with her, but the losses he bears alone. The beautiful Amarilla's mother, who is seated in front of them on the other side of the long table, looks on with great content, laughs heartily at Signore Goethe's jokes, and rejoices at the bank's success, because her daughter's little treasure increases. But a change comes over her countenance, her dark eyes no longer sparkle with delight. This change is evidently owing to the fact that Signore Wolfgang Goethe has dissolved the partnership that existed between himself and her daughter; he tendered his services as partner to Leonora, and is accepted. Not being familiar with the game, she allows Goethe to guide and direct her. She is fast losing her timidity, and is already conversing quite gayly and confidentially with the signore who eagerly gratifies all her little wishes.

The right to keep the bank now passed from Leonora to her neighbor. Goethe, however, did not offer to be her partner too, but quietly retained his place between the two lovely girls. While Amarilla, with all the animation of her southern nature, gave her exclusive attention to the game, while all the players were anxiously listening to the numbers as they were called out, and covering them on their cards with little squares of glass, Goethe sat leaning back in his chair, gazing into the beautiful countenance of his neighbor, who no longer desired to take part in the game, but preferred to cease playing, as she told Goethe naively, rather than run the risk of losing the two scudi she had already won.

"Signore, we must not tempt fortune," said she, as she

raised the little coins, which amounted to two scudi in value, in her delicate little hands, and then let them fall one by one into her lap. Unconscious of what she was doing, she continued to play with the little bajocchi and paoli, raising and letting them fall again and again into her lap.

Goethe smilingly regarded the beautiful hands as they toyed with the little coins, and thought of Correggio's celebrated painting of Danaë and the shower of gold. The thought occurred to him: "It is well that the gods no longer roam the earth tempting innocence with such a shower! Could this lovely child also have been ensnared by the shower of gold?"

"You laugh, signore," said Leonora, looking earnestly at Goethe; "you laugh, but it is, nevertheless, true! We must not tempt fortune; we are sure to suffer when we confide in fortune."

"Is Fortuna so bad a goddess?" asked Goethe, smiling.

"Fortuna is no goddess," replied Leonora, earnestly; "Fortuna is a demon, signore. She is the daughter of the tempter who spoke to the mother of mankind in the garden of Eden. If we listen to her words and allow ourselves to be ensnared by her allurements, our good thoughts vanish, and we are led astray."

"You calumniate the noble goddess, signora. You are doubly unjust to Fortuna; has she not smiled on you to-day, and are not your thoughts good and innocent?"

"I, myself, am a proof that she is a temptress, a demon," said Leonora, eagerly, but in a subdued voice. "I will tell you my thoughts, signore; there is something in your eyes that compels me to confess the truth. Listen, signore. When I, thanks to your good advice and skill, had won the first few paoli, I rejoiced over my fortune and thought to myself: 'I will give these to Theresa, the old woman I see on the steps of the Santa Marie della Pace, every morning when I attend mass at this church.' Old Theresa invariably stretches out her withered, trembling hand, and I am so

rarely able to give her any thing, for my brother is not rich, signore, and we are compelled to economize his earnings. It always grieves me to have to pass by the poor woman without giving her any thing. I rejoiced over the first few paoli I had won, calculating that I could have them changed into copper coins and give Theresa one each day for a whole week. At this moment you handed me a few more paoli, telling me that I had already won an entire scudo. But what followed! Old Theresa's image vanished from my heart; it occurred to me that my brother had recently wished for a new cravat, and that I could now purchase it with my scudo. You are laughing at me, signore, are you not? You are right; it is very bold in me to impart my foolish, girlish thoughts to so wise a gentleman as yourself."

"No, signora, I am not laughing at you," said Goethe, in such tender tones that she looked up in surprise and listened attentively, as though his words were sweet music. "I was only amused because your own words rebutted your accusations against Fortuna. The goddess has awakened good thoughts only in your bosom!"

"But I have not yet finished, signore! Only wait a little! My old beggar-woman was forgotten, and I had determined to devote my scudo to the purchase of the silk cravat for my brother. But I won, again and again, and you poured the little paoli into my hand, and observed laughingly: you are now rich, signora, for you have already won more than two scudi! Your words startled me; I now heard a tempting voice whispering in my breast: 'Play on, Leonora; play on. Win one more scudo, and then you will have enough to buy the coral earrings you recently admired so much, but were unable to buy. Play on, Leonora; win money enough to purchase this jewelry.' I was about to continue playing, thinking neither of the old woman nor of my brother, but only of my own desires. But I suddenly remembered the last words my confessor, Father Ignatio, had spoken to me in Milan when I took leave of him. He said: 'My child, when you hear the tempter's voice, pray for strength to resist his allurements;' and I did pray, signore. While we were praying, I vowed to the holy virgin that I would not purchase the jewelry, but would expend my scudi for my brother and my poor old Theresa only. I will keep my vow. Now you will admit that Fortuna is a demon, a daughter of the temptress who spoke to our mother Eve, and was the cause of the expulsion of mankind from Paradise, will you not?"

Goethe did not reply; with an inward tremor that was inexplicable to himself, he gazed at the lovely being whose cheeks were flushed with animation, and whose countenance shone with the holy light of purity and innocence. Her sweet voice still rang in his ear after she had ceased speaking.

"Confess, signore!" repeated Leonora, eagerly.

Goethe gave her a look of infinite mildness and tenderness. "Signora, you, at least, are still in Paradise, and may the avenging angel with the flaming sword never touch the pure brow which the angel of innocence has kissed and sanctified."

"We have finished, the game is at an end!" cried the imperious voice of Amarilla's mother. In the bustle which ensued, Leonora, who was listening breathlessly, failed to catch the words which Goethe added in a low tone.

The company had arisen from the table, and formed little groups in various parts of the pavilion. Goethe had stepped to an open window and was looking out at the lake, that glittered in the last rays of the setting sun. Suddenly a hand was laid heavily on his shoulder; he slowly turned and saw Signora Frezzi, Amarilla's mother, standing at his side. Her countenance was grave, her brow clouded, and the accustomed smile was wanting on her lips.

"Signore Goethe, you are a stranger, and are, of course, not familiar with the usages of our favored land," said she, in subdued, reproachful tones.

"Have I sinned, signora?" asked he, gayly. "Have I been guilty of an impropriety?"

"Yes, signore, you have, and as Amarilla's mother, I must say that I cannot suffer the innocent child to be affronted."

"But, signora," he asked, in alarm, "how can I have affronted your daughter?"

"I will tell you, signore. You have known my daughter since your concert in Rome, and, when we met here in Castel Gandolfo a week ago, you showed a disposition to cultivate her acquaintance. Since then you have been her companion on all our walks and excursions. It is recognized as your right by all our friends and acquaintances, and no one would dream of attempting to take your place at her side. It is a good old custom for each young lady and gentleman to select a special friend during their summer sojourn in the country. It binds the young lady and gentleman who have associated themselves in this manner, to the most enduring and delicate attentions to each other until they return to Rome, when, of course, all obligation ceases."

"What impropriety have I committed?"

"This impropriety, signore: for the last week you have been recognized by every one as the *amico* of my daughter, and now, when you have scarcely made the acquaintance of her friend Leonora, you transfer the attentions hitherto shown to my daughter to this young lady. This is not proper, signore, and I must request you—"

"I have a request to make of you first, signora," said Goethe, interrupting her in severe and imperious tones. "I must request you not to forget that I am a stranger, and cannot give up the customs and usages of my own country. In Germany it is c stomary for gentlemen to be polite to all ladies. This, it seems to me, is better and more agreeable than to show exclusive attention and devotion to *one* lady to the neglect of all others. You will have to permit me to pursue the course I deem the most proper."

He left her side, and walked through the pavilion to the bay-window in which the two young ladies were standing. They both smiled as he approached. Amarilla had just broken off a twig of blooming myrtle from the vine that clung to the lattice-work of the pavilion, and was fastening it in Leonora's hair. She pointed proudly to her friend:

"See how beautiful she is, signore! Does she not look like the goddess of love with the flowers of love in her hair?"

Leonora blushed and turned her head hastily toward the open window. Th myrtle fell from her hair to the floor, at Goethe's feet. He stooped down and picked it up. His heart beat tumultuously, and a feeling of wondrous delight ran through his whole being as he handed it to Amarilla to be replaced in Leonora's hair.

"How long will it be," said Amarilla, smiling, as she again fastened the myrtle in her friend's hair; "how long will it be before I adorn this golden hair with a real bridal wreath!"

She looked smilingly at Goethe as she uttered these words, and this look made his heart quake. How composed this heart had hitherto been since his sojourn in Italy! How carefully had Goethe avoided awakening it from this state of dreamy repose! How sedulously had he avoided women, living only for art and nature! Now, when he hardly knew that he had a heart, it suddenly beat tumultuously, and filled his breast with all the sweet sensations and stormy desires of former days!

He was so astonished and bewildered by this revelation, that he was unable to take part in the conversation going on around him, or to appear indifferent to this charming girl. He left the pavilion and sought out the most solitary part of the park, where he walked to and fro for hours, listening to the sweet voices that were whispering in his soul. He smiled when he remembered how Moritz had entreated the gods to melt his icy heart; his friend's wish was being gratified in a charming manner!

"I thank you, ye eternal gods, for having accorded me this highest revelation of poetry here in Italy; I thank you for having enkindled in my heart the holy flames of love. I laughed at you, Venus Aphrodite, and you are punishing the

sinner with your sweetest wrath; you are permitting him to
feel that undying youth is still glowing in his bosom. For
love is eternal youth, and I love! Yes, I love!"

It was late at night, and his friends had long since retired
to rest, but Goethe was still walking to and fro in the gloomy
avenues of the park—in the avenues in which the pious
fathers of the order of the holy Ignatius had formerly wandered, forming plans to divert the power and glory of the
whole world into their hands.

The palace that now belonged to the wealthy Mr. Jenkins
had formerly been the summer residence of the general of
this order. The monastery was situated at the other end of
the park. Pope Urban had once walked arm in arm with his
friend the Jesuit general in these avenues, and together they
had considered how they were to subjugate princes and
nations, and make themselves masters of the world.

Goethe thought of this as he stepped into the main avenue,
and saw before him the grand old palace.

"Truly," murmured he, "this is the work of the holy
fathers. They have thrown a Jesuit's cloak over the mischievous god. In this disguise, he has dogged my footsteps,
and, while I fondly believed myself to be conversing with an
honest priest on learned topics, this impudent knave has so bewitched me that I have abjured all wisdom, and am about to
become a fool among fools."

"But what is to come of this, you fool?" asked he of himself. "Where is your love for this beautiful child to lead
you?"

He listened, as if expecting an answer from the night wind
that rustled by. He looked up at the moon, to see if a solution of this mystery of the future could be found in its
shining countenance. In his heart the mocking words of his
own song were all the while ringing, singing, and laughing
in low tones:

" Heirathen, Kind, ist wonderlich Wort,
Hör' ich's, möcht ich gleich wieder fort!" *

* When marriage is spoken of, my child, I feel like leaving at once.

He repeated these words again and again, as he slowly walked toward the house, endeavoring to convince himself that they embodied his own sentiments. But the moonbeams are strange sorcerers; over the glittering waters of the murmuring cascades, and in every open myrtle-blossom, he saw the countenance of a lovely girl, who seemed to greet him with her dark, starlike eyes, and whose golden hair encompassed her angel countenance as with a halo of beauty and innocence.

Goethe smiled, and whispered the following lines of the same song:

> " Heirathen wir eben,
> Das übrige wird sich geben !" *

CHAPTER X.

A DREAM OF LOVE.

STRONG and mighty, harnessed, and full of life, as Minerva had sprung forth from the head of Jupiter, had love suddenly arisen in Goethe's heart. A single day had awakened it, a single night had sufficed to make it strong, mighty, and confident of victory.

When Goethe, after having passed a night of delightful dreams, left his apartments on the following morning, and repaired to the large saloon in which the Jesuit general had formerly entertained his devout guests, and in which merry artists and men of the world, and joyous and beautiful women, were now in the habit of assembling, his countenance wore a glad smile. He had bravely resolved to permit himself to be borne onward on the seething, silver waves of feeling, regardless of whither they tended—satisfied that they would bear him to some one of the enchanted isles of bliss, on the fragrant shores of which two white arms would embrace him, and two

---

* Let us only marry, the rest will take care of itself.

radiant eyes would whisper wondrous music in his listening heart,

He was alone in the large room. The artists had returned at a late hour from their excursion of the previous day, and had not yet left their apartments. Angelica Kaufmann, who, with her husband, the old painter Zucchi, was always the first to take her seat at the breakfast-table, had to-day sent down word that she was tormented with headache, and would breakfast in her apartments. Signora Frezzi avoided the parlor, because she did not desire to meet Goethe, whose abrupt behavior of the day before had offended her.

The newspapers that had arrived yesterday were lying around on the little tables. Goethe seated himself at one of these tables, and opened one of the large English papers which are so great a solace to the blue-eyed daughters of Albion.

Two joyous, girlish voices interrupted his reading, causing him to throw his paper hastily aside, and sending the hot blood to his cheeks.

The voices were those of Amarilla and Leonora, who had come from the park, and now entered the parlor. They were attired in simple morning dresses, and looked charming with their fresh, rosy cheeks, and the blossoming sprigs of pomegranate in their waving hair.

Amarilla's quick, roving eye detected Goethe first, and she uttered a joyous greeting as she hurried forward with extended hands.

Leonora stood at a distance, but her smiling lips and the timid glance of her large eyes were more eloquent than Amarilla's words could possibly be.

He stepped forward and extended his hand to Leonora, and, when she laid her little hand in his, timidly, and yet with an expression of childlike confidence, his soul exulted, his heart overflowed with joy, and his countenance beamed with delight.

Amarilla did not observe this, as she was busily engaged in

pouring out the coffee at one of the tables. Leonora turned
pale under Goethe's glances, blushed, and then turned pale
again, and withdrew her hand with a quick, convulsive movement. She slowly raised her eyes, and looked at Goethe so
reproachfully, so anxiously, that a tremor of joy and emotion
ran through his whole being.

"Be firm, my heart, do not yield so soon to this sweet en-
chantment! First inhale the fragrance of this purple blossom which we call love, before you pluck it and press it to
your heart. Be firm, and enjoy the pure delight of the dawning sunlight!"

She glided slowly from his side, and now, when she stood
at the table assisting Amarilla, her anxious look vanished;
the timid little dove felt safe under the protecting wing of
the older and stronger dove; she had instinctively heard the
rustle of the falcon's wings, but now that she was at the side
of her sister dove she no longer feared.

Leonora smiled again, took part in the merry conversation
which Amarilla had begun with Signore Wolfgang, and seated
herself at his side at the breakfast-table, which Amarilla had
arranged for the three. It was a beautiful morning; the
fresh breeze wafted clouds of fragrance into the room through
the broad, open glass doors; the rustling of the orange and
myrtle trees, and the murmuring and plashing of the cascades, greeted the ear like soft music.

To Goethe, the two lovely girls between whom he sat seemed
as bright and fair as the morning. Their ingenuous conversation seemed to him more charming and instructive than
any conversation he had ever had with the most intellectual
women, or the greatest scholars on the most profound subjects.

His attention was, however, chiefly directed to the fair
daughter of Milan, the maiden with the light hair, dark eyes,
and the delicate, transparent cheeks—the maiden, whose
countenance was but the mirror of her soul, the mirror in
which her every thought and impulse was reflected.

Amarilla had taken one of the English newspapers, had

folded it into a cap in imitation of the *fazzoletta* of the Albanian peasant-women, and placed it jauntily on her pretty head. She was dancing around in the room, and singing in a low voice to the melody of the tarantella, one of those little love-ditties which gush so harmoniously from the lips of Italian maidens.

"She flies about like the bee, sipping sweets from every blossom, and fancies the world a vast flower-garden, created only for her delight."

"Are you of that opinion, beautiful Leonora?" asked Goethe, with a tender glance.

She shook her head slowly. "No," said she; "I know that both the bee and the flower are of but little importance in the great economy of the universe. I often think," she continued, in a low voice, and with a charmingly thoughtful air, "I often think that we poor, simple girls are nothing more in the sight of God than the bee and flower, and that it is immaterial whether we live or die."

"You have too poor an opinion of yourselves," said Goethe, in low and impassioned tones. "You do not know that the Almighty sometimes takes pity on men, and sends an angel of innocence, grace, and beauty, to console the human soul and refresh the human heart. You do not know that you are such an angel to me!"

She shook her lovely little head dissentingly. "I only know, signore, that I am a poor ignorant girl, and that I often long to cast off my stupidity, and be able to understand what wise men say. It is, however, not altogether my own fault that I am so stupid, that—"

"You are unjust to yourself," cried Goethe, interrupting her; "you should not confound the divine ignorance of innocence with stupidity."

"I speak the truth only," rejoined Leonora; "and you see that I am attempting to excuse myself by telling you that it is not wholly our own fault that we are so foolish and ignorant. Our parents and instructors, in their anxiety for our welfare, fear to open our eyes, believing it best that a girl should learn and know nothing. They do not teach us to write, because they fear that we would do nothing but write love-letters; nor would they teach us to read, if it were not to enable us to use our prayer-books. We are scarcely taught to express ourselves well in our own language; and it occurs to none to have us instructed in foreign languages, and give us access to the books of the world." *

"Would you like to be able to read in these books of the world, Leonora?"

"I would give all I possess to learn English! Whenever I hear Mr. Jenkins and my brother, or Madame Zucchi and her husband, conversing in English, it makes me feel sad, and a feeling of envy comes over me that I never experience at other times. See, Signore, Amarilla has made a *fazzoletta* from one of these large English papers, and is skipping around with it on her head, while I—I would give every thing to be able to read and understand what is written in the papers, which I know bring us intelligence from the whole world."

"You say you would give every thing to be able to read these papers? What will you give me if I teach you how to do so?"

"Do teach me," she cried, clapping her little hands joyfully; "oh, do teach me! I will be so thankful, so very thankful! You will make me so happy, and I know that you are noble and generous, and will find your best reward in having made a poor ignorant girl happy."

"Do you, then, really believe me to be so disinterested, signora?" asked Goethe, gazing earnestly into her animated countenance. "No, Leonora, you are mistaken in me! I am not so godlike as you suppose!"

At this moment the ringing tones of Amarilla's voice were wafted in from the terrace. She was singing to the charming air so well known to every Italian maiden and youth, and so familiar even to the orange groves and flowers, because they

---

* Leonora's own words.—See Goethe's Works, vol. xxiv., p. 135.

have so often heard it resounding from the cooing, exulting lips of lovers:

"Io ti voglio ben' assai
Ma tu non pens' a me !"

Alarmed by the impassioned tones of Goethe's voice, Leonora turned her head quickly toward the terrace. She smiled when she saw Amarilla skipping about from tree to tree, singing like a humming-bird, as she plucked a blossom or a sprig here and there, and arranged them into a bouquet.

"See, signore," whispered Leonora as she raised her delicate little hand and pointed to her friend. "I told you before that we were not taught how to write, for fear that we would write love-letters. See what we poor ignorant girls resort to when we wish to write a love-letter. Instead of using the letters of the alphabet we take flowers, that is the whole difference."

"Do you mean to say that Amarilla is writing a love-letter with her flowers?"

"Be still, do not betray her, signore. Look down, that no profane glance may desecrate the letters which God and the sun have created!"

"But I may look at that young man who is stealing out from behind the evergreen-hedge, may I not?"

"Of what young man are you speaking?" asked Leonora, in alarm.

"Of the young Comaccini, who is cautiously peering through those bushes, and for whom the fragrant love-letter, which Amarilla holds aloft so triumphantly, is probably intended."

"No, do not look that way, signore," cried Leonora, with an air of confusion, as she hastily took one of the papers from the table and handed it to Goethe.

"You said you would teach me to read these papers, to make out these difficult English words. Please do so, signore. I will be a very thankful scholar!"

Goethe smiled as he took the paper and unfolded it. He had laid his left arm on the back of the chair, in which Leonora sat; with his right hand he held the paper before her lovely countenance. He began to read and translate, word for word, the passage at which her rosy finger pointed. She listened with breathless attention, utterly unconscious that their heads were side by side, that her cheeks almost touched his, and that her fair, fragrant hair was intermingled with his brown locks. Her whole soul was filled with the determination to impress each word that Goethe uttered indelibly on her mind. Her glances flew like busy bees from the paper to his lips, unconscious that they bore a sting which was infusing sweet poison into the heart of her zealous teacher.

To be the teacher of a beautiful young girl is a dangerous office for a man who is young, and impetuous, and whose heart is not preoccupied. To read out of one book, cheek by jowl, so near to each other that the breath of his lips is mingled with hers, and that he can hear her heart's quick throbs—when has a woman done this with impunity, unless it was her lover or her husband with whom she was reading! Francesca da Rimini would not have been murdered by her jealous husband, if she had not read Launcelot with her handsome brother-in-law Paolo Malatesta.

> " One day we were reading for our delight,
> Of Launcelot, how love did him enthrall;
> Alone we were and without any fear.
> Full many a time our eyes together drew,
> That reading, and drove the color from our faces;
> But one point only was it that o'ercame us.
> When as we read of the much longed-for smile,
> Being by such a noble lover kissed,
> This one, who ne'er from me shall be divided,
> Kissed me upon the mouth all palpitating.
> Galeotto was the book and he who wrote it,
> That day no further did we read therein." *

They too were reading for their delight, and were alone without any fear.

Amarilla sang and danced about on the terrace, and paid no attention to the two who were sitting so close together and studying the English newspaper so earnestly. The passage at

* Dante Alighiere's Divine Comedy, canto v.—Translated by H. W. Longfellow.

which Leonora pointed, chanced to be the simple, touching history of a young man and a girl who loved each other devotedly, but could not be united because the man was already married. The girl, unable to conquer her love, and yet tormented with remorse and anguish, had buried her love and her sorrows in the dark waters of the Thames. Her lover poisoned himself when he learned the sad intelligence, leaving a letter, in which he begged that they might be permitted to rest in one grave.

Leonora's attention was so entirely absorbed in the translation of the separate words that the meaning of what they were reading escaped her. In breathless excitement she listened to the words of glowing passion that fell from her teacher's lips, and stored them away in her memory, as newly-acquired precious treasures. She cried out with delight, when, after they had translated the passage for the second time, she succeeded in comprehending its meaning, and could render whole sentences and periods in her own language. She was so beautiful in her innocent joy, her countenance was so animated, her eyes so radiant, the smile on her lips was so charming, that a tremor of delight ran through Goethe's being as he gazed at the fair creature. He said to himself that it must be enchanting to open the treasures of knowledge to this charming child of Nature, and to learn from her while giving her instruction.

They were still absorbed in the English lesson, and did not observe that the door was noiselessly opened, and that a young man with a merry countenance and bright smile appeared on the threshold. But, when he saw the two, seated side by side, shoulder to shoulder, cheek to cheek, she gazing fixedly at the paper, he regarding her with an expression of passionate tenderness—when the young man saw this, his merry expression vanished, and he cast a look of anger and hatred towards the readers. Leonora had just succeeded in translating the whole narrative, unassisted by her teacher, and now uttered the concluding words in a loud voice: "They found it sweeter to die in love than to live without love!" The pale young man with the angry countenance slowly withdrew, closing the door as noiselessly as he had before opened it. They observed nothing of this, and continued reading until a number of their friends and acquaintances entered the room, when they laid the paper aside, with a sigh and a mutual look of regret and tenderness.

The servants now appeared and were soon hastily engaged in preparing the breakfast table for the numerous guests who were sojourning in the house. Angelica Kaufmann, who had just entered the room on Mr. Jenkins's arm, stepped forward and greeted Goethe, cordially, mildly reproaching him with having neglected and forgotten her.

Goethe replied to this reproach, but not in his usual gay and unrestrained manner, and her keen glance detected a change in his countenance.

"One of the muses or goddesses of Olympus has paid you a visit this morning," said she. "Her kiss is still burning on your cheeks, and the heavenly fire is still flaming in your eyes. Tell me, my friend, which muse or which goddess was it that kissed you?"

"Why must it have been an immortal woman, Angelica?" asked Goethe, laughing.

"Because no mortal woman can touch your hard heart. You know your friend Moritz always called you the polar bear, and maintained that you had an iceberg in your breast instead of a heart. He was right, was he not?"

"Woe is me, if he was not, but is to be!" sighed Goethe, thinking of the dire visitation Moritz had called down upon his head.

Breakfast was announced, and the guests began to seat themselves at the table. The place of honor was generally conceded to be at Goethe's side, Mr. Jenkins therefore requested Angelica Kaufmann to take the seat on Goethe's right hand. While he was looking around, considering to whom he should accord the second place of honor on Goethe's left, Leonora stepped forward and quietly seated herself in the coveted place at her instructor's side.

"I cannot separate myself from you, maestro," said she, smiling. "You must repeat, and explain to me, a few words of our lesson. Only think, I have already forgotten the sentence which commences: 'Sweet it is to die in love.'"

Angelica's astonished look convinced Goethe that she had heard these words, and this confused him. His embarrassed manner, when he replied to Leonora, betrayed to Angelica the mystery of his sudden change of color when she had first spoken to him on entering the room. "I was mistaken," said she, in a low voice, and with her soft smile, "it was not a goddess or a muse who visited you. The god of gods himself has kissed your heart and opened your eyes that you might see."

Yes, these flaming eyes did see, and love had softened the poet's hard heart with kisses. His soul was filled with rapture as in the days of his first boyish love; every thing seemed changed—seemed to have become brighter and fairer. When he walked in the park with his friends after breakfast it seemed to him that his feet no longer touched the earth, but that his head pierced the heavens, and that he beheld the splendor of the sun and the lustre of the stars. He had gone to the pavilion, where he had first seen Leonora, hoping to find her there now. Amarilla had drawn her aside, after breakfast, and whispered a few words in her ear. Goethe had seen her shudder, turn pale, and reluctantly follow her friend from the room. He hoped to find her in the pavilion. She was, however, not there; a few groups of ladies and gentlemen were standing at the open windows, looking at the beautiful landscape.

Goethe stepped up to one of these windows and gazed out at the lovely lake with its rippling waves and wooded banks. It had never before looked so beautiful. He did not view this picture with the eye of an artist, who desires to reproduce what he sees in oil or aquarelle, but with the eye of an enraptured mortal, before whom a new world is suddenly unfolded, a world of beauty and of love.*

Suddenly he heard Amarilla's merry, laughing voice, and his heart told him that she also was near—she, the adored Leonora! Goethe turned towards the entrance. Yes, there was Leonora; there she stood on the threshold, at her side a young man, with whom she was conversing in low and eager tones.

"Here you are, Signore Goethe," cried Amarilla, stepping forward. "We have been looking for you everywhere, we—"

"Signore," said Goethe, interrupting her, and laying his hand gently on her arm, "pray tell me who that young man is with whom your friend Leonora is so eagerly conversing?"

"We have been looking for you to tell you this, and to make you acquainted with young Matteo. He has come to tell Leonora that the rich old uncle whose only heir he is, has suddenly died, and that no impediment to his marriage now exists."

"What does it concern your friend whether this Mr. Matteo has grown rich, and can now marry or not?"

"What does it concern her?" said Amarilla, laughing. "Well, I should think it concerned her a great deal, as she is betrothed to this Mr. Matteo, and their marriage is to take place in a week."

Not a muscle of his face quivered, not a look betrayed his anguish. He turned to the window, and stared out at the landscape which had before shone so lustrously in the bright sunlight. How changed! All was now night and darkness; a film had gathered over his eyes.

While he stood there, immovable, transfixed with dismay, he observed nothing of the little drama that was going on behind him; he did not feel the earnest gaze of the two pairs of eyes that were fastened on him: the eyes of Leonora, with tender sympathy; the eyes of the young man, with intense hatred.

* See Goethe's Works, vol. xxiv., p. 37.—"Trip to Italy."

"I saw him turn pale and shudder," hissed Matteo in Leonora's ear. "It startled him to hear that you were my betrothed. It seems that you have carefully concealed the fact that you were my affianced, and about to become my bride?"

"I have not concealed it, Matteo, I had only forgotten it."

"A tender sweetheart, truly, who forgets her betrothal as soon as another, perhaps a handsomer man, makes his appearance."

"Ah, Matteo," whispered she, tears gushing from her eyes, "you do me injustice!"

He saw these tears and they made him furious. "Come now, and introduce me to this handsome signore," commanded Matteo, grimly; "tell him, in my presence, that our marriage is to come off in a week. But if you shed a single tear while telling him this, I will murder him, and—"

"Step aside, signore, if you please," said a voice behind him; "step aside, and permit me to pass through the doorway."

The voice was cold and composed, as was also the gaze which Goethe fastened on the young man. He did not even glance at Leonora; he had no words for the fair-haired girl, who looked up into his countenance so timidly and so anxiously. He passed out into the open air, down the steps and into the garden, leaving behind him her who but yesterday had seemed to him as the dawn of a new day, the glorious sunshine of a new youth—her, who to-day had cast a pall over his soul, and had cried into his sorrowing, quivering heart the last adieu of departing youth.

He passed the confines of the park, strode rapidly into the forest and sought out its densest solitude. There, where the stillness was unbroken, save by the rustling of trees and the dreamy song of birds—there he threw himself on a bed of moss, and uttered a cry, a single, fearful cry, that made the forest ring, and betrayed to God and Nature the mystery of the anguish of a noble, human heart, that was struggling with, but had not yet overcome, its agony.

Goethe did not return home from the forest until late in the evening. He retired to his room and locked himself in, desiring to see no one, to speak to no one, until he had subdued the demons that were whispering words of wild derision and mocking despair in his heart. He would not be the slave of passion. No one should see him until he had mastered his agony. Early the next morning he again wandered forth into the forest with his portfolio under his arm; leaving a message at the house for his friends to the effect that they must not expect him back to dinner, as he had gone out to draw, and would not return till late in the evening.

His friends, and *she* above all, should not know what he suffered! The forest is discreet, the trees will not betray the poor child of humanity who lies at their feet struggling with his own heart.

"I will not suffer, I will not bear the yoke! Did I come to Rome for any such purpose? did I come here to see my peace and tranquillity of mind burn like dry straw, under the kindling glances of a beautiful girl? No! I will not suffer! Pain shall have no power over me! It will and shall be conquered! Away with you, hollow-eyed monster! I will tread you under foot, will grind you in the dust as I would an adder!"

He sprang up from his bed of moss, and stamped on the ground, furiously. He then walked on deeper into the forest, compelling himself to be calm, and to contemplate Nature.

"Goethe, I command you to be calm," cried he, in stentorian tones. "I will collect buds and mosses, and choose butterflies and insects. Help me, Spirit of Nature! aid me, benign mother. Give me peace, peace!"

With firmer tread, his head proudly erect, he walked on in the silent forest, still murmuring from time to time: "I will have peace, peace!"

While Goethe was struggling with his heart, in the depths of the forest, and striving to be at peace with himself, another heart was undergoing the same ordeal, in silence and solitude. The heart of a tender, young girl, who hoped to attain by prayer what the strong man was determined to achieve by the power of his will.

She did not even know what it was that had so suddenly darkened her heart; she only felt that a change had taken place—that she was transformed into another being. An unaccountable feeling of anxiety had come over her—a restlessness that drove her from place to place, through the long avenues of the park, in search of solitude. She only asked herself this: What had she done to cause Signore Goethe to avoid her so studiously? Why had he left the house so early in the morning, and returned so late in the evening, for the past three days? Why was it that he conversed gayly with others when he returned in the evening, but had neither word nor look for her?

These questions gave her no rest; they tormented her throughout the entire day. "What wrong have I done him? Why is he angry with me? Why does he avoid me?" She sat in the pavilion repeating the questions that had made her miserable for the last three days, when suddenly Matteo, who had followed her, stepped forward and regarded her with such anger and hatred that she trembled under his glance like the dove under the claws of the falcon.

"What is the matter with you, Leonora?" he asked, gruffly. "Why are you weeping?"

"I do not know, Matteo," murmured Leonora. "Please be patient with me, it will soon pass away."

He laughed derisively. "You do not know! Then let me tell you. You have no honor! You have no fidelity! You are a vile, faithless creature, and not worthy of my love."

"How can you speak so, Matteo? What have I done?"

"I will tell you what you have done," he cried, furiously. "You have listened to the honeyed words of the tempter. Be still, do not contradict me! I saw you seated together— he, breathing sweet poison into your heart; and you, eagerly inhaling it. I hate and despise him, and I hate and curse you! There! I hurl my engagement ring at your feet, and will never take it back again—no, never! We are separated! Matteo will not stoop to marry a girl who has broken faith with him."

"I—with you? Matteo, that is false! That is false, I tell you."

"False, is it?" he cried, furiously. "Well then, swear by the holy virgin that your heart is pure; swear by all the saints that you love me, and that you do not love him, this Signore Goethe!"

She opened her mouth as if to speak, but no words escaped her lips. Her lovely features assumed an expression of dismay; she stared into vacancy, and stretched out her arms as if to ward off some horrible vision that had arisen before her.

"Speak!" cried he. "Swear that you do not love him!"

Her arms sank helplessly to her side, and a deathly pallor spread over her countenance as she slowly, but calmly and distinctly murmured: "I cannot swear, Matteo! I know it now, I feel it now: I do love him!"

Matteo responded with a cry of fury, and struck Leonora with his clinched fist so forcibly on the shoulder, that she fell to the ground with a cry of pain. He stood over her, cursing her, and vowing that he would have nothing more to do with the faithless woman. With a last imprecation, he then turned and rushed out of the pavilion and down into the garden. All was still in the pavilion. Leonora lay there with closed eyelids, stark and motionless, her countenance of a deathly pallor.

A pale woman glided in through the open door, looked anxiously around, and saw the form of the poor girl extended on the floor. "She has fainted! I must assist her!"

It was Angelica Kaufmann who uttered these words. She had been painting outside-on the porch, had heard every word that was spoken in the pavilion, and now came to help and console the poor sufferer.

She knelt down by her side; rested her head on her knees,

drew a smelling-bottle from her dress-pocket and held it to
the poor girl's nose.

She opened her eyes and gazed dreamily into the kind,
sympathetic countenance of the noble woman who knelt over
her.

"It is you, Signora Angelica," murmured Leonora. "You
were near? You heard all?"

"I heard all, Leonora," said the noble artiste, bending
down and kissing her pale lips.

"And you will betray me!" cried she, in dismay. "You
will tell him?"

"No, Leonora, I will not betray you to any one. I will tell
no human being a word of what I have overheard."

"Swear that you will not, signora. Swear that you will
keep my secret, and that you will not betray it to *him*, even
though my life should be at stake."

"I swear that I will not, Leonora. Have confidence in me,
my child! I have suffered as you suffer, and my heart still
bears the scars of deep and painful wounds. I have known
the anguish of hopeless love!"

"I too, suffer; I suffer terribly," murmured Leonora. "I
would gladly die, it would be a relief!"

"Poor child, death is not so kind a friend as to hasten to
our relief when we call him! We must learn to endure life,
and to say with smiling lips to the dagger when we draw it
from the bleeding wound: 'Paete, paete, non dolet!'"

CHAPTER XI.

ADIEU TO ITALY.

WRITHING in agony for three days and three long nights,
at length Goethe found relief in the omnipresent balsam, all-
healing Nature!

The poet-eagle was healed! The pinions of his soul had
recovered from the wounds inflicted by Cupid's envenomed

arrow. Six days of solitude, six days of restless wandering, six days of communing with God and Nature, six days of struggling with his own weakness—these six days have made him six years older, taught him to conquer pain, and restored him to joyousness and confidence in himself.

On the morning of the seventh day, Goethe entered the room where his friends were assembled, and greeted them with all his former gayety and cordiality. No change was observable in his countenance, except that he had become a little paler, and that his large brown eyes looked still larger than usual. Only once did an anxious expression flit over his countenance, and that was when he asked Signore Zucchi why his dear friend Angelica had not come down to breakfast with her husband.

"She is not here," replied Zucchi. "She has been in Rome for the past three days."

"In Rome?" repeated Goethe, with astonishment. "We intended making an excursion together through the Albanian Mountains, and now she has left us! When will she return?"

"That the physicians alone can tell you," replied Zucchi.

"Is Signora Angelica ill?" asked Goethe, with alarm.

"Oh, no, not she! But the young girl, the beautiful Leonora, has suddenly fallen ill. Angelica found her lying insensible on the floor of the pavilion. She interested herself in the poor girl, did all she could to cheer and console her, and even attempted to reconcile her to her affianced, from whom she had been estranged. Leonora, however, declared that she would never marry young Matteo—that she would become no man's wife, but would always remain with her brother. At her earnest request, Angelica took her to Rome, to her brother's house. She had hardly arrived there before she was taken violently ill with an attack of fever. She is in a very precarious condition, and Angelica, instead of finishing the large painting for which an Englishman has offered four thousand scudi, has made herself this poor girl's nurse."

Goethe had listened to this narrative in silence, his head

bowed down on his breast. When Zucchi ceased speaking, he raised his head, and cast a quick glance around the room. He saw gay and unconcerned countenances only. No one observed him—the story of his anguish was known to none of his friends.

He also seemed to be perfectly quiet and composed—to be occupied solely with his paintings and drawings. When his friends suggested that the time had now arrived to carry out their projected tour through the Albanian Mountains, Goethe declined to accompany them, telling them that an alteration which his friends in Germany desired him to make in his "Egmont," necessitated his speedy return to Rome.

Goethe returned to the city on the evening of the same day, and repaired, immediately on his arrival, to the house of Signore Bandetto, to inquire after his sister's condition. She was still dangerously ill, and the physicians gave but little hope. Signora Angelica was with her, nursing her like a tender mother. He returned to the house for the same purpose later in the evening, and so on each ensuing day. Gradually, the bulletins were more favorable, and he was told that she was steadily improving.

Goethe had been in Rome for two weeks, and had neither written nor painted during this time; he had even avoided the gods of the Belvidere and the holy halls of St. Peter's. The wounds of his heart were not yet quite healed. Leonora's illness still made them smart.

To-day, he had again repaired to Signor Bandetto's house, had seen Angelica Kaufmann, and had been told that all danger was now over. A weight of care was removed from his soul, and he now entered his studio with a gay and unclouded countenance for the first time during his stay in Rome. His studio was a scene of wild confusion; books, papers, drawings, chairs, and tables, were in the greatest disorder. The Juno Ludovisi's head was gray with dust, and the impious chambermaid had thrown the poet's dressing-gown over the figure of Cupid, as though the god of love were a clothes-rack.

Goethe laughed loudly, laughed for the first time in long, long weeks, and relieved the poor god of his disgraceful burden.

He then bowed profoundly, and looked intently into the mischievous god's smiling countenance, as if to defy him to do his worst.

From this hour Goethe was once more himself. All grief had vanished from his heart, and he was again restored to his former peace and gayety. He once more belonged to the gods and muses, to poetry and to nature. But, above all, to poetry! In the hours of his anguish the arts had not been able to rescue and strengthen him, but wondrous thoughts and sublime feelings had taken root in his soul.

Pain was overcome, as was also love. When he saw Leonora, after her recovery, and when she thanked him, in faltering tones, for his sympathy, and his frequent inquiries during her illness, Goethe smiled, and treated her as a kind father treats his child, or a brother his sister.

She fully understood the meaning of this smile, and shed many bitter tears in her little room in the stillness of the night, but she did not complain. She knew that this short-lived passion had fallen from Goethe, as the withered blossom falls from the laurel-tree, and that she would be nothing more than a remembrance in his life.

This consciousness she wore as a talisman against all sorrow; the roses returned to her cheeks, her eyes once more shone lustrously, and never in her after-life did she forget Goethe, as he never forgot her. The remembrance of this beautiful girl shone as a bright, unclouded star throughout Goethe's entire life; and in the days of his old age, when the heart that had throbbed so ardently in Rome had grown cold, Goethe said and wrote of this fair girl: "Her remembrance has never faded from my thought and soul."

Another painful awakening soon followed this short dream of love—the awakening from the dreamy, enchanting life in Italy, the return to Germany. It was a pain and a joy at the same time. The deep pain of separation from Rome, and the joyful prospect of returning to his home and friends, and, above all, to his friend Charlotte von Stein?

"It was for her sake that I conquered this passion," said Goethe to himself. "I told her that I would return to her, unfettered in hand and heart, and I will keep my promise. Charlotte's love, Charlotte's friendship, shall console me for what I have denied myself here, for what I leave behind me! You, too, will be there, Muses; you will follow me to the fatherland, and assemble lovingly around the poet in the little house in Weimar. A poet I am; that I feel; of that I am now convinced. In the next ten years of work that will at the utmost be vouchsafed me, I will strive to accomplish, by diligent application, as much that is good and great as I achieved without hard study in the days of my youthful vigor and enthusiasm. I will be diligent and joyous! I will live, create, and enjoy, and that I can do as well in Weimar as in Rome! I will bear the Italian heaven within me; I will erect 'Torquato Tasso' as a monument to Italy and myself. Farewell, sublime, divine Roma! A greeting to you, you dear little city, in which the prince lives whom I love, and the friend who belongs to my soul. A greeting to you, Weimar!"

BOOK IV.

CHAPTER I.

THE RETURN.

To-day is the anniversary of the birthday of the beautiful Princess Ferdinand, and is to be celebrated by a grand reception in the royal palace of Berlin. The rank and fashion of Berlin are invited. The ladies of the aristocracy are occupied with nothing but their toilette, this object of first and greatest importance to the fair creatures who form so marked a contrast to the lilies of the field, which neither toil nor spin, and are yet so gorgeously arrayed. Nor do these beautiful lilies of the parlor toil or spin; nor do they wait for the Lord to array them, but take this care upon themselves, and make it an affair of state in their lives. To the Countess Moltke it is also an affair of state, and all the more so as her waning beauty demanded increased attention to the arts of the toilette. The rose-colored satin dress lies on the sofa, awaiting the garland of roses destined to encircle its skirt. Her rich black hair is also to be adorned with a wreath of roses, for the countess has a decided penchant for them and fancies the color of her robe and flowers will be reflected in her countenance, and impart to it a youthful, rosy hue. The flowers had been ordered a week before at the establishment of Marie von Leuthen, the first manufacturer of them in the city, and the countess was now awaiting the return of the servant she had sent after them. For the past two years, and since the day on which she had opened her store on Frederick Street, Marie von Leuthen had furnished flowers for all the ladies of high rank in Berlin.

It was considered *bon ton* to buy one's wreaths, bouquets, and garlands from her. No one arranged them so prettily as she, no one understood imitating Nature in so beautiful and artistic a manner; moreover, it gave one the appearance of patronizing the unfortunate young woman, whose fate had been the all-engrossing topic of conversation in good society for an entire week. Her flowers were also very dear, and it was therefore all the more honorable to be able to say: "I purchased them from Madame von Leuthen. True, she is exceedingly dear, but her work is good, and, moreover, it is a sort of duty to assist her with our patronage. She is, as it were, one of us; we have been entertained by her, and have enjoyed many agreeable evenings at her house."

Marie von Leuthen had ceased to be a lady of fashion, but she had become the fashionable flower-manufacturer of the city, and, as we have already said, it was considered essential to adorn one's self from her establishment.

Madame von Moltke was therefore not a little dismayed when the servant returned, and announced that the flowers were not ready, and that Madame von Leuthen begged to be excused for not having been able to furnish them.

"But did you not tell her that I must necessarily have them?" asked the countess.

"My lady, I not only told old Trude so, but I reproached her violently for having accepted an order which her mistress could not execute; but the old woman shut the door in my face, and gave me no other answer than this: 'The flowers are not ready.'"

"But they can perhaps still be got ready," said the countess. "Probably she has a great deal of work on hand for this evening, and it will perhaps only be necessary to offer her a higher price in order to secure the preference above her other customers. Let my carriage be driven to the door. I will see and speak with this inconsiderate person myself!"

A quarter of an hour later the countess's carriage stopped in front of the store in Frederick Street, over the door of which was written in large letters: "Marie von Leuthen, manufacturer of flowers."

The servant hurried forward to open the door, and the countess glided majestically into the store, and greeted the old woman, who advanced to meet her, with a proud, and almost imperceptible inclination of the head.

"I wish to speak with Madame von Leuthen herself," said the countess, imperiously.

"Her ladyship, however, well knows that none of Madame von Leuthen's customers have had the pleasure of seeing her in the last two years," rejoined the old woman in sharp tones. "Her ladyship, like all the other inquisitive ladies, has often attempted to see and speak with my mistress, but always in vain. Madame von Leuthen has neither time nor inclination to be chatted with or stared at. She does the work and I receive the orders. Her ladyship must therefore have the goodness to say what she has to say to old Trude."

"I have come for my flowers," said the countess, angrily. "My servant tells me that he received the very impertinent message that they not only were not, but would not be, ready. I can, however, scarcely credit his statement, for I ordered these flowers myself, and when an order has been accepted, it must of course be filled at the proper time."

"Your servant told you the truth," replied old Trude, in grumbling tones, "the roses will not be ready."

"And why not, if I may be permitted to ask?"

"Certainly, why should you not ask? Of course you may ask," rejoined Trude, shrugging her shoulders. "The answer is: The roses have not been got ready, becau e Madame von Leuthen has not worked."

"Has your mistress then done so well that she is on the point of retiring from business?" asked the countess.

Trude raised her eyes with a peculiar expression to her ladyship's haughty countenance, and for a moment her withered old face quivered with pain. But this emotion she quickly suppressed, and assumed her former peevish and severe manner.

"What does my lady care whether my little Marie desires to retire to rest or not, or whether the good Lord wills that she shall do so," said she, gruffly. "Enough, the roses cannot indeed be ready, and if her ladyship is angry, let her scold old Trude, for she alone is to blame, as she never even gave Madame von Leuthen your order."

"This is, however, very wrong, very impertinent," cried the countess. "Pray, why did you accept the order?"

"True, that I ought not to have done," murmured the old woman to herself, "but I thought she would grow better, and instead—my lady," said she, interrupting herself. "I have nothing more to say, and must beg you to content yourself with my reply. No more flowers will be furnished to-day, and I will immediately lock the front door."

"She is a rude person," cried the countess, angrily. "If she dares to insult those who assisted her impoverished mistress out of benevolence and pity, in this shameless manner, the consequence will be that her customers will withdraw their patronage and give her no more orders."

"As you please, my lady," said old Trude, sorrowfully. "But be kind enough to go, if you have nothing further to say."

The countess gave the presuming old woman an annihilating glance, and rustled out of the store and into her carriage.

Trude hastily locked the door behind her, and pulled down the blind on the inside. "Who knows whether I shall ever unlock this door again!" sighed she. "Who knows whether she shall ever make flowers again!"

The old woman sank down on a chair and burst into tears. She quickly dried her eyes, however, and assumed an air of gayety when she heard her name called in the adjoining room, and walked hurriedly into the apartment from which the voice had proceeded.

"Here I am, my little Marie," said she, on entering; "here I am." She hurried forward to the pale lady, who was sitting in the arm-chair at the large round table.

Was that really Marie? Was this pale woman with the

large lustrous eyes, with the hectic flush on her hollow
cheeks—was this really that proud beauty who had laid aside
rank and wealth with royal contempt—who with joyous courage had determined to create for herself a new life, and, after
having avenged herself on her unworthy husband and her unnatural mother, had gone out into the world to earn a subsistence with the work of her hands? The figure of that
woman had been tall and full—the figure of this woman was
shrunken, and, in spite of the heavy woollen dress which she
wore, it was evident that nothing of their former beauty and
fulness remained to these shoulders, to these arms, and to this
unnaturally slight figure. And yet, although this pale woman
had retained so little of her former beauty, there was still an
inexpressible, a touching charm in her appearance. Disease
had laid waste her fair form, but disease had not been able to
deprive these eyes of their lustre, nor these cheeks of their
rosy hue. To be sure, the same lustrous eyes and flushed
cheeks were the fatal evidences of that disease which gives
those whom it destroys the appearance of improvement, and
permits them to hope until the last moment. Her brow was
clear and transparent, and a soft, tranquil smile rested oftener
on her thin, delicate lips than formerly. True, her figure
was thin and unattractive, but this attenuation gave to her
appearance something spirituelle. When she glided lightly
and noiselessly through the room, the thought would occur
to you that she was not a woman of earth, but must really be
one of those of whom we read in song and story—one who,
for some fault committed in heaven, or in the realm of spirits,
is compelled to descend to the earth to make atonement by
learning to suffer and endure pain like mortals! She had
been working flowers of every variety. Roses and lilies,
violets and forget-me-nots, tulips and pinks, and whatever else
the names of these lovely children of the spring and sun may
be, lay on the table in the greatest confusion. They were in
the varied stages of completion, some half finished, and others
wanting only a leaf or the stem. Marie held a bunch of lilies

in her delicate hand, and Trude sighed when she observed it. It seemed to her that her darling looked like the angel of death, standing on the brink of the grave, and waving her lilies in a greeting to the new life that was dawning for the dying mortal!

"Trude, who was it I heard speaking in the other room, who spoke in such loud tones?" asked Marie, as she leaned back in the arm-chair, as if exhausted by her work.—"Why do you not answer? Why do you not tell me who was there? Good heavens!" she cried, suddenly, "it cannot have been— O Trude, for God's sake, tell me, who was it? And if it was he, Trude—if he has at last come, then—"

"Be still, Marie!" answered the old woman, interrupting her, and assuming an air of gayety. "You are still the same young girl, just as impatient as ever! No, no, it was not he! It was only Countess Moltke, who wished to speak with you about a garland of roses."

"Countess Moltke!" repeated Marie, thoughtfully. "She, too, was present on that terrible day when—"

"Do not speak of it, do not think of it!" entreated the old woman. "You know the doctor told you that if you desired to grow healthy and strong again, you should lay aside all sad thoughts, and endeavor to be right cheerful."

"I am cheerful, Trude," replied Marie, smiling. "Each day brings him nearer, each fleeting hour shortens our long separation. I now bless the disease that attacked me two months ago, for, under the impression that I was about to die, you then did what I never would have done, you caused good Professor Gedicke to write to him and tell him to come home, as his Marie was very ill. I thank you, good Trude, for confessing this, and for giving me the blessed assurance that he will soon be here. But yet it was cruel to terrify and alarm him! I hope, however, that the professor has again written since then, and told him that all danger is over, and that I am very greatly improved!"

"And he did so, Marie; he wrote immediately after the

receipt of his letter from Rome, announcing his departure for home, and requesting that further intelligence, as to your condition, should be sent to him at the post-office in Stuttgart. Mr. Moritz knows that all danger is over, and that you are doing well. You are certainly doing well, are you not, dear Marie?"

"Yes, I am doing well, very well indeed, and better each day. I feel, at times, as though I had wings, and had flown high above the earth; when I look down, every thing seems small and indistinct, as though far away in the dim distance. You, however, are always near me, as is also his dear countenance; his large dark eyes are ever shining into my heart like two stars. I feel so happy when I see them—so light and free, that I seem to have bidden adieu to all earthly care and sorrow. Only at times my eyes grow a little dim, and my hands tremble so when I wish to work, and then something pains me here in the breast occasionally! But this need not disquiet you, Trude, it only pains a little, and it will soon pass away."

"Yes, indeed, it will soon pass away!" said Trude, turning aside, and hastily wiping away the tears which rushed to her eyes in spite of her endeavors to repress them. "Certainly, Marie, you will soon be entirely restored to health and strength; this weakness is only the result of your long illness."

Marie did not reply, but cast a quick, searching glance at old Trude's kind face, and then slowly raised her eyes toward heaven with an expression of earnest entreaty. But then a soft smile flitted over her countenance, and the ominous roses on her cheeks burned brighter.

"Yes, I will soon recover, Trude," she said, almost gayly. "Under such treatment I cannot fail to recover. You nurse me as tenderly as a mother nurses her child. And it is very necessary that I should, good Trude, for our supply of flowers is almost exhausted, and our purse is empty. This is the case, is it not? You gave Countess Moltke no garland of roses because we had no more."

"Yes, such is the case, Marie, if you must know. The roses are all sold, but that is easily accounted for, as no elegant lady is willing to wear any flowers but yours. You are quite right, Marie, you must make haste and get well, so that you can make a fresh supply of beautiful roses. But, in order to be entirely restored to health, you must rest and do no work whatever for the next few weeks."

"The next few weeks!" repeated Marie, in a slightly mocking tone of voice. "The next few weeks! Trude, that seems like an almost inconceivable eternity, and— But, good heavens! you do not believe that weeks will pass before Philip comes?"

"But why should I believe any thing of the kind, Marie?" said the old nurse, in tranquillizing tones. "He left Rome long ago, and Mr. Gedicke says we may expect him at any hour."

"How pleasantly that sounds! what music lies in your words, Trude!" sighed Marie. "We may expect him at any hour! Do you know, good Trude, that I am still nothing more than a foolish child! I have been awaiting Philip these two long years, and during this time I have always been joyous and patient, for I know that this separation was necessary, and would be a blessing to him I loved. 'Before the roses bloom, the thorns grow, and we are wounded by them when we pluck the lovely flowers!' This I have constantly repeated to myself during these two long years, and have borne the pain which the thorns caused me without murmuring. But now, when I know that I will soon see him again—now, each hour is magnified into an eternity of torment, and all reasoning is in vain, and all patience exhausted. I feel as though I could die for very longing to see him. And yet, I am determined not to die; I must live—live to pluck the roses after having suffered so much from the thorns. But, alas! Trude, if my sufferings shall have been too great—if I should die of these many wounds! Sometimes it seems to me as though my strength were entirely exhausted, and— There, the thorn is again piercing my heart! How it pains!"

She sank back groaning, and pressed her quivering hand to her breast. Trude hurried forward, rubbed her cold, damp brow with strengthening essences, and then ran to the closet to get the little phial of medicine which the physician had prescribed for such attacks of weakness.

"Open your lips, Marie, and swallow these drops; they will relieve you."

She slowly opened her eyes, and her trembling hand grasped the spoon which Trude had filled from the phial, and carried it to her pale lips.

"That will do you good, my dear child," said the old nurse, in a firm voice, that knew nothing of the tears which stood in her eyes. "The doctor said these little attacks were harmless, and would cease altogether by and by."

"Yes, they will cease altogether by and by," whispered Marie, after a pause. "Cease with my life! I will not die! No, I will not!"

With a quick movement, she arose and walked rapidly to and fro in the little room. A few roses and violets were swept from the table by Marie's dress, and fell to the floor. In passing, Marie's foot crushed them. She stood still and looked down sadly at these flowers.

"See, Trude," said she, with a faint smile, "a few moments ago I was complaining of having suffered so much from thorns, and now it looks as if Fate intended to avenge me. It strews my path with flowers, as for a bride on her way to the altar, or for a corpse that is being borne to the grave."

"But, my child, what strange words these are!" cried Trude, with assumed indignation. "The physician says that all danger is past, and that you are steadily improving; and you say such sad and ominous things that you make me feel sad myself, and make the tears gather in my eyes. That is not right, Marie, for you well know that the doctor said you must carefully avoid all agitation of mind, and endeavor to be uniformly cheerful."

"It is true, good nurse, I ought to be cheerful, and I will

be cheerful. You see it is only because I so long to live—so long to pluck a few roses after having been wounded by so many thorns. You must not scold me on this account," continued Marie, as she entwined her arms lovingly around her old nurse. "No, you must not scold me!"

"I am not scolding you, you dear, foolish child," said Trude, laughing. "I, too, so long to see you live; and if I could purchase life for you with my heart's blood—well, you know I would gladly shed my blood for you, drop by drop."

"Yes, I know you would," cried Marie, tenderly, as she rested her head on Trude's shoulder.

"Fortunately, however, it is not necessary," continued the old nurse. "Marie will live and be happy without old Trude's assistance. Professor Philip Moritz will make us healthy and happy."

"You, too?" asked Marie, a happy smile lighting up her countenance.—"Really, Trude, I believe you love him too, and I suppose I ought to be jealous of you for daring to love my Philip."

"Yes, I not only love him, but am completely bewitched by him," rejoined Trude, laughing. "I long for him, day and night, because I desire to see my child happy. Like a good, sensible girl, you must endeavor to recover your health and strength, in order that your Philip may rejoice when he arrives, and not suppose you to be still unwell."

"You are right, Trude, Philip will be alarmed if I am not looking well and strong. But then I really am well; all that I want is a little more strength. But that will soon come, as I intend to guard against all agitation and sad thoughts. These thoughts, however, return, again and again, particularly at night, when I am lying awake and feel feverish; they sit around my bed like ghosts, and not only tell me sad legends of the past but also make gloomy prophecies for the future. At night I seem to hear a cricket chirping in my heart in shrill, wailing tones: 'Marie, you must die, you have made many roses for others, but life has no roses for you, and'—but this is nonsense, and we will speak of it no longer."

"We will laugh at it," said Trude, "that will be still better." She stooped down to pick up the flowers Marie had trodden under foot, and availed herself of this opportunity to wipe the tears from her eyes. "The poor things! look, Marie, you have completely crushed the poor little violets!"

"There is a beautiful and touching poem about a crushed violet," said Marie, regarding the flowers thoughtfully. "Philip loved it, because his adored friend, Goethe, had written it. One day when I showed him the first violets I had made, he smiled, pressed the little flowers to his lips and repeated the last lines of this poem. It seems to me that I still hear the dear voice that always sounded like sweet music in my ear. 'And if I die, 'tis she who takes my life; through her I die, beneath her feet!' "

"There you have commenced again," sighed Trude. "No more sad words, Marie, it is not right!"

"You are right, nurse," cried Marie, throwing the flowers on the table. "What care we for crushed violets! We will have nothing to do with them! We will be gay! See, I am ascending my throne again," she continued, with mock gravity, as she seated herself in the arm-chair. "Now I am the princess in the fairy-tale, and you are the old housekeeper whose duty it is to see that her mistress is never troubled with ennui. Begin, madame; relate some story, or the princess will become angry and threaten you with her bunch of lilies."

"I am not at all afraid," said Trude, "I have a large supply of pretty stories on hand. I learned a great deal while attending to your commissions yesterday, Marie."

"My commissions? Ah yes, I recollect, I asked you to look at the little monument on my father's grave. It has already been placed there, has it not?"

"Yes, Marie, and the large cross of white marble is beautiful; the words you had engraved on it in golden letters are so simple and touching that the tears rushed to my eyes when I read: 'He has gone to eternal rest; peace be with him and with us all! His daughter, Marie, prays for him on earth; may he pray for her in heaven!' The golden words shone beautifully in the sun."

"They came from my heart, Trude. I am glad that I can think of my father without sorrow or reproach. We were reconciled; he often came to see me, and looked on at my work for hours together, rejoicing when I had finished a flower."

"It is true," said Trude, "your father was entirely changed. I believe his conscience was awakened, and that he became aware of how greatly he had sinned against a good and lovely daughter."

"Do not speak so, Trude. All else is forgotten, and I will only remember that he loved me when he died. The blessing uttered by his dying lips has wiped out his harsh words from my remembrance. Let it be so with you, too, Trude! Promise me that you will think of my father with kindness only."

"I promise," said the old woman, hesitatingly, "although— well, let the dead rest, we will speak of the living. Marie, whom do you suppose I met on my return from the church-yard? Mrs. General von Leuthen!"

"My mother," exclaimed Marie, raising her hand convulsively to her heart, "my mother!"

"Yes, your unnatural mother," cried Trude, passionately; "the woman who is the cause of all your misfortunes and sorrows—the woman I hate, and will never forgive—no, not even in my hour of death."

"I have already forgiven her, although my hour of death is, as I hope, far distant. Where did you see her?"

"Riding in a beautiful carriage, and very grand and stately she looked, too. Happening to see me, she called out to the servant, who sat by the coachman's side, to halt. The carriage stopped, and her ladyship had the wondrous condescension to beckon to me to approach."

"And you did so, I hope?" said Marie, eagerly.

"Yes, I did, but only because I thought you would be angry with me if I did not. I stepped up to the carriage, and her ladyship greeted me with the haughtiness of a queen, and inquired after the health of my dear mistress. She wished to know if you were still happy and contented, and whether you never regretted what you had done. To all of which I joyously replied, that you were happy and contented, and were about to be married to the dear professor who was expceted to arrive to-day. Her ladyship looked annoyed at first, but soon recovered her equanimity, and said she was glad to hear it. She then observed that something of a very agreeable nature had also occurred to her a short time ago, and that her exalted name and high connections had at last been a great service to her. She had become lady stewardess of the Countess von Ingenheim's household, and at her particular request his majesty the king had permitted her to resume her family name, and call herself Countess Dannenberg. She had a large salary, a waiting-maid, and a manservant. Moreover, the king had given her a pair of beautiful horses and a magnificent carriage, with her coat of arms painted on the door. The king was very gracious to her, as was also Countess Ingenheim. I tell you, Marie, her ladyship was almost delirious with joy, and exceedingly proud of her position. You know who this Countess Ingenheim is, do you not?"

Marie shook her head slowly. "I believe I did know, but I have forgotten."

"This Countess Ingenheim is the wife of the left hand of our king; her maiden name was Julie von Voss, and she was maid of honor to the queen-dowager. The king made her a countess, and his bad councillors and favorites told him he could marry her rightfully, although he already had a wedded wife. These exalted interpreters of God's Word told the king that it was written in the Bible: 'Let not your right hand know what the left does,' and that this meant: 'It does **not**

concern the wife of your right hand, although you should take
another on your left.' The king was easily persuaded of this,
and the pious Privy-councillor Wöllner, who is an ordained
priest, performed the ceremony himself, and is on this account
in high favor at court. The newly-created Countess von
Dannenberg has become lady stewardess to the newly-created
Countess Ingenheim; she is proud of it, too, and does not
consider it beneath her dignity to be in the service of the wife
of the right hand. To have a celebrated professor as son-in-
law was not enough for her—that she called a disgrace. But
she bends the knee to gilded disgrace, and acts as if she were
not well aware that the wife of the left hand is no better than
the mistress, and that the ancient nobility of the Countess
von Dannenberg is sullied when it comes in such close contact
with the brand-new nobility of the Countess Ingenheim."

"Say no more, Trude, do not give way to passion," said
Marie, wearily. "I am glad that she has at last found the
happiness and content she has so long been seeking. On
earth each one must seek out his happiness in his own way,
and we can reproach no one because his is not ours."

"But we can reproach every one who seeks it in a dishonor-
able way, and that her ladyship has done, and—"

"Be still, Trude!" interrupted Marie; "you forget that
she is my mother."

"Why should I remember it?" cried Trude, passionately;
"why should not I also, at last, forget what she has forgotten
throughout her entire life? I hate her!"

"And I," said Marie, softly, as she folded her hands piously
and looked upward, "I forgive her with my whole heart, and
wish her all the happiness she can desire."

"Ah, Marie," cried the old woman, as she hurried forward,
seized Marie's hands and covered them with kisses, "how
good an angel my Marie is, and how wicked, how abominable
an old woman I am! Forgive me, my child, I, too, will endeavor to be better, and to learn to be good and pious from
you."

"As if you were not so already, my dear nurse!" cried
Marie, as she entwined her arms lovingly around the old
woman, who had seated herself on a stool at her feet and was
looking up at her tenderly.   "As if you were not the best,
the most loving, the kindest and the bravest of women!
What would have become of me without you?   How could I
have survived these two long, terrible years, if you had not
stood at my side like a mother?   Who has worked with me
and kept my little household in good order?   Who nursed me
when I was sick?   Who cheered me in my hours of sadness,
and laughed with me in my hours of gladness?   You, my
dear, kind nurse, you did all this: your noble, honest, brave
heart has supported, guarded, and protected me.   I thank
you for all this; I thank you for your love, and if I should
die, my last breath of life and my last thought will be a blessing for my dear, good nurse!"

They held each other in a long and close embrace, and for
a time nothing was heard but sighs and suppressed sobbing.
Then old Trude released her darling, with a last tender kiss.

"Here we are in the midst of emotions and tears," said she,
"although we had determined to be cheerful and gay, in order
that we might give our dear Philip a joyous reception if he
should happen to come to-day, and not have to meet him with
tear-stained countenances."

"Do you, then, really consider it possible that he may come
to-day?" asked Marie, eagerly.

"Professor Gedicke said we might expect him at any hour,"
replied Trude, smiling.   "Let us, therefore, be gay and
merry; the days of pain and sorrow are gone, and hereafter
your life will be full of happiness and joy."

"Do you really believe so, Trude?" asked Marie, fastening
her large luminous eyes in an intent and searching gaze on
the pale, wrinkled countenance of her old nurse.   She had
the courage to smile, and not to falter under the anxious gaze
of her darling.

"Certainly I do," said she; "and why should I not?   Is

not your lover coming back after a separation of two years? are we not to have a wedding, and will we not live together happily afterward? We are not poor; we have amassed a little fortune by the labor of our hands. To be sure, we cannot keep an equipage for our Marie, but still she will have enough to enable her to hire a carriage whenever she wishes to ride, and it seems to me it is all the same whether we drive with four horses or with one, provided we only get through the dust and mud. But listen, Marie, I have not yet given you all the news, I have something to tell that will be very agreeable."

"Then tell me quickly, Trude, I love to hear good news."

"My child, you have often asked me if I had heard any thing of Mr. Ebenstreit, and if I knew what had become of him. In your goodness you have even gone so far as to observe that you have been hard and cruel toward him."

"And I have been, Trude, I presumed to play the rôle of fate and take upon myself the punishment which is God's prerogative only. True, I had bitter cause of complaint against him, and he was to blame for my unhappiness, but I am not free from blame either, and he, too, had just cause of complaint against me. I had stood before God's altar with him—had, at least, recognized him as my husband before the world, and yet I have hated and detested him, and have fulfilled none of the duties which devolved upon me from the moment of our marriage."

"But you were never married, Marie. You did not utter a single word at the wedding? You did not pronounce the 'Yes.'"

"Do not speak so, Trude; we deceive our conscience with such pretences, and only persuade ourselves that we have done no wrong. But when we lie sleepless on our couches during the long night, as I do, then the slumbering conscience awakens, all self-deception vanishes, and we see things as they really are. Yes, I know that I have not behaved toward Ebenstreit as I ought to have done, and I wish I knew where he is, so that I could write to him and make peace with him before—"

"Before you marry, you would say, Marie? Then, listen! I know where Mr. Ebenstreit is. I also know that he is doing well, and that he, too, longs to see and speak with you. What do you say to this news, my child?"

"I am glad to hear it, Trude, and wish to see Ebenstreit as soon as possible, for all things are uncertain on earth, and if he came later—"

"Yes, if he came later," said Trude, interrupting her, "our dear professor might be here, and then we would not have time to occupy ourselves with any one else. You see I thought of this when I saw Mr. Ebenstreit, and therefore—"

"What? You have seen and spoken with him?"

"Of course I have, my child. From whom could I have otherwise learned all this? He entreated me to procure him an interview with you. I told him to come here in two hours and wait outside, promising to call him in if you should permit me to do so. The two hours have now passed, my child. Will you see him?"

"Wait a moment," said Marie, turning pale. "I must first collect my thoughts, I must first nerve myself. You know I am very weak, Trude, and—there! I feel that thorn piercing my breast again! It pains fearfully!"

She closed her eyes, threw herself back in the chair, and lay there quivering and groaning. Trude remained standing near the door tearfully, regarding the pale, attenuated countenance, which was still her ideal of all that was lovely and beautiful.

Slowly Marie opened her eyes again. "You may bring him in, Trude, but we will be composed and avoid speaking of the past."

Marie followed Trude with a sorrowful gaze, as she walked noiselessly to the door and out into the hall. "The good, faithful old nurse!" murmured she. "Does she really believe that I shall recover, or is she only trying to make me believe so? I so long to live, I so long for a little happiness on earth!"

CHAPTER II.

RECONCILIATION.

THE door opened again, and Trude entered, followed by a tall, thin gentleman. His cheeks were hollow, and his light hair and brown beard had turned gray, and yet it seemed to Marie that he was younger and stronger than when she had last seen him, two years before, on that fearful day of vengeance. His countenance now wore a different, a firmer and more energetic expression, and the eyes that had formerly been so dim, now shone with unusual lustre, and were fastened on Marie with an expression of tender sympathy.

He hurried forward, grasped the two pale, attenuated hands which Marie had extended toward him, hid his countenance in them and wept aloud.

For a time all was silent. Trude had noiselessly withdrawn to the furthest corner of the room, where she stood, half-concealed by the bed-curtains, endeavoring to suppress her sobs, that her darling might not hear them.

" Marie, my friend, my benefactress," said Ebenstreit, after a long pause, " I have come to thank you. I came here from New Orleans, with no other intention and no other wish than the one that is now being gratified: to kneel before you, holding your hands in mine, and to say: I thank you, my benefactress! You have made a new being of me; you have driven out the demons, and prepared the altar for good spirits. I thank you, Marie, for through you I have recovered happiness, peace, and self-esteem! Marie, when we last saw each other, I was a sordid being, whose soul was hardened with egotism and vanity. You were right in saying there was nothing but cold calculation, and the miserable pride of wealth, in the place where the warm human heart should beat. You stepped before me like the avenging angel with the flaming sword. In your sublime, your divine anger, you thrust the sword so deep into my breast, that it opened like the box of Pandora, permitting the evil spirits and wicked thoughts to escape, and leaving, in the depths of the heart that had been purified by pain, nothing but hope and love. When I left you at that time and rushed out into the street, I was blinded and maddened. I determined to end an existence I conceived to be worthless and disgraced. But the hand of a friend held me back, the voice of a friend consoled me; and then, when I was again capable of thought, I found that these words were engraven in my heart and soul, in characters of living flame: 'Marie shall learn to esteem me, I will make of myself a new man, and then Marie will not despise me.' These words have gone before me on the rough path, and through the darkness of my life, like a pillar of flame. It was my sun and my star. I looked up to it as the mariner looks at his guiding compass when tossed about on the wide ocean. This pillar of flame has at last led me back to the avenging angel, whom I now entreat to become an angel of reconciliation. I entreat you, Marie, forgive me for the evil I have done you, forgive me for the unhappiness I have caused you, and let me try to atone for the past!"

Marie had at first listened to him with astonishment, and then her features had gradually assumed an expression of deep emotion. Her purple lips had been tightly compressed, and the tears which had gathered in her large eyes were slowly gliding down over the cheeks on which the ominous roses were once more burning brightly. Now, when Ebenstreit entreated her to forgive him, when she saw kneeling in the dust before her the man whose image had stood before her conscience for the past two years as an eternal reproach, and as a threatening accusation, a cry of pain escaped her heaving breast. She arose from her arm-chair, and stretched out her hands toward heaven.

"Too much, too much, O God!" she cried, in loud and trembling tones. "Instead of passing judgment on the sinner, you show mercy! All pride and arrogance have vanished from my soul, and I bow myself humbly before Thee and before this man, whom I have wronged and insulted!'

And before Ebenstreit—who had arisen when he saw Marie rise from her chair in such great agitation—could prevent it, Marie had fallen on her knees before him, and raised her folded hands, imploringly.

"Ebenstreit, forgive me, I entreat you! I have wronged and insulted you, have lived at your side in hatred and anger, instead of striving to be a blessing to you—instead of endeavoring to seek out with you the path of goodness and justice from which we had both wandered so far. But look at me, Ebenstreit! behold what these years of remorse have made of me—behold her who was once the proud tyrant who presumed to command, but has now become a poor penitent who humbly begs forgiveness. Speak, say that you forgive me! No, do not attempt to raise me up! Let me remain on my knees until you take pity on me in your magnanimity—until you have uttered the words for which my soul thirsts."

"Well, then, Marie," sobbed Ebenstreit, his countenance flooded with tears, "I will do your will. Marie, I forgive you with my whole soul—forgive you for all my sufferings and tears, and tell you that out of these sufferings consolations, and out of these tears hopes, have blossomed. God bless, protect, and reward you, my benefactress, my friend!"

With folded hands, and in breathless suspense, she listened to his words, and a joyous smile gradually illumined her countenance.

"I thank you, my friend; I thank you," she murmured, in low tones; and lightly and airily, as though borne up by her inward exaltation, she arose and stood before Ebenstreit, a radiant smile on her lips.

"Do not weep, my friend," she said, "all sorrow and sadness are past, and lie behind us. Let us rejoice in the good fortune that brings us together once more for a short time, after our long separation and estrangement. You shall narrate the history of your life during this period, and tell me where and how you have lived and struggled."

"No," he said, tenderly, "let me first hear your history."

"My friend," she replied, smiling, as she slowly seated herself in the arm-chair, "look at this table, look at these poor flowers made out of cloth, wire, and water-colors. These lilies and violets are without lustre and fragrance. Such has been my life. Life had no roses for me; but I made roses for others, and I lived because one heavenly flower blossomed in my life—I lived because this one flower still shed its fragrance in my heart. This is the hope of seeing my beloved once more!

"Do not ask me to tell you more; you will soon see and learn all; and I know you will rejoice in my happiness when my hope becomes beautiful, blissful reality!"

"I will, indeed," said Ebenstreit, tenderly, "for your happiness has been my constant prayer since our separation; and not until I see you united to the noble man from whom I so cruelly and heartlessly separated you—not until then will I have atoned for my crime, and I conceive of the possibility of a peaceful and happy future for myself."

She extended her hand and smiled. But this smile was so touching, so full of sadness, that it moved Ebenstreit more profoundly than lamentations or despairing wails could have done.

"Tell me of your life," said Marie, in a soft voice. "Seat yourself at my side, and tell me where you have been and how you have lived."

He seated himself as she had directed. Old Trude came forward from the background, and listened eagerly to Ebenstreit's words.

"I cannot illustrate my history as you did yours when you pointed to these flowers," he said, smiling. "In order to do this I should have to show you forests felled by the axe, fields made fruitful, rivers dammed up, and huts and barns erected after hard toil. When I rushed from your presence, in mad desperation, I met the banker Splittgerber on the sidewalk. He had been standing at the door, awaiting me. I endeavored to tear my self from his grasp, but he held me firmly. I cried out that I wanted peace, the peace of the grave, but he only held me the more firmly, drew me away with irresistible force, raised me like a child, and placed me in his carriage, which then drove rapidly to the densest part of the zoological garden. I was wild with rage, and endeavored to jump out of the carriage. But on the side on which I sat, the carriage door was not provided with a handle, and I found it impossible to open it. I endeavored to pass Splittgerber and get out at the other door, and cried: 'Let me out! No one shall compel me to live! I will die, I must die!' But the old man held me with an iron grasp, and pressed me down on my seat again. A loud and terrible voice resounded in my ear, like the trumpet of the day of judgment, and to this hour I have not been able to convince myself that it was no other than the voice of good old Splittgerber. This terrible voice uttered these words: 'You have no right to die, for you have not yet lived. First go and learn to live, in order to deserve death!' I was, however, completely overcome by these fearful words, and sank back in a state of insensibility."

" 'You have no right to die, for you have not yet lived,' " repeated Marie, in a low voice. "Have I then lived, and is it for this reason that—" she shuddered and interrupted herself: "Go on, my friend—what happened further?"

"Of what further occurred I have no knowledge. I have a vague remembrance that I was like a departed soul, and flew about from place to place through the universe, seeking a home and an asylum everywhere, and finding none. I sojourned in hell for a long time, and suffered all the tortures of the damned. I lay stretched on the rack like Prometheus, a vulture feeding on my vitals, and cried out vainly for mercy. When my wandering soul again returned to earth and to its miserable tenement—when I awakened to consciousness, they told me that I had been ill and delirious for a long time. Good old Splittgerber had nursed me like a father, and, when I recovered, made me the most brilliant offers. Among many other similar propositions, I was to become his partner, and establish a branch house in New York. I rejected all; I could hear nothing but the trumpet-tones of that voice, crying: 'You have no right to die, for you have not yet lived. Go and learn to live, in order to deserve to die!' I wished to deserve to die; that was my only thought, and no one should help me in achieving this end. I wished to accomplish this alone, entirely unaided! After having converted the paltry remnants of my property into money, I suddenly took my departure without telling any one where I was going. I was wearied of the Old World, and turned my steps toward the New. I longed to be doing and struggling. I bought a piece of land in America, large enough to make a little duchy in Germany. I hired several laborers, immigrants in whose countenances sullen despair was depicted, and with them I began my work; and a vast, gigantic work it was. A morass and a dense forest were to be converted into fruitful fields. What the Titans of mythology could perhaps not have accomplished, was achieved by poor mortals to whom despair gave courage, and defiance of misfortune superhuman strength. We worked hard, Marie, but our labors were blessed; we had the satisfaction of knowing that they were not in vain, and of seeing them productive of good results. The forest and morass I then bought have now been converted into a splendid farm, on which contented laborers live in cleanly cottages, rejoicing in the rewards of diligence. In the midst of this settlement lies my own house, a simple log-house, but yet a sufficiently comfortable dwelling for a laborer like myself. Over the door stands the following inscription: 'Learn to work, that you may enjoy life,' and on the wall of my humble parlor hangs a board on which is written: 'Money is temptation, work is salvation. True riches are, a good heart and the joyousness resulting from labor.'"

"You are a good, a noble man," whispered Marie, regarding him earnestly. "I thank you for having come, I rejoice in your return."

"I have not returned to remain," said Ebenstreit, pressing her hand to his lips. "I only returned to see you, Marie, and to render an account to Heaven, through the avenging angel, whose flaming sword drove me from my sins. You see, Marie, there is something of my former accursed sordidness in me still; I dare to speak of accounts even to God and to you, as if the soul's burden of debt could ever be cancelled! No, while I live I will be your debtor.—And your debtor, too, Trude," said he, turning, with a smile, to the old woman, who was regarding him wonderingly.

"I'm sure I don't know how that can be," said she, thoughtfully; "you have received nothing from me but abuse; that however you certainly still owe me. If you propose to return this now, and call me a short-sighted fool, and an abominable person, as I have so often called you, you will be perfectly justifiable in doing so. I must say that you have the right, and I am glad that I am compelled to say so. You have become a good man, Mr. Ebenstreit, and the good Lord himself will rejoice over you, for it is written in the Bible: 'When the unjust man returns to God there is more joy over him in heaven than over a hundred just men.' Therefore, my dear Mr. Ebenstreit, pay me back for all my abuse, and then give me your hand and say: 'Trude, we now owe each other nothing more, and after all you may be a very good old woman, whose heart is in the right place, and—her mouth too!'"

Ebenstreit extended his hand, with a kindly smile. "Let us shake hands; the abuse you shall, however, not have. I am your debtor in a higher and better sense; your brave and resolute countenance was often before me, and at times, when a task seemed almost impossible, I seemed to hear a voice at my side, saying: 'Work, work on! Ransom your soul with the sweat that pours from your brow, you soul-seller, for otherwise old Trude will give you no peace, either on earth or in heaven! Work, work on! Earn your bread by the sweat of your brow, otherwise you can never enter the kingdom of heaven, you soul-seller!' You will remember that this was the only title you accorded me in former days?"

"Well, Mr. Ebenstreit, I had others for you, to be sure," said the old woman, blushing, "but that was the main title on account of the five hundred dollars that—"

"Be still!" interrupted Marie, as she slowly arose, and leaned forward in a listening attitude. "Did you hear nothing, Trude?"

"No, my darling. What could I have heard?"

"A carriage stopped before the door, and my heart suddenly ceased to beat, as if expecting a great joy or a great sorrow. I seemed to hear steps in the passage. Yes, I recognize this step—it is his; he—be still! do you hear nothing?"

They all listened for a moment in breathless suspense. "Yes, I seem to hear some one walking in the outer hall," murmured the old woman. "Let me go and see whether—"

"Some one is knocking," cried Marie. "Trude, some one is—"

"Be composed, my darling, be composed," said Trude, in soothing tones; "if you excite yourself so much, it will be injurious. Some one knocks again, and—"

"Trude, be merciful!" cried Marie. "Go and open the door. Do not let me wait; I believe I have but a little while longer to live, and I cannot wait! Go!"

Trude had hurried to the door, and opened it. She started, waved her hand, closed the door again, and turned to Marie, who stood erect, in breathless suspense.

"Marie," said she, vainly endeavoring to speak with composure, "there certainly is some one at the door, who desires to speak with me, but it is no stranger; perhaps he wishes to order some flowers. I will go and ask him."

She was about to open the door again, but Marie ran forward and held her back. "You are deceiving me, Trude.

You well know who it is, and I know too. My heart tells me
it is he! Philip! my Philip! Come to me, Philip!"

"Marie!" cried a loud, manly voice from the outside. The
door was hastily thrown open, and he rushed in, with extended
arms. "Marie! where are you, Marie!"

She uttered a loud, piercing cry of joy, and flew to her
lover's heart. "My Philip! My beloved! God bless you
for having come!"

"My Marie, my darling!" murmured he, passionately.
"God bless you for having called me!"

CHAPTER III.

GRIM DEATH.

THEY held each other firmly embraced, heart to heart. All
sorrow and sadness were forgotten; they were oblivious of the
whole world, and of all that was going on around them.
They did not see old Trude standing near by, with folded
hands, her face radiant with delight; they did not see her
follow Mr. Ebenstreit, who had glided noiselessly out of the
room. They did not hear the door creak on its hinges, as she
closed it behind her, and left them alone and unobserved in
the silent chamber. And, though the two had remained,
though hundreds and hundreds of eyes had been fastened on
them inquiringly, what would they have cared? They would,
nevertheless, have still been alone with love, with happiness,
and with the joy of reunion.

Her head still rested on his breast; he still pressed her to
his heart. "Marie, the dream of my whole life is now fulfilled; I hold you in my arms, you are mine! The restless
wanderer has at last crossed the threshold of the promised
land, and love and peace bid him welcome."

"Yes, my Philip," she murmured, softly, "love and peace
bid him welcome. Pain has left us for evermore, and we
shall be happy!"

"Yes, happy, Marie! Look up, darling, that I may read love in your dear eyes!"

With his hand he attempted to raise her head, but she only pressed it the more firmly to his breast.

"No, Philip, let my head still rest on your bosom; let me dream on for a little while."

"Marie, I have yearned to see these dear eyes for two long years; look up, my darling!"

"Not yet, Philip," she whispered, entwining her arms more closely around her lover, her countenance still hid in his bosom. "Let me first tell you something, Philip! I have been ill, very ill, and it was thought I would die. If you should find me a little changed, a little pale, my beloved, it will only be because I have not yet quite recovered, but am only steadily improving. Remember this, and do not be alarmed. Look at me! Welcome, welcome, my Philip!"

When she raised her head, a radiant expression of happiness rested on her features; her lips were crimson, her eyes shone lustrously, and the death-roses on her cheeks burned brightly. Death had, perhaps, been touched by the supreme happiness of these two beings, who had been wandering under a thunder-cloud of sorrow for long years, and who now fondly believed that they had at last found a refuge from the storms of life, and a balsam for all pain. Death, who comes from God, had, perhaps, been moved with divine pity, and had lain concealed behind these flushed cheeks and crimson lips, permitting joy to illumine Marie's countenance with a last golden ray of the setting sun, and to give her for a brief moment the appearance of health and strength.

Philip, at least, did not see the grim messenger; he was deceived by these death-roses, by this ray of sunshine. He had expected to find Marie in a much worse condition. Gedicke's letter had carried the conviction to his heart that he would find her in a hopeless, in a dying condition, and that nothing buoyed her up, and withheld her from the clutches of the grave, but her longing to see him once more.

Now she stood before him with rosy cheeks, with a bright smile on her lips, and with eyes that sparkled with joy.

"Marie, my jewel, my longed-for happiness, how lovely, how beautiful you are! Why speak of illness and of pale cheeks! I see nothing of all this; I see you healthy, happy, and beautiful—as beautiful as when I often saw you in my dreams in the long nights of the past—as beautiful as I have ever conceived you to be when standing before the Madonnas of Raphael and Giulio Romano in Rome and Florence. 'Gaze at me with your dark eyes,' I said to them. 'You would ask me whether I admire and adore you. True, you are lovely, but I know a Marie who is lovelier and purer than you all! I know a Marie whose eyes are radiant with the light of womanhood, purity, and virtue. She is not so coquettish as you are, Maria della Ledia; her eyes are not so dreamy as yours, Maria di Fuligno. But they are resplendent with holy love, and noble thoughts dwell on her chaste brow!' And now I have thee, and now will I hold thee, my Marie, and nothing can separate us more!"

"No," she said, thoughtfully, "nothing henceforth can now separate us but death!"

"Death has nothing to do with us, my darling. We shall live, and live a joyous, happy life!"

"Yes, live, live!" she cried, in such longing, passionate tones, and with so sad an expression of countenance, that Moritz's heart quaked. It seemed to him as though a string had broken on the harp on which she had just begun to play the joyous song of life and of love, and at this moment he saw grim death peering forth from behind the roses on her cheeks, and the smile on her crimson lips.

"Come, my darling, let us be seated. There is your throne, and here at your feet lies he who adores you, looking up at his Madonna, at his Marie, with ecstacy."

He bore her tenderly to the arm-chair, and then seated himself at her feet. He looked up at her with an expression of deep devotion, his folded hands resting on her lap. She

bowed down over him and stroked with her pale little hand
his black, curly hair, and the broad forehead she had once
seen so gloomy and clouded, and which was now as clear and
serene as the heaven in her own breast.

"I have thee at last once more, thou star of my life! When
I regard thee, I feel that life is, indeed, beautiful, and that
one hour of bliss is not too dearly purchased with long years
of suffering and want. We paid dearly, Philip, but now we
have the longed-for happiness. We have it and will hold it
fast; nothing on earth shall tear it from us?"

"No, nothing on earth, my beloved! Like Odysseus, I
have now returned from my wanderings through life, and
here I lie at the feet of my Penelopeia; like him, I have
driven off the suitors who aspired to the favor of my fair one.
Was it not a suitor, who slipped out at the door when I
entered?"

"A suitor of the past," replied Marie, smiling. "Did you
not recognize him?"

"Have I ever known him? But what do we care, now that
he has gone! I am not compelled to drive him off, nor yet
to hang old Trude as a go-between, as Odysseus did the old
woman of whom Homer tells us."

Philip and Marie both laughed. It was the innocent childlike laughter with which happiness illumines even the gravest
countenances, and which permits those who have been sorely
tried, and have suffered greatly, to find the innocence of
youth and the smile of childhood again on the threshold of
paradise regained.

"Marie, how beautiful you are when you laugh! Then it
seems as though all these years of sorrow had not been—as
though we had only been dreaming, and now awake to find
that we are again in the little room under the roof. You
are once more my charming young scholar, and Professor
Moritz has just come to give Miss von Leuthen a lesson in the
Italian language. Yes, that is it, we are still the same; and
see! there lie the flowers on your table, just as they were when

old Trude conducted me to your room to give you your first lesson."

He took a handful of flowers from the table and held them between his folded hands. "You dear flowers! She is your god and your goddess! Like God she made you of nothing, and, like the goddess Flora, she strews you over the pathway of humanity; but to-day you shall receive the most glorious reward for your existence—to-day you shall adorn her, my fair Flora!"

He sprang up, seized whole handfuls of violets, pinks, lilies, and forget-me-nots, and strewed them over Marie's head, in her lap, and all over and about her.

"Let me strew your path with flowers for the future, my darling. May your tender little feet never more be wounded by the sharp stones! may you never again be compelled to journey over rough roads! Flowers shall spring up beneath your footsteps, and I will be the gardener who cultivates them."

"You are my heaven-flower yourself, my imperial lily," said she, extending her hands. He took them in his, pressed them to his lips, and then resumed his former seat at her feet.

"How handsome you are, Philip, and how strong you look, tanned by the sun of Italy and steeled by the combat with life! Misfortune has made a hero of you, my beloved. You are taller and prouder than you were."

"And are you not a heroine, Marie, a victorious heroine?"

"A victorious heroine!" she said, sadly. "A heroine who is struggling with death! Do not look at me with such consternation, Philip—I am well. It is only that joy and surprise have made me feel a little weak. You do not find that I look ill, and therefore I am not ill; you say I will recover, and therefore I will recover. Tell me once more that I am not ill, that I will recover!"

"You will recover; you will bloom again in happiness and joy."

"You say these words in a sad voice, as though you did not

believe them yourself! But I will not die; no, I will not! I am too young; I have not lived long enough. Life still owes me so much happiness. I will not die! I will live—live!"

She uttered this in loud tones of anguish, as though Life were an armed warrior to whom she appealed to defend her against Death, who was approaching her with a murderous dagger in his bony hand. But Life had no longer a weapon with which to defend her; it timidly recoiled before the king who is mightier than the King of Life, and whose sceptre is a scythe with which he mows down humanity as the reaper harvests the grain of the fields.

"Philip, my Philip," cried Marie, her countenance quivering with pain, "remain with me, my beloved! It is growing so dark, and— There, how my breast pains me again! Alas, you have scattered flowers at my feet, but the thorns have remained in my heart! And they pain so terribly! It is growing dark—dark!—Trude!"

The old woman, who had been waiting at the threshold with the humility of a faithful dog, threw the door open and rushed forward to her darling, who lay in the arm-chair, with closed eyes, pale and motionless, her head resting on Moritz's arm.

"Trude, call the physician!" cried he, in dismay. "Run for assistance! Run! run! She must not die! She shall not leave me! O God, Thou canst not desire to tear her from me! Thou permittedst me to hear her voice when in Rome, when widely separated from her, and I answered this call and flew here on the wings of the wind. It cannot be Thy will that I am to be surrounded by eternal silence—that I am never more to hear this dear voice!—Help me, Trude! Why do you not call the physician?"

"It is useless, dear sir, useless," whispered Trude, whose tears were still flowing in torrents. "All the physicians say that her case is hopeless; they told me that this would occur, and that all would then be at an end. But perhaps this is only a swoon; perhaps we can awaken her once more."

Was it the strengthening essence with which Trude rubbed her forehead, the strong musk-drops which she poured between Marie's parted lips, or was it the imploring voice in which Moritz called her name, and conjured her not to leave him?—Marie opened her eyes and cast a look of ineffable tenderness at the pale, horror-stricken countenance of her lover, who was again kneeling at her feet, his arms clasped convulsively around her person, as if in a last despairing effort to withhold her from the King of Terrors, who had already stretched out his skeleton arm to grasp his victim.

"I am dying, Philip!" murmured Marie, in low tones, and her voice resounded on his ear like the last expiring notes of an Æolian harp. "It is useless to deceive you longer; the truth is evident, and we must both bear it as we best may."

"Marie, I cannot, cannot bear it!" he sobbed, burying his countenance in her lap. "God is merciful; He will take pity on me, on my agony, on my love! God will grant you recovery!"

"The only recovery God vouchsafes me is at hand," whispered Marie. "Recovery is death! I have felt it approaching for many, many days—in the long, fearful nights I have lain awake struggling with this thought, unable to comprehend it, and doubting God's mercy and goodness. My defiant heart refused to submit humbly to God's will, and still continued to entreat a little more life, a little happiness, of Him who is inexorable, and upon whose ear the wail of man strikes in as low tones as the last breath of the insect we tread under foot. I comprehended, finally, that all complaints were useless—that nothing remained but to submit, to humble myself, to thank God for each hour of life as for a gracious boon, and to consider each ray of sunshine shed on my existence as a proof of His goodness. I have conquered myself; my stubborn heart has been softened, and no longer rebels against the hand of the Almighty, to whom men are as worms, and as the grain of sand to the mighty glacier that touches the clouds. You, too, must be gentle and submissive, my Philip. Learn to submit to the eternal laws of God!"

"No, I cannot," said he, in heart-rending tones; "I cannot be submissive. My heart is rebellious; in my anguish I could tear it from my breast when I see you suffer!"

"I am not suffering, Philip," said she, her countenance radiant with a heavenly smile. "All pain has now left me, and I feel as though I floated in a rosy cloud, high above all earthly sorrow. From this height I see how paltry all earthly sorrows are, and how little they deserve a single tear. Here below, all is paltry and insignificant—above, all is great and sublime. Oh, Philip, how sweet it will be to meet you once more up there! In blissful embrace, our spirits will soar from star to star, and the glories of all worlds and the mysteries of all creations will be made manifest to us, and our life will be bliss and joy unending! The cloud is soaring higher and higher! Philip, I see thee no longer!"

"But I see thee, my darling," cried Philip, despairingly, as he clasped her sinking head between his hands, and covered it with tears and kisses. "Do not leave me, Marie; stay with me, thou sole delight of my life! Do not leave me alone in the world."

His imploring voice had that divine power which, as we are told by the Greeks, breathed life into stone, and transformed a cold, marble statue into a warm, loving woman. His imploring voice recalled the spirit of the loving woman to the body already clasped in the chilly embrace of death.

"You shall not be solitary, Philip," she murmured; "it is so sad to have to struggle alone through life. I must go, Philip, but you shall not be left alone."

"But I will be if you leave me, Marie; therefore stay! Oh, stay!"

"I cannot, Philip," gasped Marie, in low tones. "You must place another at your side! Another must fill my place. Hear my last wish, my last prayer, Philip. Take a wife, marry!"

"Impossible, Marie, you cannot be so cruel as to desire this."

"I have thought of this a great deal, have struggled with my own heart, and am now convinced that you must do so. You must have a wife at your side who loves you. Swear that you will seek such a wife. Swear this, and accord me a last joy on earth."

She raised her hand once more, and her dying gaze was fastened on him imploringly. He could not resist it; he clasped the pale fingers in his quivering, burning hands, and swore that he would do as she bade him.

A faint smile flitted over her countenance, and her eyes sought out the faithful old woman, who had loved her like a mother, and who found it no longer necessary to conceal her tears, as she had been doing for many months, in holy and heroic deception.

"Trude," whispered Marie, "you have heard his vow, and you must remind him of it, and see that he keeps it, and marries within the year. Kiss me, Trude, and swear that you will do so!"

Old Trude had no other words than her tears, no other vow than the kiss which her trembling lips pressed on her darling's brow, already covered with that cold, ominous perspiration which gathers, like the morning dew of another world, on the countenances of those who stand on the threshold of the grave, and is symbolical of the new life to which they will awaken on high.

"Philip, my beloved, you too must kiss me!" whispered Marie, in eager tones, "Kiss me! Hold me fast! Drive death, grim, fearful death, away!"

He kissed her, entwined his arms around her, and pressed her to his bosom. Trude stretched out her arms imploringly into empty space, as if to ward off "grim death!"

But he is king of kings, and claims as his own all who live on earth!

Silence reigned in the little chamber. Holy is the hour

of separation—holy the moment in which the immortal soul is torn from its earthly abode, and this holy moment must not be desecrated with lamentations and tears!

After a long interval, the heart-rending cry of a man, and the low wail of a woman broke in upon the stillness.—Marie had died, but a smile still rested on her lips.

CHAPTER IV.

GOETHE'S RETURN FROM ROME.

GOETHE has returned! Goethe is once more in our midst! He arrived quite unexpectedly yesterday evening, repaired at once to his summer-house in the park, raised the little draw-bridge, and has yet seen no one!

This was the intelligence that ran like wildfire through the good city of Weimar on the morning of the nineteenth of June, 1788, exciting joy and expectation in the minds of many, and perhaps also some little discontent in the minds of others. All were anxious to see the poet once more, who had been enthroned in Weimar as the genius of gayety and happiness, and who had taken these two most beautiful ideals of humanity with him on leaving the capital of Thuringia. Weimar had changed greatly since Goethe's departure. It had, as the Duke Charles August often complained to his friends, become dull, and "terribly old fogyish." The genial freedom from care and restraint, and the poetic enthusiasm and exaltation had all vanished with Goethe. Weimar lay slumbering in its dullness and tranquillity on the banks of the murmuring Ilm, and the staid and honest burghers of the good city considered it a positive blessing that this restless spirit had departed. The court was also very quiet—so quiet that the genial Duchess Amelia could no longer endure it, and was preparing to journey to Italy in the company of her friends, Wieland and Herder, to indemnify herself under the bright skies of Italy, and in the midst of rare works of art, for the dull life she had led for the past few years.

No wonder that the intelligence of Goethe's return agitated the little city, and infused a little life and excitement into slumbering society!

Goethe's servant had appeared at the ducal palace at an early hour on the following morning, had communicated the glad tidings of his master's arrival to the duke's chamberlain, and had begged to be informed at what hour the privy-councillor would be permitted to pay his respects. The duke had briefly replied that he would send the privy-councillor word; nothing more! But half an hour later, instead of sending word, the duke quietly left his palace, crossed the Market Square with hasty footsteps, and passed on through the streets, into the park, and along its shady avenues to Goethe's little summer-house.

The bridge was raised, but the Ilm was almost completely dried up by the summer heat, and but a narrow, shallow rivulet flowed in the midst of its sandy bed. What cared he, the genial duke, although his boots and Prussian uniform should become somewhat soiled in wading across to the little island? He had not come to pay a visit of state, but only to call on his dear friend in an unceremonious manner, and to give him a warm embrace, after a long separation. Therefore, forward, through mud and water! On the other side lies the modest little house of his cherished friend! Forward!

Goethe's servant had not yet returned from the city; no one was there to announce the duke, and, if there had been, Charles August would have preferred coming unannounced into his friend's presence; he desired to surprise him. Noiselessly he crept up the stairway, and threw the door open.

"Welcome, my Wolf! A thousand welcomes! To my arms, beloved brother!"

"His highness the duke! How unexpected an honor!"

Goethe rose hastily from the sofa, and bowed profoundly to the duke, who still stood before him with extended arms.

"And in this manner you receive your friend, Wolf? Truly, I came running here like a lover to a rendezvous with his adored, and now you receive me with a cold greeting?"

"I beg leave to assure your highness, that the heart of your humble servant is also filled with joy, in beholding his dear master once more, and that this moment reconciles me to my return, and—"

"Wolf, tell me are you playing a comedy? Are you only jesting, or has your sojourn in Rome really made you the stiff and courtly old fellow you appear to be?"

"I a stiff old fellow? I a courtly old fellow?" asked Goethe, with sparkling eyes; and now he was again the Goethe with the Apollo countenance, as he had been in Rome and Castel Gandolfo—once more the poet of Italy, and no longer the privy-councillor of Weimar.

As the friends now looked at each other—as the duke's merry brown eyes encountered Goethe's fiery, passionate gaze—the last vestiges of the privy-councillor fell from the poet. His handsome countenance brightened, and with a cry of joy he sprang forward, threw himself into the duke's arms and kissed his eyes and lips.

"May God forgive me if I am guilty of disrespect! I had determined to return home as a well-trained and respectable privy-councillor and courtier. But I am not to blame if the sight of your dear countenance scatters all my good resolutions to the winds. Let me embrace, let me kiss you once more, my dear duke and friend!"

And he did so, again and again, with great ardor. The duke's laughter while submitting to this embrace seemed to be only assumed in order to conceal his emotion, and to make his friend believe that the tears which stood in his eyes had not come from the depths of his heart, but were only the consequence of his violent laughter.

"I see you are still the same wild, unaccountable genius, Wolf! You are as capricious as a beautiful woman, and as imperious as a tyrant! You are still the same Goethe!"

"Not at all times, my duke. I have determined that the
sober-minded world here in Weimar, shall behold in me a
sober-minded privy-councillor, and that I will give no further
cause of offence to madame the Duchess Louise, and all other
sensitive souls, by my wild behavior. But, for a quarter of
an hour, and in the presence of my dear master, I let the
mask fall, and am once more the old Goethe or the young
Goethe. Your Goethe, my duke and friend!"

"Thanks, Wolf, thanks! I hardly knew what to make of
you, and was quite ill at ease when I saw you standing before
me with your formal manner and courtier countenance. I
thought to myself, 'This is not the Goethe you expected to
see; this is only his outward form; the inner man has remained in Italy.'"

"Alas! that such should be the case, my duke, but it is
so," sighed Goethe. "The inner man has not yet quite returned; only after a painful struggle will it be able to tear
itself from the beautiful home of art and poetry. But since
I see you, my dear friend—since I behold your brave, handsome countenance, I feel that my wounds are healing—that I
am coming home! They are healing under your loving
glances, and I begin to rejoice in my return, and to consider
what I did only from a sense of duty as a real pleasure."

"Then you did not return gladly, Wolf? It was reason,
and not your heart, that prompted you to return!"

"It was reason only, my duke—the conviction that it was
necessary for my well-being. Do not be angry with me for
saying so, but in this hour my heart must be laid bare to my
friend, and he must see and read its every quivering fibre.
No, my duke, my heart did not prompt me to return. I returned only because I recognized the necessity of so doing, if
I hoped to accomplish any thing great and beautiful. I was
compelled to flee from Italy, the siren in whose toils I lay
bound, and by whom my being was about to be divided, making of the poet that I really am, or at least can become, a
talent-monster, who acquires a certain artistic ability in many

things, without attaining to perfection in any one of them. Had I remained in Italy, I would perhaps at last have been able to paint a tolerably good aquarelle picture, and to make a passably good statue according to all the rules of art, and might also have manufactured dramas and poems in my hours of leisure; but I would have knocked in vain at the temple-gates of each individual art. Not one of them would have been thrown open to permit me to enter, as the elect, the chosen! At the door of each temple I would have been turned away, and advised to apply for my reward at the abode of another art, and thus I would be considered a worthy applicant nowhere! He who desires to accomplish something great and complete, must bend all the energies of his soul to the accomplishment of one end. He must not diffuse his talents, but must concentrate them in the attainment of one object. He must strive upward; in the spirit he must see before him a summit to which he is determined to climb, removing all obstacles that may retard his progress. This conviction forces itself upon me, and I also became convinced that I possessed only one talent—that is, but one great talent—that could carry me to the summit, and this talent is my talent of poetry. All others are but secondary; and when I take this view of myself, I am reminded of the magnificent marble group in Rome, 'the Nile, with its Tributaries.' There lies the godlike form in its manliness, strength, grandeur, and sublimity. On his sinewy arms, mighty shoulders, and muscular legs, a number of beautiful little boys are gracefully dancing, reclining, and playing with his limbs. These are the tributaries of the god Nile, who lies there in sublime composure. He would still be a god although he were entirely alone. We would still admire him and rejoice in his beauty, although he were not surrounded by these graceful, boyish forms. But they would be nothing without him, would not be able to stand alone, and would be passed by as unworthy of attention, if they were not reposing on the grand central form. Thus it is with all my other talents and capac-

ities: they are only the little boys of the statue, and with me
the poet is the main figure. Yes, your highness, thus it is
with me. My poetic talent is my Nile, and my other little
talents are the tributaries that flow into my being to strengthen
me, to make the waves of poetry surge higher, and fill the air
with music that shall resound throughout the world, and find
an echo in heaven and in hell!"

"Oh, Wolf!" cried the duke, now that Goethe had paused
for a moment, "how happy I am to have you once more in
our midst! It is as though the sun had returned, and I had
just stepped out of a dark cellar into the fresh, free air, and
were walking hand in hand with a friend toward a glittering
temple that had been closed to me during his absence. Wolf,
I was becoming a very prosaic and stupid fellow, and had
almost begun to consider the dark cellar in which I was sojourning an agreeable dwelling. I thank God that you have
come to relieve me from this curse! Speak on, my friend;
your words are as sweet music that I have not heard for a
long time."

"I must speak on, my duke; I must unburden my heart
completely, for who knows whether it will often open itself
again, and lay aside the covering in which I enveloped the
poor thing when I took leave of bright, sunny Italy? But I
must admit that, since I crossed the borders of Germany, I
have been twenty times on the point of retracing my footsteps, in defiance of reason and conviction—on the point of
giving up every thing, and deciding rather to live in Italy as
a happy, worthless dilettante, than to dwell in Germany as a
high official and celebrated poet. I am angry with myself,
but I must nevertheless make the admission. I feel that I
have been disenchanted since my return to Germany: I now
view, with sobered sight, many things that memory painted
in glowing colors, and the result is that I am by no means
pleased. I long to return to Italy; and yet, in my inmost
soul, I feel that I must remain here, in order to become that
for which Fate has destined me. I feel like crying, as a bad

boy over his broken playthings, and I could box my own ears for entertaining such a desire. I now conjure you, my duke and friend, stand at my side and help me to allay the fury of the storm that is raging in my inmost being. See, what an infamous irony this is on my being! I have happily passed the stormy period of my poetic labors, and have freed myself from the bombast of sentimentality. I despise all this from the bottom of my heart, and am at times so angry with myself about that sentimental fellow, 'Werther,' that I would gladly disown him. Now a new storm is raging within me in its former fury, and my heart longs for Italy as for a lost paradise. So help me, duke; help me to become a sensible man once more!" Goethe stamped furiously on the floor as he uttered these words, and his eyes sparkled with anger.

"Now you look like the Thunderer, like Jupiter," said the duke, regarding him lovingly. "You have returned handsomer and sublimer than when you departed, and I can readily comprehend that all the goddesses and nymphs of Italy have endeavored to retain in their happy land the heavenly being in whom the sublimity of Jove and the beauty of Apollo are united."

"Duke!" cried Goethe, furiously, "I conjure you, speak seriously! Do not annihilate me with your ridicule!"

"Well, then, we will be serious," said Charles August, tenderly. "Come here, Wolf, and seat yourself at my side on this little sofa, where we have so often sat together in brotherly love. Thus it shall be to-day again. I see, to my joy, Wolf, that you are unchanged, and your quick temper and fierce anger against yourself are therefore refreshing to your old friend. Now let us see what can be done; but this I tell you in advance—you must overcome your longing to return to Italy, you must remain here, for only in tranquillity and peace can you attain the high ends of your existence, and climb to the summit of which you were speaking. Of this you were convinced yourself, and on this account you left Italy and returned home. Therefore be true to yourself, you dear, great fellow, and journey on toward your high aim with undaunted heart and steadfast gaze! Accomplish your sublime mission as poet, and I will endeavor to procure you the leisure and honorable retirement essential to your poetic labors."

"My duke and master, you are indeed my savior!" cried Goethe; "you have spoken what I scarcely dared utter! Yes, that is it! Leisure and retirement I must have. My official sprang wholly from my personal relations to your highness. Let our old ones be modified—let a new relation hereafter exist between us. Let me fill the whole measure of my existence at your side, so that my strength may be concentrated and made available, like a newly-opened, collected, and purified spring situated on an eminence, from which your will can readily cause its waters to flow in any direction! Continue to care for me as you have heretofore done; thus you will do more for me than I could accomplish for myself, more than I can desire or demand. Yes, I hope that I will become more to you than I have hitherto been, if you will only command me to do that which no one can do but myself, and commission others to do the rest. I can only say: 'Master, here am I, do with me as you will.' " *

"Let me first tell you, Wolf, what it is that no one but yourself can do: gladden my heart, elevate my mind, and restore sunshine to our little city. During your absence I have made a fearful discovery concerning myself; I am fast becoming an 'old fogy,' and if new life and activity are not infused into my sluggish spirit, I greatly fear that my case will soon be hopeless. As it is, I resemble the stagnant waters of a ditch. In its depths swims many a fine fish and blossoms many a fair flower, but the concealing duck-weed covers its surface and hides the treasures that lie below. You and you alone can brighten the mirror of my soul. And if you but now called yourself my servant, I can reverse your poetic

* Goethe's own words.—See correspondence of Duke Charles August with Goethe, vol. ii.

phrase, and say to you: 'Servant, here am I—do with your master as you will.' "

" See, my duke, you make me blush for shame. You alone are master, and you only can do as you will."

" Then let me tell you what my will is, Wolf, and I will be brief, for I observe that the quarter of an hour to which you proposed to limit your outpouring of the heart is almost at an end, and the worthy face of my cabinet president and privy-councillor is already peering forth from behind the god-like countenance of the poet. I wish you to retain the rank and dignities with which you were invested when you left for Italy. You are herewith relieved of the duty of presiding in my cabinet and in the war office. You, however, still retain the right to attend the various meetings, if you should find time to do so, and whenever you appear you will seat yourself in the chair set apart for me. I will see that instructions to this effect are issued. On the other hand, you will retain the superintendence of the mining commission, and all other in- stitutions of science and art which you now hold. Your chief occupation will, however, be to stand at my side as friend and councillor, and to tell me the plain, unvarnished truth at all times. These are your duties, and you will now perceive that I have known how to read your soul, although we were widely separated, and that I have endeavored to make your future honorable, and not too burdensome. And, that you may not suppose, Wolf, that these are only fine phrases and that these thoughts first occurred to me in your presence to-day, I have brought you the written order addressed to the bureau of my cabinet, and the letter in which I acquainted you with all these matters, and which I was about to forward to you in Rome when the letter came announcing your departure from that city."

" As if my dear, my noble duke ever needed witnesses to confirm his statements," cried Goethe, as he gently refused to receive the papers which the duke held in his extended hand.

"Ah, I perceive the cabinet president is himself once more," cried the duke, laughing. "I must now retire to my ducal palace. Others will, I have no doubt, think I have played the barbarian and tyrant by remaining with you so long, and thereby robbing them of the time to which they imagine they have a fairer title."

"Duke, I know of no one who has a higher and better title to my time and person than yourself, my dear patron and friend."

"Wolf, it is well that I alone have heard these words," cried Charles August, gayly; "I believe there is a woman in whose ears they would have had a discordant sound. The responsibility must not rest on me, if a difficulty should arise on your first meeting. Therefore I am going, Wolf, although I am very curious to hear of your promised land and of your discoveries and purchases, but for this I will have to wait till the afternoon. You will, of course, dine with me to-day, Wolf, and dispense a little of the incense of your eloquence on the altar of my household gods. Farewell till we meet again, my returned wanderer! I must, however, request you not to come as the privy-councillor, but as the poet. You may show your official mask and the star on your breast to the court, but appear before me with your Apollo countenance and the stars of your eyes."

"My dear duke," said Goethe, affectionately, "your presence has cheered and strengthened me; I feel as though I had been bathing in nectar, and had been refreshed with ambrosia. When I am with you, nothing will be wanting to my joy and happiness. You must, however, not be angry, my dear duke, if I should sometimes appear grave and stiller than usual in the presence of others, and you will then know that it is only the longing after the distant land of the gods that is tormenting me."

"I will know how to account for it, Wolf, and will respect your longing; I very much doubt, however, whether others will be equally considerate—I doubt whether one person of whom I am thinking will be particularly pleased with such conduct on your part. Have you see her already, Wolf?"

"Whom does your highness mean?" asked Goethe, with a perfectly innocent expression of countenance.

The duke laughed. "Oh, Wolf, Wolf, I hope you have not exchanged names, as Hector and Patroclus exchanged armor, and become Von Stein.* I hope you return to your old love, faithful and true. Ah, there I have made a pun without intending it. Excuse me, I entertained no evil design, but now that I have said it I will repeat it. You return to your old love, faithful and true. Remain here, you must not accompany me; I came *sans cérémonie*, and I will take my departure in like manner. It is understood that we dine together to-day. Adieu!"

A cloud gathered on Goethe's brow as the duke left the room. "My old love!" said he to himself, in low tones. "I wish he had not spoken that word; it sounds so ridiculous!"

CHAPTER V.

ESTRANGEMENT.

CHARLOTTE VON STEIN sat before her mirror, anxiously regarding her countenance, and carefully examining each feature and every little wrinkle that was observable on her clear forehead and cheeks.

"No," said she, with an air of joyous confidence, "no, it is not visible; no one can read it in my face! It is a secret between myself and my certificate of baptism!"

As intelligent as she was, Charlotte von Stein was yet subject to that cowardly fear of her sex—the fear that her age might be read in her countenance. She, too, was wanting in that courage which contents itself with the eternal youth of

* Von Stein, the name of Goethe's sweetheart—anglicized: *Stone.*

the mind, and does not demand of its covering that it retain no traces of the rude, unfeeling hand of Time.

A woman who loves has invariably the weakness to desire not to become old, at least in the eyes of him whose image fills her heart—in the eyes of him she loves. She does not consider that, in so doing, she insults the intelligence of the object of her devotion, by admitting that he thinks more of the outward form than of the inner being, and loves with the eyes only, and not with the mind.

In the first years of their acquaintance, and in the incipient stage of their attachment, Charlotte von Stein had always listened to Goethe's protestations of love with a merry smile, and had invariably replied: "I am too old for you! Remember that I am some years older than you—that I am old enough to be your mother." When she made this reply, Goethe would laugh, and kiss with passionate tenderness the fair hand of the woman who offered him motherly friendship, and whom he adored with all the ardor of a lover.

But ten long years had passed since then! Charlotte thought of this while looking at herself in the mirror, and she sighed as she admitted to herself that she had committed a fault—a great fault, for she had left the cool regions of motherly tenderness, and had permitted herself to be carried away by the tide of Goethe's passion; the two flames in her heart had been united into the one godlike flame of love. It had seemed so sweet to be adored by this handsome man, and to listen to his tender protestations and entreaties! It had been so charming to receive each morning a letter filled with passionate assurances of love, and vows of eternal fidelity! She had continued to read these ardent letters until their words glowed in her own heart—until, at last, that day came for the lovers of which Dante says: "On that day they read no more"—the day on which Charlotte confessed to her enraptured lover that his love was reciprocated.

A few days later, Goethe had written: "My FIRST AND BEST FRIEND! I have always had an ideal wish as to how I desired to be loved, and have vainly sought its fulfilment in my illusive dreams. Now that the world seems lighter to me each day, I see it realized in such a manner that it can never be lost again. Farewell, thou fairest prospect of my whole life; farewell, thou only one, in whom I need lose nothing, in order to find all!'' *

Charlotte had placed this little letter in a golden locket, from which she was never separated; it had been her blissful assurance, her talisman of eternal youth and joy.

She now turned from the mirror that utterly refused to say any thing agreeable, and drew from her bosom her talisman, the locket that contained the relic, the source of so much happiness, love, and delight.

Relics! Alas, how much that we consider real, present, and full of life, is only a relic of the past! How few men there are in whose hearts the love they once vowed should be eternal, is no more than a relic!—the crumbling bone of a saint, to whom altars were once erected, and who was adored as an immortal, unchangeable being. Alas, Love, thou poor saint, how often are thy altars overthrown, and how soon do thy youth and beauty fade, leaving nothing of thee but a little dust and ashes—a relic!

Charlotte von Stein held the letter in her hands, but the thought did not occur to her that it too was only a relic; she still considered it the eloquent witness of passionate love. While reading the letter, a bright smile had illumined her features, and imparted to them a more youthful and beautiful expression. She now kissed the sheet of paper, and replaced it in the locket which she wore on a golden chain around her neck.

What need had she of written evidences? Was not *he* near? would not *his* lips soon say more, in a single kiss, than thousands of written words could tell?

"But he might have come sooner," whispered a voice in Charlotte's heart; "it is very late."

---

* Goethe's correspondence with Madame von Stein, vol. ii., pp. 170, 171. Literal translation.

Her beautiful brown eyes cast an anxious look toward the door, and she smiled. Her heart throbbed in advance of time; it was still so early in the morning, that it would hardly have been considered proper for him to call at an earlier hour.

But now her heart beat quicker—she heard a step in the antechamber.

"It is he! Be firm, my heart, do not break with delight, for—yes, it is he! it is he!"

She flew forward to meet him, with extended hands, her countenance radiant with delight. "Welcome, Goethe, a thousand welcomes!"

"A thousand thanks, Charlotte, that your faithful, loving heart bids me welcome!"

His large black eyes regarded her with all their former tenderness, and then—then he kissed her hand.

Charlotte could scarcely restrain a sigh, and could not repress the terror that pervaded her whole being. He felt the tremor in the hands which he held in his own, and it was perhaps on this account that he released them, threw his arms around her and pressed her to his heart.

"Here I am once more, Charlotte, and, as God is my witness, I return with the same love and fidelity with which I left you! You can believe this, my beloved, for it was on your account chiefly, or on your account solely, that I returned at all. You must therefore love me very dearly, Charlotte, and reward me, with faithful love and cordial friendship, for the sacrifice I have made for your sake."

"It was, then, a sacrifice?" said she, with a touch of irony in her voice that did not escape Goethe.

"Yes, my dearest, this return to cold, prosaic Germany, from the warm, sunny clime of happy Italy, was a sacrifice."

"Then I really regret that you did not remain there," said she, with more sensitiveness than discretion.

He looked at her wonderingly. "You regret that I have returned? I supposed you would be glad."

" I can rejoice in nothing that I have attained by a sacrifice on your part."

" My love, do not let us quarrel over words," said he, almost sadly. " We will not unnecessarily pour drops of bitterness into the cup of our rejoicing at being together once more. We have met again, and will endeavor to hold each other fast, that we may never be divided."

" If an effort is necessary, then we are already half divided."

" But I have come home in order that we may be reunited, wholly and joyfully," said Goethe, moved to kindness and generosity by the tears which stood in her eyes, and the annoyance and sadness that clouded her countenance, rendering it neither younger nor more beautiful.

But remembrances of the past smiled on him in the lustrous eyes of the woman he had loved so ardently for ten years, and it was still a very comforting feeling, after having been tossed about by the storms of life for so long a time, to return once more to his heart's home, to lie once more in the haven of happiness and love, where there were no more storms and dangers, and where the wearied wanderer could enjoy peaceful rest, and dream sweet dreams.

He seated himself at Charlotte's side on the sofa, laid his arm around her neck, took her hand in his own, looked lovingly into her countenance, and began to tell her of his journey—of the little accidents and occurrences that can only be verbally imparted.

She listened attentively; she rejoiced in his passionate eloquence, in his glowing descriptions of his travels, and yet—and yet, as interesting as this was there was nevertheless another theme that would have been far more so—the theme of his love, of his longings to see her, and of his delight in being once more reunited with his Charlotte, and in finding her so beautiful, so unchanged.

But Goethe did not speak of these things; and, instead of contenting herself with reading his love in his tender glances, his smiles, and his confiding and devoted manner, her heart thirsted to hear passionate assurances of love fall from his lips. Her countenance wore a listless expression, and she did not seem to take her usual lively interest in his words. Goethe observed this, and interrupted his narrative to tell her that he was delighted to be with her once more, and that she was still as beautiful and charming as ever. Hereupon Charlotte burst into tears, and then suddenly embraced him passionately, and rested her head on his breast.

"Oh! let no estrangement occur between us; do not become cold and reserved to me too, as you are to the rest of the world!"

"Am I that?" asked he, with an offended air. From her at least he had not deserved this reproach, and it affected him disagreeably, casting a damper over the gayety with which he had been narrating his adventures. "Am I really cold and reserved?" he asked, as she did not reply, for the second time.

"Yes, Wolf," said she, with vivacity, "you know that you are; the world accuses you of being so."

"Because I am not like a market-place, open to the inspection of every fool, and in which the inquisitive rabble can gaze at, handle, and criticise every thing, as though the holiest thoughts of the soul were mere wares exposed for sale!—because I am rather to be compared to a fortress surrounded by a high wall, which opens its well-guarded gates to the initiated and chosen only. In this sense I admit that that which is called the world, and which is in reality only the inquisitive, gossipping rabble, composed chiefly of individuals who make great pretensions to intellectuality, but are generally empty-headed—that this world calls me cold and reserved, I admit. But have I ever been so toward my friends, and, above all, toward you?"

"No, Heaven be thanked! no, my beloved Wolf!" cried Charlotte, in eager and tender tones, well aware that she had committed an error, which she wished to repair; "no, toward me you have always been friendly, communicative, and open, and therefore—"

"And therefore, my love," said he, interrupting her, " therefore you should not have reproached me, undeservedly, in the hour of our reunion." He arose and took his hat from the table.

"Oh, Wolf!" cried she, anxiously, "you are not going?"

"I must, my dearest! I must first pay a few formal visits, to avoid giving offence. I must call ón some friends I expect to meet at the ducal table to-day."

"Perhaps it was only on this account that you visited me?" said Charlotte, the tears which she could no longer repress, gushing from her eyes. "Wolf, did you visit me solely because you expected to meet me in the ducal palace to-day?"

He regarded her with a look of distress and astonishment. "Charlotte, dear Charlotte, is it possible that so great a change has come over you in two short years?"

She started, and a glowing color suffused itself over her countenance; the poor woman thought of what her mirror had told her but a short time before, and Goethe's question awakened bitter reflections. "Am I really so changed?" sighed she, and her head sank wearily upon her breast.

"No," cried he, earnestly, "no, Charlotte, you cannot have changed; it is only that this first moment of reunion after a long separation has affected us strangely. We will soon be restored to each other completely, we will soon be reunited in love and friendship. Charlotte, it is impossible that two years of separation can have torn asunder the holy union of our souls! Let us strive to prevent so unhappy a consummation; it would be a misfortune for me—yes, I may say, a misfortune for you, too! I think we love each other so tenderly that we should both endeavor, with the whole strength of our souls, to ward off misfortune from each other. Let these be my farewell words, darling, and, as I have just learned that you too will dine at court to-day, I can joyfully say—till we meet again!"

He embraced her, and pressed a kiss on her lips, a kiss that wounded her heart more than a cold leave-taking would have done; for this gentle, friendly kiss seemed to her but as the second echo of what her mirror had said! As the door closed behind his loved form, Charlotte sank down on her knees, buried her face in the cushions of the sofa, and wept bitterly.

His head erect, his countenance grave and earnest, Goethe walked on to pay his calls; and those whom he thus honored found that he had come home colder and more reserved than when he had departed. But, at the banquet, in the ducal palace, he was neither cold nor reserved; there he was eloquent and impassioned,—there enthusiastic words of poetic description flowed like golden nectar from his smiling lips; there his eye sparkled and his cheek glowed, and his illustration of life in Italy awakened delight and admiration in the hearts of all—of all, except Charlotte von Stein! She sat at Goethe's side, and he often turned his lightning glance on her, as though speaking to her alone, but Charlotte felt only that what he said was intended for all. Had he but attempted to whisper a single word in her ear, had he given her hand a gentle pressure, had he but made her some secret sign understood by herself only, and permitted her to feel that something peculiar and mysterious was going on in which they two alone participated! In society, Goethe had formerly, before his journey to Italy, availed himself of every little opportunity that arose to press her hand and whisper loving words in her ear. To-day he was wanting in these delicate little attentions—in these little love-signals, for which she had so often scolded him in former times! She was therefore very quiet, and did not join in the applause of the rest of the company. But, amidst the admiration evoked by his eloquence, Goethe listened only to hear a word of approval from Charlotte, and, when his friend still remained silent, his animation vanished and his countenance darkened.

But they had loved each other too long and too tenderly not to be alarmed by the thought of a possible coolness and separation. True, Charlotte often wept in the solitude of her

chamber, and accused him of ingratitude; true, Goethe often
grumbled in silence, and lamented over Charlotte's irritability
and sensitiveness, but yet he was earnest in his desire to avoid
all estrangement, and to restore to their hearts the beautiful
harmony that had so long existed.

He resumed the habit that had formerly given him so much
delight—that of writing to Charlotte almost daily. But her
sensitive woman's ear detected a difference in the melody of
his letters; they were no longer written in the same high,
passionate key, but had been toned down to a low, melancholy
air. Her own replies were of a like character, and this annoyed Goethe greatly. He abused the gloomy skies of Germany, and lamented over the lost paradise of Italy; and
Charlotte could not help comprehending that she was the
cause of his discontent and anger.

But still he visited her almost every day, and was always
animated and communicative in her society. He read portions of his newly-commenced drama "Torquato Tasso," with
her, told her of his plans for the future, and permitted her to
take part in his intellectual life. Then she would soon forget
her little sorrows and her woman's sensitiveness, and become
once more the intelligent friend, with the clear judgment and
profound understanding.

On an occasion of this kind, Goethe requested his "beloved
friend" to return the letters he had written to her during the
two years of his sojourn in Italy.

Charlotte looked at him in astonishment. "My letters—
the dear letters I have kept so sacred that I have not shown a
single one of them to my most intimate friends—these letters
you desire me to return?"

"Certainly, my dear, I beg you to do so. I intend having
an account of my Italian journey published—have also promised Wieland some fragments for his "Mercury," and, in
order to prepare these for the press, it will only be necessary
to have the letters I have written to you copied."

"Can this be possible, Wolf?" asked she, in dismay. "Do

you really intend to have the letters, written by you to me, read and copied by a third person?"

"As a matter of course, I will first correct these letters, and leave nothing in them addressed to you personally and intended for your dear eyes only," replied Goethe, laughing. "I always had this end in view while writing to you in Italy, and you will have observed that my letters were always divided, to a certain extent, into two portions. The first is addressed to you only, my dear Charlotte—to you, my friend and my beloved—and this was filled with the words of love and longing that glowed in my own heart. The second portion is a mere narrative and description of what I have seen, heard, and done while in Italy, and was intended for publication."

"But this is unheard of," cried Charlotte, angrily; "this experiment does great honor to your cold calculation, but very little to your heart."

"Charlotte, I am not aware of ever having done any thing discreditable to my heart in my relations to you!"

"Relations to me!" she repeated, offended. "Certainly, this is an entirely new name for the ardent love you once protested could never expire in your heart."

"Charlotte, dear, beloved Charlotte!" he sighed, sadly, "do take pity on us both. Be yourself once more. You were once so noble, so lofty-minded; do not now fall from this high estate, but take a quiet, unprejudiced view of our relations. Why should you reproach me for desiring to have a portion of your letters published? Will they be any the less your letters on that account?"

"They are not, and never were mine!" she replied, angrily; "they merely chanced to be addressed to me—these letters, which you intended for publication even while writing them, and which were so well concocted that it will only be necessary to extract a few little elements of feeling and sentiment to make the manuscript complete and ready for the press. And I, poor, blinded simpleton, imagined that this Goethe, who could leave me to go to Italy—I imagined that this Goethe, whom my soul had followed with its sighs of affectionate longing, still loved me. I was generous enough to believe that the thoughts, love, and confidence contained in his letters were addressed to me only; but now I must learn that I was nothing more to him than the representative of the great hydra-headed monster, the public, and that he was only informing it when he seemed to be speaking to me!"

"Charlotte, I conjure you, do not continue to talk in this manner; you cannot know how your words grieve my heart! Charlotte, by the brightest and most beautiful years of my life, I conjure you, do not step forth from the pure and radiant atmosphere in which you have heretofore appeared to me. I conjure you, my friend, by all the adoration, esteem, and love which I have consecrated to you, do not descend from the altar on which my love has placed you; do not join the throng of those women who are unnecessarily jealous when they fancy their lovers not quite so tender as usual. You are not one of them; remain, therefore, on your altar, and allow me to worship you as I have heretofore done."

"You do well to say 'as you have done,' but as you no longer do," cried Charlotte, bursting into tears, without considering that woman's tears are but poor weapons to use against men, and that the woman must be very young, very beautiful, and the object of great adoration, who can afford to disfigure her countenance with tears and clouds of discontent.

Goethe looked at her in surprise and alarm, and his glance rested on her countenance inquiringly, as though seeking the charm that had formerly attracted him so irresistibly. Then, as she fastened her tear-stained eyes on his countenance, he started and turned hastily aside, as though some unwelcome vision had arisen before him.

The conviction now dawned on Charlotte that she had committed a grave error; she quickly dried her eyes, and, with that power peculiar to women, she even forced a smile to her lips.

"You turn from me, Wolf," said she, in tender tones, "you do not reply?"

"My dear," said he, gently, "as you have asked me no question, what can I answer? You asserted that I no longer loved and adored you as in former days. To such an assertion, Charlotte, I can make no reply; I would consider it a sacrilegious breach of the union that has been sanctified and confirmed by long years of love and fidelity, and that should be elevated above all doubt and protestations."

"Then you love me, Wolf? You still love me?"

"Yes," said he; and it seemed to Charlotte as though he had laid a peculiar emphasis on this little word. It sounded like another echo of the ominous whisperings of her mirror.

For a moment both were silent, perhaps because Charlotte was too completely absorbed in her own thoughts. When they conversed again it was on an entirely different topic.

After a short time Goethe tenderly took leave of Charlotte, and left the house; he hurried through the streets and entered the park, to the densest and most obscure retreats of which he had so often revealed his thoughts in past years. This park had been Goethe's true and discreet friend for many years, and he now turned his footsteps once more toward the favorite retreat in which he had so often poured out his sighs and complaints in former days, when Charlotte had cruelly repelled the advances of her tender friend and lover. Goethe suffered to-day also, but his sufferings were not to be compared to those he had formerly experienced in the same shady avenues. Then his soul was filled with a despair that was tempted with hope and joyousness. For was there ever a true lover whose ladylove had driven him to despair by her cruelty, who did not nevertheless entertain a joyous hope that her hard heart would at last be softened, and that he would yet become a *happy* lover? Then these avenues had often resounded with Goethe's sighs and lamentations, and there the tears of wounded pride had often filled his eyes. To-day he neither sighed nor lamented, and his eyes were tear-

less, but he looked gloomy, and an expression of annoyance
rather than of sadness rested on his countenance. In silence
he walked to and fro with hasty strides; suddenly he raised
the light cane which he held in his hand and struck a sprig
of blossoming woodbine from a vine that overhung the walk,
so violently that it fell to his feet; and then his lips murmured: "She is very much changed. She has become an old
woman, and I—I cannot make myself ridiculous by playing
the lover—no!"

He ceased speaking, without having finished his sentence,
as if alarmed at his own words. He then stooped down,
picked up the sprig of woodbine, and regarded it thoughtfully.

"Poor blossom," said he, gently, "I did wrong to strike
you! You are not beautiful, but you are very fragrant, and
it is for this reason probably that the kindly and delicate feeling of the people has given you so pretty a name. They call
you, 'The longer, the dearer!' I will not tread you under
foot, you poor 'the longer the dearer;' your fragrance is very
delightful, and somehow it seems to me as though Charlotte's
eyes were gazing at me from out your tiny cups."

He placed the flower in a button-hole of his coat, and, as
though his little "the longer the dearer" blossom had given
him a satisfactory solution of his heart-troubles, he left the
shady retreat and went toward an opening in the park. He
walked rapidly, and was on the point of turning into a path
that led to his garden-house, when he saw a young girl approaching from the other side of the road. She was unknown
to Goethe, and her whole appearance indicated that she did
not belong to that favored class that claims to constitute what
is called "society." The simple calico dress which enveloped
her full and graceful figure, the coarse shoes in which her little feet were enclosed, and the white and delicate little un-
gloved hands, proclaimed that she did not belong to
"society." Moreover, the light little hat which ladies of rank
wore jauntily on one side of their powdered hair at that time,

was wanting. Her hair was uncovered, and surrounded her lovely little head with a mass of sunny curls. Her countenance was radiant with youth, innocence, and freshness; she blushed as her eyes encountered Goethe's lightning glances. Her large blue eyes rested on him with an expression of gentle entreaty and tender humility, and a soft smile played about her pouting, crimson lips. This youthful, charming apparition resembled but little the pale, faintly-colored blossoms of the flower which he wore in his button-hole; she was more like the rich mossrose-bud which nestled on the fair girl's bosom, and with which she had confined the two ends of the lace shawl that hung loosely over her beautiful shoulders.

Goethe now stood before her, regarding her with inquiring, wondering glances. With a graceful movement the young girl raised her right hand, in which she held a folded paper.

"Mr. Privy-Councillor, I beg you to take this and read it."

"What does this document contain?" asked Goethe, in tender tones.

"It is a petition from my brother in Jena," murmured her clear, silvery voice. "I promised him to give it to the privy-councillor myself, and to entreat him right earnestly to grant my dear brother's request. Dear privy-councillor, please do so. We are such a poor and unhappy family; we are compelled to work so hard, and we earn so little. We have to study such close economy, and there are so few holidays in our life! But it would be a glorious fête-day for us all if the privy-councillor would grant what my dear brother so ardently desires."

Goethe's eyes were still fastened on the lovely apparition that stood before him like an embodied Psyche. In her rich, youthful beauty she seemed to him like some myrtle-blossom wafted over from sunny Italy. "What is your name, my dear girl?" asked he.

"My name is Christiane Vulpius, Mr. Privy-Councillor," murmured she, casting her eyes down.

"Not the daughter of that good-for-nothing drunkard, who—"

"Sir, he is my father," said she, interrupting him in such sad, reproachful tones, that Goethe felt heartily ashamed of his inconsiderate words, and took off his hat as he would have done to a lady of rank. "Forgive me, mademoiselle, I did wrong. Excuse my thoughtless words. But now I can readily comprehend that your family must be poor and unhappy. It seems to me that misfortune has, however, not dared to touch these rosy cheeks and lustrous eyes with its rude fingers."

She smiled. "I am still so young, sir; youth is lighthearted and hopes for better times. And then, when I grow weary of our dark little room, I run here to the park. The park is every one's garden, and a great delight for us poor people. Here I skip about, seek flowers in the grass, and sing with the birds. Is not this enough to make me happy, although hard work, poor fare, and much abuse, await me at home?"

"But it seems to me," said Goethe, taking the hand, which still held the petition, gently in his own, "it seems to me that this fair hand has no right to complain of hard work. It is as white as a lily."

"And this hand has made a great many lilies," rejoined she, smiling. "My work consists in making flowers. I love flowers, and roam through the woods all day long on Sundays, seeking beautiful flowers to copy from. My field-flower bouquets are great favorites, and the milliners pay me well for them. They are very fashionable, and the high-born ladies at court all desire to wear field-flower bouquets on their hats. Day before yesterday I furnished a field-flower bouquet, which the milliner sold to Madame the Baroness von Stein, on the same day, and yesterday I saw it on her hat."

The hand which but now had clasped the white tapering fingers of the young girl so tenderly, trembled a little, and a shadow flitted over his smiling countenance. Madame von

Stein's name sounded strangely on the young girl's lips; it seemed like a warning of impending danger. He looked grave, and released her hand, retaining only the petition. "Tell me what it contains," said he, pointing to the paper. "I would rather read it from your lips than from the paper?"

"Mr. Privy-Councillor, it concerns my poor, dear brother. He is such a brave, good fellow, and so diligent and learned. He lives in Jena, translates books from the Italian and French, and sells them to publishing houses. The office of secretary of the university library, in Jena, is now vacant, and my brother desires it, and would be so happy if he should receive the appointment! He has dared to address you, Mr. Councillor, and to entreat you earnestly to use your influence to secure him the situation. I have undertaken to deliver the petition, and to say a great many fine phrases besides. Ah, Mr. Privy-Councillor, I had written down a whole speech that I intended to make to you."

"Then let me hear this speech, my fair girl. The nightingales and bulfinches have hushed their songs, and are waiting for you to begin."

"Sir," murmured she, blushing, "I do not know why it is, but I cannot."

He bent forward, closer to her side, so close that the wind blew her golden locks against his cheek. "Why is it that you cannot, my fair child? Why not let me hear your beautiful little speech?"

"Because, because—I have hitherto only seen you at a distance, and then you looked so exalted, and walked with so much stiffness and dignity, that I entertained the most profound respect for the proud old privy-councillor, and now that I am near you I see, well—"

"Well?"

"Well," cried she, with a joyous peal of laughter, "I see that you are much too young, that my speech is entirely inappropriate."

"Why so?" asked Goethe, smiling. "Try it, let me hear it, nevertheless."

She looked up at him with an inquiring, childlike expression. "Do you believe that my beautiful speech would influence you and promote my brother's interests? If you believe that, I will speak, for my brother is a dear, good fellow, and I will do any thing to make him happy!"

"Then let us hear it," replied Goethe, delighted with the fair young girl, whose beauty, grace, and naïveté, reminded him of the lovely Leonora in Rome. Yes, it was she, it was Leonora, with this difference only, that this fair girl was a northern version of the Leonora of the south, but was none the less beautiful on that account. "Oh, Leonora, you child of the sun and of Nature, am I really to be so blessed, am I to find you here again—here where my heart was congealing, and longing for the sunny rays of delight from a fair woman's eyes? Yes, Leonora, this is your sweet smile and kindling, childlike glance; it is you, and yet it is not you. God and Nature were reflected in your countenance, a whole heaven shone in your features. Fair Nature is reflected in this lovely countenance also, but I seek the divinity in vain, and instead of heaven I find the joyous earth enthroned therein!"

Goethe was occupied with these thoughts while Christiane, blushing, smiling, half-ashamed at times, and then again bold and fearless, was declaiming her well-prepared speech. Too much of what was passing in Goethe's mind must have been reflected in the tender, ardent glances which rested on her countenance, for she suddenly broke off in the midst of a sentence, murmured a few embarrassed words, blushed, courtesied, and then turned and fled like a startled doe.

CHAPTER VI.

THE TWO POETS.

"SHE is bewitching," murmured Goethe, as the beautiful girl was lost to view behind the green bushes that skirted the avenue. "I had no idea that dull, sober Weimar contained such a treasure, and—"

"Goethe! Welcome, Goethe!" cried the joyous voice of a woman behind him; "how delighted I am to meet you here!"

He turned hastily, and saw Madame von Kalb standing before him, on the arm of a tall, fair-haired gentleman. This was the cause of Christiane's flight. The beautiful girl had seen this lady and gentleman coming. She was, therefore, not only beautiful, she was also discreet and modest. Goethe said this to himself, while he kissed Madame von Kalb's extended hand, and gayly responded to her greeting.

"The two gentlemen are, of course, acquainted," said she.

"I believe I have never had the honor," replied Goethe, who had again assumed the cold reserve of the privy-councillor.

"Who does not know the greatest and most celebrated of Germany's poets?" said the other gentleman, a slight flush suffusing itself over his pale, hollow cheeks. "I have known the poet Goethe for a long time; I was present when he visited the Charles School in Stuttgart. He, of course, did not observe the poor scholar, but the latter was delighted to see the poet Goethe. And he is now delighted to make the acquaintance of the Privy-Councillor Goethe!"

Perhaps there was a slight touch of irony in these words, but his large blue eyes beamed as mildly and lovingly as ever. A slight shadow flitted over Goethe's brow.

"You are right," said he, "in reminding me that there are hours in which the poet must be contented to perform the duties of an official. By the document which I hold in my hand, you will perceive, my lady, that I am an official who has duties to fulfil, and I trust that you will, therefore, excuse me." He bowed formally, and passed on in the direction of his garden-house.

"He is becoming colder and more reserved each day," said Madame von Kalb. "He has been completely transformed since I first saw him here in Weimar. Then, radiant and handsome as Apollo, flaming with enthusiasm, carrying all hearts with him by his impetuosity and genial manner—then we were forced to believe that earth had no barriers or fetters for him, but that he could spread his pinions and soar heavenward at any moment; now, a stiff, unapproachable, privy-councillor, reserved and grandly dignified! Schiller, no woman could change so fearfully, or become so false to herself! Goethe's appearance has saddened me so much that I feel like crying!"

"And I," said Schiller, angrily, "I feel like calling myself a simpleton for having addressed a kindly greeting to so haughty a gentleman. He despises me, and looks down upon the unknown dramatic writer with contempt; he—"

"Frederick," said Madame von Kalb, gently, "my Frederick, such petty envy does not beseem a genius like yourself; you—"

"Nor do I envy him," said Schiller, interrupting her; "in my breast also glows the holy fire that was not stolen from heaven by Prometheus for him alone! My spirit also has pinions that would bear it aloft to the sun, if—yes, if it were not for the paltry fetters that bind my feet to earth!"

"And yet, my beloved friend," rejoined Charlotte, passionately, "and yet I will be only too happy to share these fetters with you—and I would rather live with you in a modest cottage, than in the most magnificent palace at the side of an unloved man."

"You are an angel, Charlotte," murmured Schiller; "you over-estimate me, and I know only too well how little I resemble the sublime image your lively imagination has made of me."

He did not look at Charlotte while uttering these words, his manner was embarrassed, and his eyes turned heavenward. He suffered Charlotte to lead him by the hand, and walked at her side like a dreaming, confiding child.

She led him to the darkest and most solitary avenue—to the same retreat in which Goethe had walked restlessly to and fro but a short time before. The little branch of woodbine which Goethe had struck down with his cane, and from which he had plucked a blossom and placed it in his button-hole, still lay in the middle of the road. Charlotte carelessly trod it under foot, never dreaming that these crushed blossoms could have told a tale that might have served her as a warning.

But of women's hearts the same may be said that Mirabeau said of princes: "They have learned nothing and forgotten nothing!"

No; they, too, learn nothing and forget nothing, these poor women's hearts. Never have they learned by the fate of another woman that love is not immortal, and that the vows of men, as Horace says, "are wafted away like the leaves of the forest." Never have they forgotten these vows, and on the leaves of the forest do they still erect air-castles, which they fondly hope will stand forever.

They seated themselves on a rustic bench that had been placed in a flowery niche, cut out of the hedge that skirted the path in which they had been walking. There they sat, hand in hand, Charlotte's eyes fastened on Schiller's noble, thoughtful countenance, with an expression of mingled pain and tenderness.

"Frederick, you have nothing to say to me?"

He raised his eyes slowly, and in the vehemence of her own feelings she failed to observe that his glance was somewhat embarrassed and anxious.

"It is very beautiful here," he said in low tones. "This

solitude, this eloquent silence of Nature, is very delightful, particularly when I can enjoy it at your side, my beloved friend. Our souls are like two harps that are tuned to the same tone, and are so near together that, when the strings of the one are touched, those of the other echo a response in the same accord."

"God grant that it may ever be so, my Frederick! God grant that no storm break in upon the harmony of these harps!"

"And from whence should such a storm come, my dear friend, beloved sister of my soul? No, I am sure that this can never be. The love which unites us is exalted above all change and illusion. I can conceive of no purer or more beautiful relation than that of a brother to his sister, when they are loving, and live in a proper understanding of their duties to each other. Let this thought truly console us and strengthen our hearts, Charlotte, if other wishes entertained by me for a long time, as you well know, should never be fulfilled. Charlotte, I am not one of those whose lives flow on in a smooth, unbroken current, and over whose desires auspicious stars shine in the heavens. To forego has ever been my fate, and you, my dearest, have given me painful instruction in this bitter lesson. You will remember how I knelt at your feet in Manheim, passionately entreating you to sunder the fetters which bound you to the unloved man, and to become mine, my wife! It was, however, in vain; and now, when your heart is at last inclined to grant the fulfilment of our wishes and hopes—now, when you would dare to become my wife, another obstacle presents itself that seems to render it impossible that we should ever be outwardly united."

"What obstacle, Frederick? Who can prevent it?"

"Your husband, Charlotte. It seems that he loves you truly, and cannot bear to entertain the thought of separation."

"Have you spoken with him, Frederick? Have you honestly and openly told him of our wishes, and have you entreated him to fulfil them?"

"I have often attempted to do so, but he always avoided

coming to the point. Whenever he observed that I was endeavoring to turn our conversation in that direction, he would break off abruptly and introduce another topic of conversation. This convinced me that he loved you dearly, and the thought that I am about to grieve this good and noble man and rob him of a treasure that my own feelings teach me must be very dear to him, pains me to the heart's core."

"Frederick," said she, softly, "how fearful it is to see the most beautiful flowers of spring fade and die, sometimes cut off by a nipping frost, sometimes parched by the too great warmth of the sun!"

"I do not understand you, Charlotte," said Schiller, in a little more confusion than was entirely compatible with his "not understanding."

"And I," cried she, with sparkling eyes, "I wish I did not understand you! Tell me, Frederick, is your heart really mine? Are your feelings toward me unchanged?"

He raised his eyes, and gazed into her agitated countenance earnestly and thoughtfully. "Charlotte, you ask a question which God alone can answer. Who can say of himself that he has a true and exact knowledge of his own feelings? All is subject to change; the sea has its ebb and flow, the sun rises and sets. But the sea ever and again returns to the beach it had before deserted, and the sun ever rises again after the dark night. As the sea and sun, with all their changes, are still eternally constant, so it is also with true love. At times it would seem as though it were withdrawing, and leaving a bleak, sandy desert behind; in the next hour its mighty waves surge back impetuously over the barren strand, chanting, in holy organ-tones, the song that love is eternal."

"Wondrous words!" cried Charlotte; "the paraphrase to a glorious song which I hope the poet Frederick Schiller will one day sing to the world! But I ask the poet, whether these are also the words of the man Frederick Schiller? Did the hymn to love, just uttered by the poet's lips, also resound in the heart of the man, and was it addressed to me?"

"And why these questions, my dearest? The poet and the man are one, and the utterances of the poet's lips are the thoughts of the man; when he consecrates an enthusiastic hymn to love, while at your side, be assured that it is addressed to you!"

He laid his arm around her neck, and drew her head to his breast, as he had so often done before in hours of tenderness. But Charlotte felt that there was, nevertheless, a difference between then and now: the arm that embraced her did not rest on her neck with the same warm pressure as of yore. She, however, repressed the sigh that had nearly escaped her lips, nestled closer to his bosom, and whispered in low tones: "Frederick, your hymn has found an echo in my heart; Frederick, I am very grateful to God for your love!"

He was silent, his only response was a warmer pressure of the arm entwined around her neck. Then both were silent. Deep stillness reigned; it seemed as though Nature were holding divine service in her green halls under the dome of heaven; at first with silent prayer, then a joyous song of praise resounded from the hidden chorus in the foliage of the tall trees, until the breeze rustled through the leaves in holy organ-tones, and silenced the feathered songsters.

To these deep organ-tones, to this rustling of the wind in the foliage, listened the two lovers, who sat there on the little rustic bench in a trance of delight and devotion. Both were silent, and yet so eloquent in their silence. He, with his pale countenance turned upward, gazing intently at the blue dome of heaven, as though seeking to fathom its mysteries; she, with her head resting on his bosom, seeking no other, now that she had found this heaven. But the wind now rustled through the trees in deeper and more solemn tones, and awakened Charlotte from her sweet repose. A leaf torn from the branches by the wind was borne against her cheek; it glided over her face like the touch of a ghostly finger, and fell into her hands, which lay folded in her lap. She started up in alarm, and looked down at this gift of the wind and trees.

They had given her a withered, discolored leaf. Like the harbinger of coming autumn had this withered leaf touched her face, and rudely awakened her from her heavenly summer dream.

"A bad omen," she murmured, tearing the leaf to pieces with her trembling fingers.

"What does this murmuring mean, Charlotte?" asked Schiller, who had been completely absorbed in his own thoughts, and had not observed this little by-play in the great tragedy of the heart. "What alarmed you so suddenly?"

"Nothing, it is nothing," said she, rising. "Come, my friend, let us go; I fear that a storm is gathering in the heavens."

He looked up at the clear blue sky in amazement. "I do not see a single cloud."

"So much the better, Frederick!" rejoined Charlotte, quickly, "so much the better! Nothing will therefore prevent our taking the contemplated drive to Rudolstadt."

Her large eyes fastened a quick, penetrating glance on his countenance while uttering these words, and she saw that he colored slightly, and avoided encountering her gaze.

"We will carry out our intention of driving to Rudolstadt to-morrow, will we not, my friend? I have been promising to pay Madame von Lengefeld a visit for a long time, and it will afford me great pleasure to see her two daughters again. Caroline von Beulwitz is a noble young woman, and bears the cruel fate entailed upon her by her unfortunate marriage with true heroism. At the side of this matured summer-rose stands her sister Charlotte, like a fair young blossom of the spring-time."

Schiller, his countenance radiant with pure joy, gave Charlotte a tender, grateful look; and this look pierced her heart, and kindled the consuming flames of jealousy. Poor Charlotte! The wind had dashed a withered autumn-leaf against her face, and but now she had called the woman who was henceforth to be her rival "a fair young blossom of the spring-time."

"How beautifully you paint with a few strokes of the brush, Charlotte!" said Schiller, gayly. "Your portrait is an excellent one, and portrays Madame von Lengefeld's daughters as they really are. Caroline, as the full-blown rose, and Charlotte as a lovely, fragrant violet."

"And which of these flowers do you most admire?"

"It is hard to choose between them," replied Schiller, laughing. "It is best to admire them together; I can scarcely conceive of their being separated; separation would destroy the harmony of the picture!"

Charlotte felt relieved. Then he loved neither. His heart had not chosen between them.

"I am so glad," said she, "that my friends chance to be yours also! How did you become acquainted with the Von Lengefeld family?"

"We are old acquaintances!" replied Schiller, smiling. "I made the acquaintance of these ladies four years ago while residing in Madame von Wollzogen's house, soon after my flight from Stuttgart, and it was her son, my friend, William von Wollzogen, who took me to see them in Rudolstadt." *

"Rumor says that Mr. William von Wollzogen loves his cousin Caroline devotedly."

"And for once, rumor has, as I believe, told the truth. Wollzogen loves his beautiful cousin passionately."

"And Caroline, does she love him?"

"Who can fathom the heart of this noble woman! Her lips are sealed by the solemn vow which united her with her unloved husband, and Caroline von Beulwitz is too noble and chaste a woman to become untrue even to an unloved husband, and—" Schiller hesitated; he now felt how deeply his words must have wounded the woman who stood at his side— the woman over whom he had just pronounced judgment. But women have a wonderful knack of not hearing what they do not wish to hear, and of smiling even when stabbed to the heart.

* Schiller's Life, by Caroline von Wollzogen, p. 115.

Charlotte von Kalb smiled on Schiller as though his words had not wounded her in the slightest degree.

"And has Charlotte, has this poor child, at last recovered from her unhappy love? Have the bleeding wounds of her young heart at last been healed?"

Madame von Kalb, her countenance wreathed in smiles, had drawn the dagger from her own heart and plunged it into her lover's. "Paete, Paete, non dolet!"

He felt the blow and found it impossible to force a smile to his lips. "What do you mean?" asked he, gloomily. "Who has dared to wound the heart of this fair girl?"

"I am surprised, indeed, that you should have heard nothing of this affair, my dear friend," said Charlotte, the smile on her lips becoming more radiant as she felt that the dagger was entering deeper and deeper. "Charlotte von Lengefeld was affianced to a noble young man whom she loved devotedly, and it was the most ardent wish of both to be united for life. But, unfortunately, the wealth of their feelings formed a cutting contrast to the poverty of their outward circumstances. Madame von Lengefeld, a lady of experience and discretion, informed the lovers that their union was out of the question, as they were both poor. Yielding to stern necessity they separated, although with many tears and bleeding hearts. The young man entered the Hessian army and went to America, never to return, The young girl remained behind in sorrow and sadness, and, as it is said, took a solemn vow never to marry another, as fate had separated her from the man she loved."

And after Charlotte, with the cruelty characteristic of all women when they love and are jealous, had dealt this last blow, she smiled and gave her lover a tender glance. But his countenance remained perfectly composed, and Charlotte's narrative seemed rather to have appealed to the imagination of the poet than to the heart of the man.

"It is true," said he, softly, "each human heart furnishes material for a tragedy. All life is, in reality, nothing more

than a grand tragedy, whose author is the Eternal Spirit of
the universe. We, little children of humanity, are nothing
more than the poor actors to whom this Eternal Spirit has
given life for no other purpose than that we might play the
rôles which He has assigned us. We poor actors fancy ourselves independent beings, yes, even the lords of creation,
and talk of free agency and of the sublime power of the
human will. This free agency is nothing more than the self-
worship of the poor slave.—Come, Charlotte," cried Schiller,
suddenly awakening from his thoughtful contemplation;
"come, my dear friend, let us go. Thoughts are burning in
my heart and brain, the poet is being aroused within the man.
I must write; work only can restore me to peace and tranquillity!"

"Do you no longer find peace and tranquillity with me,
Frederick? Have they ceased to ring the festive bells of our
union of hearts? Do they no longer call our souls together,
that they may impart light and warmth to each other like two
rays of sunshine?"

"Charlotte, souls too are untuned at times, although the
accord of love is ever the same. Remember this, and do not
be angry if storms should sometimes break in upon the harmony of our souls."

"I am never angry with you," said she, in tones of mingled
sadness and tenderness. "Your peace and your happiness is
all I desire, and to give you this shall be the sole endeavor of
my whole life. I believe that this is the holy mission with
which fate has entrusted m , and for which I have been placed
in the world. To do my utmost to add to your happiness and
to give joyousness to your heart and gayety to your soul.
Yes, you shall be gay! Your good genius smiles on your
labors and relieves the laurel-crowned head of the poet of all
care, giving him honor and glory. But I—I will give you
happiness and gayety, for I love you; and you, you have told
me a thousand times that you loved me, and that my heart
was the home of your happiness. I will believe this sweet as-

surance, Frederick, and will hold fast to it forever and ever-more. I will look into the future with a glad heart, hoping that we may, at last, overcome all obstacles and belong to each other wholly. You say that my husband always avoids this subject, refusing to understand you. I will compel him to understand us. I, myself, will tell him of our hopes and wishes!"

"No, Charlotte," said he, "this duty devolves upon me! A time will come when all his endeavors to avoid this subject will be futile, and I will avail myself of this moment to speak for us both. Do not look at me so doubtingly, Charlotte. You have instructed me in the trying art of patience! Be patient yourself, and never forget that the stars of our love will shine forever!"

CHAPTER VII.

THE FIRST MEETING.

On the next morning Schiller and Madame von Kalb drove to Rudolstadt to pay the Lengefeld family a visit. Charlotte did not fail to observe that Schiller's countenance grew brighter and brighter the nearer they approached the little Thuringian village, that was so beautifully situated in the midst of wooded hills.

Madame von Lengefeld received her welcome guests, at the door of her pretty little house, with dignity and kindness. Behind her stood her two lovely daughters; the eyes of both fastened on Frederick Schiller, to whom they extended their hands, blushingly bidding him welcome.

Charlotte von Kalb, although conversing in an animated manner with Madame von Lengefeld, nevertheless listened to every word Schiller uttered, and observed his every glance. She heard him greet the two sisters with uniform cordiality, and she saw that his gaze rested on both with the same kindliness.   Madame von Kalb's countenance assumed a more joyous expression, and a voice in her heart whispered, exultingly: "He does not love her, he has no preference for either one of them.   He told me the truth, he entertains a brother's affection for *them*, but his tenderness and love are for *me!*"   And now that her heart had come to this joyful conclusion, Charlotte von Kalb's whole manner was gay and animated; she laughed and jested with the two young ladies, was devoted in her attentions to Madame von Lengefeld, and treated Schiller with the most tender consideration.   Her conversation was very gay and witty, and the most piquant and brilliant remarks were constantly falling like sparkling gems from her smiling lips.

"How intelligent and amiable this lady is!" said the elder of the two sisters, Caroline von Beulwitz, to Schiller, with whom they were walking in the flower-garden, behind the house, while dame von Kalb remained with Madame von Lengefeld in the parlor.

Schiller walked between the sisters, a pretty snow-white hand resting on either arm.   His countenance shone with happiness, and his step was light and buoyant.   "I should like to ascend straightway into Heaven with you two," said he, joyously; "and I think it highly probable that I will do so directly.   Nothing would be impossible for me to-day, and it seems to me as though Heaven had descended to earth, so that I would have no obstacles to overcome, and could walk right in, with you two ladies on my arms."

"Then let us return to the house at once, in order to guard against any such ascension," said Caroline von Beulwitz, smiling.

"Oh, Caroline," exclaimed Charlotte, laughing joyously, "I wish we could take this flight to Heaven!   How surprised they would be, and how they would look for us, while we three were taking a walk up there in the clouds!"

"And how angry Madame von Kalb would be with us, for having enticed her dear friend away!" said Caroline, ironically.

" I would enjoy it all the more on that very account," rejoined Charlotte, laughing.

" And I, too," protested Schiller. " It would be very pleasant if we could sometimes cast aside all earthly fetters and rise, like the bird, high above the noisy, sorrowing earth, and float in the sunbright ether with the loved one in our arms. My dear friends, why not make this ascension to-day?"

" To-day! no, not to-day," said Charlotte, exchanging a meaning glance with her sister. " It will not do to leave the earth to-day, will it, Caroline? We expect to have too pleasant a time here below to think of making the ascension to-day!"

" What does this mystery—what do these sly glances mean?" asked Schiller. " Something extraordinary is about to occur. Tell me, Lolo, what does all this mean?"

" I will tell nothing," said Charlotte, laughing merrily, and shaking her brown locks. " It is useless to ask me."

" But you, dear Caroline, on whose sweet lips the truth and goodness are ever enthroned, you, at least, will tell me whether I am wrong in supposing that a mystery exists that will be unravelled to-day."

" Yes, my dear friend," said she, smiling, " there is a little surprise in store for you, but I hope you are satisfied that we would never do any thing that—"

" And I believe," said her younger sister, interrupting her, " I believe that the solution of this mystery is at hand, for I hear a carriage approaching. Listen, it has stopped at our door! Yes, this is the mystery! Come, my friend, the solution awaits you!"

She was about to lead Schiller to the house, when Caroline gently drew her back. " One moment, Lolo! Tell me, my friend, do you place sufficient confidence in us, to follow without question and without uneasiness, even when we confess that we are leading you to the solution of a mystery?"

Schiller clasped the right hands of the two sisters and pressed them to his heart. " I will gladly and proudly follow you wherever you may choose to lead me. I place such confidence in you both that I could lay my life and eternal happiness in your dear hands, and bid defiance to all the mysteries of the world!"

"But yet you would like to know what this mystery is, would you not?" asked Lolo.

"No," replied Schiller, with an expression of abiding faith; "no, the solution of the mystery which my fair friends have in store for me will unquestionably be agreeable. Let us go."

"We are much obliged to you for your confidence, Schiller," said Caroline. "We will, however, not permit you to be surprised, as the other ladies had determined you should be. It will depend upon your own free-will whether you enter into the plans agreed upon by your friends, or not. Schiller, you heard a carriage drive up to our door a few moments since? Do you know who were in that carriage? Madame von Stein and Goethe!"

"Is not that a surprise?" cried Lolo, laughing.

"Yes," he said, with an expression of annoyance, "yes, a surprise, but not an agreeable one. The Privy-Councillor Goethe showed no desire to cultivate my acquaintance, and I would not have him think that I desire to intrude myself on his notice. If he deems my acquaintance undesirable, the world is wide enough for us both, and we can easily avoid each other. As much as I admire Goethe's genius, I am not humble enough to forget that I too am a poet to whom some consideration is due. Nothing could be less becoming than for Schiller to advance while Goethe recedes, or even stands still."

"But this is not so, Schiller; it could not be!" exclaimed Charlotte earnestly, while Caroline gazed at him with sparkling eyes as though rejoicing in his proud bearing and energetic words. "Join with me, Caroline, in assuring him that is not the case! Tell him how it is."

"My friend," said Charlotte, in a low voice, "Goethe knew as little of your presence here as you of his. The two ladies,

Madame von Stein and Madame von Kalb, arranged the whole affair, and we were only too glad to assist them in bringing together the two greatest poets of our day, the two noblest spirits of the century, in order that they might become acquainted, and lay aside the prejudices they had entertained concerning each other. While we are conversing with you here, this same explanation is being made to Goethe by the ladies in the house. Charlotte von Stein is also there, and, as you will readily believe, holds the honor of her beloved friend Schiller in too high estimation to permit Goethe to suppose for a moment that you had connived at this meeting, or were anxious to make an acquaintance which he might deem undesirable."

"Come, my friends, let us return to the house," said Schiller, smiling sadly. "It is but proper that I should make the first advances to my superior in rank and ability, and—"

He ceased speaking, for at this moment Goethe and the two Charlottes appeared on the stairway.

"You see," whispered Caroline, "Goethe thinks as you do, and he, too, is willing to make the first advances."

In the meantime Goethe had walked down into the garden, still accompanied by the two ladies, with whom he was engaged in an animated conversation. But when he saw Schiller approaching, Goethe hastened forward to meet him.

"Madame von Kalb has reproached me for having withdrawn so abruptly when we met in the park a few days since," said Goethe, in kindly tones. "I admit that I was wrong, but, at the same time, I must confess that it did not seem appropriate to me that we should make each other's acquaintance under such circumstances—as it were by the merest chance."

"And yet it is chance again that enables me to greet the poet Goethe, to-day," replied Schiller, quickly.

"But this time it has been brought about by fair hands," cried Goethe, bowing gracefully to the ladies, "and, with the ancients, I exclaim: "'What the great gods vouchsafe can only be good and beautiful!'"

But, as though he had conceded enough to his friends' wishes, and shown Schiller sufficient consideration, Goethe now turned again to the ladies, and resumed the conversation in which he had been engaged on entering the garden. They had been questioning him about Madame Angelica Kaufmann, the painter, and Goethe was telling them of her life, her genius, and her nobility of mind, with great animation and in terms of warm approval. Afterward, when the company were assembled around the table at dinner in the garden pavilion, Goethe, at Charlotte von Stein's request, told them of his travels, of the Eternal City, and of that charming life in Italy which he considered the only one worthy of an artist, or of any really intellectual man. Carried away with enthusiasm, his countenance shone with manly beauty, originating rather from his inward exaltation than from any outward perfection of form and feature.

The ladies were fascinated by this handsome countenance, these lustrous eyes, and the eloquent lips which described sunny Italy, the land of promise, of art and poetry, in such glowing colors.

Schiller sat there in silence, listless, his eyes cast down, rarely adding a low word of approval to the enthusiastic applause of the ladies, and never addressing a question or remark to Goethe; nor did the latter ever address himself directly to Schiller, but spoke to all with the air of a great orator who feels assured that *all* are listening to his words with deference and admiration.

"I am not satisfied with our success to-day," sighed Madame von Kalb, while returning with Schiller to Weimar in the evening. "I had promised myself such glorious results from this meeting with Goethe. I hoped that you would become friends, learning to love each other, but now you seem to have passed like two stars that chance to meet on their heavenly course, yet journey on without attracting each other. Tell me, at least, my dear friend, how you were pleased with Goethe."

"Ask me how I am pleased with a glacier, and whether I feel warm and cheerful in its vicinity. Yes, this Goethe is a glacier, grand, sublime, and radiant, like Mount Blanc, but the atmosphere that surrounds him is cold, and the little flowers of attachment that would so gladly blossom are frozen by his grandeur. To be in Goethe's society often, would, I confess, make me unhappy. He never descends from this altitude, even when with his most intimate friends. I believe him to be egotistic in an eminent degree. He possesses the gift of enchaining men, and of placing them under obligations to himself, by little as well as great attentions, while he always manages to remain unfettered himself. He manifests his existence in a beneficent manner, but only like a god, without revealing himself—this, it seems to me, is a consistent and systematic rule of action, based on the highest enjoyment of self-love. Men should not permit such a being to spring into existence in their midst. This, I confess, makes me detest him, although I love his intellect, and have a high opinion of his ability." *

"But you will yet learn to love him as a man, Frederick."

"It is quite possible that I may," said Schiller, thoughtfully. "He has awakened a feeling of mingled hatred and love in my bosom—a feeling, perhaps, not unlike that which Brutus and Cassius may have entertained toward Cæsar. I could murder his spirit, and yet love him dearly." †

While "Brutus" was giving utterance to this feeling of mingled hatred and love, "Cæsar" was also pronouncing judgment over "Brutus;" this judgment was, however, not a combination of hatred and love, but rather of pride and contempt. The hero who had overcome all the difficulties of the road, and whose brow was already entwined with the well-deserved laurel, may have looked down, from the sublime height which he had attained, with some proud satisfaction and pitying

---

* Schiller's own words.—See "Schiller's Correspondence with Körner," vol. ii., p. 21.

† Ibid.

contempt upon him who had not yet overcome these difficulties, who had not yet vanquished the demons who opposed
his ascent.

"My dear Wolf," said Madame von Stein to Goethe, while
returning to Weimar, "I had hoped that you would meet
Schiller in a more cordial manner. You scarcely noticed
him."

"I esteem him too highly to meet him with a pretence of
cordiality when I really dislike him," replied Goethe, emphatically. "I have an antipathy to this man that I neither
can nor will overcome."

"But Goethe is not the man to be influenced by antipathies
for which he has no good reasons."

"Well, then," cried Goethe, with an outburst of feeling,
such as he had rarely indulged in since his return from Italy,
"well, then, I have good reasons. Schiller destroys what I
have toiled to create; he builds up what I fancied I had overthrown—this abominable revolution in the minds of men, this
heaven-storming conviviality, this wild glowing, and reeling,
so very indistinct and cloudy, so replete with tears, sighs,
groans, and shouts, and so antagonistic to lucid, sublime
thought, and pure enthusiasm. His 'Robbers' I abhor—this
Franz Moor is the deformed creation of powerful but im-
mature talent. I found, on my return from Italy, that
Schiller had flooded Germany with the ethic and theatrical
paradoxes of which I had long been endeavoring to purify
myself. The sensation which these works have excited, the
universal applause given to these deformed creations of an in-
toxicated imagination, alarm me. It seems to me as though
my poetic labors were all in vain, and had as well be discontinued at once. For, where lies the possibility of stem-
ming the onward tide impelled by such productions—such
strange combinations of genuine worth and wild form? If
Germany can be inspired by the robber, Charles Moor, and
can relish a monstrous caricature like the brutal Franz Moor,
then it is all over with the pure conceptions of art, which I

have sought to attain for myself and my poems—then my labors are useless and superfluous, and had best be discontinued." *

"But you are speaking of Schiller's first works only, my dear friend; his later writings are of a purer and nobler nature. Have you not yet read his 'Don Carlos?'"

"I have, and I like it no better than 'The Robbers.' It is useless to attempt to reconcile us to each other. Intellectually, we are two antipodes, and more than one diameter of the earth lies between and separates us. Let us then be considered as the two poles that, in the nature of things, can never be united." †

"How agitated you are, my dear friend!" sighed Charlotte. "It seems there is still something that can arouse you from your Olympian repose and heartless equanimity, and recall you to earth."

"'*Homo sum, nihil humani a me alienum puto,*'" rejoined Goethe, smiling. "Yes, Charlotte, I learned in Italy to appreciate the vast distance between myself and the great gods of Olympus, and I say with all humility: 'I am a man, and a stranger to nothing that is human.'"

"I wish you had never been in Italy," sighed Charlotte.

"And I," rejoined Goethe, "I wish I had never left Italy to return to Germany, and to exchange a bright sky for a gloomy one."

"How cruel you are, Goethe!" cried Charlotte, bursting into tears.

"Cruel!" repeated he, in dismay. "Good heavens! are we never to understand each other again! Does Charlotte no longer sympathize with me in my sorrows, as in my joys? Can you not comprehend the deep sadness that fills my heart when I think of Italy?"

"Certainly I can," cried Charlotte. "Since you told me of your love-affair with the beautiful Leonora, I comprehend

* Goethe's words.—See "Goethe's Works," vol. xxiii.
† Goethe's words.

and understand all. I know that you left your heart in Italy, and that it is the longing of love that calls you back to the sunny land from the bleak north."

He gave her a lingering, reproachful look. "Charlotte, it is now my turn to call *you* cruel, and I can do so with perfect justice. That which you should consider the best proof of my love and friendship—the unreserved and complete confession I made when I told you of this affair—this same confession seems rather to have made you doubt me, than to have carried the conviction to your heart that you are the being I love most dearly on earth!"

"I thank God that I have no confession to make to you," cried Charlotte. "I have not forgotten you for a moment. My soul and heart were ever true to you, and, while you were kneeling at the feet of the beautiful Leonora, I knelt at the feet of God, and entreated Him to bless and preserve the faithless man who was perhaps betraying me at that very hour, and who now carries his cruelty so far that he dares to complain and lament over his lost Italian paradise in my presence, and—"

"Charlotte, do not speak so, I conjure you," cried Goethe, interrupting her. "You cannot know what incalculable pain your words inflict. My friend, my beloved, is nothing sacred? is every temple to be overthrown? is every ideal to be destroyed? Charlotte, be yourself once more; do not give way to this petty jealousy. Be the noble, high-souled woman once more, and lay aside these petty weaknesses. Know that the holy bond of love in which we are united is indestructible, and still exists even when fair blossoms of earth spring into life beside it. Be indulgent with me and with us both, and do not desire that I, at forty years of age, should be an ascetic old man, dead to all the little fleeting emotions of the heart."

"These sophistries are incomprehensible to me," said she, sharply, "and it seems to me that what you call fleeting emotions of the heart are simply infidelity and a desecration

of the love which you vowed would be eternal and unchangeable."

Goethe bowed his head sadly. "It really looks as though
we could no longer understand each other," said he, gently.
"I admit, however, that I am to blame, and beg you to pardon me. In the future I will be more cautious. I will make
no more communications calculated to offend you."

"That is, you will withdraw your confidence, but you will
not cease to do that which must offend me."

His countenance quivered, his eyes sparkled with anger,
and his cheeks turned pale, but he struggled to repress the
indignant words that trembled on his lips.

Charlotte turned pale with alarm. Goethe looked sternly
on his beloved for the first time. She read indifference in
his features for the first time. A loud cry of anguish escaped
her lips, and the tears gushed from her eyes.

Goethe did not attempt to console her, but sat at her side
in silence, his gaze resting gloomily on her countenance.
"It is a cruel destiny that women should be compelled to give
vent to their grief in tears, for their beauty is seldom en-
hanced thereby," said he to himself. "The tears of offended
love are becoming in youthful faces only, and Charlotte's is
not youthful enough. She looks old and ugly when she
cries!"

Poor Charlotte!

Late in the evening of this day Goethe left his house
through a side door that led from his garden into a narrow
little street. His hat was pressed down over his forehead,
and a long cloak enveloped his figure. In former days, before his trip to Italy, he had often slipped through this small
door in the early hours of the morning, and in the twilight,
to take the most direct and quiet route to his beloved Charlotte; the side door had also been often opened to admit the
beautiful Madame von Stein when she came to visit her dear
friend Goethe. To-day, Goethe had waited until it grew so
dark that it was impossible that his curious neighbors could

observe his departure, and on this occasion he did not
direct his footsteps toward the stately house in which madame the Baroness von Stein resided.   He took an entirely
different direction, and walked on through streets and alleys
until he came to a poor, gloomy, little house.   But a light
was still burning in one window, and the shadow of a graceful, girlish figure flitted across the closed blind.   Goethe
tapped twice on the window, and then the shadow vanished.
In a few moments the door was cautiously opened.   Had any
one stood near he would soon have observed two shadows on
the window-blind—two shadows in a close embrace.

CHAPTER VIII.

WILHELMINE RIETZ.

THEY were victorious, the pious Rosicrucians and Illuminati, who held King Frederick William the Second entangled
in their invisible toils.   They governed the land; by their
unbounded influence over the king's mind *they* had become
the real kings of Prussia.   General von Bischofswerder stood
at the king's side as his most faithful friend and invoker of
spirits.   Wöllner had been ennobled and advanced from the
position of chamberlain to that of a minister of Prussia, and
to him was given the guidance of the heart and conscience of
the nation.   This promotion of Wöllner to the position of
minister of all affairs connected with the church and public
schools, took place at the end of the year 1788, and the first
great act of the newly-appointed minister was the promul-
gation of the notorious Edict of Faith, intended to fetter the
consciences of men, and prescribing what doctrines appertaining to God and religion they should accept as true and
infallible.   They were no longer to be permitted to illumine
the doctrines of the church with the light of reason, and to
reveal what it was intended should remain enveloped in mystical darkness.   It was strictly forbidden to subject the com-

mandments of the church and the doctrines of revealed religion to the *fallacious* tests of reason.   Unconditional and implicit obedience to the authorities of the church was required
and enforced.

But the minister Von Wöllner was far too shrewd a man
not to be fully aware that this edict of faith would be received
with the greatest dissatisfaction by the people to whom
Frederick the Great had bequeathed freedom of thought and
faith, as his best and greatest legacy.   He had fettered reason
and intelligence in matters appertaining to religion, but he
knew that they would seek revenge in severe criticisms and
loud denunciations through the public press.   It was necessary to prevent this, but how could it be done?   Wöllner de-
vised the means—the censorship of the press.   This guillotine
of the mind was erected in Prussia, and at the same time the
good King of France and Doctor Guillotine were, from
motives of humanity, devising some means of severing the
heads of criminals so quickly from their bodies that death
would be instantaneous and painless.   Good King Louis the
Sixteenth and his philanthropical physician invented an instrument which they believed would answer these requirements, and baptized it "Guillotine," in honor of its inventor.
Good King Frederick William caused his misanthropical physician Wöllner to erect an instrument that should kill the
noblest thoughts and mutilate the mind.   This guillotine of
the mind, called censorship of the press, was Wöllner's second stroke of policy.   With this instrument he effectually
destroyed Frederick the Great's work of enlightenment; and
yet this same pious, holy, orthodox man published the
"Works of Frederick the Great," the royal freethinker and
mocker at religion.   For these works there was, however, no
censorship.   The publication of Frederick the Great's writings was a source of great profit to the wily minister Von
Wöllner, who worshipped with greater devotion at another
than the shrine before which he bowed the knee in the church—
at the shrine of mammon.

The great king now lived in his writings only; the men who had served him faithfully, Count Herzberg above all, had been dismissed from office, and were powerless; the laws which he had made to protect freedom of thought were annulled, the light which he had diffused throughout his kingdom was extinguished, and darkness and night were sinking down over the minds and hearts of a whole nation! The promise which the circle directors had made to the grand-kophta on the night of Frederick the Great's death was fulfilled: "The kingdom of the church and of the spirits embraced all Prussia, and the power and authority of the government were in the hands of the pious fathers. The invisible church and its visible priests now ruled in Prussia. The king was restored to the true faith, and lay in the dust at the feet of the Invisibles, who ruled him and guided his mind and conscience as they saw fit."

There were still a few brave men left who refused to submit to their control, and bade defiance to this guillotine of censorship—men who warred against these murderers of thought and freedom. There was Nicolai, and Büsching, and Leuchsenring, the former instructor of the prince royal, who never wearied of warning the people, and who unceasingly endeavored to arouse those whom the pious executioners desired to destroy. "Nicolai's Berlin Monthly Magazine" was the arena of these warriors of enlightenment, and in this magazine the combat against darkness and ignorance was still carried on, in defiance of censorship and the edict of faith. The practical and intelligent editor, Nicolai, still attacked these new institutions with bitter sarcasm; the warning voice of Leuchsenring was still heard denouncing these Rosicrucians. But Wöllner's guillotine vanquished them at last, and the "Berlin Monthly Magazine" fell into the basket of the censors, as the heads of the French aristocrats fell into the executioner's basket when severed by the other guillotine in France.

But King Frederick William the Second submitted to the

will of the Invisibles, and obeyed the commands of the holy fathers, announced to him through their representatives, Bischofswerder and Wöllner. Let these men rule, let them take care of and discipline minds and souls; the king has other things to do. The minds belong to the Rosicrucians, but the hearts are the king's.

In her palatial residence, "under the linden-trees," in Berlin, sat the king's friend, in brilliant attire, her hair dressed with flowers, and her beautiful neck and bare arms of dazzling whiteness adorned with rich jewelry. She was reclining on her sofa, and gazing at her reflection in a large mirror of Venetian glass that stood against the wall on the opposite side of the boudoir; the frame of this mirror was of silver, richly studded with pearls and rubies, and was one of the king's latest presents. A proud and happy smile played about her full, rosy lips as she regarded the fair image reflected in this costly mirror.

"I am still beautiful," said she, "my lips still glow, and my eyes still sparkle, while *she* is fading away and dying. Why did she dare to become my rival, to estrange the king's heart from me? She well knew that I had been his beloved for long years, and that the king had solemnly vowed never to desert me! She dies with the coronet of a countess on her pale brow, while I still live as Madame Rietz—as the self-styled wife of a valet. I have life and health, and, although I am not yet a countess, I can still achieve the coveted title. Have I not sworn that I will yet become either a countess, a duchess, or, perhaps, even a princess? Neither the royal wife of the right nor of the left hand shall prevent me; while I rise, they will descend. While I am riding in my splendid equipage, emblazoned with a coronet, they will be riding to the grave in funeral-cars. And truly, it seems to me that it must be more agreeable to ride in an equipage, even as plain Madame Rietz, than to journey heavenward as Countess Ingenheim."

She burst into laughter as she said this, and saluted her

image in the mirror with a playful nod. The brilliants and rubies on her neck and arms sparkled like stars in the flood of light diffused through the room by the numerous jets of gas in the splendid chandeliers, richly adorned with crystal pendants. This, as well as all the other apartments of Wilhelmine Rietz's residence, was furnished with a degree of luxury and splendor befitting a royal palace. The king had kept the promise made to his darling son, Count Alexander von der Mark, in Charlottenburg. The affectionate father had given his handsome son the longed-for palace under the linden-trees; and the young count, together with his mother and sister, had taken up his abode in this palace. But the little Count von der Mark had not long enjoyed the pleasure of standing with his beautiful mother at the windows of his residence, to look at the parades which the king caused to be held there on his account. On such occasions the king had always taken up his position immediately beneath the windows of his son's palace, in order that they might obtain a better view of the troops. The little count had worn his title and occupied his palace but one year, when he died.* The king's grief had been profound and lasting, and never had the image of his handsome boy grown dim in the heart of his royal father. The loss of his son had driven Frederick William to the verge of despair, and Wilhelmine had been compelled to dry her own tears and suppress her own sorrow in order to console the king. Wilhelmine Rietz had manifested so much love and tenderness for the king during this trying period, and had practised so much self-denial, that the king's love and admiration for his "dear friend" had been greatly increased.

"You are a noble woman, and a heroine," said he. "Any other woman would weep and lament—*you* are silent, and your lips wear a smile, although I well know what pain this smile must cost your tender mother's heart. Any other woman would tremble and look with care and anxiety into the

* In the latter part of the year 1787.

future, because the death of the son might be prejudicial to her own position; she would have hastened to obtain from me an assurance that she should not suffer in consequence of this loss. You have done nothing of all this; you have wept and sorrowed with me; you have cheered and consoled me, and have not once asked, who was to be the heir of my little Alexander, and what souvenir he had left you."

Wilhelmine Rietz shook her head, and smiled sadly, well knowing how becoming this smile was to her pale countenance.

"I need no souvenir of my son," said she; "his memory will ever live in my heart. I have not asked who Alexander's heir was to be, because I have never supposed that he could have left an inheritance, for all that I and my children have belongs to the king, and is his property, as we ourselves are. I have not trembled for my own security, because I confide in my king and master as in my God, and I feel assured that he will ever observe his solemn oath and will never abandon me."

"No, never, Wilhelmine," cried the king. "You are a noble woman! You are, and will ever remain, my dear, adored friend, and my love for you will be more enduring than my love for any other woman. Lay aside all care and fear, Wilhelmine, and confide in me. All the efforts and intrigues of your friends to injure you shall be unavailing. All else will pass away, but my love for you will endure until death; and no woman, though I love her passionately, will be able to banish you from my side!"

"Will you swear this, Frederick William! Will you lay your finger on this scar on my hand and swear that my enemies shall never succeed in banishing me from your side, and that you will ever accord me a place in your heart?"

The king laid his hand on this scar, and it recalled to his memory the hour in which Wilhelmine had intentionally given her hand a wound in order that he might record his vow of love and fidelity in her own blood. "I lay my hand on this scar," said he, "and swear by the memory of my dear son, Alexander, that I will never neglect or forget his mother, but will love, honor, and cherish her until the end. And here is a proof that I *have* not forgotten you," cried the king, as he threw his arms around her neck, kissed her cheek, and handed her a deed of the palace under the linden-trees, and of all else that had belonged to Count Alexander von der Mark.

Wilhelmine Rietz and her daughter continued to reside in the palace under the linden-trees. Her house was one of the most popular resorts in Berlin, and the most select and intelligent society was to be found in her parlors. To be sure the rustle of an aristocratic lady's silk robe was never heard on the waxed floors of this stately mansion, but Wilhelmine's social gatherings were, perhaps, none the less animated and agreeable on that account. Her guests were charmed with her vivacity, brilliant wit, and fine satire, and the most eminent scholars, artists, and poets, esteemed it a great honor to be permitted to frequent Wilhelmine Rietz's parlors. She loved art and science, was herself somewhat of a poetess, and possessed above all else a mind capable of quickly comprehending what she saw and heard, and of profiting by intercourse with scholars and artists. It was a favorite plea with the gentlemen who visited her house, that Wilhelmine Rietz was the protectress of art and science, and, moreover, a very intelligent lady, of whom they were in justice compelled to say that she possessed fine sense, much knowledge, and very agreeable manners.

The king himself, an intellectual man, and a patron of art and science, often took part in Madame Rietz's social gatherings. In her parlors he was sure to find the relaxation and enjoyment which he sought in vain in the society of his beautiful and aristocratic wife of the left hand.

The beautiful Julie von Voss, entitled Countess Ingenheim, had never forgiven herself for having at last yielded to the wishes of her family, to the entreaties of her royal lover, and to the weakness of her own heart, by consenting to become the king's wife of the left hand, although a wife of the right hand still lived. Her reason and her pride told her that this little mantle of propriety was not large enough to hide her humiliation. Her soul was filled with grief and remorse; she felt that her glittering, apparently so happy existence, was nothing more than a gilded lie—nothing more than shame, garnished over with titles and honors.

The king often found his beautiful, once so ardently loved Julie in tears; she was never gay, and she never laughed. Indeed she often went so far as to reproach herself and her royal lover.

But tears and reproaches were ingredients of conversation which were by no means pleasing to Frederick William, and he fled from them to the parlors of his dear friend, Wilhelmine, where he was certain to find gayety and amusement.

Wilhelmine Rietz thought of all this while reclining on her sofa, awaiting the arrival of invited company—she thought of this while gazing at the reflection of herself (adorned with jewelry and attired in a satin dress, embroidered with silver), in the magnificent Venetian mirror. She had always found these conversations with her image in a mirror very interesting, for these two ladies kept no secrets from each other, but were friends, who imparted their inmost thoughts without prudery and hypocrisy.

"You will yet be a countess," said Wilhelmine. "Yes, a countess, and whatever else you may desire."

The lady in the mirror smiled, and replied: "Yes, a countess, or even a princess, but certainly not one who heaps reproaches upon herself, and dies of remorse; nor yet one of those who seek to reconcile themselves to the world, and to purchase an abode in heaven, by unceasing prayer and costly alms-giving. No, I will be a countess who enjoys life and compels her enemies to bend the knee—who seeks to reconcile herself to the world by giving brilliant entertainments and good dinners, and cares but little for what may take place after her death—a countess who exclaims with her great model, the Marquise de Pompadour, '*Après moi, le déluge!*' "

CHAPTER IX.

HUSBAND AND WIFE.

WILHELMINE was now interrupted in her animated conversation with her reflection by the abrupt entrance of her "self-styled husband," the Chamberlain Rietz.

She saw him in the mirror, and she saw, too, how the friend with whom she had been conversing, colored with displeasure and frowned. Without rising, or even turning her head, she allowed the chamberlain to approach until he stood in front of her, and then she cried, in an imperious voice: "Where were my servants? Why do you come unannounced to my presence?"

Rietz, the king's chamberlain and factotum, laughed loudly. "For fear of being turned away, ma belle, and because I considered it more appropriate to come unannounced to my wife's presence. Once for all, my dearest, spare me this nonsense, and do not embitter our lives unnecessarily! Let your courtiers, your dukes, princes, counts, and professors, wait in the antechamber, and come announced, if you will, but you must receive me as you receive the king, that is, unannounced. On the other hand, I promise you, never to make use of this privilege when you are entertaining company, or are engaged in some agreeable little *tête-à-tête*. Are you satisfied? Is this agreed upon?"

"It shall be as you say," said Wilhelmine, pointing to a stool that stood near the sofa. "Seat yourself and let me know why you honor me with your presence."

But Rietz, instead of seating himself on the stool, proceeded with the greatest composure to roll forward a splendid arm-chair, on the back of which a royal coronet was emblazoned.

"I suppose I am entitled to use this chair when the king is not present," said he, seating himself; "moreover, I like to sit comfortably. Now, I am installed, and the conference between the two crowned heads can begin. Do you know, or have you the slightest conception of, what the subject of this conference will be?"

"No," replied Wilhelmine, placing her little foot with its gold-embroidered satin slipper on the stool, and regarding it complacently, "no, not the slightest, but I beg you to tell me quickly, as I am expecting company."

"Ah, expecting company! Then I will begin our conference, Carissima, by telling you to order your servant to inform your visitors that you have been suddenly taken ill and beg to be excused."

"Before giving this command I must first request you to give me your reasons."

"My reasons? Well, I will give you one reason instead of many. It might not be agreeable to your guests to have the glass from the window-panes and the stones which have shattered them flying about their heads in your parlor."

"My friend," said Wilhelmine, still regarding the tips of her feet, "if you feel an irresistible inclination to jest, you will find an appreciative audience among the lackeys in my antechamber."

"Thank you, I prefer to converse seriously with my wife in the parlor. But if you desire it I will ring for one of these impudent rascals, and order him, in your name, to admit no visitors. Moreover, it would be well to have the inner shutters of all the windows of your palace closed. The latter must, of course, be sacrificed, but the shutters will, at least, prevent the stones from entering your apartments and doing any further damage. Are your windows provided with shutters?"

"I see you are determined to continue this farce," said Wilhelmine, shrugging her shoulders. "Without doubt you have wagered with some one that you could alarm me, and the closing of the shutters is to be the evidence that you have won the wager. Such is the case, is it not?"

"No, Carissima, such is not the case, and I beg you to

play the rôle of the undaunted heroine no longer; it becomes you very well, but you cannot excite my admiration and—"

"Nor have I any such intention," said she, leaning back on the sofa, and stretching herself like a tigress that appears to be quite exhausted, but is, nevertheless, ever ready to spring upon the enemy.

"Enough of this, my friend!" cried the chamberlain, impatiently. "Listen! If you consider it a bagatelle to have your palace demolished, and yourself accused of being a poisoner, it is, of course, all the same to me, and I have nothing more to say, except that I was a fool to consider it my duty to warn you, because we had formed an alliance, offensive and defensive, and because I could not look on calmly while your enemies were plotting your destruction."

The tigress had bounded from her lair, her eyes glowing with great excitement.

"You are in earnest, Rietz? This is not one of your jokes? My enemies are plotting my destruction! They are about to attack me! Speak, be quick! What was it you said about poisoning? Do they accuse me of being a poisoner?"

"Certainly they do, and I am glad that this magical word has recalled my sleeping beauty to life. Yes, your enemies accuse you of being a poisoner. It is truly fortunate that I have spies in every quarter, who bring me early intelligence of these little matters."

"And whom have I poisoned?"

"Countess Ingenheim, of course. Whom should you have poisoned but your rival?"

"My rival!" repeated Wilhelmine, with a contemptuous shrug of her shoulders. "Countess Ingenheim was ill. Is she worse?"

"Countess Ingenheim is dying!"

"Dying!" echoed Wilhelmine, and a ray of joy gleamed in the eyes of the tigress, but she quickly repressed it. "This is, of course, an exaggeration of the physicians, who will afterward attribute to themselves the merit of having effected her recovery from so hopeless a condition. I have heard of instances of this kind before. Four days ago the countess was comparatively well; I met her in the king's little box at the theatre, on which occasion her affability and condescension were truly surprising."

"Yes, and it is alleged by your enemies that you committed the crime on that very occasion. The countess complained of heat and thirst, did she not?"

"Yes, she did, and when she sank back in her chair, almost insensible, the king begged me to assist her."

"To which you replied that a composing powder was what she required, and that you, fortunately, always carried a box of these powders in your pocket. Hereupon you opened the door, and ordered one of the lackeys who stood in the entry to bring you a glass of water and some sugar. When he brought it, you took a small box from your pocket, and emptied a little paper of white powder into the water; when this foamed up, you handed the glass to the countess, who immediately drank its contents. Am I accurate?"

"You are, and I admire this accuracy all the more, because no one was present in the box but us three."

"You forget the lackey who brought the water, and saw you pour the powder into the glass. This morning the countess was suddenly attacked with a violent hemorrhage; whereupon the lackey immediately told her brother, Minister von Voss, the whole story. Her high connections and the entire court have been aroused, and if the countess should die to-day, as her physicians say she will, a storm will arise out of this glass of water, with the aid of which your enemies hope to hurl you from your eminence and consign you to prison."

"Foolish people!" said Wilhelmine, contemptuously. "The king will not only discredit their revelations, but will also hold them to a strict account for their slander. Let this be my care."

"My dearest, before proceeding to punish these slanderers,

I would advise you to consider your own safety a little. I tell you this matter is graver than you suppose, my proud, undaunted lady. The whole pack is let loose, and Bischofswerder and Wöllner are lashing the conspirators on, and heaping fuel on the flames. They immediately convoked a meeting of the holy brotherhood, and issued a secret order. This order I have seen. You must know that I was received into this holy band some two weeks since, as serving brother of the outer temple halls. What do you think of the title, 'serving brother of the outer temple halls?'"

And the chamberlain burst into so loud and mocking a peal of laughter, that his colossal stature fairly trembled.

"Suppress your merriment for a moment, if you please, and tell me how this secret order of the Rosicrucians reads."

The chamberlain's countenance quickly assumed an air of gravity. "The order is as follows: 'All the brothers serving in the outer temple halls will repair, at ten o'clock this evening, to your palace, for the purpose of engaging in the charming recreation of battering your windows with the stones that lie piled up in great plenty in this vicinity, in places where the pavement is being renewed; while so occupied, they are to cry—'Murderess! poisoner! Curses upon her! Down with this murderess!' A charming chorus, my angel of innocence!"

"Yes, a chorus over which the angels in heaven will rejoice, even if they should not be such angels of innocence as I am in this affair. I thank you for this communication; it is really of great importance."

"I must, however, beg you, my dear madame, to take this fact into consideration. By making this communication, I not only imperil my salvation, but am probably already wholly lost, and have certainly forfeited all prospects of ever entering the sanctuary of the temple, and becoming an Invisible Brother. Each brother is required, on his admission, to register a fearful oath, to the effect that he will never, although his own life or that of his parents or children should be at stake, betray the secrets of the holy fathers; and I, frail mortal, have betrayed the confidence of my superiors! Alas, alas! I am a lost soul! The Invisible Fathers will expel me from the brotherhood if they should ever hear of this."

"Give yourself no disquiet, I will never betray you," said Wilhelmine, laughing. "I am only surprised that you should ever have been admitted into the brotherhood, and that such an order should have been issued in your presence."

"My fairest, they are not aware that the Mr. Müller of Oranienburg, who was received into the holy order by the general assembly some two weeks since, is no other than the veritable Chamberlain Rietz. You must know that it is impossible to recognize each other in these assemblies, as they are held in a mystical gloom, and that the brothers are known to each other when they meet in the world by certain words, signs, and pressures of the hand, only. My dear, twenty of these Rosicrucians might meet at a party, without dreaming that they were so closely connected. The names of all the brothers are known only to the circle directors, and I was of course not such a fool as to write my real name on the slip of paper which I deposited in the urn after having paid the admission-fee of four Fredericks d'or, and received in return the holy symbol of initiation in the solemn twilight of the outer temple halls. The exalted fathers, Bischofswerder and Wöllner, would be astonished, and any thing but delighted, to learn that I was present at the meeting of to-day, and was one of the favored individuals who heard the order given concerning the demolition of your palace."

"By all that I hold dear, these traitors shall pay dearly for this malice!" exclaimed Wilhelmine, frowning angrily. "This conflict must be brought to a conclusion. I am weary of this necessity of being constantly on the alert to guard against the stratagems and attacks of my enemies. I will have peace, and either *they* or *I* must be conquered."

"If I might be permitted to give the goddess Minerva my advice, I would say: 'Make peace with *these* enemies, and secure the support and assistance of the dear Rosicrucians against your other enemies, the aristocrats and court conspirators.' Believe me, I give you this advice in all honesty and sincerity, and why should I not? Are we not allies, and have we not sworn to assist each other at all times and everywhere? In *this* respect my charming wife has been a most excellent companion; she has kept her promises faithfully. Thanks to her assistance, I have attained all I desired, and there are few men who can say this of themselves. I desired influence, power, and money, and I have them all. By the king's favor I have achieved influence and power, and have amassed wealth by the folly of the persons sent me by you, my dearest, with their petitions for patents of nobility and decorations. In the three years of our reign I have created at least two hundred noblemen, and of this number twenty counts in the first year alone."

"Yes, indeed, these counts are well known," said Wilhelmine, laughing; "the gentlemen of the old nobility call them by no other name than 'the batch of 1786.'" *

"Moreover, the number of crosses of St. John, and orders of the Eagle, conferred by me upon deserving individuals, is legion, and goodly sums of money have they brought into my coffers!" said Rietz, laughing. "I desired a well-provided table, at which I could entertain a few gentlemen of rank and convivial spirits; and now gentlemen of this stamp are only too anxious to obtain invitations to my dinners, and to enjoy the delicious pasties for which my French cook is so justly celebrated. I lead a life of enjoyment, and, as I am in a great measure indebted to your recommendation and patronage for this enjoyment, it is but natural that I should be grateful, and should endeavor to serve you to the best of my ability."

"I thank you, *cher ami*," said Wilhelmine, in kindly tones. "You, too, have always been a good and efficient friend, and it was partly through *your* influence that my debts were paid,

* See "Private Letters," vol. iii.

my income doubled, and myself made the mistress of this beautiful palace. I still desire a great many things, however. You are aware that I am so unfortunate as to be ambitious, and—"

"And, in your ear, the name Madame Rietz is not exactly the music of the spheres."

"Not exactly, my dear friend, although I must admit that the name is rather musical. But I—"

The door of the antechamber was hastily opened, and a lackey appeared on the threshold, holding in his hand a silver waiter on which a folded note lay.

"This note has just been left here for Chamberlain Rietz," said the lackey.

Rietz took the note and opened it. "Madame," said he, after the door had closed behind the servant, "madame, my worst fears are realized. Countess Ingenheim is dead!"

"Dead!" repeated Wilhelmine, shuddering. "Poor woman, she has paid dearly for her short-lived triumph, and those who assert that the poor person was poisoned, are probably right; the shame attendant upon her position, her pangs of conscience and her remorse—these were the drops of poison which she daily imbibed, and of which she has now died. Truly, to be the beloved of a king requires a firm heart and very strong nerves. Poor woman, I pity her!"

"Truly, you are worthy of the greatest admiration," said Rietz. "You lament the sad fate of your rival, while you yourself are in the greatest danger on her account. You must now decide whether you will receive your company or not."

"Oh, my friend," sighed Wilhelmine, "how can you suppose me capable of indulging in the delights of social intercourse at a time when I have suffered so sad a loss? No, the king's grief is my grief also, and instead of being merry and laughing with others, I will weep with the royal widower."

"You are an incomparable woman," cried Rietz, with a loud peal of laughter; "as wise, as beautiful, as much the demon as the angel! No wonder you are fearless! Your power rests on an adamantine foundation."

Wilhelmine made no response, but rang the bell, and told the servant who answered her call, to inform the porter than no soirée would take place that evening, and that he was to tell all visitors that mourning for the sudden death of Countess Ingenheim would compel her to forego the pleasure of seeing them for that evening and the following week.

"I beg you to leave me now, my friend," said Wilhelmine, beginning to divest herself of the sparkling jewels that encircled her neck and arms. "I must hasten to lay aside these worldly garments, in order that the king may find me attired in sable robes when he arrives."

"How! Do you believe the king will visit you at a time when his wife of the left hand has but just breathed her last?"

"I feel assured that he will. His majesty knows how deep an interest I take in all that concerns him. He knows where to look for sympathy; he knows that I laugh with him when he is glad, and weep with him when he is sad. To whom should he flee in his hour of grief but to me?"

"You are right," said Rietz, smiling, "to whom should he flee, in his hour of grief, but to his first sultana? I am going, and I truly promise you that if his majesty, in the depth of his grief, should chance to be forgetful of this haven of rest, I will suggest it to our dear, chastened king."

"Do so, my friend, and hasten to his majesty's side, or my enemies will forestall you, and perhaps console the king in a different manner."

"I am going, sultana. But these shutters—shall I order them to be closed?"

"And why, pray? I am not afraid of a few stones, and if they should be showered upon us too plentifully, we can retire to one of the back rooms and observe the bombardment in perfect security. When did you say it was to begin?"

"As soon as it has grown dark; the deeds of these pious

fathers shun the light of day. The calendar says moonlight until ten o'clock; it is therefore probable that the sovereign people, as the rabble of Paris now calls itself, will not honor you with a call until that hour. It would be well to notify the police of the flattering attentions awaiting you, and to solicit a guard for the protection of your palace."

"I will take good care not to do so," rejoined Wilhelmine, smiling. "Let the sovereign people amuse themselves by breaking my windows if they choose. The louder they howl and call me poisoner the better, for the king will hear them and he will pity me."

"Wilhelmine," cried Rietz with enthusiasm, "it is a pity you are already my wife; if you were not I should certainly address you. I could love you to distraction!"

"Do not, my friend, I pray you," said Wilhelmine; "you would cut but a sorry figure in the rôle of a disconsolate lover. But now go; it is already eight o'clock, and I hear a great many carriages coming and going."

The chamberlain pressed her beautiful hand to his lips, and then took his departure. She regarded him with a contempt-uous smile as he left the room, and when the door had closed behind him, a clear and ringing peal of laughter escaped her lips. "To think that this Caliban has the honor of being called my husband," said she, "and that I am still the wife of a valet! And why? Merely because I am not of noble birth, like—like these sensitive puppets, whose shame is gar-nished over with noble titles and robes of ermine, and who nevertheless succumb and die under the burden of their self-acquired dignities. I can bear the precious burden! I—will not die! No, not I!"

CHAPTER X.

THE ATTACK.

HALF an hour later the folding-doors of the reception-room were thrown open to admit the king, who came without ceremony, and without attendants, as he was in the habit of doing. Wilhelmine hurried forward to meet him; her lovely countenance wore a sad expression, and her beautiful figure was attired in sable mourning-robes. One might have supposed she had lost her mother or a sister, so mournful was her manner, so full of sadness was her glance as she slowly raised her eyes to the king's pale countenance. "My dear master," murmured she, "how kind your majesty is, to think of me, and honor me with a visit, in this your hour of sore trial!"

He stroked her soft, shining hair tenderly, and drew her head to his bosom. "I never forget you, my friend, and the thought of your radiant eyes and lovely countenance always consoles me when I am troubled with care or grief, which is unfortunately very often the case."

"Your majesty's grief has been so great to-day! The divine being whom we all loved and honored has gone from us!"

"Yes," said the king, with a deep-drawn sigh, his expression more indicative of ennui than of sorrow, "yes, Countess Ingenheim died this afternoon. But her death did not surprise me; the good countess had been in very bad health ever since the birth of her son, more than a year ago, and my physician had long since told me that she had the consumption, and would not live through the autumn. The poor countess had been very tearful of late; she wept a great deal when I was with her, and was constantly reproaching herself. This was unpleasant, and I visited her but rarely during the last few weeks for fear of agitating the poor invalid. Moreover, she kept up a pretence of being well," continued the king, seating himself in the arm-chair, in which Rietz had been so comfortably installed a few minutes before. "Yes, she wished to impose on the world with this pretence, as if it were possible to avoid observing the traces of her terrible disease in her pale, attenuated countenance! She always held herself erect, went to all the parties, and even visited the theatre, four days ago. You remember it, doubtlessly, as you were present?"

"Yes, I remember," murmured Wilhelmine, as she seated herself on a stool at the king's feet, folded the hands, that contrasted like white lilies with her flowing black-lace sleeves, on his knees, and gave him a tender, languishing glance. She knew how effective these glances were—she knew that she could always bind her lover to herself again with these invisible toils.

"If poor Julie had but had your eyes and your health!" sighed the king. "But she was always ailing, and in the end nothing becomes more disagreeable than a sickly woman. But let us speak of this no longer, it makes me sad! It is well that my poor Julie has, at last, found a refuge in the grave from her unceasing remorse and her jealous love."

And thus Frederick took leave of the spirit of the affectionate woman who had sacrificed all through her love for him. The consciousness that his love for her had long since died, and that she was nothing more than a burden to him, had killed her.

Having taken leave of the spirit of his dead love, the king now assumed a cheerful expression, and this expression was immediately reflected in Wilhelmine's countenance. She smiled, arose from her stool, threw her soft, white arms around the king's neck with passionate tenderness, and exclaimed: "How is it possible to die when one can have the happiness of living at your side!"

The king drew her to his heart and kissed her. "*You* will live, Wilhelmine! You love me too dearly to think of dying of this miserable feeling of remorse. You have been tried and found true, Wilhelmine, and nothing can hereafter separate us."

"Nothing, my dear king and master!"

"Nothing, Wilhelmine; not even a new love. The flames of tenderness that glow in my heart may sometimes flare up and seem to point in other directions, but they will ever return to you, and never will the altar grow cold on which the first love-flames burned so brightly in the fair days of our youth."

"God bless your majesty for these words!" cried Wilhelmine, pressing the king's hands to her lips.

"Let us have no more of this formality, I pray you," said Frederick William, wearily. "We are alone, and I am heartily tired of carrying the royal purple about with me wherever I go. Relieve me of this burdensome mantle, Wilhelmine, and let us dream that the days of our youthful happiness have come back to us."

"My Frederick is always young," whispered she; "eternal youth glows in your heart and is reflected on your noble brow. But I—look at me, Frederick William! I have grown old, and the unmerciful hand of Time has been laid ungently on my brow."

The king looked at Wilhelmine, and could find no evidence of this in the fresh, smiling countenance of his enchantress. He listened to her siren voice, and its music soothed his soul and dissipated all care and sorrow. As the hand of the clock neared the tenth hour, and while Wilhelmine was engaged in a charming *tête-à-tête* with the king over a delightful supper of savory dishes and choice wines, the smiling siren told him of the danger that threatened her, of the new intrigue of her enemies at court, and of their determination to incite a mob to attack her palace.

"There can be nothing in all this," said the king, smiling; "this story has only been concocted to alarm you. If your enemies had formed any such plan, my superintendent of police would certainly have heard of it, and have taken measures to prevent it."

Wilhelmine inclined her rosy lips to the king's ear, and narrated in low accents what Rietz had told her concerning the order issued by the Rosicrucians.

The king started with surprise and alarm. "No," said he, "this is impossible; Bischofswerder and Wöllner are my most faithful friends; they will never undertake to harm you, for they know that you are dear to me, and that your presence is necessary to my peace and contentment—yes, I may even say to my happiness!"

"It is for this very reason that they desire to effect my banishment. They hope to gain unbounded control over you, by driving from your side the only being who dares to tell you the truth, and who loves in you the dear, noble man, and not the king! My disinterested love for you, Frederick William, is in their eyes a crime, and they accuse me of having committed another crime, for the purpose of tearing me from your heart and treading me under foot like a noxious weed!"

"They shall not succeed!" protested Frederick William. "But I cannot believe that—" The king ceased speaking; at this moment a deafening roar, as of the sea when lashed to fury by the storm, was heard in the street; it came nearer and nearer, and then the windows of the palace shook with the fierce cries: "Murderess! Poisoner! Curses upon the murderess!"

Wilhelmine, an air of perfect serenity on her countenance, remained seated at the king's feet, but he turned pale and looked toward the window in dismay. "You perceive, my master," said she, with an air of perfect indifference, "you perceive that these are the exact words agreed upon in the Rosicrucian assembly this morning. This is the war-cry of my enemies."

"Murderess! Poisoner!" resounded again upon the night air. "Curses upon the murderess!"

"I knew they would dare to make this attack," murmured Wilhelmine, still smiling. "Had I felt guilty, I would have fled or have solicited protection of my king. But I wished your majesty to see how far my enemies would go in their malignity—what cruel measures they would take to effect my banishment."

"You have done well," said the king, earnestly; "you have acted like a heroine, and never—"

He was interrupted by a loud crash, and something hissed through the broken window. With a loud, piercing cry, Wilhelmine threw herself over the king's person and clasped him in a close embrace, as if determined to protect him against the whole world.

"They may murder me, but they shall not harm a hair of your dear head, my beloved!"

These words, uttered in loud, exulting tones, sounded in the king's ear like an inspiring hymn of love, and he never forgot them.

The stone had fallen to the floor, with a loud noise, but no second one followed it. Curses still resounded from below, but the mob seemed nevertheless to have been alarmed by their own boldness, and hesitated before commencing a new attack.

Wilhelmine now released the king from her protecting embrace, and with gentle force compelled him to rise from his chair.

"Come, my beloved, danger threatens you here! They will soon make another attack."

"Wilhelmine," said he, with emotion, "give me that stone."

As she stooped to pick up the stone that lay at her feet, the black lace shawl fell to the floor, disclosing a purple stripe on her snow-white shoulder.

"You are wounded, Wilhelmine, you are wounded!" cried the king, in dismay. She had arisen in the mean while, and now handed him the stone, with her siren smile.

"It is nothing, my king; the dear people's cannon-ball merely grazed my shoulder. To be sure, it hurts a little, but my arms are not broken."

"And it was for me that you received this wound!" said

the king, in deep emotion. "You shielded and protected me with your fair form. Wilhelmine, I will never forget this; this stone shall be a lasting memorial of your love and heroic devotion!"

For the second time a loud crash was heard, and now the stones came flying through the broken windows in quick succession. At this moment several lackeys, pale with fright, rushed into the room to report that the populace were endeavoring to batter down the doors of the palace, and that these were already giving way.

"Save yourself, my king, flee from this palace!" cried Wilhelmine. "Permit my butler to lead you through the garden to the little gate that opens into Behren Street; from there your majesty will be able to return to your palace in safety."

"And you, my dearest?" asked the king.

"And I," said she, with heroic composure, "I will await my enemies; if they kill me I can die with the proud consciousness that I have saved the life of my king, and that he, at least, is convinced of my innocence!"

Another shower of stones succeeded, and the parlor was now a scene of fearful confusion. While fierce curses upon the head of the murderess, and denunciations of the poisoner, resounded from the street below, chairs, mirrors, vases, and marble tables, were being broken and scattered in every direction by the stones that poured in through the windows in an uninterrupted shower. In the midst of this din and clatter Wilhelmine's voice could be heard from time to time, conjuring the king to fly, or at least to repair with her to one of the apartments in the rear of the palace.

But the king remained firm; and issued his commands to the trembling servants, in a loud voice. He ordered them to close the inner shutters, and they did as he bade them. Creeping timidly on their hands and knees to the windows, they withdrew the bolts and closed the shutters with a sudden jerk. The king now ordered one of the lackeys to hasten through the garden to the office of his superintendent of police, to acquaint him with the state of affairs, and to request him to disperse the insurrectionary populace. After this messenger had been despatched, and now that the stones were falling harmlessly from the closed shutters, the king dismissed the servants who were present. He was now once more alone with the beloved of his youth.

"Wilhelmine," said he, "I can never forget your heroism and devotion. You shall have complete satisfaction for the insults offered you to-day, and those who sought your destruction shall bend the knee before you."

Half an hour later all was still, and the stones were no longer flying against the windows. The chief of police had made a requisition on the military authorities for a body of troops, and the populace had fled in terror from the threatening muskets and glittering sabres.

The king had taken his departure in the carriage that had been ordered to await him in Behren Street. He had, however, taken the stone with him that had struck Wilhelmine's shoulder. On taking leave he kissed her tenderly, and told her to await him in her palace at twelve o'clock on the following day, when she should receive the promised satisfaction.

Wilhelmine was now alone; with a proud, triumphant smile, she walked to and fro in the parlor, seeming to enjoy the scene of confusion and destruction. At times, when her foot touched one of the stones, she would laugh, push it aside, and exclaim: "Thus you shall all be thrust aside, my enemies! I will walk over you all, and the stones which you have hurled at me shall serve as a stairway for my ascent!— I have managed well," said she, continuing to walk restlessly to and fro. "I have opened the king's eyes to the malignity and cunning of his friends, and have shown my enemies that I am not afraid of, and scorn to fly from them. Messrs. Von Bischofswerder and Wöllner will soon come to the conclusion that they will be worsted in this conflict, and had better seek to form an alliance with their formidable enemy!"

As she continued walking amid the surrounding stones and ruins, the blood trickled slowly down her shoulder; and this, with her glittering eyes, gave her once more the appearance of a tigress—of a wounded tigress meditating revenge.

Wilhelmine was now interrupted in her train of thought by a noise in the street that sounded like the distant roll of thunder. She opened one of the shutters, behind which nothing remained of the window but the frame, and looked out into the night, and down into the broad street of the linden-trees, now entirely deserted. But the noise grew louder and louder, and the street seemed to be faintly illumined in the distance. This light soon became a broad glare; and then Wilhelmine saw that it was a funeral procession. She saw a number of dark, shrouded figures bearing gleaming torches, and then a long funeral car, drawn by four black horses. A coffin lay on this car. Its silver ornaments shone brightly in the reflection of the torches; a coronet at the head of the coffin glittered as though bathed in the dawning light of a new day. Torch-bearers followed the funeral car, and then came a number of closed carriages. It was the funeral procession of Countess Julie von Ingenheim, conveying the corpse to the estate of the family Von Voss, to deposit it in the ancestral vaults. Wilhelmine stood at the window and saw this ghostly procession glide by in the stillness of the night. She remained there until it had disappeared in the distance, and all was again silent. When she stepped back her countenance was radiant with a proud, triumphant smile. "She is dead!" said she, in low tones; "the coronet now glitters on her coffin *only*. I still live, and a coronet will yet glitter on my brow. A long time may elapse before I attain this coveted gem; but this wound on my shoulder may work wonders. I can afford to wait, for I— I do not intend to die. I will outlive you all—you who dare contend with me for the king's heart. Our love is sealed with blood, but the vows which he made to you were cast upon the wind!"

On the following day, the king repaired to Madame Rietz's palace at the appointed hour. He came with a brilliant suite; all his ministers and courtiers, and even his son, the Prince Royal Frederick William, accompanied him. The young prince had come in obedience to his father's command, but a dark frown rested on his countenance as he walked through the glittering apartments. When he met the mistress of all this magnificence, and when the king himself introduced her to his son as his dear friend, a glance of contemptuous anger shot from the usually mild eyes of the prince royal upon the countenance of the smiling friend.

She felt the meaning of this glance; it pierced her heart like a dagger; and a voice seemed to whisper in her ear: "This youth will destroy you! Beware of him, for he is the avenging angel destined to punish you!"

But she suppressed her terror, smiled, and listened to the king, who was narrating the occurrences of the riot of the day before, and pointing to the stones which, at the king's express command, had been allowed to remain where they had fallen.

"It was an insurrection," said the king—"an insurrection of the populace, that now fancies itself sovereign, and would so gladly play the master and ruler, and dictate terms to its king. I hate this rabble and all those who make it subservient to their ends—who use its rude fists to execute their own plans—and never will I pardon or take into favor such rebels and traitors."

As the king concluded, he fastened an angry glance on Bischofswerder and Wöllner, the covert meaning of which these worthies seemed to have divined, for they cast their eyes down and looked abashed.

The king now turned to Wilhelmine, raised the lace shawl from her shoulder with a gentle hand, and pointed to the wound which she had received the day before.

"Look at this, gentlemen! Madame Rietz received this wound while interposing her own body to protect her king;

the stone that inflicted this wound would, but for her devotion and heroism, have struck me in the face. My son, you see before you the protectress of your father; kiss her hand and thank her! And you, too, gentlemen, all of you, thank the heroic woman who shielded your king from danger."

This was indeed a glorious satisfaction! Wilhelmine's ambitious heart exulted with joy as she stood there like a queen, her hand extended to be kissed by a prince royal, by generals, ministers, and courtiers, whose words of thanks were unceasingly resounding in her ear. But there was one drop of bitterness in all this honey; and the warning voice again whispered, "Beware of the prince royal, for he is the avenging angel destined to punish you!"

The prince royal had given her a second threatening glance when he stooped to kiss her hand, at the king's command; and she alone knew that his lips had not touched her hand.

The king had looked on with a smile while his ministers and courtiers were doing homage to his "protectress." He now turned to the portrait of his favorite son, Count von der Mark. His boy's soft, mild eyes seemed to gaze down on his father.

"My son," said the king, in a loud, agitated voice, "I swear to your blessed spirit, surely in our midst in this hour, I swear that I will reward the mother you so tenderly loved, for all the affection which she lavished upon my boy, and that I will never forget her devotion in risking her own life to preserve mine. My son, I swear to you that I will be grateful to the preserver of my life while I live, and that her enemies shall never succeed in lowering her in my high estimation. My son, in witness of this my solemn vow, I kiss the wound which your noble mother received in my defence!"

Frederick William stooped and kissed the wound on Wilhelmine's shoulder.

It was a grand, an impressive moment, and Wilhelmine's ambitious heart exulted. Visions of a brilliant future arose before her soul, and, as she stooped to kiss the king's hand, she vowed that these visions should be realized!

But, when she raised her head, she shuddered. She had again encountered the prince royal's glance. The dagger pierced her heart for the third time, and the warning voice in her soul whispered for the third time: "Beware of the prince royal! He is the avenging angel destined to punish you!"

CHAPTER XI.

YOUTH VICTORIOUS.

CHARLOTTE VON STEIN sat in her garden pavilion, anxiously awaiting him for whom it had never been necessary to wait in former days. She had already given him three invitations to pay her a morning visit in the little pavilion in which his protestations of love had so often resounded. But these tender invitations had not been accepted. He had always found some pretext for avoiding this *tête-à-tête* in Charlotte's pavilion; he was too busy, had commenced some work which he desired to finish without interruption, or was troubled with toothache.

But Charlotte would not understand that he made these excuses in order to give the dark cloud that hung over them both time to pass away. With the obstinate boldness so often characteristic of intelligent women who have been much courted, and which prompts them rather to cut the Gordian knot with the sword than to unravel it slowly with their skilful fingers, Charlotte von Stein had for the fourth time entreated him to grant the desired interview, and Goethe at last consented.

Charlotte was now awaiting him; she gazed intently at the doorway, and her heart beat wildly. But she determined to be composed, to meet him in a mild and gentle manner. She knew that Goethe detested any exhibition of anger or violence in women. She was also well aware that he was very restive under reproach. Charlotte knew this, and was determined

to give him no cause for displeasure. She desired to see this
monarch bound in her silken toils once more; she desired to
see the vanquished hero walk before her triumphal car as in
the past. "I cannot break with him," said she, "for I feel
that I still love him; moreover, it would be very disagreeable
to be spoken of by posterity as the discarded sweetheart of
the celebrated poet! No, no! I will be reconciled to him,
and all shall be as it was before! All! And now be quiet,
my heart, be quiet!"

She took a book from the table before which she was sitting, regardless of what it might be; her object was to collect
her thoughts, and compel her mind to be quiet. She opened
the book, and looked at it with an air of indifference. It
was a volume of Voltaire's works, which Goethe had sent the
day before, when she had written him a note requesting him
to let her have something to read. She remembered this
now, and also remembered that she had as yet read nothing
in the volume. Perhaps she would still have time to make
good this omission; Goethe might ask her about the book.
She read listlessly, in various parts of the work; suddenly
this passage attracted her attention:

> "Qui n'a pas l'esprit de son âg
> De son âge n'a que la malheur !"*

Strange words these! She felt as if a chilly hand had been
laid on her warm, quivering heart. Was the spirit of her
age wanting in her? was nothing but its unhappiness por-
trayed in her faded countenance? With an angry movement
she threw the book aside, arose from her seat, and went to
her mirror.

"Am I really old? Is the unhappiness of old age really
depicted in my countenance, while the spirit of youth and
love is at the same time burning in my heart?"

She anxiously scanned her features in search of the handwriting of this inexorable enemy of women, who stalks

---

* He who has not the spirit of his age
Has nothing but the unhappiness of his age.

pitilessly behind their youth and beauty, is their invisible
companion on all the rosy paths of life, and who, when he at
last becomes visible, drives away all those who had loved,
adored, and done homage to their beauty.   Charlotte sighed;
she recognized this handwriting; the enemy was becoming
but too plainly visible! She sighed again.

" Yes, it is written there that I am forty-six years old, and
every one can read it!   He, too—alas! he, too!" But after
a short pause her countenance grew brighter.   " Charlotte,
you should be ashamed of yourself—you insult your friend
and lover!   He loves you for your beauty of heart and mind,
and not for your outward beauty.   It was your mind that attracted him, your heart that enchained him, and they have
not undergone any change, have not grown older.   He loves
you for the eternal youth that glows in your heart and mind,
and he cares not for the mask with which age has covered
your countenance!   Yes, thus it is, and thus it always will
be, for Goethe is not like other men; he cares not for outward appearances, he looks at the inmost being.   This it is
that he loves, and ever will love in me, for this is and ever
will be unchanged!   Be joyous, Charlotte, be happy! Do
not dread the unhappiness of old age.   Voltaire was wrong,
and I will take the liberty of correcting Voltaire.   His sentence should read:

> " Qui n'a pas l'esprit de la jeunesse
> N'aura que le malheur de la vieillesse."

"Yes, thus it should read: 'Who does not bear the spirit
of youth within himself, to him old age brings nothing but
unhappiness!' "

As her dear friend soon afterward entered the pavilion,
Charlotte advanced to meet him with the reflection of enduring youth resting on her brow, and a glad smile on her lips.

But he did not observe it, his countenance was grave and
earnest.   He came with the conviction that the thunder
storm that had been long gathering overhead would now burst
upon them in all its fury.   He had come armed for the fray

with this outward sternness of manner, while his soul was filled with grief and tenderness.

"Goethe," she murmured, extending both hands to greet him, "Goethe, I thank you for having come."

"Charlotte," said he, gently, "how can you thank me for doing what is as gratifying to me as to yourself?"

"And yet I was compelled to entreat you to do so for the fourth time. Three times you excused yourself with pretexts," she cried, forgetful of her good resolutions, and carried away by her sensitiveness.

"Pretexts?" repeated Goethe.—"Well, if you will have it so, I must admit that they were pretexts, and this should convince you, Charlotte, of my anxiety to avoid offending you; for to any one else I would plainly and openly have said: 'I will not come.' It will be better for us both if we avoid any further explanation. It would perhaps have been wiser, my dear Charlotte, if you had endeavored to master this irritation in silence, instead of bringing about the explanations which it would have been better for us both to have avoided."

"I have nothing to avoid; I can give every explanation. I can lay bare my heart and soul to you, Wolf, and give an account of my every thought and deed. No, I have no cause to avoid explanations. I love you and have always been true to you, but you, you—"

"My love," he said, interrupting her, "do not reproach me again; my soul's pinions are already drooping under the weight of reproaches that retard the flight of my imagination!"

"Now you are reproaching me!" cried Charlotte. "I am to blame that the pinions of your soul are drooping! O Wolf, how can you be so cruel! To reproach me!"

"No, Charlotte, I do not reproach you, and how could I? If you have to bear with me in many things, it is but right that I, too, should suffer. It is much better to make a friendly compromise, than to strive to conform to each other's requirements in all things, and, in the event of our endeavor being unsuccessful, to become completely estranged. I would, however, still remain your debtor in any agreement we might make. When we reflect how much we have to bear from all men, my love, it will teach us to be considerate with each other." *

"Then we are no longer to endeavor to live together in happiness, but only in an observance of consideration toward each other?" cried Charlotte.

"I had hoped that consideration for each other's weaknesses would lead us back to happiness. I, for my part, will gladly be indulgent."

"I was not aware that I stood in need of your indulgence," said Charlotte, proudly.

"I will, however, be indulgent, nevertheless. And I will gladly say—that is, if you care to hear it—that your discontent and many reproaches have left no feeling of anger in my heart, although they inflicted great pain."

"This is surely to be attributed to the fact that candor compels you to admit that my reproaches are just, and my discontent, as you call my sadness, but natural under the circumstances. Tell me, Wolf, what reproaches have I ever made that were not fully warranted by your changed manner and coldness?"

"There it is!" cried Goethe, beginning to lay aside his kindly manner, and to resent Charlotte's haughtiness; "therein lies the reproach, and, I must say, the unmerited reproach. This is the refrain that I have been compelled to listen to ever since my return. I am changed, I love you no longer. And yet my return and my remaining here, are the best and most conclusive proofs of my love for you! For your sake, I returned—for your sake I tore myself from Italy, and all the beauties that surrounded me, and—"

"And also from the beauty who had entwined herself around your faithless heart," added Charlotte.

* Goethe's own words.—See "Goethe's Correspondence with Madame von Stein," vol. ii., p. 326.

He did not notice this interruption, but continued in more animated tones: "And for your sake have I remained here, although I have felt that this life was scarcely endurable ever since my return. I saw Herder and the duchess take their departure; she urged me to take the vacant seat in her carriage, and journey to Italy in her company, but I remained, and remained on your account. And yet I am told, over and over again, that I might as well have remained away— that I no longer take an interest in my fellow-man, and that it is no pleasure to be in my company." *

"That I have never said."

"You have said that and much more! You have called me indifferent, cruel, cold-hearted! Ask all my other friends if I am indifferent to them, less communicative, or take less interest in all that concerns them, than formerly. Ask them if I do not belong more completely to them and to society than formerly."

"Yes, indeed, so it is! You belong more to them and society, because you belong less to me; you have abandoned our intimate, secret, and peculiar relation, in order to devote yourself to the world in general. This relation is no longer pleasant, because all confidence is at an end between us."

"Charlotte," cried he, in angry tones, "whenever I have been so fortunate as to find you reasonable and disposed to converse on interesting topics, I have felt that this confidence still existed. But this I must admit," he continued, with increased violence, and now, that the floodgates were once opened, no longer able to repress his indignation; "this I must admit, the manner in which you have treated me of late is no longer endurable. When I felt disposed to converse, you closed my lips; when I was communicative, you accused me of indifference; and when I manifested interest in my friends, you accused me of coldness and negligence. You have criticised my every word, have found fault with my manner, and have invariably made me feel thoroughly ill at

* Goethe's own words.

ease. How can confidence and sincerity prosper when you
drive me from your side with studied caprice?" *

"With studied caprice?" repeated Charlotte, bursting
into tears. "As if my sadness, which he calls studied
caprice, were not the natural result of the unhappiness which
he has caused me."

"I should like to know what unhappiness I have caused
you. Tell me, Charlotte; make your accusations; perhaps I
can succeed in convincing you that you are wrong."

"It shall be as you say," cried Charlotte, passionately.
"I accuse you of being faithless, of having forgotten the love
which you vowed should live and die with you—of having
forgotten it in a twofold love, in a noble and in an unworthy
one."

"Charlotte, consider well what you say; weigh your words
lest they offend my soul."

"Did you weigh your words? You have offended my soul
mortally, fearfully. Or, perhaps, you suppose your telling
me to my face that you had loved another woman in Italy,
and had left there in order to flee from this love, could not
have inflicted such fearful pain."

"Had left there in order to preserve myself for *you*, Charlotte; to remain true to *you*."

"A great preservation, indeed, when love is already lost.
And even if I admit that the beauty of the charming Italian
girl made you for the moment forgetful of your plighted
faith, what shall I say to what is now going on here in Weimar? What shall I think of the great poet, the noble man,
the whole-souled, loving friend, when he finds his pleasure in
secret, disreputable intercourse with a person who has neither
standing nor education, who belongs to a miserable family,
and who, in my estimation, is not even worthy to be my
chambermaid? Oh, to think, to know, that the poet Goethe,
the privy-councillor Goethe, the scholar Goethe—that he

* Goethe's own words.—See " Goethe's Correspondence with Madame von Stein,"
vol. iii., p. 327.

steals secretly to that wretched house in the evening to visit the daughter of a drunkard! To think that *my* Goethe, my heart's favorite, my pride, and my love, has turned from me to a person who is so low that he himself is ashamed of her, and only visits her clandestinely, anxiously endeavoring to avoid recognition!"

"If I did that, it was for your sake," cried he, pale with inward agitation, his lips quivering, and his eyes sparkling. "If I visited her clandestinely, I did so because I knew that your noble perception was dimmed, and that you were no longer capable of looking down upon these petty, earthly relations from a more exalted stand-point. If you were wise and high-hearted, Charlotte, you would ignore a relation that lies entirely out of the sphere in which we both live. Of what nature is this relation? Upon whose rights does it trespass? Who lays claim to the feelings I bestow upon this poor creature? Who claims the hours that I pass in her company?" *

With a loud cry of anguish, Charlotte raised her arms toward heaven, "O God, he admits it! He admits this fearful relation!"

"Yes," said he, proudly, "he does, but he also entreats you to aid him in preventing the relation you so greatly abhor, from degenerating—to aid him in keeping it as it is. Confide in me again, look at this matter from a natural point of view, permit me to reason with you on the subject, and I may still hope to bring about a good understanding between us." †

"Not I!" she cried, with a proud toss of her head. "No good understanding can exist between us while this person stands in the way—this person who makes me blush with shame and humiliation, when I reflect that the hand which grasps my own has, perhaps, touched hers; that these lips—oh, Wolf, I shudder with anger and disgust, when I reflect

* Goethe's own words.—See " Correspondence with Madame von Stein," vol. iii., p. 328.
† Ibid. U—MUHLBACH—VOL. 17

that you might kiss me after having kissed her a short time before!"

"There will be no further occasion for such disagreeable reflections," said he, gruffly, his countenance deathly pale. "Out of love I have endured much from you, but you have now gone too far! I repeat it, you will never again have to overcome the disgust of being kissed by me, and while I, as you observed, have perhaps kissed another but a short time before! And as for this other woman, I must now confess that you were quite right in reproaching me for visiting her clandestinely, and making a mystery of our relation. You are right, this is wrong and cowardly; a man must always avow his actions, boldly and openly; and this I will do! Farewell, Charlotte, you have shown me the right path, and I will follow it! We now separate, perhaps to meet no more in life; let me tell you before I go that I owe to you the happiest years of my life! I have known no greater happiness than my confidence in you—the confidence that has hitherto been unbounded. Now, that this confidence no longer exists, I have become another being, and must in the future suffer still further changes!" *

He ceased speaking, and struggled to repress the tears that were rushing from his heart to his eyes. Charlotte stared at him in dismay and breathless anxiety. Her heart stood still, her lips were parted, but she repressed the cry of anguish that trembled on her lips, as he had repressed his tears. A warm, tender, forgiving word might perhaps have called him back, and all misunderstanding might have vanished in tears, remorse, and forgiveness; but Charlotte was too proud, she had been too deeply wounded in her love and vanity to consent to such a humiliation. She had exercised such great power over Goethe for the past ten years, that she perhaps even now believed that he would return, humble himself before her, and endeavor to atone for the past. But the thought did not occur to her that a man can forgive the woman who mistrusts

* Goethe's own words.--See "Correspondence with Madame von Stein, vol iii., p. 330.

his love, but that he never will forgive her who wounds his pride and his honor.

Charlotte did not speak; she stood motionless, as in a trance, and saw him take up his hat, incline his head, and murmur: " Farewell! dearest, beloved Charlotte, farewell!"

Then all was still, and she saw him no longer! She glanced wildly and searchingly around the room, and when the dread consciousness that he had gone, and that she was surrounded by a terrible solitude, dawned upon her, Charlotte sank down on her knees, stretched out her arms toward the door through which his dear form had vanished, and murmured, with pale, quivering lips: " Farewell! lost dream of my youth, farewell! Lost delight, lost happiness, lost hope, farewell! Night and solitude surround me! Youth and love have departed, and old age and desolation are at hand! Henceforth, no one will love me! I shall be alone! Fearfully alone! Farewell!"

While Charlotte was wailing and struggling with her grief, Goethe was pacing restlessly to and fro in the shady little retreat in the park to which he had so often confided his inmost thoughts in the eventful years that rolled by. When he left the park, after hours of struggling with his own heart, an expression rested on his noble and handsome countenance that had never been observed there before. An expression of mingled gloom and determination was depicted in his features. His eyes were luminous, not with their usual glow of enthusiasm, but with subdued and sudden flames. " Descended into hell, and arisen again from the dead!" murmured he, with a derisive smile, as he walked on through the streets to the wretched little house in which Christiane Vulpius's drunken father and his family lived.

She came forward to greet him with an exclamation of joyous surprise, for it was the first time Goethe had visited, in the light of day, the little house in which she lived. She threw herself into his extended arms, entwined hers around his neck and kissed him.

Goethe pressed her lovely head to his bosom, and then
raised it gently between his hands. He gazed long and
tenderly into her large blue eyes. "Christiane," murmured
he, "Christiane, will you be my wife?"

A dark glow suffused itself over her face and neck, and then
a clear ringing peal of laughter, like the joyous outburst of a
feathered songster, escaped her coral lips, displaying two
rows of pearly teeth. "I, your wife, my good friend? Why
do you jest with poor little Christiane?"

"I am not jesting, Christiane. I ask you in all earnestness, Will you be my wife?"

"In all earnestness?" repeated she, the gaze of her large,
soft eyes fastened with an expression of astonishment on
Goethe, who stood regarding her intently, his countenance
radiant with a tender smile.

"Give me an answer, Christiane."

"First, give *me* an answer, my good friend. Answer this
question. Do you love me? Am I still your pet, your sing-
ing-bird, your little love, your fragrant violet?"

"You still are, and will ever remain my pet, my singing-
bird, my little love, and my violet."

"Then let me remain what I am, my dear sir. I am but
a poor little girl, and not worthy to be the wife of a gentleman of high rank; I would cut but a poor figure at your
side, as the wife of the mighty privy-councillor, and you
might even suppose I had only accepted your love because I
had seen the altar and this magnificence in the background."

"I could not think so, my darling; I know that you love
me."

"Then I wish you to understand, good sir, that I must remain as I am, for you are pleased with me as I am. Let me
still remain your violet, and blossom in obscurity, observed
by no one but you, my good friend and master. I will serve
you, I will be your maid-servant, and will work and sew and
cook for you. For this I am suited; but I cannot become a
noble lady worthy to bear your celebrated name. If I were

your wife, you would often have cause to blush for me; if I remain your love, I can perhaps amuse you by my little drolleries, and you would have no cause to be ashamed of the ignorant girl who craved nothing except to be near you, and to have you smile on her sometimes." *

"Christiane, you shall ever be near me; I will always smile on you!" protested Goethe, deeply moved.

"Always near you!" repeated Christiane, in joyous, exulting tones. "Oh, do let me be with you, good sir! Let me be your servant—your housekeeper. I will serve and obey you, I will honor you as my master, and I will love you as my dearest friend!"

"And I," said Goethe, laying his hand on her golden hair, "I swear, by the Eternal Spirit of Love and of Nature, that I will love you, and that your happiness shall be the chief end of my life. I swear that I will honor you as my wife, protect and cherish you as my child, and be to you a husband and father until death."

He stooped and kissed her shining hair and fair brow, and gazed tenderly into her lustrous eyes. "And now, my pet, get ready and come with me!"

"To go where? You cannot intend to walk with me through the public streets in the broad light of day?"

"Through the public streets, and in the broad light of day, at your side!"

"But that will not do," said she, in dismay. "It would not be proper for a noble, celebrated gentleman to be seen in public with a poor, humble creature like myself. What would the world say?"

"Let the world say what it will! Come, my violet, I will transplant you to my garden, and there you shall blossom in the future."

She no longer resisted, but threw her shawl over her shoulders, covered her golden tresses with the hat adorned with

* Christiane Vulpius really rejected Goethe's offer of marriage. See Lewes's Life of Goethe, vol. ii. p. 121.

roses of her own manufacture, stepped with Goethe from beneath the roof of her father's wretched house, and walked at his side through the streets to the stately mansion on Market Square, henceforth destined to be her home.

Goethe conducted her up the broad stairway, through the antechamber, and into his reception-room. Both were silent, but the countenances of both were radiant with happiness.

With a gentle hand he relieved her of her shawl and hat, pressed her to his bosom, and then, with upturned eyes, he cried, in loud and impressive tones: " Oftmals hab' ich geirrt, und habe mich wieder gefunden, aber glücklicher nie; nun ist dies Mädchen mein Glück! Ist auch dieses ein Irrthum, so schont mich, ihr klügeren Götter, und benehmt mir ihn erst drüben am kalten Gestade." *

CHAPTER XII.

SCHILLER'S MARRIAGE.

THE two great intellects, whose genius shed such rays of light over Weimar, and over all Germany, neither knew nor loved each other. These two heroes of poetry still kept at a distance from each other, and yet there was a wondrous uniformity in their inner life, although their outward existence was so different. Goethe, the recognized poet, the man of rank, who had never known want or care: Schiller, still struggling, creating much that was great and beautiful, but aspiring to, and foreseeing with prophetic mind, a future of greater and more brilliant success—Schiller, the man of humble standing, who was still wrestling with want and care. His anxiety and poverty were not destined to be relieved by the appointment which Schiller received in the year 1789, as Professor

---

* Often have I erred, and always found the path again, but never found myself happier; now in this maiden lies my happiness. If this, too, is an error, oh spare me the knowledge, ye gods, and let me only discover it beyond the grave!"

of History at the University of Jena, for—no salary was attached to this professorship!

"A Mr. Frederick Schiller," wrote (not the poet, but) the Minister Goethe—a report forwarded to the Duke Charles August at that time—"a Mr. Frederick Schiller, who has made himself known to the world by his History of the Netherlands, is disposed to take up his abode at the University of Jena. The possibility of this acquisition is all the more worthy of consideration from the fact that it could be had gratis."

Gratis! The Dukes of Weimar, Meiningen, Altenburg, and Gotha, the patrons of the University of Jena, could offer nothing but a professorship without salary to the poet of "Don Carlos," of "Fiesco," of "Louise Müllerin," and of "The Robbers"—to the poet of so many glorious songs, to the author of "The History of the Netherlands!" They had but one title, but one appointment, to bestow upon the man to honor whom was to honor themselves, and this appointment was made to save expense!

Schiller accepted this professorship with the nobility of mind of the poet whose soul aspired rather to honor and renown than to pecuniary reward, and who had, for those who profited by his labors while withholding all compensation, nothing but a contemptuous shrug of the shoulders and a proud smile. Schiller's friends were, however, by no means satisfied with this appointment; his practical friend Körner called his attention to the fact, that the necessities of life were also worthy of some consideration, advising him to inform the minister of state that the addition of a salary to his title of professor was both desirable and very necessary. But Schiller was too proud to solicit as a favor what had not been accorded from a sense of duty. He would not beg bread for the *professor*, hoping that the poet would be able to support him. He had been accustomed to study close economy, and to struggle with want; care had been his inseparable companion throughout his entire life. The poet had ever looked up to .

heaven in blissful enthusiasm, rejoicing in the glory of God, and had been "with Him" while the world was being divided among those who understood looking after their pecuniary interests better than the poet. His heart was rich, and his wants were few. He did not desire wealth, and had refused the rich lady tendered him in marriage by his friend Körner. His loving heart should alone be his guide in the selection of a wife.

His loving heart! Had not Schiller a Charlotte, as well as Goethe? The year 1789 had been an eventful one in Goethe's heart's history, and had effected a final separation between Goethe and his Charlotte: the same year was also destined to be an important one in Schiller's heart's history, and to bring about a crisis in his relations to his Charlotte.

The experience of the two women at this period was of a similar nature. Charlotte von Kalb had often entreated Schiller to pay her a visit, but in vain. He had invariably excused himself with the plea that the duties of his professorship in Jena were of such a nature that it was impossible to leave there even for a single day.

At last Charlotte despatched a messenger to Jena with this laconic letter: "If you do not come to me in Weimar, I will go to you in Jena. Answer." And Schiller's answer was— "I am coming!"

She was now awaiting him, gazing fixedly at the door; a nameless fear made her heart throb wildly.

"He shall not find me weak," murmured she; "no, I will neither weep nor complain. No, my pride must give me strength to conceal my anguish, and to hear the decision, whatever it may be, with a smiling countenance. I will cover my heart with a veil, and it shall rest with him to withdraw it with a loving hand, if he will."

"Here you are at last, my Frederick!" she said to Schiller on his arrival. "It seems, however, that a threat was necessary to bring you!"

"No, dearest friend," replied Schiller, gayly, "the threat

was unnecessary! You know that I love you with my whole soul, and my heart has always ye rned to see you once more. The duties of my professorship are such that I find it almost impossible to leave Jena."

A bitter smile rested for a moment on Charlotte's lips, but she quickly repressed it. "It is but natural that the new professor should be so busily engaged as not to be able to find time to pay his friend a visit. And yet, Frederick, it was necessary that I should speak to you; life has now brought me to a point where I must decide upon taking one of two paths that lie before me."

"Charlotte, I am convinced that your heart and your wisdom will prompt you to take the right path," said Schiller.

She inclined her head in assent. "At our last interview I was excited and agitated; I reproached you for not having spoken to my husband. I believe I even wept, and called you faithless and ungrateful."

"Why awaken these remembrances, Charlotte? I have endeavored to forget all this, and to bear in mind that we should make allowance for words uttered by our friends when irritated. We have both dreamed a sweet dream, my friend, and have, unfortunately, been made aware that our romantic air-castles are not destined to be realized in this prosaic world."

"Do you call the plans we have both made for our future, romantic air-castles?"

"Yes," replied Schiller, with some little hesitation, "I am unhappily compelled to do so. A marriage with you was the brightest and most glorious air-castle of my fantasy; and may the egotism of my love be forgiven if I once dreamed that this castle might on some blissful day descend to earth and open its portals to admit us within its radiant halls! But sober thought followed quickly upon this trance of ecstasy, and told me that these heavenly dreams could not be realized."

"Why not?"

"Because I can offer you no compensation for the great

sacrifice you would be compelled to make, and because the
thought that you might live to regret what you had done fills
me with horror. You are a lady of rank, accustomed to the
comforts and luxuries of an aristocratic house. I am only a
poor professor, accustomed to hardships and want, and not in
a condition to provide a comfortable home for a wife. Who-
ever takes me must enter upon life with modest expectations,
and begin an existence at my side that offers little for the
present but hopes and prospects. It would even require much
self-denial on the part of a young girl, who is but just beginning life, to become the wife of a poor professor and poet.
How much more would it require on the part of a lady of
high rank to exchange a palace for an humble cottage, and
to relinquish wealth, rank, and even the son she so dearly
loves? What could I give her in return after she had relinquished all these blessings? Charlotte, to live with me is to
labor, and labor would wound your tender hands. Therefore,
forgive the enraptured poet, who thought only of his own
happiness when he dared to hope you might still be his,
without reflecting that he had no right to purchase his happiness at the expense of that of his idol."

"You are right, my dear friend; we must never permit
love to make us selfish, and we must consider the happiness
of the object of our love more than our own. We will both
consider this and act accordingly. You have my happiness at
heart; let me, therefore, consider yours. Schiller, I conjure
you by the great Spirit of Truth and Love, now surely hovering over us, tell me the truth—answer the question I am
about to ask as truthfully as you would before God: Do you
love me so firmly, so warmly, and so exclusively, that my
possession can alone make you happy?"

"Charlotte, this is, indeed, a question that I could only
answer before God."

"God dwells in the breast of each human being, and, by
the God of Love, who has stretched out His hand over me, I
demand of you a truthful answer to my question: Do you

love me so firmly, so warmly, and so exclusively that my possession can alone make you happy?"

A pause ensued—a long pause. The God of Truth and of Love, whose presence Charlotte had so solemnly proclaimed, alone beheld the pale countenances of the two beings who stood face to face with the bitter feeling that nothing on earth is constant, and that all is subject to change and destruction— even love!

"No!" said Schiller, in a low voice, "no, I do not love you so firmly, so warmly, and so exclusively. Nor do I believe we would be happy together, for it is only when no passion exists that marriage can unite two beings in an eternal union; and then, Charlotte, you are also too exalted for me, and a woman who is a superior being cannot, I believe, make me happy. I must have a wife whom I can educate, who is my creation, who belongs to me alone, whom I alone can make happy, and in whose existence I can renew my own—a wife who is young, inexperienced, and gentle, not highly gifted, devoted to me, and eager to contribute to my comfort and peace." *

"In a word, a woman who is young," said Charlotte, with proud composure, "or rather, a young girl who is like a sheet of white paper, on which your love is to write the first word."

"Yes, Charlotte, so it is! You understand my heart as you have always understood it."

"I relinquish from to-day all further claim to any such understanding, and I can only give you one last piece of advice, and that is, to ask Mademoiselle von Lengefeld if she is not desirous of being the sheet of paper on which you could write your name. I advise you to marry Mademoiselle von Lengefeld; she seems to possess all the required qualifications: she is not gifted, has no experience, and can certainly not be called a superior being."

"But a noble, an amiable being," cried Schiller, passionately; "a being full of innocence and goodness, a fair creature full of heart and feeling, full of gentleness and mildness;

* Schiller's own words.—See "Schiller's Correspondence with Körner," vol. ii.

moreover, she has a noble heart, and a mind capable of great cultivation. She has understanding for all that is intellectual, reverence for all that is great and beautiful, and is at the same time modest, affectionate, playful, and naïve."

"In brief, she is an ideal," said Charlotte, derisively. "But let your thoughts sojourn with me for a moment longer. At my request you have told me the truth, now you shall hear the truth from my lips. We might have spared ourselves all these explanations, but I desired to probe your heart to assure myself that I would not wound you too deeply by telling you what I must now avow. Now that I am no longer uneasy on that score, you shall hear the truth from my lips. My air-castles have vanished also—vanished so long since, that I scarcely have a recollection of them, and can only think of them as of a foolish dream, that neither could nor should have been realized. I have awakened, and I will remain what I am, the wife of Mr. von Kalb, and the mother of my son. I live once more in the present, and the past with all its recollections and follies is obliterated." *

"I am glad to hear this," said Schiller, in a clear and composed voice, the gaze of his large blue eyes fastened on Charlotte's cold and haughty countenance with an expression of severity. "I am glad to hear that the past is obliterated from your remembrance, as it is from mine. I can now speak to you freely and openly of the happiness which the future has, as I hope, in store for me. I love Charlotte von Lengefeld, and now that you have discarded me, I am at liberty to ask her to become my wife."

"Do so," said she, quietly. "We are about to separate, but my blessing will remain with you; any correspondence between us in the future would, of course, be annoying, and as our letters of the past have become meaningless, I must request you to return mine." †

"As you had already written to me on this subject several

---

* Charlotte's own words.—See "Schiller's Life of Caroline von Wollzogen."
† Charlotte's own words.—See "Charlotte: A Life Picture," p. 80.

times, I took the precaution of bringing these letters with me
to-day. Here they are. I have preserved them carefully and
lovingly, and I confess that it gives me great pain to part with
these relics of the past."

He handed her the little sealed package which he had drawn
from his breast-pocket; she did not take it, however, but
merely pointed to the table.

"I thank you, and I will now return your letters."

She walked into the adjoining room, closing the door softly
behind her. With trembling hands she took Schiller's letters
from the little box in which she had kept them. She kissed
them, pressed them to her heart and eyes, and kissed them
again and again, but when she saw that a tear had fallen on
the paper she wiped it off carefully; she then walked rapidly
to the door and opened it. On the threshold she stood still,
composed, proudly erect.

"Schiller, here are the letters!"

He approached and took them from her hand, which she
quickly withdrew. She then returned to the adjoining room,
locking the door behind her.

This was their leave-taking, this their parting, after long
years of love!

With downcast eyes and in deep sadness of heart, Schiller
left the house of the woman he had once loved so ardently.
But this soon passed away and gave place to the blissful feeling that he was once more free—free to offer his heart, his
hand, and his life, to the woman he loved!

A few days later his heart's longing was gratified. He went
to Rudolstadt and received a loving and cordial welcome from
both sisters. Both! But only one of the sisters was at liberty
to bestow her hand. Caroline was not! Her hand was fettered by her plighted troth, and even if her husband's consent to a separation could have been obtained, there were
other fetters. She was in her sister's confidence. She knew
that Charlotte loved Schiller tenderly.

They were together in the quiet little parlor, they three

alone, for the mother was absent on a little journey. Schiller sat between the sisters, his countenance radiant with happiness.

"Oh, my fair friends, how delighted I am to be with you once more!"

"Schiller," whispered Caroline, laying her hand gently on his shoulder, "Schiller, I have a word to say to you. Come!"

She conducted him to a window-recess, and inclined her head so close to his ear that her trembling lips kissed one of his fair locks. "Schiller," whispered she, "you love my sister, and I know that she loves you. Courage, confess your love, and God bless you both!"

Having said this, she walked noiselessly from the room, retired to her solitary chamber, closed the door behind her, and sank down on her knees. She shed no tears, and the brave soul of this noble woman was exalted above all pain in this hour of her great sacrifice. Her chaste lips would not express the noble secret in words, even before God. But her Maker may have read her sacrifice in the expression of anguish and resignation in her upturned countenance.

"Be happy, Schiller! God bless you both! Be happy! then I will be happy, too."

On returning to the parlor, Caroline's countenance shone with pleasure, and her lips parted in a happy smile when she saw the two lovers in a close embrace, heart to heart.

"Oh, dear Caroline, she has confessed; you were certainly right! She loves me, she is mine. And so are you, Caroline, you are also mine, and we three will belong to each other for evermore!"

"Yes, for evermore, my friend, my brother!" She gently entwined her arms around Schiller's and Lottie's neck; and now the three were joined in one close and loving embrace.

"I have at last entered the haven of happiness," said Schiller, in deep emotion. "I have, at last, found my home, and eternal peace and repose are mine. I am encircled with your love as with a halo, ye beloved sisters; and now all the great expectations which you have entertained concerning me will be realized, for happiness will exalt me above myself. Charlotte, you shall never again have cause to tell me I look gloomy, for your love will shed a flood of sunshine on my existence hereafter. You shall teach me to laugh and be merry. O God, I thank Thee for permitting me to find this happiness! I, too, was born in Arcadia!"

They held each other in a close embrace, they wept for joy, and their souls, beaming eyes, and smiling lips, exchanged mute vows of eternal love and fidelity.

These were blissful days for Schiller. Madame von Lengefeld had given her consent to the marriage of her daughter Lottie with Schiller, sooner than the lovers expected. Charles August gave the poet the title of privy-councillor, and attached a salary of two hundred dollars to his professorship, as a marriage present. The title delighted Madame von Lengefeld, and somewhat reconciled her aristocratic heart to the thought that her daughter, who had been on the point of becoming a maid of honor, should now marry a man of the people. Schiller deemed his salary of two hundred dollars quite a small fortune, and hoped that this, together with the fruits of his poetic labors, would be sufficient to provide a comfortable home for his darling, and—" space in the smallest cottage for a happy and loving pair!"

They were a " happy, loving pair;" and the serene heaven of their happiness was undimmed by the smallest cloud. Had a cloud appeared, Charlotte's quick eye would have detected and dissipated it before the lovers were aware of its existence. The sister watched over their happiness like their good genius, like a faithful sentinel.

At times, while gazing dreamily into his Lottie's soft eyes, Schiller would smile and then ask her if she really loved him, as though such happiness were incredible.

In reply, Charlotte would smile and protest that she had loved him for a long time, and that her sister, who had known her secret, could confirm her statement.

"And she it was who told me this sweet secret. Yes, Caroline was the beneficent angel who infused courage into my timid heart."

"Yes, she is an angel!" said Charlotte, thoughtfully. "I look up to her as to a being far superior to myself, and, let me confess, my beloved, that the thought sometimes torments me that she really could be more to you than I am, and that I am not necessary to your happiness."

He gazed into her lovely countenance, an expression of perfect peace resting on his own. "Your love is all I require to make me happy. The peculiar and happiest feature of our union is, that it is self-sustaining, ever revolving on its own axis in a well-defined orbit; this forbids my entertaining the fear that I could ever be less to either of you, or that I could ever receive less from you. Our love has no need of anxiety—of watchfulness. How could I rejoice in my existence unless for you and Caroline?—how could I always retain sufficient control over my own soul, unless I entertained the sweet conviction that my feelings toward both, and each of you, were of such a nature that I am not forced to withdraw from the one what I give to the other? My soul revolves between you in safety, ever returning lovingly from the one to the other, the same star, the same ray of light, differently reflected from different mirrors. Caroline is nearer to me in age, and therefore more closely akin to me in the form of her thought and feeling; but I would not have you other than you are, for all the world, Lottie. That in which Caroline is your superior, you must receive from me; your soul must expand in my love, and you must be my creation. Your blossom must fall in the spring of my love." *

"Yes," cried Charlotte, entwining her arm more closely around his neck, "I will be your creation, and happy shall I feel in the consciousness of belonging to you, and of being able to contribute somewhat to your happiness." †

* Schiller's own words.—See "Schiller's Life of Caroline von Wollzogen."
† Lottie's own words.—Ibid.

On the morning of the twentieth of February, 1790, a closed carriage drove rapidly from Rudolstadt in the direction of Jena. But this carriage stopped in the little village in the immediate vicinity of the university-city—Weningenjena—at the door of the village church with its tapering spire.

The sexton was standing at the open door in his Sunday suit; when the carriage drove up, he hastened forward to open the door. A tall gentleman, attired in black, stepped out; his countenance was pale, but a wondrous light beamed in his eyes, and noble thoughts were enthroned on his brow, while his lips were parted in a soft smile. With tender solicitude, he helped an elderly lady from the carriage. Then followed a younger lady, with pale cheeks, but with eyes that were radiant with love and peace. At last a young girl—a girl with rosy cheeks, and a timid, childlike smile on her fresh lips—was about to descend from the carriage, but the tall gentleman would not suffer her to touch the pavement with her tender little feet. He raised her fair form in his arms, and bore her over the rough stones and into the church.

The two ladies followed, and behind them came the sexton, gravely shaking his head, and ruminating over the strangely quiet nature of the approaching ceremony. He did what Pastor Schmidt, who was already standing between the burning wax-candles in front of the altar, had told him to do. He closed and locked the church doors, so that no one should see what was going on in the church.

And you, too, ye rude winter winds, hold your breath and blow softly! and thou, thou clear blue sky, look down mildly; and thou, bright sun, shed thy warmest rays through the windows into the little village church of Weningenjena. For the poet Frederick Schiller is standing before its altar at the side of his lovely bride. Charlotte weeps, but her tears are tears of emotion and of joy. The mother stands at her side, her hands folded in prayer. Caroline's eyes are upturned; and God reads the mute entreaty of her lips.

Schiller's countenance is radiant with peace and happiness,

and manly determination beams in the large blue eyes that gaze so firmly and tranquilly at the preacher, who stands before the altar, proclaiming the sacred nature of the union about to be consummated.

Subdue your fury, ye boisterous winter storms! do not touch the poet's cheeks too rudely with your cold breath. He has already suffered much from cold winter winds, he has journeyed over rough paths—has renounced and struggled, and has often seen his heart's fairest blossoms bruised and borne away by rude storms. Be tranquil, and let the spring-time come, that the buds of his hopes may put forth blossoms.

Shed thy glorious light upon this little church, thou heavenly sun! greet the poet Frederick Schiller, the poet of the German nation, who is now celebrating life's fairest festival before its holy altar! But,

> " Ah, life's fairest festival
> Ends the May of life anon;
> With the girdle, with the veil,
> Is the fond illusion gone! "

THE END.